All in One®
CHEMISTRY
Class 9

Author
Pooja Yadav

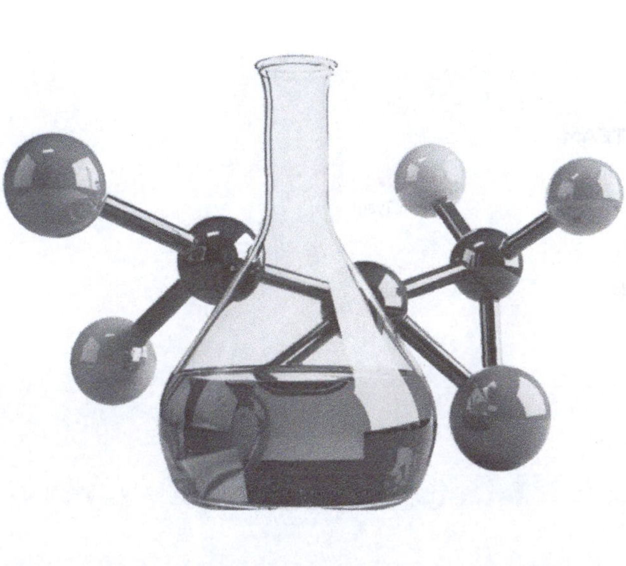

arihant
SUCCESS AND NOTHING LESS

arihant
SUCCESS AND NOTHING LESS

ARIHANT PRAKASHAN
(School Division Series)

卐 *ADMINISTRATIVE & PRODUCTION OFFICES*
Regd. Office
'Ramchhaya' 4577/15, Agarwal Road, Darya Ganj, New Delhi -110002
Tele: 011- 47630600, 43518550; Fax: 011- 23280316
卐 *Head Office*
Kalindi, TP Nagar, Meerut (UP) - 250002, Tel: 0121-7156203, 7156204

卐 *SALES & SUPPORT OFFICES*
Agra, Ahmedabad, Bengaluru, Bareilly, Chennai, Delhi, Guwahati, Hyderabad, Jaipur, Jhansi, Kolkata, Lucknow, Nagpur & Pune.

PO No : TXT-XX-XXXXXXX-X-XX

Published By Arihant Publications (India) Ltd.

For further information about the books published by Arihant, log on to www.arihantbooks.com or e-mail at info@arihantbooks.com
Follow us on

卐 *PRICE* ₹215.00

PRODUCTION TEAM

Publishing Managers
Mahendra Singh Rawat & Keshav Mohan

Cover Designer
Salman Shaikh

Inner Designer
Ankit Tyagi

Project Head
Akansha Tomar

Page Layouting
Sanjay Yadav

Proof Reader
Akhil

Index *cum* Study Planner

One Book- Endless Features

to Help you Succeed

CHAPTER 01

The Language of Chemistry

CHAPTER OUTLINES

• Chemical Symbols • Valency • Chemical Formulae • Radicals • Chemical Equation • Relative Atomic Mass (Atomic Weight) • Relative Molecular Mass (Molecular Weight) • Percentage Composition

In this Chapter

At the start of each chapter, all the chapter topics have been listed, so that students may know what they are going to study.

Valency

The combining power (or capacity) of an element is called its **valency**. It can be used to find out how the atoms of an element will combine with the atom(s) of another element to form a chemical compound. It is also referred to the number of electrons that atom can gain, lose or share during a chemical reaction. The electrons that are present in the outermost shell are known as **valence electrons**.

The loss or gain of electrons in an atom depends upon valence shell electrons.

- Elements that have one, two or three electrons present in their outermost shell are known as

Simplified Theory

It contains the necessary study material well supported by Definitions, Facts, Figures, Flowcharts, etc.

Check Your Learning

A set of 4-6 Questions given in between the text, helps students to remain connected with the text while studying. They can instantly assess themselves for their understanding.

Check Your LEARNING...

1 Write the balanced equation for the follong reaction.

$$Na_2O_2(s) + H_2O(l) \longrightarrow NaOH(aq)$$

2 Which of the following reactions is balanced, *A* or *B*?

$A: 2NaCl + 2H_2O \xrightarrow{\text{Electricity}} 2NaOH + 2Cl_2 + H_2\uparrow$

$B: Ca(OH)_2 + Cl_2 \longrightarrow CaOCl_2 + H_2O$

3 What is the value of amu in grams?

4 Complete the following.
Relative atomic mass is defined as the number of times a given atom is heavier than .... of the mass of 1 atom of carbon-12.

5 What will be the mass of hydrogen atom in amu?

6 Calculate the percentage composition of K in $KClO_3$.

Example 3. Calculate percentage of oxygen in water. Given that the relative atomic masses of H = 1, O = 16.

Sol. Relative molecular mass of $H_2O = 1 \times 2 + 16 = 18$

Percentage composition of oxygen

$$= \frac{\text{Mass contributed by oxygen}}{\text{Total molecular mass of water}} \times 100$$

$$= \frac{16}{18} \times 100 = 88.89\ \%$$

∴ Percentage composition of oxygen in water is 88.89%.

Solved Examples

To explain the application of concept, Solved Examples have been given in between the theory. These examples have been solved in Step-by-Step manner, so that students can learn the problem solving process completely.

One Book- Endless Features

to Help you Succeed

QUICK Revision

At the end of each chapter, QUICK Revision is given. It contains crux of the chapter in pointer form.

QUiCK Revision

- **Symbols of elements** are derived from one or two letters of names of the elements in English, Greek, Latin, German, etc. First letter is written in capital and second one in small, e.g. iron, Fe(from ferrum).
- **Valency** is the combining capacity of an element and it is charge in case of ions.
- An **Ion** is a positively or negatively charged atom (or group of atoms) which is formed by loss or gain of electrons by an atom (or group of atoms).
- Elements with one, two or three electrons in their outermost shell (valence shell) are usually metals. Out of the elements that have four electrons in the outermost orbit-carbon is a non-metal, silicon and germanium are metalloids and the rest are metals.
- Elements with five, six or seven electrons in their outermost shell are normally non-metals.

(iv) In the formula, the positive and negative charges must balance each other and the overall structure must be neutral.

- **Radical** is an atom or a group of atoms, which behave as a single unit, having their own combining capacity and has positive or negative charge.
- **Chemical equation** is the symbolic representation of a chemical reaction that describes a chemical change in terms of symbols and formulae.
- **A balanced chemical equation** is that, in which the total number of atoms of each element are equal on both sides of the equation.
- The method involved for balancing chemical equation is hit and trial method.
- **Hit and trial method** This method consist of counting the number of atoms of each element on both sides and try to

Chapter Practice

Section-I

a. Multiple Choice Questions

1. The abbreviations used in the chemistry
   (a) to represent name of elements
   (b) to represent reactions
   (c) Both (a) and (b)
   (d) None of the above

Sol. (c)

2. Modern atomic symbols are based on the method proposed by
   (a) Berzelius (b) Bohr (c) Dalton (d) Newton

Sol. (a)

3. The symbol for carbonate ion is
   (a) CO (b) CO_3^- (c) CO_3^{2-} (d) CO_2

Sol. (c)

4. Valency of copper in Cu_2Cl_2 and $CuCl_2$ are respectively
   (a) 2, 1 (b) 1, 2
   (c) 1, 1 (d) 2, 2

Sol. (b)

5. The valency of iron in Fe_2O_3 is
   (a) + 1 (b) + 2
   (c) + 3 (d) Both (b) and (c)

Sol. (c)

6. The formula of compound represents
   (a) a radical (b) a molecule
   (c) a particle (d) an atom

Sol. (b)

7. The correct chemical formula of aluminium oxide is
   (a) AlO (b) AlO_3 (c) Al_2O_3 (d) Al_3O_2

Sol. (c)

8. The number of carbon atoms in a hydrogen carbonate radical is
   (a) one (b) two (c) three (d) four

Sol. (a)

9. The chemical reaction,
   $$(NH_4)_2Cr_2O_7 \xrightarrow{\Delta} N_2 + 4H_2O + Cr_2O_3$$
   is an example of
   (a) two reactants and two products
   (b) one reactant and two or three products
   (c) two reactants and one product
   (d) two reactants and three or four products

Sol. (b)

10. In water, the hydrogen-to-oxygen mass ratio is
    (a) 1 : 16 (b) 1 : 32 (c) 1 : 8 (d) 1 : 64

Sol. (c)

b. Fill in the Blanks

11. Dalton used symbol .... for oxygen and ...... for hydrogen. [O], [⊛], [H], [Δ]

Sol. [O], [H]

12. Usually symbol represents ...... atom(s) of an element. (one, two, three)

Sol. one

13. Nitrite is .... and ...... radical.

Sol. NO_2^-, monovalent,

14. Nitride is .... and .... radical.

Sol. N^{3-}, trivalent

15. Nitrate is .... and .... radical.

Sol. NO_3^-, monovalent

16. The formula of caustic potash is .... (KOH, NaH, K_2CO_3)

Sol. KOH

17. The formula of washing soda is .... (Na_2CO_3, $NaHCO_3$, Ca_2SO_4)

Sol. Na_2CO_3

18. Limestone is .... ($CaCO_3$, $Ca(OH)_2$, Na_2SO_4)

Sol. $CaCO_3$

19. Formula of iron (III) carbonate is .... (Fe_2CO_3, $Fe_2(CO_3)_3$, $FeCO_3$)

Sol. $Fe_2(CO_3)_3$

20. Sodium chloride has two radicals. Sodium is ...... radical, whereas chloride is ...... radical. (acid, basic, neutral)

Sol. basic, acidic

21. Essential condition for a chemical equation is that it must be .... and should be .... (balanced, molecular, unbalanced)

Sol. balanced, molecular

22. $2H_2O + 2Cl_2 \longrightarrow$ .... $+ O_2$ (4HCl, 5HCl, 3HCl)

Sol. 4HCl

23. $2NaHCO_3 \longrightarrow$ .... $+ H_2O + CO_2$ (Na_2CO_3, $2NaCO_3$, $NaHCO_3$)

Sol. Na_2CO_3

Chapter Practice

The Exercise contains questions in that format in which these are asked in the examinations. Questions have been categorised as 1 mark questions, 2 marks questions, 3 marks questions, 4 marks questions. All the questions given here are fully solved.

Chapter Assessment

It is the Assessment exercise for the complete chapter. With this exercise, students can assess their understanding of the chapter and can prepare for it accordingly.

Chapter Assessment

Section-I

a. Multiple Choice Questions

1. The symbol of neon is
   (a) NE (b) ne (c) Ne (d) nE
2. The chemical formula of sodium chlorate is $NaClO_3$ then the chemical formula of sodium hypochlorite is
   (a) NaClO (b) $NaClO_2$
   (c) $NaClO_4$ (d) Na_2ClO_2
3. Oxygen, nitrogen and platinum are respectively
   (a) trivalent, trivalent, tetravalent
   (b) divalent, trivalent, trivalent
   (c) divalent, tetravalent, trivalent
   (d) divalent, trivalent, tetravalent
4. Cl^-, F^-, K^+ and Na^+ are the examples of
   (a) basic radical
   (b) acidic radical
   (c) simple radical

c. Give One Word or a Phrase

11. The symbol 'S' represent for.
12. The name of two elements, which show variable valency.
13. One example of bivalent cations.
14. The cation and anion present in the CH_3COONa
15. One example of trivalent anion.

d. Match the Columns

16. Match the following columns.

	Column I (Name)		Column II (Radicals)
A.	Dichromate	1.	$Cr_2O_7^{2-}$
B.	Nitrite	2.	ZnO_2^{2-}
C.	Mercuric	3.	NO_2^-
D.	Zincate	4.	Hg^{2+}

One Book- Endless Features
to Help you Succeed

Olympiad Section

It includes some special questions based on the pattern of Olympiad and other competitions to give the students a taste of the questions asked in competitions. These are not meant for school examinations.

Olympiad Section*

Brain Teasing Questions asked in Previous Olympiads

1. What is the mass percentage of nitrogen in the following active compounds present in fertilizers?
(i) Ammonium nitrate and (ii) Ammonium sulphate

	(i)	(ii)
(a)	35	40
(b)	32	21
(c)	35	21
(d)	21	35

2. Iron present in spinach can be estimated by titrating it with potassium permanganate. Small amounts of spinach leaves are weighed and dissolved in acid to extract the iron in solution. The solution is then titrated and the following reaction takes place during this titration.

$$Fe^{2+} + MnO_4^- + H^+ \longrightarrow Mn^{2+} + Fe^{3+} + H_2O$$

When properly balanced with the simplest set of whole number coefficients, the sum of the coefficients in the balanced equation is
(a) 16 (b) 18
(c) 22 (d) 24

3. Valence electron in Cl^- ion is
(a) 16 (b) 8
(c) 17 (d) 18

4. The formulae of an oxide of an element *M* is *M*O. The formulae of its phosphate is
(a) $M_3(PO_4)_2$ (b) MPO_4
(c) $M_2(PO_4)_3$ (d) M_3PO_4

5. What is the formula of carbon tetrachloride?
(a) CCl_4 (b) CCl_3
(c) CCl_2 (d) CCl

6. An example of a homo atomic molecule is
(a) ozone (b) ammonia
(c) methane (d) sulphur dioxide

7. Chemical formula of lime stone is
(a) $Ca(OH)_2$ (b) $CaCO_3$
(c) $CaCl_2$ (d) CCl_4

8. Which of the following statement is not true about an atom?
(a) Atoms are not able to exist independently
(b) Atoms are the basic units from which molecules and ions are formed
(c) Atoms are always neutral in nature
(d) Atoms aggregate in large numbers to form the matter that we can see, feel or touch

Answers

1. (c) 2. (a) 3. (b) 4. (a) 5. (a) 6. (a) 7. (b) 8. (d)

SAMPLE QUESTION PAPER 1

A HIGHLY SIMULATED Sample Question Paper for ICSE Class IX

Chemistry (Solved)

Time : 2 hours Max. Marks : 80

GENERAL INSTRUCTIONS

- Answer to this Paper must be written on the paper provided separately.
- You will not be allowed to write during first 15 minutes.
- This time is to be spent in reading the question paper.
- The time given at the head of this Paper is the time allowed for writing the answers.
- **Section A** is compulsory. Attempt any **four** questions from **Section B.**
- The intended marks for questions or parts of questions are given in brackets [].

Section-A [40 Marks]

(Attempt all questions from this section.)

1. Choose the correct answers to the questions from the given options. [15]

(i) The salt which is deliquescent
(a) washing soda (b) glauber's salt
(c) iron (III) chloride (d) sodium chloride

(ii) An alkaline earth metal is
(a) potassium (b) calcium
(c) lead (d) copper

(iii) In the periodic table, alkali metals are placed in the group
(a) 1 (b) 11 (c) 17 (d) 18

(iv) The products of neutralisation reaction are
(a) salt and oxygen (b) salt and hydrogen
(c) hydrogen and oxygen (d) salt and water

(v) The reaction, $2Cu + O_2 \longrightarrow 2CuO$ is an example of
(a) oxidation reaction (b) reduction reaction
(c) redox reaction (d) None of these

(vi) The formula of calcium hydrogen carbonate is
(a) $CaHCO_3$ (b) $Ca(HCO_3)_2$
(c) Ca_2HCO_3 (d) $Ca(HCO_3)_3$

(vii) Which of the following is not a balanced equation ?
(a) $Ca(OH)_2 + CO_2 \longrightarrow CaCO_3 + H_2O$
(b) $Fe + Cl_2 \longrightarrow FeCl_3$
(c) $Zn + H_2SO_4 \longrightarrow ZnSO_4 + H_2$
(d) $2KBr + Cl_2 \longrightarrow 2KCl + Br_2$

(viii) Which among the following carbonates do not decompose on heating ?
(a) Magnesium carbonate (b) Zinc carbonate
(c) Calcium carbonate (d) Potassium carbonate

(ix) Catalyst used to convert sulphur dioxide to sulphur trioxide is
(a) iron (b) vanadium pentaoxide
(c) ammonia (d) ozone

(x) The metal which burns with lilac flame is
(a) sodium
(b) chromium
(c) potassium
(d) sodium and potassium both

(xi) Which of the following isotope is used for determination of age of fossil fuels ?
(a) ${}^{12}_{6}C$ (b) ${}^{2}_{1}H$ (c) ${}^{14}_{7}N$ (d) ${}^{13}_{6}C$

(xii) Elements which loose electrons are known as
(a) ionic atom
(b) electropositive elements
(c) electronegative element
(d) covalent

(xiii) Element used in atomic clock is
(a) cesium (b) lithium
(c) rhodium (d) gallium

(xiv) When a metal '*X*' reacts with water, the reaction is exothermic and violent. Identify *X*.
(a) Copper (b) Calcium
(c) Potassium (d) Iron

(xv) 78°C is equal to
(a) 351 K (b) 330 K (c) 376 K (d) 350 K

Internal Assessment of Practical Work

To make this book complete in all aspects, experiments based on latest syllabus have been given.

Internal Assessment of Practical Work

Experiment 1

Identification of Gases

S. No.	Experiment	Observations	Inferences
1.	**Detection of Hydrogen (H_2)**		
	• Dilute hydrochloric acid (HCl) or dilute sulphuric (H_2SO_4) acid is added to one of the active metals (e.g. Mg). • **Reaction** $Mg + \underset{dil.}{H_2SO_4} \longrightarrow MgSO_4 + H_2\uparrow$ • Moist blue litmus and a burning splinter is brought near to the mouth of test tube.	• A colourless, odourless gas is evolved which is neutral towards litmus. • It put off the burning wooden splinter after giving a pale blue flame and producing a pop sound.	Presence of H_2 is confirmed.
2.	**Detection of Oxygen (O_2)**		
	• Lead dioxide is strongly heated in a boiling tube. • **Reaction** $2PbO_2 \xrightarrow{\Delta} 2PbO + O_2\uparrow$ • Moist blue litmus paper and a burning splinter is brought near to the mouth of test tube.	• A colourless, odourless gas is evolved which is neutral towards litmus.It increased the glow of burning wood splinter.	Presence of O_2 is confirmed.
3.	**Detection of Carbon Dioxide (CO_2)**		
	• Dilute sulphuric acid (H_2SO_4) or dilute hydrochloric acid (HCl) is added to metal carbonate. • **Reaction** $ZnCO_3 + Dil.\ 2HCl \longrightarrow ZnCl_2 + CO_2 + H_2O$ • Moist blue litmus paper is brought near to the mouth of the test tube. • Pass the evolved gas through lime water, $Ca(OH)_2$.	• A colourless, odourless gas is evolved which turned moist blue litmus paper red. • It put off the burning wooden splinter and turned lime water milky.	Presence of CO_2 is confirmed.
4.	**Detection of Chlorine (Cl_2)**		
	• Concentrated HCl is added to the lead oxides (Pb_3O_4 or PbO_2) or manganese oxide (MnO_2). • **Reaction** $PbO_2 + 4HCl \longrightarrow PbCl_2 + 2H_2O + Cl_2\uparrow$ $Pb_3O_4 + 8HCl \longrightarrow 3PbCl_2 + 4H_2O + Cl_2\uparrow$ $MnO_2 + 4HCl \longrightarrow MnCl_2 + H_2O + Cl_2\uparrow$ • Moist blue litmus paper and moist a stach iodide paper is brough near to the mouth of test tube.	• A greenish yellow gas with pungent smell is evolved which turned moist blue litmus paper first red and then decolourised it. • It turned moist starch iodide paper blue black.	Presence of Cl_2 is confirmed.

Sample Question Papers

To make students practice of examination in real sense, there are 5 Sample Question Papers at the end. All these Sample Questions Papers are exactly prepared on the latest syllabus & pattern of examination.

Latest Course Structure

There will be one paper of **two hours** duration of 80 marks and Internal Assessment of practical work carrying 20 marks.

Note: All chemical reactions should be studied with reference to the reactants, products, conditions, observations and the (balanced) equations.

1. The Language of Chemistry

(i) Symbol of an element; valency; formulae of radicals and formulae of compounds. Balancing of simple chemical equations.

- Symbol – definition; symbols of the elements used often.
- Valency - definition; hydrogen combination and number of valence electrons of the metals and non-metals; mono, di, tri and tetra valent elements.
- Radicals – definition; formulae and valencies.
- Compounds – name and formulae.
- Chemical equation – definition and examples of chemical equations with one reactant and two or three products, two reactants and one product, two reactants and two products and two reactants and three or four products; balancing of equations. (by hit and trial method).

(ii) Relative Atomic Masses (atomic weights) and Relative Molecular Masses (molecular weights): either - standard H atom or 1/12th of carbon 12 atom.

- Definitions
- Calculation of Relative Molecular Mass and percentage composition of a compound.

2. Chemical Changes and Reactions

(i) Types of chemical changes.

- Direct combination
- Decomposition
- Displacement
- Double decomposition

(The above to be taught with suitable chemical equations as examples).

(ii) Energy changes in a chemical change.

Exothermic and endothermic reactions with examples – evolution/absorption of heat, light and electricity.

3. Water

(i) Water as a universal solvent.

- Solutions as 'mixtures' of solids in water; saturated solutions.
- Qualitative effect of temperature on solubility (e.g. solutions of calcium sulphate, potassium nitrate and sodium chloride in water).

(ii) Hydrated and anhydrous substances.

(a) Hydrated substances:
Water of Crystallisation – meaning and examples.

(b) Anhydrous substances:
Meaning and examples only

(c) Properties:

- Efflorescence
- Deliquescence
- Hygroscopy
- Removal of hardness

(i) By boiling
(ii) By addition of washing soda

(Definition and examples of each of the above).

(iii) Drying and Dehydrating Agents
Meaning and examples only.

(iv) Soft water and Hard water

- Meaning, (in terms of action of soap)
- Advantages and disadvantages of soft water and hard water.
- Types and causes of hardness.

4. Atomic Structure and Chemical Bonding

(i) Structure of an Atom, Mass Number and Atomic number, Isotopes and Octet Rule.

- Definition of an atom

- Constituents of an atom - nucleus (protons, neutrons) with associated electrons; mass number, atomic number.
- Electron distribution in the orbits - $2n^2$ rule, Octet rule. Reason for chemical activity of an atom.
- Definition and examples of isotopes (hydrogen, carbon, chlorine).

(ii) Electrovalent and Covalent Bonding, Structures of Various Compounds – Orbit Structure

(a) Electrovalent Bond
- Definition
- Atomic orbit structure for the formation of Electrovalent compounds (e.g. NaCl, $MgCl_2$, CaO);

(b) Covalent Bond
- Definition
- Atomic orbit structure for the formation of Covalent molecules on the basis of duplet and octet of electrons (examples: hydrogen, chlorine, oxygen, nitrogen, hydrogen chloride, water, ammonia, carbon tetrachloride, methane.)

5. The Periodic Table

Dobereiner's Triads, Newland's law of Octaves, Mendeleev's contributions; Modern Periodic Law, the Modern Periodic Table. (Groups and periods)

- General idea of Dobereiner's triads, Newland's law of Octaves, Mendeleev's periodic law.
- Discovery of Atomic Number and its use as a basis for Modern Periodic law.
- Modern Periodic Table (Groups 1 to 18 and periods 1 to 7).
- Special reference to Alkali metals (Group 1), Alkaline Earth metals (Group 2) Halogens (Group 17) and Zero Group (Group 18).

6. Study of the First Element - Hydrogen

Position of the non-metal (Hydrogen) in the periodic table and general group characteristics with reference to valency electrons, burning, ion formation applied to the above mentioned element.

(i) Hydrogen from: water, dilute acids and alkalis.

(a) Hydrogen from water:
- The action of cold water on sodium potassium and calcium.
- The action of hot water on magnesium.
- The action of steam on aluminium, zinc, and iron; (reversibility of reaction between iron and steam).
- The action of steam on non-metal (carbon).

Students can be shown the action of sodium and calcium on water in the laboratory. They must be asked to make observations and write equations for the above reactions.

Application of activity series for the above mentioned reactions.

(b) Displacement of hydrogen from dilute acids:
- The action of dilute sulphuric acid or hydrochloric acid on metals: Mg, Al, Zn and Fe.

(To understand reasons for not using other metals and dilute nitric acid)

(c) Displacement of hydrogen from alkalis:

The action of Alkalis ((NaOH, KOH) on Al, Zn and Pb –unique nature of these elements.

(ii) The preparation and collection of hydrogen by a standard laboratory method other than electrolysis.

In the laboratory preparation, the reason for using zinc, the impurities in the gas, their removal and the precautions in the collection of the gas must be mentioned.

(iii) Industrial manufacture of hydrogen by Bosch process
- Main reactions and conditions.
- Separation of CO_2 and CO from hydrogen.

(iv) Oxidation and reduction reactions

Differences in terms of addition and removal of oxygen / hydrogen.

7. Study of Gas Laws

(i) The behaviour of gases under changes of temperature and pressure; explanation in terms of molecular motion (particles, atoms, molecules); Boyle's Law and Charles' Law; absolute zero; gas equation; simple relevant calculations.

- The behaviour of gases under changes of temperature and pressure; explanation in terms of molecular motion(particles, atoms, molecules).
- Boyle's Law: statement, mathematical form, simple calculations.
- Charles' Law: statement, mathematical form, simple calculations.
- Absolute zero Kelvin scale of temperature.
- Gas equation $p_1 V_1 / T_1 = p_2 V_2 / T_2$; simple relevant calculations based on gas equation.

(ii) Relationship between Kelvin scale and Celsius Scale of temperature; Standard temperature and pressure.

Conversion of temperature from Celsius Scale to Kelvin scale and vice versa. Standard temperature and pressure. (Simple calculations).

8. Atmospheric Pollution

(a) Acid rain – composition, cause and its impact.

Sulphur in fossil fuels giving oxides of sulphur when burnt. High temperatures in furnaces and internal combustion engines produce oxides of nitrogen. (Equations to be included). Acid rain affects soil chemistry and water bodies.

(b) Global warming: Greenhouse gases – their sources and ways of reducing their presence in the atmosphere.

(Water vapour, carbon dioxide, methane and oxides of nitrogen)

(c) Ozone depletion

- Formation of ozone – relevant equations
- Function in the atmosphere.
- Destruction of the ozone layer – chemicals responsible for this to be named but reactions not required.

INTERNAL ASSESSMENT OF PRACTICAL WORK

Candidates will be asked to observe the effect of reagents and/or of heat on substances supplied to them. The exercises will be simple and may include the recognition and identification of certain gases listed below.

Gases Hydrogen, Oxygen, Carbon dioxide, Chlorine, Hydrogen chloride, Sulphur dioxide, Hydrogen sulphide, Ammonia, Water vapour, Nitrogen dioxide.

Candidates are expected to have completed the following minimum practical work.

Simple Experiments on:

1. Action of heat on the following compounds:
   (a) copper carbonate, zinc carbonate
   (b) washing soda, copper sulphate crystals
   (c) zinc nitrate, copper nitrate, lead nitrate
   (d) ammonium chloride, iodine, ammonium dichromate

   Make observations, identify the products and make deductions where possible.

2. Action of dilute sulphuric acid on the following substances. (warm if necessary)
   (a) a metal
   (b) a carbonate
   (c) a sulphide
   (d) a sulphite

   Make observations, identify the gas evolved and make deductions

3. Apply the flame test to identify the metal in the unknown substance.
   (a) a sodium salt
   (b) a potassium salt
   (c) a calcium compound

4. Simple experiments based on hard water and soft water – identification of hardness – simple softening – by heating the temporary hard water, using washing soda and advantage of using detergents over soap in hard water.

5. Find out the sources of pollution of water bodies in the locality. Suggest preventive steps to control it.

CHAPTER 01

The Language of Chemistry

CHAPTER OUTLINES

• Chemical Symbols • Valency • Chemical Formulae • Radicals • Chemical Equation • Relative Atomic Mass (Atomic Weight) • Relative Molecular Mass (Molecular Weight) • Percentage Composition

The abbreviation is an important fact, which is used in every field of study to save space, time and labour. In chemistry, the names of elements and compounds are abbreviated by using symbols and formulae.

Earlier, Alchemists and Dalton tried to represent the substance that they used for their experiments by different pictograph symbols such as triangle (Δ) for earth, circle [O] for oxygen etc.

Afterwards, **John Berzelius** suggested that the initial letter of an element should represent the atom of that particular element. For example, O for oxygen, H for hydrogen and so on. This method led to the foundation of IUPAC system of chemical symbols and formulae.

In this chapter, we will discuss about symbols of elements, formulae of radicals and compounds, equations of chemical reactions and balancing of simple chemical equations.

Chemical Symbols

A chemical symbol represents the abbreviation for the full names of the element. In another words, it is the short form for the atom of an element. When the first letter of more than one element is same then the symbol of elements incorporates two letters.

The first letter is capital while the second is small. e.g.

- Carbon is denoted by C.
- Cadmium is denoted by Cd.

The symbol of an element has qualitative as well as quantitative significance as explained below

- Qualitatively, symbol represents name of the element.
- Quantitatively, symbol represents one atom of the element.

e.g. The symbol C represents

Qualitatively (a) Carbon
Quantitatively (b) One atom of carbon
(c) 12 parts by weight of carbon

Different Ways to Write the Symbols of Elements

The symbols of elements can be written in the following ways

- In few cases, first letter of the name of the element is taken as its symbol and written in capital.
  e.g. Carbon-C, Oxygen-O, Nitrogen-N
- In few cases, the symbol of element have been derived from their Latin names.
  e.g. Sodium-Na (discovered from *Natrium*)
  Potassium-K (discovered from *Kalium*)
- In few cases, the symbol of element has two letters, first letter is written in capital and second letter is written in small.
  e.g. Calcium-Ca, Cobalt-Co, Nickel-Ni
- In the present days, the symbol of element having atomic number more than 100, have three letters, first letter is written in capital then two letters are written in small.e.g. Unnilbium : Unb

Symbols for Some Elements

Element	Symbol	Element	Symbol	Element	Symbol
Aluminium	Al	Cobalt	Co	Neon	Ne
Argon	Ar	Chromium	Cr	Nitrogen	N
Barium	Ba	Copper	Cu	Oxygen	O
Boron	B	Fluorine	F	Silicon	Si
Bromine	Br	Hydrogen	H	Sulphur	S
Calcium	Ca	Iodine	I	Uranium	U
Carbon	C	Magnesium	Mg	Zinc	Zn
Chlorine	Cl	Lithium	Li	Manganese	Mn

Symbols of Some Elements based upon their Latin Names

Element	Latin name	Symbol
Sodium	*Natrium*	Na
Potassium	*Kalium*	K
Iron	*Ferrum*	Fe
Copper	*Cuprum*	Cu
Lead	*Plumbum*	Pb
Mercury	*Hydragyrum*	Hg
Gold	*Aurum*	Au
Tin	*Stannum*	Sn
Silver	*Argentum*	Ag

Symbols of Some Elements Involving Three Letters

Element	Symbol
Unnilbium	Unb
Unniltrium	Unt
Unnilquadium	Unq

Check Your LEARNING...

1 Why is it necessary to use symbol for the elements?

2 Give the correct symbol in each case.

(i) Cadmium (ii) Sodium

(iii) Barium (iv) Nitrogen

3 Why the symbols of few elements, like sodium, do not start with the initial letter of the name?

4 Name any two elements (other than sodium and potassium) whose symbols do not start with the first letter of their name.

5 Write the Latin name of the following elements.

(i) Sodium (ii) Potassium

Valency

The combining power (or capacity) of an element is called its **valency**. It can be used to find out how the atoms of an element will combine with the atom(s) of another element to form a chemical compound. It is also referred to the number of electrons that atom can gain, lose or share during a chemical reaction. The electrons that are present in the outermost shell are known as **valence electrons.**

The loss or gain of electrons in an atom depends upon valence shell electrons.

- Elements that have one, two or three electrons present in their outermost shell are known as **metals**.
- Metals form univalent, divalent, trivalent and tetravalent **cation** (positive ions) by losing their valence electrons.
- Elements that have five, six or seven electrons present in their outermost (valence) shell are known as **non-metals**. They form univalent, divalent, trivalent and tetravalent anion (negative ions) by gaining electrons. The valency of an ion is equal to the charge on that ion.
- Valency in terms of hydrogen is defined as the number of hydrogen atoms that are attached with the elements. e.g.

(i) One atom of hydrogen is attached with one atom of chlorine to form a molecule of hydrogen chloride. So, the valency of chlorine is one.

H—Cl

(ii) Two atoms of hydrogens are attached with one atom of oxygen to form a molecule of water. So, the valency of oxygen is two.

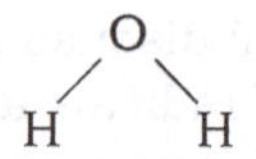

(iii) Three atoms of hydrogens are attached with one atom of nitrogen. So, the valency of nitrogen is three.

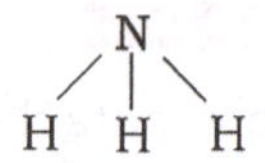

Names, Symbols and Valency of Some Ions

Valency	Ion of metallic element	Symbol	Ion of non-metallic element	Symbol	Polyatomic ions	Symbol
1.	Sodium	Na^+	Hydrogen	H^+	Ammonium	NH_4^+
	Potassium	K^+	Hydride	H^-	Hydroxyl	OH^-
	Silver	Ag^+	Chloride	Cl^-	Nitrate	NO_3^-
	Copper (I)*	Cu^+	Bromide	Br^-	Hydrogen Carbonate (bicarbonate)	HCO_3^-
			Iodide	I^-		
2.	Magnesium	Mg^{2+}	Oxide	O^{2-}	Carbonate	CO_3^{2-}
	Calcium	Ca^{2+}	Sulphide	S^{2-}	Sulphite	SO_3^{2-}
	Zinc	Zn^{2+}			Sulphate	SO_4^{2-}
	Iron (II)*	Fe^{2+}				
	Copper (II)*	Cu^{2+}				
3.	Aluminium	Al^{3+}	Nitride	N^{3-}	Phosphate	PO_4^{3-}
	Iron (III)*	Fe^{3+}	Phosphide	P^{3-}		
4.	Lead (IV)	Pb^{4+}	Carbide	C^{4-}		

Note *These elements show more than one valency, i.e. variable valency. Here, the roman numeral written in brackets shows their valency.

e.g. $Cu_2O \rightarrow$ Copper oxide is written as copper (I) oxide.

$CuO \rightarrow$ Copper oxide is written as copper (II) oxide.

Chemical Formulae

The shortest way to represent a compound with the help of symbols and valency of elements is known as **chemical formula**. It shows constituent elements and the number of atoms of each combining element. In ionic compounds, the charge on each ion is used to determine the chemical formula of a compound.

A chemical formula is also known as **molecular formula** as it denotes the molecule of an element or of a compound, e.g. 2NaCl represents two molecules of sodium chloride and each molecule contains one atom of sodium and one atom of chlorine. In other words, the symbolic representation of a molecule is known as **formula** or **molecular formula**.

Writing Chemical Formula

To write the chemical formula for simple compounds

Step 1. Write the symbols of constituent elements and their valencies.

Step 2. Write the symbol of cation first followed by the symbol of anion.

Step 3. Then criss-cross their charges or valencies to get the formula.

- In the formula, the positive and negative charges must balance each other and the overall structure must be neutral.

Note The simplest compounds made up of two different elements are also called **binary compounds**.

e.g. **Hydrogen sulphide**

Symbols	H	S
Charges	1	−2
Formula	H_2S	

Note When the subscript is 1, then it is not written.

Carbon tetrachloride

Symbols	C	Cl
Charges	4	−1
Formula	CCl_4	

Magnesium chloride

Symbols	Mg	Cl
Charges	+2	−1
Formula	$MgCl_2$	

Calcium oxide

Symbols	Ca	O
Charges	+2	−2
Formula	Ca_2O_2 or CaO	

Note When the valency of both elements are numerically equal, the subscripts are not written.

Aluminium oxide

Symbols	Al	O
Charges	+3	−2
Formula	Al_2O_3	

Sodium nitrate

Symbols	Na	NO_3
Charges	+1	−1
Formula	$NaNO_3$	

Potassium carbonate

Symbols	K	CO_3
Charges	+1	−2
Formula	K_2CO_3	

Aluminium hydroxide

Symbols	Al	OH
Charges	+3	−1
Formula	$Al(OH)_3$	

Ammonium sulphate

Symbols	NH_4 ✕ SO_4
Charges	+1 −2
Formula	$(NH_4)_2SO_4$

Note We use brackets when we have two or more of the same ions in the formulae.

Tin (IV) oxide

Symbols	Sn ✕ O
Charges	+4 −2
Formula	Sn_2O_4 or SnO_2

Note All subscripts must be reduced to lowest term (except for molecule or covalent compound).

Importance of Chemical Formula

The chemical formula of a compound has quantitative significance /importance. It represents

- the respective numbers of different atoms present in one molecule of the compound.
- the ratios of the respective masses of the elements present in the compound.
- both the molecule and the molecular mass of the compound.
  e.g. The formula CO_2 represents that
  (i) the chemical formula of carbon dioxide is CO_2.
  (ii) each molecule contains one carbon atom joined by chemical bonds with two oxygen atoms.
  (iii) the molecular mass of CO_2 is 44 g as the atomic mass of carbon is 12 g and that of oxygen is 16 g.

Naming Chemical Compounds

Following rules are followed while naming the chemical compound from chemical formula.

- In binary compounds with one metal atom and a non-metal atom, the metal is named first and non-metal is named at the end with suffix 'ide'.

  e.g. $Na_2O \longrightarrow$ Sodium oxide
  $Ca_3N_2 \longrightarrow$ Calcium nitride

- The compounds containing two non-metals are named by using prefix mono, di, tri, etc.

  $PCl_3 \longrightarrow$ Phosphorus trichloride
  $PCl_5 \longrightarrow$ Phosphorus pentachloride

- The name of the oxygen containing compounds, depends on the number of oxygen atoms present in the compound.
- The prefix 'hypo' is used, if the number of oxygen atoms is less than 2. The suffix 'ite' is used, if the number of oxygen atom is 2.
- The suffix 'ate' is used if the number of oxygen is 3. The prefix 'per' is used if the number of oxygen atom is more than 3.

  e.g. $NaClO \longrightarrow$ Sodium hypochlorite
  $NaClO_2 \longrightarrow$ Sodium chlorite
  $NaClO_3 \longrightarrow$ Sodium chlorate
  $NaClO_4 \longrightarrow$ Sodium perchlorate

- The acids containing two elements where one atom is hydrogen that combines with one non-metal are named by adding prefix *hydro* and suffix-*ic* to the name of second element.

  Bases are named as hydroxides after the name of the metal or radical.

  $HCl \longrightarrow$ Hydrochloric acid (acid)
  $NH_4OH \longrightarrow$ Ammonium hydroxide (base)

Radicals

Radical is an atom or group of atoms having a charge (positive or negative) and shown as a single unit in chemical reaction.

Radicals have their own valencies and chemical formulae. e.g. In Na_2CO_3, sodium radical (Na^+), combining power ± 1 and carbonate (CO_3^{2-}), combining power is 2.

Types of Radicals

There are four types of radicals

(i) **Acid radicals** Radicals having negative charge on them are called acid radicals. e.g. F^-, CO_3^{2-}, SO_4^{2-}, etc.

Those acidic radicals which carry a negative charge are also called **electronegative radicals** or **anions**.

(ii) **Basic radicals** Radicals having positive charge on them are called basic radicals. e.g. Na^+, NH_4^+, Zn^{2+}, etc.

Those basic radical that carry a positive charge are also called **electropositive radicals or cations.**

(iii) **Simple radicals** These are made up of only one kind of atoms e.g. F^-, Na^+, K^+, etc.

(iv) **Compound radicals** These are made up of two or more type of atoms (polyatomic). e.g. CO_3^{2-}, OH^-, NH_4^+, etc.

List of Some Common Acid Radicals (Electrovalent Negative Ions)

Radicals having –1 charge (Monovalent)		**Radicals having –2 charges** (Divalent)		**Radicals having –3 charges** (Trivalent)		**Radicals having –4 charges** (Tetravalent)	
Hydride	– H^-	Carbonate	– CO_3^{2-}	Nitride	– N^{3-}	Carbide	– C^{4-}
Chloride	– Cl^-	Sulphite	– SO_3^{2-}	Phosphide	– P^{3-}	Pyrophosphate	– $P_2O_7^{4-}$
Bromide	– Br^-	Sulphate	– SO_4^{2-}	Phosphite	– PO_3^{3-}	Ferrocyanide	– $[Fe(CN)_6]^{4-}$
Cyanide	– CN^-	Oxide	– O^{2-}	Phosphate	– PO_4^{3-}		
Nitrite	– NO_2^-	Chromate	– CrO_4^{2-}	Ferricyanide	– $[Fe(CN)_6]^{3-}$		
Nitrate	– NO_3^-	Dichromate	– $Cr_2O_7^{2-}$				
Acetate	– CH_3COO^-	Oxalate	– $C_2O_4^{2-}$				
Chlorate	– ClO_3^-	Peroxide	– O_2^{2-}				
Bicarbonate	– HCO_3^-						
Bisulphate	– HSO_4^-						

List of Some Common Basic Radicals (Electrovalent Positive Ions)

Radicals having +1 charge (Monovalent)		**Radicals having +2 charges** (Divalent)		**Radicals having +3 charges** (Trivalent)		**Radicals having + 4 charges** (Tetravalent)	
Hydrogen	– H^+	Magnesium	– Mg^{2+}	Ferric	– Fe^{3+}	Stannic [Tin (IV)]	– Sn^{4+}
Lithium	– Li^+	Calcium	– Ca^{2+}	Chromium	– Cr^{3+}	Platinic [Platinum (IV)]	– Pt^{4+}
Sodium	– Na^+	Cobalt	– Co^{2+}	Aluminium	– Al^{3+}	Plumbic [Lead (IV)]	– Pb^{4+}
Ammonium	– NH_4^+	Nickel	– Ni^{2+}	Bismuth	– Bi^{3+}		
Silver	– Ag^+	Zinc	– Zn^{2+}				
Cuprous	– Cu^+	Ferrous	– Fe^{2+}				
Mercurous	– Hg^+	Cupric	– Cu^{2+}				

Check Your LEARNING...

1 What is the role of valency in the combination of atoms?

2 Give the symbol and valency of the following ions.
(i) Hydroxide ion (ii) Carbonate ion

3 Write the nature and combining power of different radicals of given compounds ?
(i) $(NH_4)_2CO_3$ (ii) $NaClO_3$

4 Give the names of following compounds.
(i) $HClO_3$ (ii) $HClO_2$

5 Write the formula of following compounds.
(i) Magnesium sulphate (ii) Sodium bromide
(iii) Calcium chloride (iv) Potassium nitrate
(v) Sodium phosphate (vi) Aluminium phosphate

Chemical Equation

A chemical equation is the symbolic representation of a chemical reaction. In this equation, the symbols and formulae of the reactant substances are written on the left hand side of the arrow and product substances written on the right hand side of the arrow.

e.g. The reaction of burning of methane gas can be written in words as

$$\underset{\text{(Reactants)}}{\text{Methane + Oxygen}} \xrightarrow{\Delta} \underset{\text{(Products)}}{\text{Carbon dioxide + Water}}$$

This equation is called **word equation**. The word equation can be change into a chemical equation by writing symbol and formulae of the substance in place of their name.

$$\underset{\text{Methane}}{CH_4(g)} + \underset{\text{Oxygen}}{2O_2(g)} \xrightarrow{\Delta} \underset{\text{Carbon dioxide}}{CO_2(g)} + \underset{\text{Water}}{2H_2O(g)}$$

Chemical reactions may involve

- One reactant and two or more products.

$$CaCO_3 \longrightarrow CaO + CO_2$$

- Two and more reactants and one product.

$$NH_3 + HCl \longrightarrow NH_4Cl$$

- Two and more reactants and two products.

$$Na_2SO_4 + BaCl_2 \longrightarrow BaSO_4 + 2NaCl$$

- Two and more reactants and three or more products.

$$Cu + 2H_2SO_4 \longrightarrow CuSO_4 + 2H_2O + SO_2$$

Writing a Chemical Equation

Various important points related to writing a chemical equation are as follows

- A chemical equation shows change of reactants to products through an arrow (→) placed between them.
- On the left hand side (LHS) of the arrow, reactants are written with a plus sign (+) between them. Similarly, on the right hand side (RHS), products are written with a plus sign (+) between them.
- The arrow head points toward the products and shows the direction of the reaction.

  e.g. The reaction between magnesium (Mg) and oxygen (O_2) resulting into the formation of magnesium oxide can be written as

$$\underset{\text{(Reactants)}}{2Mg + O_2} \longrightarrow \underset{\text{(Product)}}{2MgO}$$

Balanced Chemical Equation

A balanced chemical equation is that in which the total number of atoms of each element are equal on both sides of the arrow.

According to the law of conservation of mass, the mass can neither be created nor destroyed during a chemical reaction.' It means that in a chemical reaction total mass of reactants should be equal to total mass of products.

e.g. Balanced equation,

$$CaCO_3 \longrightarrow CaO + CO_2$$

In this reaction, the number of Ca, O and C on both side is the same.

Following method is used for balancing an equation.

Hit and Trial Method

This method consists of counting the number of atoms of each element manually on both the sides and try to equalise them.

Several steps involved in balancing a chemical equation are as follows

Step I. Write unbalanced equation and enclose the formulae in brackets.

$$\underset{\text{Sodium}}{(Na)} + \underset{\text{Water}}{(H_2O)} \longrightarrow \underset{\text{Sodium hydroxide}}{(NaOH)} + \underset{\text{Hydrogen}}{(H_2)}$$

Step II. Making list of elements as shown in unbalanced equation.

Element	Number of atoms in reactants (LHS)	Number of atoms in products (RHS)
Na	1	1
H	2	3
O	1	1

Step III. **Balancing first element** From the table [in step (b)], it is clear that it is only the hydrogen atoms, which are unbalanced. So, firstly we try to balance it.

Atoms of H	In reactants	In products
Initially	2 (in H_2O)	3 (1 in NaOH and 2 in H_2)
To balance	2×2	2×1 in NaOH, 2 in H_2 = 4H-atoms

Thus, the equation becomes

$$(Na) + 2(H_2O) \longrightarrow 2(NaOH) + (H_2)$$

Step IV. **Balancing second element** We examine the obtained equation and select another element which is still unbalanced. In the above equation, Na is still unbalanced. To balance the number of Na-atoms

Atoms of Na	In reactants	In products
Initially	1 (in Na)	2 (in NaOH)
To balance	2×1	2

Thus, after balancing Na and removing the brackets, we get the equation

$$2Na + 2H_2O \longrightarrow 2NaOH + H_2$$

Step V. **Balancing other elements** If we further examine the reaction, no element is found to be unbalanced. This method of balancing chemical equation is called **hit and trial method.**

Step VI. **Checking the correctness of equation** To check the correctness of the equation, we further tabulate the atoms of each element separately.

Element	Number of atoms in reactants	Number of atoms in products
Na	2	2
H	4	4
O	2	2

The above table clearly reveals that the obtained equation is a balanced chemical equation.

Example 1. Balance the following equation.

$$C_2H_6 + O_2 \longrightarrow CO_2 + H_2O$$

Sol. First of all enclose all the formulae in brackets.

$$(C_2H_6) + (O_2) \longrightarrow (CO_2) + (H_2O)$$

Hydrogen possesses maximum number of atom.

So, first of all to balance hydrogen multiply H_2O molecules by 3.

$$(C_2H_6) + (O_2) \longrightarrow (CO_2) + 3(H_2O)$$

Now, to balance carbon atom multiply CO_2 molecules by 2.

$$(C_2H_6) + (O_2) \longrightarrow 2(CO_2) + 3(H_2O)$$

There are 7 O-atoms on RHS (product side). To make 7 O-atoms at LHS (reactant side), we have to write 7/2 before O_2 but we can use only whole number to balance the equation, so we write 7/2 before O_2 and multiply the whole equation by 2.

$$\left[C_2H_6 + \frac{7}{2}O_2 \longrightarrow 2CO_2 + 3H_2O\right] \times 2$$

Thus, on removing the brackets from equation, the equation becomes

$$2C_2H_6 + 7O_2 \longrightarrow 4CO_2 + 6H_2O$$

Making a Chemical Equation More Informative

The following facts remain unexplained in a chemical equation shown in step (d).

- Physical states of substances
- Reaction conditions
- Evolution/absorption of energy

Some of these limitations of a chemical equation can be overcome by adding the following symbols or information as discussed below.

- The physical state of the reactants and products can be represented by using the symbols, (s) *for solid,* (*l*) *for liquid,* (*g*) *for gas and* (*aq*) *for aqueous solution,* alongwith their respective formulae. The word aqueous (*aq*) is used, if the reactant or product is present as a solution in water.

$$2Na(s) + 2H_2O(l) \longrightarrow 2NaOH\,(aq) + H_2(g)$$

Precipitate can also be represented by using an arrow pointing downwards (↓) instead of using symbol (s) for solid.

In the same way, the gaseous state of an evolved gas can be represented by using an arrow pointing upward direction (↑) instead of using symbol (*g*) for gas.

e.g. Magnesium reacting with dilute sulphuric acid is represented by the chemical equation.

$$\underset{\text{Magnesium}}{Mg(s)} + \underset{\text{Sulphuric acid}}{H_2SO_4\,(aq)} \longrightarrow \underset{\text{Magnesium sulphate}}{MgSO_4\,(aq)} + \underset{\text{Hydrogen}}{H_2\uparrow}$$

- The specific conditions of the reaction like temperature, pressure, catalyst, etc., are written above or below the arrow in the chemical equation.

$$\underset{\text{Carbon monoxide}}{CO(g)} + \underset{\text{Hydrogen}}{2H_2(g)} \xrightarrow{340\text{ atm}} \underset{\text{Methanol}}{CH_3OH(l)}$$

- Evolution of heat or absorption of heat can be indicated by writing [+ Heat] on the right hand side or left hand side of the equation, respectively.

e.g. Burning of carbon in the presence of air.

$$\underset{\text{Carbon}}{C(s)} + \underset{\text{Oxygen}}{O_2(g)} \longrightarrow \underset{\text{Carbon dioxide}}{CO_2(g)} + \text{Heat}$$

- The reaction which are reversible can be shown by the sign of reversibility ($\rightleftharpoons$).

e.g. $3Fe + 4H_2O \rightleftharpoons Fe_3O_4 + 4H_2$

Note Although it is not always necessary to mention the physical states and reaction conditions in a balanced chemical equation. So, you can left this step until it is asked in the question.

Information Conveyed by a Balanced Chemical Equation

- A chemical equation gives us information about the substance (reactants and products) participating in a chemical reaction.
- It give information about the symbol and formulae of all the substances involved in a particular reaction.
- It tells us about the physical state of the reactants and products.
- It gives us information whether heat is evolved or absorbed during a chemical reaction.
- It ensures that number of atoms present in reactants (LHS) is equal to the number of atoms present in products (RHS).
- It tells us about the weights of reactant consumed and of product formed, the number of atoms or molecules of reactants and products that are involved in a reaction, the number of gram of atoms or gram moles of the substance that are participating in the reaction, etc.
- It also proves the law of conservation of mass.

Limitations of Chemical Equation

- A chemical equation does not tell us about the feasibility of a chemical reaction. It means we cannot predict whether a particular reaction will take place or not.
- It does not tell us whether a particular reaction will proceed at a slow, moderate or fast speed or rate.

Relative Atomic Mass (Atomic Weight)

It is defined as the number of times a given atom is heavier than $\frac{1}{12}$th of mass of 1 atom of carbon-12 (C-12) or it is the average mass of the atom as compared to $\frac{1}{12}$th the mass of one carbon-12 atom.

Thus, Relative atomic mass

$$= \frac{\text{Mass of 1 atom of the element}}{\frac{1}{12}\text{th the mass of one C-12 atom}}$$

Atomic Mass Unit

It is defined as the mass unit equal to exactly 1/12th of the mass of one atom of C-12 isotope. Earlier, it was abbreviated as amu but according to latest recommendation of IUPAC, it is now written as 'u'–unified mass.

$$1 \text{ amu or } /u = 1.6605 \times 10^{-24} \text{ g}$$

Note Mass of an atom of hydrogen $= 1.6736 \times 10^{-24}$ g

Thus, in terms of amu,

Mass of hydrogen atom $= \frac{1.6736 \times 10^{-24} \text{ g}}{1.66056 \times 10^{-24} \text{ g}}$

$= 1.0078 \text{ amu} = 1.0080 \text{ amu}$

Relative Molecular Mass (Molecular Weight)

It is defined as the ratio of the average mass of one molecule of an element or compound to one–twelfth of the mass of an atom of carbon-12 isotope.

Relative molecular mass of a compound is the sum of relative atomic masses of the atomic species as given in the chemical formula.

Example 2. Calculate relative molecular mass of (i) ammonia (NH_3) and (ii) sugar ($C_{12}H_{22}O_{11}$).

Sol.

(i) Relative mass of NH_3,

Mass of 1 atom of nitrogen is $1 \times 14 = 14$ amu

Mass of 3 atoms of hydrogen is $3 \times 1 = 3$ amu

So, mass of NH_3 is $1 \times 14 + 3 \times 1 = 14 + 3 = 17$ amu

(ii) Relative mass of sugar ($C_{12}H_{22}O_{11}$)

= Mass of 12 atoms of carbon + Mass of 22 atoms of hydrogen + Mass of 11 atoms of oxygen

$= 12 \times 12 + 22 \times 1 + 11 \times 16$

$= 144 + 22 + 176$

$= 342$ amu

Percentage Composition

The percentage composition of an element in a compound is the percentage of the mass contributed by the element to the total mass of the compound.

Or

Percent composition of a compound is the percentage by weight of each element present in it. It is obtained by dividing mass of that element in the compound by the total mass of the compound and multiplying by 100. i.e.

Percentage composition of element

$$= \frac{\text{Mass contributed by the element}}{\text{Total molecular mass of compound}} \times 100$$

Example 3. Calculate percentage of oxygen in water. Given that the relative atomic masses of H = 1, O = 16.

Sol. Relative molecular mass of $H_2O = 1 \times 2 + 16 = 18$

Percentage composition of oxygen

$$= \frac{\text{Mass contributed by oxygen}}{\text{Total molecular mass of water}} \times 100$$

$$= \frac{16}{18} \times 100 = 88.89\ \%$$

∴ Percentage composition of oxygen in water is 88.89%.

Check Your LEARNING...

1 Write the balanced equation for the follong reaction.

$Na_2O_2(s) + H_2O(l) \longrightarrow NaOH(aq)$

2 Which of the following reactions is balanced, *A* or *B*?

$A: 2\,NaCl + 2H_2O \xrightarrow{\text{Electricity}} 2NaOH + 2Cl_2 + H_2 \uparrow$

$B: Ca(OH)_2 + Cl_2 \longrightarrow CaOCl_2 + H_2O$

3 What is the value of 1 amu in grams?

4 Complete the following.

Relative atomic mass is defined as the number of times a given atom is heavier than .... of the mass of 1 atom of carbon-12.

5 What will be the mass of hydrogen atom in amu?

6 Calculate the percentage composition of K in $KClO_3$.

[*Ans.* K = 31.83%]

QUiCK Revision

- **Symbols of elements** are derived from one or two letters of names of the elements in English, Greek, Latin, German, etc. First letter is written in capital and second one in small, e.g. iron, Fe(from ferrum).
- **Valency** is the combining capacity of an element and it is charge in case of ions.
- An **ion** is a positively or negatively charged atom (or group of atoms) which is formed by loss or gain of electrons by an atom (or group of atoms).
- Elements with one, two or three electrons in their outermost shell (valence shell) are usually metals. Out of the elements that have four electrons in the outermost orbit-carbon is a non-metal, silicon and germanium are metalloids and the rest are metals.
- Elements with five, six or seven electrons in their outermost shell are normally non-metals.
- **Chemical formula** is the shortest way to represent a compound with the help of symbols and valency of elements.

  There are some steps that should be kept in mind while attempting to write a formula. The method is called criss-cross method.

  (i) Write the symbols of constituent elements and their valencies.

  (ii) Write the symbol of cation first followed by the symbol of anion.

  (iii) Then criss-cross their charges or valencies to get the formula.

  (iv) In the formula, the positive and negative charges must balance each other and the overall structure must be neutral.
- **Radical** is an atom or a group of atoms, which behave as a single unit, having their own combining capacity and has positive or negative charge.
- **Chemical equation** is the symbolic representation of a chemical reaction that describes a chemical change in terms of symbols and formulae.
- **A balanced chemical equation** is that, in which the total number of atoms of each element are equal on both sides of the equation.
- The method involved for balancing chemical equation is hit and trial method.
- **Hit and trial method** This method consist of counting the number of atoms of each element on both sides and try to equalise them.
- **Relative atomic mass** of the atom of an element is defined as the average mass of the atom, as compared to 1/12th the mass of one carbon-12 atom.
- **Atomic mass unit** (amu) is equal to one twelth the mass of an atom of carbon-12.
- **Relative molecular mass** is the of the average mass of one molecule of an element or compound to one-twelth of the mass of an atom of carbon -12 isotope.
- **Percentage composition** of an element in a compound is the percentage of the mass contributed by the element to the total mass of the compound.

Chapter Practice

Section-I

a. Multiple Choice Questions

1. The abbreviations used in the chemistry
   (a) to represent name of elements
   (b) to represent reactions
   (c) Both (a) and (b)
   (d) None of the above

Sol. (c)

2. Modern atomic symbols are based on the method proposed by
   (a) Berzelius (b) Bohr (c) Dalton (d) Newton

Sol. (a)

3. The symbol for carbonate ion is
   (a) CO (b) CO_3^- (c) CO_3^{2-} (d) CO_2

Sol. (c)

4. Valency of copper in Cu_2Cl_2 and $CuCl_2$ are respectively
   (a) 2, 1 (b) 1, 2
   (c) 1, 1 (d) 2, 2

Sol. (b)

5. The valency of iron in Fe_2O_3 is
   (a) + 1 (b) + 2
   (c) + 3 (d) Both (b) and (c)

Sol. (c)

6. The formula of compound represents
   (a) a radical (b) a molecule
   (c) a particle (d) an atom

Sol. (b)

7. The correct chemical formula of aluminium oxide is
   (a) AlO (b) AlO_3 (c) Al_2O_3 (d) Al_3O_2

Sol. (c)

8. The number of carbon atoms in a hydrogen carbonate radical is
   (a) one (b) two (c) three (d) four

Sol. (a)

9. The chemical reaction,

$$(NH_4)_2Cr_2O_7 \xrightarrow{\Delta} N_2 + 4H_2O + Cr_2O_3$$

   is an example of
   (a) two reactants and two products
   (b) one reactant and two or three products
   (c) two reactants and one product
   (d) two reactants and three or four products

Sol. (b)

10. In water, the hydrogen-to-oxygen mass ratio is
    (a) 1 : 16 (b) 1 : 32 (c) 1 : 8 (d) 1 : 64

Sol. (c)

b. Fill in the Blanks

11. Dalton used symbol .... for oxygen and ...... for hydrogen. [O], [Θ], [H], [Δ]

Sol. [O], [H]

12. Usually symbol represents ...... atom(s) of an element. (one, two, three)

Sol. one

13. Nitrite is .... and ...... radical.

Sol. NO_2^-, monovalent,

14. Nitride is .... and .... radical.

Sol. N^{3-}, trivalent

15. Nitrate is .... and .... radical.

Sol. NO_3^-, monovalent

16. The formula of caustic potash is .... (KOH, NaH, K_2CO_3)

Sol. KOH

17. The formula of washing soda is .... (Na_2CO_3, $NaHCO_3$, Ca_2SO_4)

Sol. Na_2CO_3

18. Limestone is .... ($CaCO_3$, $Ca(OH)_2$, Na_2SO_4)

Sol. $CaCO_3$

19. Formula of iron (III) carbonate is .... (Fe_2CO_3, $Fe_2(CO_3)_3$, $FeCO_3$)

Sol. $Fe_2(CO_3)_3$

20. Sodium chloride has two radicals. Sodium is ...... radical, whereas chloride is ...... radical.
    (acid, basic, neutral)

Sol. basic, acidic

21. Essential condition for a chemical equation is that it must be .... and should be ....
    (balanced, molecular, unbalanced)

Sol. balanced, molecular

22. $2H_2O + 2Cl_2 \longrightarrow$ .... $+ O_2$ (4HCl, 5HCl, 3HCl)

Sol. 4HCl

23. $2NaHCO_3 \longrightarrow$ .... $+ H_2O + CO_2$
    (Na_2CO_3, $2NaCO_3$, $NaHCO_3$)

Sol. Na_2CO_3

24. A chemical equation has .... as well as .... significance. (qualitative, quantitative)

Sol. qualitative, quantitative

25. .... does not tell about the light related changes during chemical reactions. (chemical equation, physical equation)

Sol. Chemical equation

c. Give One Word or a Phrase

26. The chemical symbol of sodium is Na. Write its Latin name.

Sol. *Natrium*

27. The chemical symbol for nitrogen gas.

Sol. N_2

28. The chemical symbol for hydrogen gas.

Sol. H_2

29. The name given to combining capacity of an element.

Sol. Valency

30. An element '*Y*' shows variable valencies of 3 and 5. Write the formulae of its oxides.

Sol. Y_2O_3, Y_2O_5 are its oxides.

31. An element *Z* has a valency of 3. What is the formula of oxide of *Z*?

Sol. $\underset{+3}{Z} \times \underset{-2}{O} = Z_2O_3$

32. The chemical formula of ammonium phosphate?

Sol. $\underset{+1}{NH_4} \times \underset{-3}{PO_4} = (NH_4)_3PO_4$

33. The molecular formula of aluminium hydroxide.

Sol. $Al(OH)_3$

34. The correct formulae of sodium sulphide and sodium sulphite.

Sol. Na_2S (sodium sulphide), Na_2SO_3 (sodium sulphite).

35. If an element *X* has its valency equal to 3, what will be its formula with carbonate ion?

Sol. $\underset{+3}{X} \times \underset{-2}{CO_3} = X_2(CO_3)_3$

36. What do you mean by chemical equation?

Sol. Chemical equation is the symbolic representation of an actual chemical reaction.

e.g. $AgNO_3 + NaCl \longrightarrow AgCl + NaNO_3$

37. An example of one reactant and two products.

Sol. $MgCO_3 \xrightarrow{\Delta} MgO + CO_2$

d. Match the Columns

38. Match the following columns.

Column I (Name of radicals)		Column II (Formula of radicals)	
A.	Phosphite	1.	$[Fe(CN)_6]^{4-}$
B.	Ferrocyanide	2.	$C_2O_4^{2-}$
C.	Oxalate	3.	$P_2O_7^{4-}$
D.	Pyrophosphate	4.	PO_3^{3-}
E.	Phosphate	5.	PO_4^{3-}

Sol. A→(4), B→(1), C→(2), D→(3), E→(5)

39. Match the following columns.

Column I (Name of the compound)		Column II (Formula)	
A.	Sodium carbonate	1.	Na_2SO_4
B.	Sodium chlorate	2.	Na_2CO_3
C.	Sodium sulphate	3.	$NaClO_3$
D.	Sodium nitrate	4.	$NaNO_2$
E.	Sodium nitrite	5.	$NaNO_3$

Sol. A→(2), B→(3), C→(1), D→(5), E→(4)

40. Match the following columns.

Column I (Name of equation)		Column II (Examples)	
A.	Skeleton equation	1.	$Na + H_2O \longrightarrow NaOH + H$
B.	Balanced equation	2.	$2Na + 2H_2O \longrightarrow 2NaOH + H_2$
C.	Atomic equation	3.	$CaCO_3 + 2HCl \longrightarrow CaCl_2 + H_2O + CO_2$
D.	Molecular equation	4.	$CaCO_3 + HCl \longrightarrow CaCl_2 + H_2O + CO_2$

Sol. A→(4), B→(3), C→(1), D→(2)

e. Balanced Chemical Equation

41. Nitric acid + Calcium hydroxide ⟶ Calcium nitrate + Water

Sol. $2HNO_3 + Ca(OH)_2 \longrightarrow Ca(NO_3)_2 + 2H_2O$

42. Silver chloride ⟶ Silver + Chlorine

Sol. $2\,AgCl \xrightarrow{\text{Sunlight}} 2Ag + Cl_2$

43. Zinc sulphide + Oxygen ⟶ Zinc oxide + Sulphur dioxide

Sol. $2ZnS + 3O_2 \longrightarrow 2ZnO + 2SO_2$

44. Aluminium carbide + Water ⟶ Aluminium hydroxide + Methane

Sol. $Al_4C_3 + 12H_2O \longrightarrow 4Al(OH)_3 + 3CH_4$

45. Iron pyrites + Oxygen ⟶ Ferric oxide + Sulphur dioxide

Sol. $4FeS_2 + 11O_2 \longrightarrow 2Fe_2O_3 + 8SO_2$

Section-II

a. 2 Marks Questions

1. Which of the following symbols of element are incorrect? Write their correct symbols.

(i) Carbon—C (ii) Aluminium—AL

Sol. (i) Correct; Carbon = C, i.e. capital letter must be used. [1]

(ii) Incorrect; Aluminium = Al, i.e. 2nd letter should be small, while first letter is capital. [1]

2. Write the formulae and valency of the following radicals or ions.

(i) Oxalate (ii) Bicarbonate

Sol. (i) Oxalate $C_2O_4^{2-}$ (Valency = − 2) [1]

(ii) Bicarbonate HCO_3^- (Valency = − 1) [1]

3. Give difference between relative atomic mass and relative molecular mass.

Sol. **Relative atomic mass** It is defined as the number of times a given atom is heavier than $\frac{1}{12}$th of mass of 1 atom of carbon-12 or it is the average mass of the atom as compared to $\frac{1}{12}$th mass of one carbon-12 atom. [1]

Relative molecular mass It is defined as the ratio of average mass of one molecule of an element or compound to $\frac{1}{12}$ th of the mass of an atom of carbon-12 isotope. [1]

4. Find the percentage mass of water in epsom salt, $MgSO_4 \cdot 7H_2O$.

Sol. Relative molecular mass of $MgSO_4 \cdot 7H_2O$

$$= 24 + 32 + (16 \times 4) + 7(2 + 16)$$

$$= 24 + 32 + 64 + 126 = 246$$

246 g of epsom salt contains 126 g of water of crystallisation.

Hence, 100 g of epsom salt contains $100 \times \frac{126}{246}$

The % of H_2O in $MgSO_4 \cdot 7H_2O$ = 51.22% [2]

b. 3 Marks Questions

5. What is the valency of underlined element in the given compounds?

(i) $\underline{Ca}_3N_2$ (ii) $\underline{Zn}SO_4$

(iii) $\underline{C}Cl_4$

Sol. (i) Ca_3N_2, Valency of calcium = + 2 [1]

(ii) $ZnSO_4$; Valency of zinc = + 2 [1]

(iii) CCl_4 ; Valency of carbon = 4 [1]

6. (i) Write chemical formulae of the following compounds.

(a) Aluminium nitride

(b) Ammonium phosphate

(ii) Name an element which shows a variable valency. Write the formulae of its two chlorides.

Sol. (i) (a) AlN

(b) $(NH_4)_3PO_4$ [2]

(ii) Iron (Fe), it forms $FeCl_2$ and $FeCl_3$ with chlorine. [1]

7. Write the formulae of

(i) sodium chloride

(ii) aluminium oxide

(iii) ammonium sulphate

Sol. (i) $\underset{+1}{Na} \times \underset{-1}{Cl} = NaCl$ [1]

(ii) $\underset{+3}{Al} \times \underset{-2}{O} = Al_2O_3$ [1]

(iii) $\underset{+1}{NH_4} \times \underset{-2}{SO_4} = (NH_4)_2SO_4$ [1]

8. Write the chemical formulae, using criss-cross method.

(i) Magnesium bicarbonate

(ii) Barium nitrate

(iii) Potassium nitrate

Sol. (i) $\underset{+2}{Mg} \times \underset{-1}{HCO_3}$

Formula is $Mg(HCO_3)_2$. [1]

(ii) $\underset{+2}{Ba} \times \underset{-1}{NO_3}$

Formula is $Ba(NO_3)_2$. [1]

(iii) $\underset{+1}{K} \times \underset{-1}{NO_3}$

Formula is KNO_3. [1]

9. Write down the names of compounds represented by the following formulae.

(i) $Al_2(SO_4)_3$ (ii) $CaCl_2$

(iii) K_2SO_4 (iv) KNO_3

(v) $CaCO_3$ (vi) $CaZnO_2$

Sol. (i) Aluminium sulphate

(ii) Calcium chloride

(iii) Potassium sulphate

(iv) Potassium nitrate

(v) Calcium carbonate

(vi) Calcium zincate [6 × ½ = 3]

10. Choose simple and compound radicals out of the following.

$$Cl^-, SO_4^{2-}, S^{2-}, Na^+, NH_4^+, Ni^{2+}$$

Sol. Cl^- : Simple radical
SO_4^{2-} : Compound radical
S^{2-} : Simple radical
Na^+ : Simple radical
NH_4^+ : Compound radical
Ni^{2+} : Simple radical [6 × ½ = 3]

11. Correct the following statements.
(i) The molecular formula of water (H_2O) represents 9 parts by mass of water.
(ii) A molecule of an element is always monoatomic.
(iii) A balanced equation obeys the law of conservation of mass and hence, does an unbalanced equation.

Sol. (i) The molecular formula of water (H_2O) represents 18 parts by mass of water. [1]
(ii) A molecule of an element is not always monoatomic. [1]
(iii) A balanced equation obeys the law of conservation of mass while unbalanced equation does not. [1]

12. Write the essential or necessary requirements of a chemical equation.

Sol. (i) Chemical equation should represent a true chemical change. [1]
(ii) Chemical equation should be balanced, i.e. number of atoms of each element should be equal on both sides of the equation. [1]
(iii) Chemical equation should be molecular, i.e. all the substances present in the chemical equation should be represented in their molecular forms. [1]

C. 4 Marks Questions

13. Complete the following table.

Acid radicals → Basic radicals ↓	Phosphate	Hydroxide	Carbonate	Sulphate	Nitrate	Chloride
Magnesium	$Mg_3(PO_4)_2$	$Mg(OH)_2$	$MgCO_3$	$MgSO_4$	$Mg(NO_3)_2$	$MgCl_2$
Potassium						
Iron (II)						
Calcium						
Ammonium						
Silver						
Zinc						
Sodium						

Sol.

Acid radicals → Basic radicals ↓	Phosphate	Hydroxide	Carbonate	Sulphate	Nitrate	Chloride
Magnesium	$Mg_3(PO_4)_2$	$Mg(OH)_2$	$MgCO_3$	$MgSO_4$	$Mg(NO_3)_2$	$MgCl_2$
Potassium	K_3PO_4	KOH	K_2CO_3	K_2SO_4	KNO_3	KCl
Iron (II)	$Fe_3(PO_4)_2$	$Fe(OH)_2$	$FeCO_3$	$FeSO_4$	$Fe(NO_3)_2$	$FeCl_2$
Calcium	$Ca_3(PO_4)_2$	$Ca(OH)_2$	$CaCO_3$	$CaSO_4$	$Ca(NO_3)_2$	$CaCl_2$
Ammonium	$(NH_4)_3PO_4$	NH_4OH	$(NH_4)_2CO_3$	$(NH_4)_2SO_4$	NH_4NO_3	NH_4Cl
Silver	Ag_3PO_4	$AgOH$	Ag_2CO_3	Ag_2SO_4	$AgNO_3$	$AgCl$
Zinc	$Zn_3(PO_4)_2$	$Zn(OH)_2$	$ZnCO_3$	$ZnSO_4$	$Zn(NO_3)_2$	$ZnCl_2$
Sodium	Na_3PO_4	$NaOH$	Na_2CO_3	Na_2SO_4	$NaNO_3$	$NaCl$

[8 × ½ = 4]

14. Sodium chloride reacts with silver nitrate to produce silver chloride and sodium nitrate.
(i) Write the chemical equation.
(ii) Check whether it is balanced, if not then balance it.
(iii) Calculate the weights of reactants and products.
(iv) Write the law which satisfies this chemical equation.

Sol. (i) $NaCl + AgNO_3 \longrightarrow AgCl + NaNO_3$ [1]
(ii) It is a balanced chemical equation. [1]
(iii) Total weight of reactants = 58.5 + 170 = 228.5
Total weight of products = 143.5 + 85 = 228.5 [1]
(iv) It is based upon the law of conservation of mass, i.e. in a chemical reaction total mass of the reactants must be equal to the total mass of the products. [1]

15. Write the important limitations or drawbacks of a chemical equation.

Sol. The chemical equation does not indicate about the
(i) physical states of the reactants and products.
(ii) conditions necessary for the reaction to occur.
(iii) concentrations of the reactants and products.
(iv) time taken by the reaction for completion.
(v) rate at which the reaction takes place.
(vi) extent upto which the reaction takes place.
(vii) mechanism of the reaction. [4]

16. How are the limitations or drawbacks of a chemical equation removed?

Sol. Some of the drawbacks of chemical equation can be removed as follows

The physical states of the reactants and products can be indicated by using the symbol, i.e. (*s*) for solids, (*l*) for liquids, (*g*) for gases and (*aq*) for aqueous solutions.

e.g. $Zn(g) + 2HCl(g) \longrightarrow ZnCl_2(g) + H_2(g)$ [1/2]

The conditions necessary for the reaction to occur are represented by the arrow between the reactants and products.

e.g. $Fe(s) + S(s) \xrightarrow{Heat} FeS(s)$ [1/2]

The concentration of the solution of reactants can be shown by writing dil. for dilute and conc. for concentrated solution. e.g.

$Cu(s) + 2H_2SO_4(conc.) \xrightarrow{\Delta} CuSO_4(aq) + SO_2(g) + 2H_2O(l)$ [1/2]

The heat changes during a reaction are indicated by writing + Q kJ or – Q kJ along with the products for exothermic and endothermic reactions respectively

e.g. $2H_2(g) + O_2(g) \longrightarrow 2H_2O(l) + 572kJ$ [1/2]

$C(s) + H_2O(g) \longrightarrow CO(g) + H_2(g) - 131\ kJ$

The rate of reaction can be shown by writing slow or fast along with the products.

e.g. $2NO(g) + O_2(g) \longrightarrow 2NO_2(g)$ (Fast)
$2CO(g) + O_2(g) \longrightarrow 2CO_2(g)$ (Slow) [2]

17. Write the balanced chemical equation of the following reactions.
(i) Sodium chloride + Manganese dioxide + Sulphuric acid ⟶ Sodium hydrogen sulphate + Manganese sulphate + Water + Chlorine
(ii) Sulphur + Nitric acid ⟶ Sulphuric acid + Nitrogen dioxide + Water
(iii) Potassium dichromate + Hydrochloric acid ⟶ Potassium chloride + Chromium chloride + Water + Chlorine
(iv) Aluminium sulphate + Sodium hydroxide ⟶ Sodium sulphate + Sodium meta-aluminate + Water

Sol. (i) $2NaCl + MnO_2 + 3H_2SO_4 \longrightarrow 2NaHSO_4 + MnSO_4 + 2H_2O + Cl_2$ [1]
(ii) $S + 6HNO_3 \longrightarrow H_2SO_4 + 6NO_2 + 2H_2O$ [1]
(iii) $K_2Cr_2O_7 + 14HCl \longrightarrow 2KCl + 2CrCl_3 + 7H_2O + 3Cl_2$ [1]
(iv) $Al_2(SO_4)_3 + 8NaOH \longrightarrow 3Na_2SO_4 + 2NaAlO_2 + 4H_2O$ [1]

18. Balance the following equations.
(i) $P + HNO_3 \longrightarrow NO_2 + H_2O + H_3PO_4$
(ii) $HNO_3 + H_2S \longrightarrow NO_2 + H_2O + S$
(iii) $H_2O + Cl_2 \longrightarrow HCl + O_2$
(iv) $Pb_3O_4 + HCl \longrightarrow PbCl_2 + H_2O + Cl_2$
(v) $NO_2 + H_2O \longrightarrow HNO_2 + HNO_3$
(vi) $KOH + Cl_2 \longrightarrow KCl + KClO + H_2O$
(vii) $MnO_2 + HCl \longrightarrow MnCl_2 + H_2O + Cl_2$
(viii) $Pb_3O_4 \longrightarrow PbO + O_2$

Sol. (i) $P + 5HNO_3 \longrightarrow 5NO_2 + H_2O + H_3PO_4$
(ii) $4HNO_3 + 2H_2S \longrightarrow 4NO_2 + 4H_2O + 2S$
(iii) $2H_2O + 2Cl_2 \longrightarrow 4HCl + O_2$
(iv) $Pb_3O_4 + 8HCl \longrightarrow 3PbCl_2 + 4H_2O + Cl_2$
(v) $2NO_2 + H_2O \longrightarrow HNO_2 + HNO_3$
(vi) $2KOH + Cl_2 \longrightarrow KCl + KClO + H_2O$
(vii) $MnO_2 + 4HCl \longrightarrow MnCl_2 + 2H_2O + Cl_2$
(viii) $2Pb_3O_4 \longrightarrow 6PbO + O_2$ $[8 \times \frac{1}{2} = 4]$

d. Numerical Based Questions

19. Calculate the relative molecular mass of the following compound.

(i) Lead sulphate (ii) Calcium phosphate

(Given, atomic masses of various elements, $Ca = 40u, S = 32u, O = 16u, Pb = 207u$ and $P = 31u$)

Sol. (i) Relative molecular mass of lead sulphate ($PbSO_4$)

$= $ Atomic mass of Pb + Atomic mass of S + 4 × Atomic mass of O

$= 207 + 32 + 4 \times 16$

$= 207 + 32 + 64 = 303\,u$

(ii) Relative molecular mass of calcium phosphate $[Ca_3(PO_4)_2]$

$= 3 \times$ Atomic mass of Ca + 2 × (Atomic mass of P) + 8 × (Atomic mass of O)

$= 3 \times 40 + 2 \times 31 + 8 \times 16$

$= 120 + 62 + 128 = 310\,u$

20. Calculate the percentage composition of nitrogen in urea NH_2CONH_2.

Sol. Relative molecular mass of urea (NH_2CONH_2)

$= 2 \times$ Atomic mass of N + 1 × Atomic mass of C + 4 × atomic mass of H + 1 × Atomic mass of O.

$= 2 \times 14 + 1 \times 12 + 4 \times 1 + 1 \times 16$

$= 28 + 12 + 4 + 16$

$= 60\,u$

Percentage composition of nitrogen

$$= \frac{\text{Mass contributed by N}}{\text{Molecular mass of } NH_2CONH_2} \times 100$$

$$= \frac{28}{60} \times 100$$

$= 46.67\,\%$

21. Calculate the percentage of boron [B] in $Na_2B_4O_7 \cdot 10H_2O \cdot (H = 1, B = 11, O = 16, Na = 23)$

Sol. Molecular mass of $Na_2B_4O_7 \cdot 10H_2O$

$= 2 \times 23 + 4 \times 111 + 7 \times 16 + 10(2 + 16)$

$= 46 + 44 + 112 + 180$

$= 382$

So, % of boron in $Na_2B_4O_7 \cdot 10H_2O$

$$= \frac{44}{382} \times 100$$

$$= \frac{22 \times 100}{191}$$

% of B = 11.518%

22. Calculate the percentage of nitrogen in ammonium nitrate (NH_4NO_3).

Sol. Molecular mass of $NH_4NO_3 = 14 + 4 + 14 + 48$

$= 80\,u$

Percentage of nitrogen

$$= \frac{\text{Mass of N}}{\text{Molecular mass } NH_4NO_3} \times 100$$

$$= \frac{28}{80} \times 100$$

% of N = 35%

23. Find the percentage composition of various elements in sodium carbonate, Na_2CO_3.

Given that the relative atomic masses of O = 16, Na = 23 and C = 12.

Sol. Relative molecular mass of Na_2CO_3

$= 23 \times 2 + 12 + 16 \times 3$

$= 46 + 12 + 48 = 106$ amu

Since, 106 g of Na_2CO_3 contain 46 g of sodium,

$\therefore$ 100 g of Na_2CO_3 will contain $\frac{46 \times 100}{106}$ of sodium

$$= \frac{4600}{106} = 43.4 \text{ g of sodium}$$

Similarly, 106 g Na_2CO_3 contains 12 g of carbon.

$\therefore$ 100 g Na_2CO_3 contains $\frac{12 \times 100}{106}$

$$= \frac{1200}{106} = 11.3 \text{ g of carbon}$$

Again, 106 g of Na_2CO_3 contains 48 g of oxygen

$\therefore$ 100 Na_2CO_3 will contains $\frac{48 \times 100}{106}$

$$= \frac{4800}{106} = 45.3 \text{ g of Oxygen}$$

$\therefore$ In Na_2CO_3 : Na = 43.4%

C = 11.3% and O = 45.3%

24. Calculate the percentage mass of water in washing soda crystals $Na_2CO_3 \cdot 10H_2O$.

Sol. Relative molecular mass of $Na_2CO_3 \cdot 10H_2O$

$= 23 \times 2 + 12 + 16 \times 3 + 10(2 + 16)$

$= 106 + 180$

$= 286$ amu

286 g of washing soda contains 180 g of water of crystallisation.

$\therefore$ So, 100 g of washing soda will contain

$$\frac{180 \times 100}{286} = \frac{18000}{286} = 62.9 \text{ g of } H_2O$$

$\therefore$ The % of H_2O in $Na_2CO_3 \cdot 10H_2O$ = 62.9%

Chapter Assessment

Section-I

a. Multiple Choice Questions

1. The symbol of neon is
   (a) NE (b) ne (c) Ne (d) nE
2. The chemical formula of sodium chlorate is $NaClO_3$ then the chemical formula of sodium hypochlorite is
   (a) $NaClO$ (b) $NaClO_2$
   (c) $NaClO_4$ (d) Na_2ClO_2
3. Oxygen, nitrogen and platinum are respectively
   (a) trivalent, trivalent, tetravalent
   (b) divalent, trivalent, trivalent
   (c) divalent, tetravalent, trivalent
   (d) divalent, trivalent, tetravalent
4. Cl^-, F^-, K^+ and Na^+ are the examples of
   (a) basic radical
   (b) acidic radical
   (c) simple radical
   (d) compound radical
5. Which of the following is balanced chemical equation?
   (a) $2H_2SO_4 + C \longrightarrow CO_2 + SO_2 + H_2O$
   (b) $Na_2CO_3 + H_2SO_4 \longrightarrow Na_2SO_4 + H_2O + CO_2$
   (c) $MgCl_2 + Na_2CO_3 \longrightarrow MgCO_3 + NaCl$
   (d) $Al + NaOH + H_2O \longrightarrow NaAlO_2 + H_2$

b. Fill in the Blanks

6. Valency of an element is number of electrons ...., ... or .... by an atom of the element in order to get the stable configuration. (lost, shared, gained, vanished)
7. Chemical formula of glucose is represented as .... ($C_7H_{14}O_6$, $C_6H_{12}O_6$)
8. The prefix 'tri' is used to indicate .... atoms of an element. (two, three, four)
9. Cl^-, F^-, CO_3^{2-} and SO_4^{2-} are .... radicals. (acidic, basic, neutral)
10. The equation which simply represents the .... and .... of the various substances taking part in the chemical reaction is said to be .... equation. (chemical, formula, symbols)

c. Give One Word or a Phrase

11. The symbol 'S' represent for.
12. The name of two elements, which show variable valency.
13. One example of bivalent cations.
14. The cation and anion present in the CH_3COONa.
15. One example of trivalent anion.

d. Match the Columns

16. Match the following columns.

	Column I (Name)		Column II (Radicals)
A.	Dichromate	1.	$Cr_2O_7^{2-}$
B.	Nitrite	2.	ZnO_2^{2-}
C.	Mercuric	3.	NO_2^-
D.	Zincate	4.	Hg^{2+}

17. Match the following columns.

	Column I (Name)		Column II (Radicals)
A.	Permanganate	1.	Sn^{4+}
B.	Sulphite	2.	MnO_4^-
C.	Stannic	3.	N^{3-}
D.	Nitride	4.	SO_3^{2-}

e. Balanced Chemical Equation

18. Lime water + Carbon dioxide $\longrightarrow$ Calcium carbonate + Water
19. Magnesium + Silver nitrate $\longrightarrow$ Magnesium nitrate + + Silver
20. Butane + Oxygen $\longrightarrow$ Carbon dioxide + Water
21. Sodium hydroxide + Sulphuric acid $\longrightarrow$ Sodium sulphate + Water
22. Potassium bicarbonate + Sulphuric acid $\longrightarrow$ Potassium sulphate + Carbon dioxide + Water

Section-II

a. 2 Marks Questions

1. 'Methane burns in oxygen to form carbon dioxide and water'. Write the chemical equation for the given chemical reaction and balance it.
2. Write the significance of *s*, *l*, *g* and *aq* in a chemical equation.

b. 3 Marks Questions

3. An element '*X*' has a valency 1.
   (i) Write the chemical formula of its phosphide.
   (ii) Write the chemical formula of its chloride.
   (iii) Is element '*X*' a metal or a non-metal?
4. Discuss about the hit and trial method using a chemical equation.

c. 4 Marks Questions

5. Write the valency of
   (i) carbon in CH_4.
   (ii) phosphorus in PH_3.
   (iii) sulphur in SF_6.
   (iv) fluorine in CaF_2.
6. Ammonia, calcium chloride and water are obtained by heating a mixture of ammonium chloride and calcium hydroxide.
   Write a balanced equation of the reaction.

d. Numerical Based Questions

7. Calculate the relative molecular mass of the following
   (i) H_2SO_4 (ii) $(NH_4)_2SO_4$
8. Calculate the mass per cent of calcium, phosphorus and oxygen in calcium phosphate $Ca_3(PO_4)_2$.

For explanations scan the given QR Code

Olympiad Section*

Brain Teasing Questions asked in Previous Olympiads

1. What is the mass percentage of nitrogen in the following active compounds present in fertilizers?
(i) Ammonium nitrate and (ii) Ammonium sulphate (INJSO)

	(i)	(ii)
(a)	35	40
(b)	32	21
(c)	35	21
(d)	21	35

2. Iron present in spinach can be estimated by titrating it with potassium permanganate. Small amounts of spinach leaves are weighed and dissolved in acid to extract the iron in solution. The solution is then titrated and the following reaction takes place during this titration.

$$Fe^{2+} + MnO_4^- + H^+ \longrightarrow Mn^{2+} + Fe^{3+} + H_2O$$

When properly balanced with the simplest set of whole number coefficients, the sum of the coefficients in the balanced equation is (INJSO)

(a) 16 (b) 18
(c) 22 (d) 24

3. Valence electron in Cl^- ion is (NTSE)

(a) 16 (b) 8
(c) 17 (d) 18

4. The formulae of an oxide of an element *M* is *MO*. The formulae of its phosphate is (NTSE)

(a) $M_3(PO_4)_2$ (b) MPO_4
(c) $M_2(PO_4)_3$ (d) M_3PO_4

5. What is the formula of carbon tetrachloride? (NTSE)

(a) CCl_4 (b) CCl_3
(c) CCl_2 (d) CCl

6. An example of a homo atomic molecule is (NTSE)

(a) ozone (b) ammonia
(c) methane (d) sulphur dioxide

7. Chemical formula of lime stone is (NTSE)

(a) $Ca(OH)_2$ (b) $CaCO_3$
(c) $CaCl_2$ (d) CCl_4

8. Which of the following statement is not true about an atom? (INJSO)

(a) Atoms are not able to exist independently
(b) Atoms are the basic units from which molecules and ions are formed
(c) Atoms are always neutral in nature
(d) Atoms aggregate in large numbers to form the matter that we can see, feel or touch

Answers

1. (c) 2. (a) 3. (b) 4. (a) 5. (a) 6. (a) 7. (b) 8. (d)

* *These questions may or may not be asked in the examination, have been given just for additional practice required for olympiads Scholarship Exams etc. For detailed explanations refer Page No. 133.*

CHAPTER

02

Chemical Changes and Reactions

CHAPTER OUTLINES

- Chemical Changes
- Energy Changes in a Chemical Reactions

Various kinds of changes occur around us all the time. Some of the changes are natural, while some are man-made. These changes can be differentiated as physical and chemical changes. In a physical change, only the change in state is involved, while chemical change brings a change in chemical properties of matter.

In this chapter, we will discuss about the various types of chemical changes and the chemical reactions which represent chemical changes.

Chemical Changes

A chemical change is a permanent change in which one substance react with another substance to undergo a change in chemical composition, i.e. a change in which always a new substance is formed with new property.

In these, breaking of chemical bond of reacting substances and making of new bonds of products take place. A chemical change is also called a **chemical reaction**. e.g. Burning of coal, formation of curd from milk, etc.

Following conditions are necessary for a chemical change to occur.

Mixing (Close contact)

For a chemical reaction to occur, the reactants has to be in close proximity. In some cases, reaction easily occurs even in solid state, while some reaction requires a medium or aqueous state.

e.g. Lead nitrate (solid) and potassium iodide (solid) react to make lead iodide.

$$Pb(NO_3)_2(s) + 2KI(s) \longrightarrow 2KNO_3(s) + PbI_2(s)$$

Sodium chloride and silver nitrate react in aqueous solution to form the precipitate of silver chloride and sodium nitrate.

$$NaCl(aq) + AgNO_3(aq) \longrightarrow \underset{\text{White ppt.}}{AgCl\downarrow} + NaNO_3(aq)$$

Heat

Heating increases the kinetic energy of the molecules of the substance and thus, the substances are able to react with each other easily.

e.g. Iron (Fe) filings and sulphur (S) powder do not react through mixing but they react when this mixture is heated and produce iron sulphide (FeS) as shown below.

$$Fe + S \xrightarrow{\Delta} FeS \text{ (Δ is the symbol for heating)}$$

Light

Light is a form of energy that can facilitate certain chemical reactions. Such chemical reactions are called **photochemical reaction** which work through **photolysis.**

e.g. Hydrogen gas (H_2) and chlorine gas (Cl_2) do not react with each other readily but when the mixture of these two gases is exposed to diffused sunlight, they combine to form hydrogen chloride gas (HCl).

$$H_2(g) + Cl_2(g) \xrightarrow{\text{Diffused sunlight}} 2HCl(g)$$

Electricity

Few chemical changes or reactions can be brought by applying electrical energy to the substance. These are electrochemical reactions. e.g. Electrolysis of water. Electrolysis is the process of using electricity to decompose water into oxygen and hydrogen gas.

$$2H_2O \xrightarrow{\text{Electricity}} 2H_2\uparrow + O_2\uparrow$$

Pressure

Pressure plays an important role in carrying out certain reactions, which otherwise do not occur by bringing the particles closer.

e.g. Nitrogen and hydrogen gases usually do not react but when subjected to a high pressure (200 atm) they combine to form ammonia gas (NH_3).

$$N_2 + 3H_2 \xrightleftharpoons{\text{200 atm}} 2NH_3$$

Catalyst

A catalyst is a substance, which alters the rate of a reaction but does not participate in it. Thus, it helps the reacting substances to act faster.

Catalysts are of following two types

(i) **Positive catalyst** The catalysts which increase the rate of the reaction is known as positive catalyst.

(ii) **Negative catalyst** The catalysts which decrease the rate of reaction is known as negative catalyst.

e.g. In the formation of ammonia from nitrogen and hydrogen, iron filings act as a positive catalyst for the reaction by enhancing the rate of a reaction.

$$N_2 + 3H_2 \xrightleftharpoons[\text{Fast reaction}]{\text{Fe/200 atm}} 2NH_3$$

Similarly, phosphoric acid serves as negative catalyst in the decomposition of H_2O_2.

Role of Promoters

Promoter have the ability to increase the efficiency of a catalyst. Hence, these further help in making the reaction faster. e.g. Molybdenum acts as a promoter for iron catalyst during the formation of ammonia gas.

$$N_2 + 3H_2 \xrightleftharpoons[\text{Faster reaction}]{\text{Fe - Mo , 200 atm}} 2NH_3$$

Remember, promoter alone cannot increase the rate of reaction if there is no catalyst present.

Characteristics of Chemical Reactions

In a chemical reaction, the conversion of reactants into products result in some observable changes known as characteristics of chemical reactions.

(i) **Evolution of gas** The chemical reactions in which one of the product is gas, it usually escapes or evolves from the test tube. When sodium sulphite reacts with hydrochloric acid, SO_2 gas is evolved with effervescence.

e.g. $Na_2SO_3 + 2HCl \longrightarrow 2NaCl + H_2O + SO_2\uparrow$

Note The formation of gas bubbles in a liquid during a reaction is called **effervescence.**

(ii) **Formation of precipitate** In some chemical reactions, the formation of insoluble solid substance takes place. This insoluble solid substance is known as precipitate.

e.g. $\underset{\text{Copper sulphate}}{CuSO_4} + \underset{\text{Sodium hydroxide}}{2NaOH} \longrightarrow \underset{\text{Sodium sulphate}}{Na_2SO_4} + \underset{\text{Copper hydroxide (Blue precipitate)}}{Cu(OH)_2\downarrow}$

(iii) **Change in colour** Some chemical reactions are characterised by change in colour.

e.g. $\underset{\text{(Iron)}}{Fe} + \underset{\text{(Blue solution) Copper sulphate}}{CuSO_4(aq)} \longrightarrow \underset{\text{Iron sulphate (Green solution)}}{FeSO_4} + \underset{\text{Copper (Brown red ppt.)}}{Cu}$

(iv) **Change in state** Chemical reactions in which a change of state is observed.

e.g. $\underset{\text{Ammonia}}{NH_3(g) + HCl(g)} \rightleftharpoons \underset{\text{Ammonium chloride}}{NH_4Cl(s)}$

(v) **Change in temperature** Some chemical reactions are characterised by change in temperature.

e.g. $\underset{\text{Calcium oxide}}{CaO} + H_2O \longrightarrow \underset{\text{Calcium hydroxide}}{Ca(OH)_2}$

This change is characterised by rising in temperature.

Check Your LEARNING...

1 Give two examples of chemical change?

2 Give an example of a reaction where the following processes are involved.

(i) Heating (ii) Electricity

3 Define effervescence.

4 Write an equation showing change in colour as its characteristic.

Types of Chemical Change or Chemical Reaction

On the basis of chemical changes taking place, reactions can be divided into following types

1. Combination Reaction

A reaction, in which two or more reactants combine to form a single product, is called combination reaction. Based on the types of reactants involved, the combination reaction can take place in following manner

(i) **Two elements combine to form a compound**

(a) Burning of coal.

$$\underset{\text{Carbon}}{C(s)} + \underset{\text{Oxygen}}{O_2(g)} \longrightarrow \underset{\text{Carbon dioxide}}{CO_2(g)}$$

(b) Reaction between hydrogen gas and oxygen gas to form water.

$$\underset{\text{Hydrogen}}{2H_2(g)} + \underset{\text{Oxygen}}{O_2(g)} \longrightarrow \underset{\text{Water}}{2H_2O(l)}$$

(c) Nitrogen gas reacts with hydrogen gas to form ammonia gas.

$$\underset{\text{Nitrogen}}{N_2(g)} + \underset{\text{Hydrogen}}{3H_2(g)} \rightleftharpoons \underset{\text{Ammonia}}{2NH_3(g)}$$

(ii) **An element and a compound combine to give a new compound** Ferrous chloride (i.e. a compound) reacts with chlorine (i.e. an element) to form a new compound, ferric chloride.

$$\underset{\text{Ferrous chloride}}{2FeCl_2} + \underset{\text{Chlorine}}{Cl_2} \longrightarrow \underset{\text{Ferric chloride}}{2FeCl_3}$$

Similarly, when carbon monoxide reacts with oxygen then carbon dioxide is produced.

$$\underset{\text{Carbon monoxide}}{2CO(g)} + \underset{\text{Oxygen}}{O_2(g)} \longrightarrow \underset{\text{Carbon dioxide}}{2CO_2(g)}$$

(iii) **Two or more compounds combine to give single product** Calcium oxide (quick lime) dissolved in water, to form calcium hydroxide (slaked lime). The reaction is highly exothermic, i.e. a lot of heat is produced during the reaction.

$$\underset{\text{Quicklime}}{CaO(s)} + \underset{\text{Water}}{H_2O(l)} \longrightarrow \underset{\text{Slaked lime}}{Ca(OH)_2(aq)} + \text{Heat}$$

The photosynthesis reaction is also considered as a combination reaction, e.g. molecules of CO_2 and water used by plants to make glucose.

$$6CO_2 + 6H_2O \xrightarrow[\text{Chlorophyll}]{\text{Sunlight}} C_6H_{12}O_6 + 6O_2$$

2. Decomposition Reaction

A reaction in which a single reactant breaks down to form two or more products is known as decomposition reaction.

e.g. $$\underset{\text{Potassium nitrate}}{2KNO_3(s)} \xrightarrow{\text{Heat}} \underset{\text{Potassium nitrite}}{2KNO_2(s)} + O_2(g)$$

On the basis of the form of energy required for the reaction, these reactions are of three types

(i) **Thermal decomposition** These reactions used the energy in the form of heat for the decomposition of the reactant. e.g.

(a) $$\underset{\text{Calcium carbonate}}{CaCO_3(s)} \xrightarrow{\text{Heat or }\Delta} \underset{\text{Calcium oxide}}{CaO(s)} + \underset{\text{Carbon dioxide}}{CO_2(g)}$$

(b) $$\underset{\substack{\text{Lead nitrate}\\ \text{(White salt)}}}{2Pb(NO_3)_2(s)} \xrightarrow{\text{Heat or }\Delta} \underset{\substack{\text{Lead oxide}\\ \text{(Yellow)}}}{2PbO(s)} + \underset{\substack{\text{Nitrogen dioxide}\\ \text{(Brown fumes)}}}{4NO_2(g)} + \underset{\text{Oxygen}}{O_2(g)}$$

(c) $$\underset{\substack{\text{Potassium}\\ \text{chlorate}}}{2KClO_3(s)} \xrightarrow{\text{Heat or }\Delta} \underset{\substack{\text{Potassium}\\ \text{chloride}}}{2KCl(s)} + \underset{\text{Oxygen}}{3O_2(g)}$$

Note The symbol Δ(delta) is used to signify that heat has bring about the reaction.

(ii) **Electrolysis** These reactions involve the use of electrical energy for the decomposition of the reactant molecules. e.g.

(a) $$\underset{\text{Water}}{2H_2O(l)} \xrightarrow{\text{Electric current}} \underset{\text{Hydrogen}}{2H_2(g)} + \underset{\text{Oxygen}}{O_2(g)}$$

(b) $$\underset{\substack{\text{Molten sodium}\\ \text{chloride}}}{2NaCl(l)} \xrightarrow{\text{Electric current}} \underset{\text{Sodium}}{2Na(s)} + \underset{\text{Chlorine}}{Cl_2(g)}$$

(iii) **Photolysis or photochemical decomposition** These reactions involve the use of light energy for the purpose of decomposition. e.g.

(a) $$\underset{\text{Silver chloride}}{2AgCl(s)} \xrightarrow{\text{Sunlight}} \underset{\text{Silver}}{2Ag(s)} + \underset{\text{Chlorine}}{Cl_2(g)}$$

(b) $$\underset{\text{Silver bromide}}{2AgBr(s)} \xrightarrow{\text{Sunlight}} \underset{\text{Silver}}{2Ag(s)} + \underset{\text{Bromine}}{Br_2(l)}$$

Note
- The reaction of decomposition of silver halides is used in photography.
- Digestion of food by our body is also an example of a decomposition reaction.

3. Displacement Reaction

A reaction in which a more reactive element displaces a less reactive element from its salt solution is called displacement reaction. e.g.

(i) $$\underset{\substack{\text{Zinc metal}\\ \text{(Grey)}}}{Zn(s)} + \underset{\substack{\text{Copper sulphate}\\ \text{solution (Blue)}}}{CuSO_4(aq)} \longrightarrow \underset{\substack{\text{Zinc sulphate}\\ \text{solution (Colourless)}}}{ZnSO_4(aq)} + \underset{\text{Copper metal (Brown)}}{Cu(s)}$$

(ii) $$\underset{\substack{\text{Iron}\\ \text{metal}}}{Fe(s)} + \underset{\substack{\text{Copper sulphate}\\ \text{solution (Blue)}}}{CuSO_4(aq)} \longrightarrow \underset{\substack{\text{Ferrous sulphate}\\ \text{Or Iron (II) sulphate}\\ \text{solution (Green)}}}{FeSO_4(aq)} + \underset{\substack{\text{Copper}\\ \text{metal}}}{Cu(s)}$$

Displacement in displacement reactions occur on the basis of activity series.

Activity Series

In this series, the metals are arranged in the decreasing order of their reactivity.

K	Potassium	Most reactive element
Na	Sodium	
Ca	Calcium	
Mg	Magnesium	
Al	Aluminium	
Zn	Zinc	Reactivity decreases on going down the series
Fe	Iron	
Pb	Lead	
H	Hydrogen	
Cu	Copper	
Hg	Mercury	
Ag	Silver	
Au	Gold	Least reactive element

- The elements lying above in the activity series can displace the elements lying below in the activity series from its salt solution.
- Metals present above hydrogen in this activity series, displace it from mineral acids (HCl, HNO_3, H_2SO_4, etc.) and H_2O.

e.g. $Zn + 2HCl \longrightarrow ZnCl_2 + H_2\uparrow$

A detailed account of activity series is given in class 10th.

4. Double Displacement Reaction

The reaction in which two different ions or the group of atoms in the reactant molecules are displaced by each other is called a double displacement reaction. It is also known as double decomposition reaction.

e.g. $CuO + 2HCl \longrightarrow CuCl_2 + H_2O$

These are of two types

(i) **Precipitation reaction** Such double displacement reactions in which an insoluble salt is formed as one of the product while the other one remains in the aqueous state, are called precipitation reactions and that insoluble salt is called a precipitate (ppt.).

e.g.

(a) $\underset{\text{Sodium sulphate}}{Na_2SO_4(aq)} + \underset{\text{Barium chloride}}{BaCl_2(aq)} \longrightarrow \underset{\substack{\text{Barium sulphate}\\\text{(White ppt.)}}}{BaSO_4\downarrow} + \underset{\text{Sodium chloride}}{2NaCl(aq)}$

(b) $\underset{\text{Silver nitrate}}{AgNO_3(aq)} + \underset{\text{Sodium bromide}}{NaBr(aq)} \longrightarrow \underset{\substack{\text{Silver bromide}\\\text{(Yellow ppt.)}}}{AgBr\downarrow} + \underset{\text{Sodium nitrate}}{NaNO_3(aq)}$

(ii) **Neutralisation reaction** It is a double displacement reaction in which acid and base reacts with each other to form neutral products (salt and water).

e.g.

(a) $\underset{\substack{\text{Sodium hydroxide}\\\text{(Base)}}}{NaOH} + \underset{\substack{\text{Hydrogen}\\\text{chloride}}}{HCl} \longrightarrow \underbrace{\underset{\substack{\text{Sodium chloride}\\\text{(Salt)}}}{NaCl(aq)} + \underset{\text{Water}}{H_2O(l)}}_{\text{Neutral, neither acidic nor basic solution}}$

(b) $\underset{\substack{\text{Potassium}\\\text{hydroxide (Base)}}}{2KOH} + \underset{\text{Sulphuric acid}}{H_2SO_4} \longrightarrow \underset{\substack{\text{Potassium}\\\text{sulphate (Salt)}}}{K_2SO_4} + \underset{\text{Water}}{2H_2O}$

Note The products of neutralisation reaction are usually dissolved in aqueous state and do not form precipitate.

Check Your LEARNING...

1. Give an example of double decomposition (displacement) reaction.
2. Displacement in double decomposition reaction occur on which basis.
3. Name two salts that are used in photography.
4. Name the reaction, in which two compounds exchange their ions to form two new compounds.
5. Name insoluble substance formed in a reaction between barium chloride and sodium sulphate.

Energy Changes in Chemical Reactions

It is one of the characteristics of the chemical changes, that proceed with change in energy of the reacting substances.

The difference in total energies, before and after a reaction, is evolved or absorbed in the form of heat, light, sound, electricity, mechanical energy, etc. On the basis of energy changes, the chemical reactions are divided into following four categories

1. Exothermic Reaction

The reaction which is accompanied by the evolution of heat, is called **exothermic reaction**. It causes a rise in temperature.

In the exothermic reaction, total energy of reactants is more than the total energy of products.

e.g. Methane burns in presence of oxygen to form carbon dioxide and releases a huge amount of energy usually as heat.

(i) $\underset{\text{Methane}}{CH_4(g)} + \underset{\text{Oxygen}}{2O_2(g)} \longrightarrow \underset{\text{Carbon dioxide}}{CO_2(g)} + \underset{\text{Water}}{2H_2O(g)} + \text{Heat}$

(ii) $2Mg(s) + O_2(g) \longrightarrow 2MgO(s) + Heat$
Magnesium, Oxygen, Magnesium oxide

Respiration is an exothermic process in which complex food material is break down to release energy in presence of oxygen.

$$C_6H_{12}O_6(aq) + 6O_2(g) \longrightarrow 6CO_2(aq) + 6H_2O(l) + \text{Energy}$$

Some other common exothermic reactions are rusting and burning of coal, petrol, cooking gas, kerosene etc.

2. Endothermic Reaction

The reaction which occur by the absorption of heat/energy is called an endothermic reaction. It causes a fall in temperature.

Thus, such reactions cannot be sustained without supply of energy from an external source. It is also called **hypothermic reaction.**

In these reactions, total energy of products is more than the total energy of reactants.

e.g. (i) $\underset{\text{Mercuric oxide}}{2HgO(s)} + \text{Heat} \longrightarrow \underset{\text{Mercury}}{2Hg(l)} + \underset{\text{Oxygen}}{O_2(g)}$

(ii) $\underset{\text{Ammonium chloride}}{NH_4Cl(s)} + \text{Heat} \longrightarrow \underset{\text{Ammonia}}{NH_3(g)} + \underset{\text{Hydrochloric acid}}{HCl\,(s)}$

3. Photochemical Reaction

A chemical reaction, which occurs with the assistance of light energy (sunlight) is called **photochemical reaction.**

Some examples of photochemical reaction are as follows

(i) **Combination of hydrogen with chlorine** Hydrogen (H_2) and chlorine (Cl_2) gas combines to produce hydrogen chloride gas (HCl) in the presence of diffused sunlight.

$$H_2 + Cl_2 \xrightarrow{\text{Diffused sunlight}} 2HCl$$

(ii) **Photosynthesis** It is a series of complex photochemical reaction to produce carbohydrate (glucose) from carbon dioxide (CO_2) and water (H_2O) in the presence of sunlight and chlorophyll.

$$6CO_2 + 12H_2O \xrightarrow[\text{Chlorophyll}]{\text{Sunlight}} C_6H_{12}O_6 + 6H_2O + 6O_2\uparrow$$

Note Chlorophyll is a green pigment, found in the leaves of plants. It traps light energy and initiates the process of photosynthesis.

4. Electrochemical Reaction

A chemical reaction which proceeds by the absorption of electricity or electric energy is called electrochemical reaction.

If electrochemical reaction results in dissociation of a molecule, it is called electrolysis.

e.g. Water acidulated with little acid dissociates into hydrogen (H_2) and oxygen (O_2) gas when electric current is passed through it.

$$2H_2O \xrightarrow{\text{Electricity}} 2H_2 + O_2\uparrow$$

Note Electrochemical reaction find applications in electrochemical cells to produce electricity as well as in electrolytic cell for electroplating, production of compound, etc.

Check Your LEARNING...

1. Give one reaction which is accompanied by evolution of heat.
2. Fill the appropriate word in blank given.
   Respiration is......... reaction.
3. Endothermic reaction is also known as .... (hypothermic reaction, combustion reaction).
4. What is meant by the term photochemical reaction?
5. Photosynthesis is an electrochemical reaction. State whether true or false.
6. Give one example of the term electrochemical reaction.

QUiCK Revision

- When one or more substances (elements or compounds) undergoes a chemical change with the absorption or evolution of energy to give new substances, this change is called a **chemical reaction**.
- Breaking of the old bonds and formation of the new bonds is responsible for the occurrence of a chemical reaction.
- Conditions which facilitate the chemical change are (i) substances need to be in close proximity (ii) heat (iii) light (iv) pressure (v) catalyst (vi) electricity.
- Characteristics of chemical reactions are
  - (i) Evolution of gas
  - (ii) Formation of precipitate
  - (iii) Change in colour
  - (iv) Change in state
  - (v) Change in temperature.
- Types of chemical reaction are as follows
  - (i) A reaction in which two or more reactants combine to form a single product is called **combination reaction**. e.g. Calcium oxide dissolved in water to form calcium hydroxide.
  - (ii) A reaction in which a single reactant breaks down to form two or more products is known as **decomposition reaction**. e.g. Thermal decomposition of calcium carbonate.
  - (iii) The reaction in which a more reactive element displaces a less reactive element from their salt solutions is called **displacement reaction**.

    e.g. $CuSO_4 + Zn \longrightarrow ZnSO_4 + Cu$
  - (iv) A reaction in which two reacting molecules exchange their corresponding ions, is called a **double displacement reaction**. It is two types.
    - (a) **Precipitation reaction** Reaction in which an insoluble salt is formed as one of the product while the other remain in the aqueous state.

      e.g. $AgNO_3 + NaCl \longrightarrow NaNO_3 + AgCl \downarrow$
    - (b) **Neutralisation reaction** Reaction in which acid and base react with each other to form neutral products.

      e.g. $NaOH + HCl \longrightarrow NaCl(aq) + H_2O\ (l)$
- **Activity series** The series in which the metals are arranged in the decreasing order of their reactivity. The most reactive element displaces the less reactive element from its salt solution.
- On the basis of energy changes, the chemical reactions are of following four types.
  - (i) Reactions accompanied by the evolution of heat are called **exothermic** (e.g. respiration).
  - (ii) The reactions occurring by the absorption of heat are called **endothermic reaction** (e.g. photosynthesis).
  - (iii) The reaction which occurs with the absorption of light energy is called **photochemical reaction**.

    e.g. $2AgNO_3 \xrightarrow{\text{Sunlight}} 2Ag + 2NO_2 + O_2$
  - (iv) A chemical reaction which proceeds in the presence of electricity is known as **electrochemical reaction**, e.g. electrolysis of molten NaCl, electrolysis of acidulated water.

Chapter Practice

Section-I

a. Multiple Choice Questions

1. Chemical reaction
   (a) occurs by breaking of chemical bonds of reactant
   (b) occurs when reacting particles do not collide
   (c) is a temporary change
   (d) is easily reversible

Sol. (a)

2. Which of the following is a physical change ?
   (a) Formation of curd from milk
   (b) Ripening of fruits
   (c) Extracting salt from sea water
   (d) Burning of wood

Sol. (c)

3. Chemical change sometimes evolve energy in the form of
   (a) heat (b) light
   (c) sound (d) All of these

Sol. (d)

4. During a chemical reaction overall mass of the product formed is ...... that of reactants.
   (a) equal to
   (b) greater than
   (c) less than
   (d) sometimes less than sometimes greater than

Sol. (a)

5. In which of the following process new substance(s) are formed?
   (a) Melting of ice
   (b) Sublimation of naphthalene
   (c) Photosynthesis
   (d) All of the above

Sol. (c)

6. The catalyst used as a promotor for the formation of ammonia gas is
   (a) Fe (b) Mo
   (c) Pd (d) Ni

Sol. (b)

7. When crystals of lead nitrate are heated strongly in a dry test tube
   (a) crystals immediately melt
   (b) a brown residue is left
   (c) white fumes appear in the tube
   (d) a yellow residue is left

Sol. (d)

8. Dilute hydrochloric acid is added to granulated zinc taken in a test tube. The following observations are recorded.
   Point out the correct observation.
   (a) The surface of metal becomes shining
   (b) The reaction mixture turns milky
   (c) Odour of a pungent smelling gas is recorded
   (d) A colourless and odourless gas is evolved

Sol. (d)

9. On immersing an iron nail in $CuSO_4$ solution for few minutes, you will observe that
   (a) no reaction takes place
   (b) the colour of solution fades away
   (c) the surface of iron nails acquire a black coating
   (d) the colour of solution changes to green

Sol. (d)

10. Name the precipitate formed when barium chloride solution is mixed with sodium sulphate solution.
    (a) NaCl (b) BaO
    (c) $BaSO_4$ (d) Na_2O

Sol. (c)

11. The products formed by neutralisation reaction are
    (a) salt and water
    (b) salt and oxygen
    (c) salt and hydrogen
    (d) hydrogen and oxygen

Sol. (a)

12. Electrolysis of acidulated water is a decomposition reaction.
    The molar ratio of hydrogen and oxygen gas liberated during electrolysis of water is
    (a) 2 : 1 (b) 1 : 1
    (c) 1 : 2 (d) 4 : 1

Sol. (a)

b. Fill in the Blanks

13. Chemical changes bring a change in the .... properties of matter. (chemical, physical)

Sol. chemical

14. .... acts as a promoter during manufacture of ammonia. (Molybdenum, Platinum, Nickel).

Sol. Molybdenum

15. The formation of gas bubbles in a liquid takes place during a reaction is called .... (effervescence, precipitate).

Sol. effervescence

16. When calcium oxide reacts with water to form calcium hydroxide, the reaction is called .... reaction. (dissociation, combination, displacement)

Sol. combination

17. Decomposition of substance using heat is called .... decomposition. (electrolysis, thermal, photochemical)

Sol. thermal

18. Blue solution of copper sulphate changes to .... colour when a piece of iron is added to this solution. (red, white, green)

Sol. green

19. Colour of conc. H_2SO_4 in a test tube changes to blue on adding a small piece of .... to it (zinc, copper, iron).

Sol. copper

20. If one of the product in double displacement reaction is insoluble in aqueous medium, the reaction is called .... reaction. (precipitation, neutralisation, combination)

Sol. precipitation

21. When acid or base reacts to form neutral salt solution, the reaction is called .... reaction. (neutralisation, precipitation, combination)

Sol. neutralisation

22. In exothermic reaction, ... of heat occurs (evolution, absorption).

Sol. evolution

c. Match the Columns

23. Match the following columns.

Column I (Processes)	Column II (Reactions)
A. Combination	1. $H_2O(l) \xrightarrow{\text{Electric current}} 2H_2(g) + O_2(g)$
B. Thermal decomposition	2. $NaOH(aq) + HCl(aq) \longrightarrow NaCl(aq) + H_2O$
C. Electrolysis	3. $CaO(s) + H_2O(l) \longrightarrow Ca(OH)_2 + \text{Heat}$
D. Precipitation	4. $CaCO_3(s) \xrightarrow{\Delta} CaO(s) + CO_2(g)$
E. Neutralisation	5. $Na_2SO_4(aq) + BaCl_2(aq) \longrightarrow BaSO_4(s) + 2NaCl(aq)$

Sol. A→ (3), B→ (4), C→ (1), D→ (5), (E)→ (2)

24. Match the following columns.

Column I (Reactions)	Column II (Colour of precipitate)
A. $Pb(NO_3)_2 + 2KI \longrightarrow PbI_2 + KNO_3$	1. Grey
B. $FeSO_4 \cdot 7H_2O \xrightarrow{\Delta} FeSO_4 + 7H_2O \longrightarrow Fe_2O_3 + SO_2 + SO_3$	2. Brown
C. $2Al + 3FeSO_4 \longrightarrow Al_2(SO_4)_3 + 3\ Fe$	3. White
D. $2AgCl \longrightarrow 2\ Ag + Cl_2$	4. Yellow

Sol. A→ (4), B→ (2), C→ (3), D→ (1)

d. Give the Balance Chemical Equation

25. Carbon burns in oxygen.

Sol. $C(s) + O_2(g) \xrightarrow{\Delta} \underset{\text{Carbon dioxide}}{CO_2(g)} + \text{Heat}$

26. Reaction of ammonia and hydrogen chloride.

Sol. $NH_3 + HCl \longrightarrow NH_4Cl$

27. Heating lead sulphide in a test tube.

Sol. $PbS + 2O_2 \xrightarrow{\Delta} PbSO_4$

28. Steam is passed over red hot iron.

Sol. $3Fe + 4H_2O \rightleftharpoons Fe_3O_4 + 4H_2\uparrow$

29. Magnesium reacts with dilute HNO_3.

Sol. $Mg(s) + 2HNO_3(aq) \longrightarrow Mg(NO_3)_2(aq) + H_2(g)$

30. Magnesium ribbon burnt in an atmosphere of nitrogen.

Sol. $\underset{\text{Magnesium}}{3Mg(s)} + \underset{\text{Nitrogen}}{N_2(g)} \xrightarrow{\Delta} \underset{\text{Magnesium nitride}}{Mg_3N_2(s)}$

e. Give One Word or a Phrase

31. The process of breaking the chemical bonds of reactants and formations of new bonds to form new products.

Sol. Chemical reaction

32. Four factors that confirm the chemical reaction.

Sol. (i) Evolution of gas
(ii) Change of colour
(iii) Formation of precipitate
(iv) Change of state

33. A substance that does not take part in the reaction and remains unchanged.

Sol. Catalyst

34. Reddish brown compound formed on iron with time.

Sol. Rust

35. A substance which increases the efficiency of a catalyst.

Sol. Promoter

36. A type of chemical reaction in which heat is evolved.

Sol. Exothermic reaction

37. A type of chemical reaction in which heat is absorbed.

Sol. Endothermic reaction

38. Common name of lead oxide.

Sol. Litharge

Section-II

a. 2 Marks Questions

1. Give an example of each of the following chemical changes.
   (i) A photochemical reaction involving
   (a) silver salt (b) water
   (ii) A reaction involving the formation of
   (a) blue colour solution
   (b) dirty green precipitate

Sol. (i) (a) $2AgNO_3 \xrightarrow{\text{Sunlight}} 2Ag + 2NO_2 + O_2$

(b) $6CO_2 + 6H_2O \longrightarrow C_6H_{12}O_6 + 6\ O_2$ [1]

(ii) (a) $\underset{\text{(Brown/ pink)}}{Cu(s)} + \underset{\text{(Conc.)}}{2H_2SO_4(aq)} \longrightarrow \underset{\text{Blue}}{CuSO_4(aq)} + 2H_2O(l) + SO_2(g)$

(b) $\underset{\text{Ferrous sulphate}}{FeSO_4(aq)} + \underset{\text{Sodium hydroxide}}{2NaOH(aq)} \longrightarrow \underset{\text{(Dirty green) Ferrous hydroxide}}{Fe(OH)_2 \downarrow} + \underset{\text{Sodium sulphate}}{Na_2SO_4(aq)}$ [1]

2. Give an example of a reaction where the following are involved.
   (i) Heat (ii) Light (iii) Electricity (iv) Catalyst

Sol. (i) Example of reaction involving heat is as follows

$$\underset{\text{Copper carbonate}}{CuCO_3(s)} \xrightarrow{\Delta} \underset{\text{Copper oxide}}{CuO(s)} + \underset{\text{Carbon dioxide}}{CO_2(g)}$$

(ii) Example of reaction involving light is as follows

$$\underset{\text{Carbon dioxide}}{6\ CO_2} + 12\ H_2O \longrightarrow \underset{\text{Glucose}}{C_6H_{12}O_6} + 6\ O_2 + 6\ H_2O$$

(iii) On passing current through molten sodium chloride, sodium and chlorine are obtained separately.

$$2NaCl \xrightarrow{\text{Electricity}} 2Na + Cl_2$$

(iv) The rate of decomposition of hydrogen peroxide increases in the presence of manganese dioxide.

$$2H_2O_2 \xrightarrow{MnO_2} 2H_2O + O_2$$ [½ × 4]

3. Why do we store silver chloride in dark coloured bottles?

Sol. Dark coloured bottles interrupt the path of light such that light cannot reach to silver chloride and its decomposition is prevented. It is known that silver chloride decomposes to silver and chlorine in the presence of light. [2]

4. Why does the colour of copper sulphate solution change when an iron nail is dipped in it?

Sol. The colour of copper sulphate solution changes when an iron nail is dipped in it because iron being more reactive than copper, displaces copper metal from aqueous copper sulphate solution.

Thus, blue colour of copper sulphate disappears and green colour of ferrous sulphate is formed.

$$\underset{\text{Grey}}{Fe(s)} + \underset{\text{Blue}}{CuSO_4(aq)} \longrightarrow \underset{\text{Green}}{FeSO_4(aq)} + \underset{\text{Brown}}{Cu(s)}$$ [2]

5. What happens when dilute hydrochloric acid is added to iron filings?

Sol. Iron being a reactive metal (on reaction with dilute hydrochloric acid) produces H_2 gas along with its salt, iron (II) chloride . This is a displacement reaction.

$$\underset{\text{Iron}}{Fe(s)} + \underset{\text{Hydrochloric acid}}{2HCl(aq)} \longrightarrow \underset{\text{Iron (II) chloride}}{FeCl_2(aq)} + \underset{\text{Hydrogen}}{H_2(g)}$$

Those metals which are present above hydrogen in the reactivity series, show similar reaction with dilute HCl and H_2SO_4 and produce H_2 gas along with the corresponding salt. [2]

6. What is a precipitate? Give example.

Sol. A precipitate is a solid substance formed on mixing two solutions, e.g. in the reaction between lead nitrate and potassium iodide solution, a yellow precipitate of lead iodide appears.

$$\underset{\text{Lead nitrate}}{Pb(NO_3)_2(aq)} + \underset{\text{Potassium iodide}}{2KI\ (aq)} \longrightarrow \underset{\text{Lead iodide (Yellow ppt.)}}{PbI_2(s)} + \underset{\text{Potassium nitrate}}{2KNO_3(aq)}$$ [2]

7. Write the balanced chemical equation for the reactions that take place during respiration.
   Identify the type of combination reaction that takes place during this process and justify the name. Give one more example of this type of reaction.

Sol. $C_6H_{12}O_6(aq) + 6O_2(aq) \longrightarrow 6CO_2(aq) + 6H_2O + \text{Energy}$ [1]

It is an exothermic reaction because a large amount of heat is released, e.g. burning of natural gas.

$$CH_4(g) + 2O_2(g) \longrightarrow CO_2(g) + 2H_2O(g) + \text{Heat}$$ [1]

b. 3 Marks Questions

8. Observe the two test tubes A and B in the diagram given below and answer the following questions.
   (i) In which test tube, reaction will take place?
   (ii) Name the type of reaction.
   (iii) Give another example of this reaction.

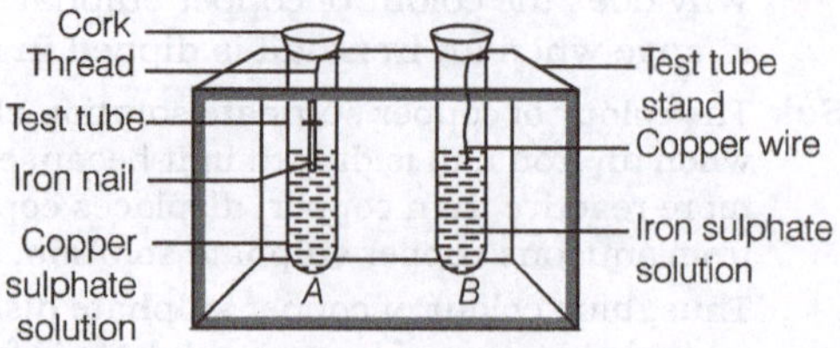

Sol. (i) In test tube A, because Fe is placed above the Cu in metal reactivity series. Thus, it displaces Cu from its $CuSO_4$ solution. [1]
(ii) Displacement reaction. [1]
(iii) Example of displacement reaction.
$$CuO + H_2 \longrightarrow Cu + H_2O$$ [1]

9. Identify the type of reaction in the following examples.
   (i) $Na_2SO_4(aq) + BaCl_2(aq) \longrightarrow BaSO_4(s) + 2NaCl(aq)$
   (ii) $Fe(s) + CuSO_4(aq) \longrightarrow FeSO_4(aq) + Cu(s)$
   (iii) $2H_2(g) + O_2(g) \longrightarrow 2H_2O(l)$

Sol. (i) Double displacement reaction [1]
(ii) Displacement reaction [1]
(iii) Combination reaction [1]

10. State the type of chemical reactions of the following.
   (i) $2Pb(NO_3)_2 \xrightarrow{\Delta} 2PbO + 4NO_2 + O_2$
   (ii) $2AgBr(s) \xrightarrow{\text{Sunlight}} 2Ag(s) + Br_2(l)$
   (iii) $C + O_2 \xrightarrow{\Delta} CO_2$

Sol. (i) Thermal decomposition reaction [1]
(ii) Photolysis [1]
(iii) Combination reaction [1]

11. A white salt on heating decomposes to give brown fumes and a residue is left behind.
   (i) Name the salt.
   (ii) Name the type of reaction.
   (iii) Write the equation for the decomposition reaction.

Sol. (i) Lead nitrate [1]
(ii) Decomposition reaction [1]
(iii) $\underset{\text{(White salt)}}{\underset{\text{Lead nitrate}}{2Pb(NO_3)_2(s)}} \xrightarrow{\text{Heat}} \underset{\text{(Residue)}}{\underset{\text{Lead oxide}}{2PbO(s)}} + \underset{\text{(Brown fumes)}}{\underset{\text{Nitrogen dioxide}}{4NO_2(g)}} + \underset{\text{Oxygen}}{O_2(g)}$ [1]

12. (i) Give an example for a combination reaction which is exothermic.
   (ii) Name any two metals which do not react with water.
   (iii) Name the metal lies at the top of reactivity series.

Sol. (i) $\underset{\text{Calcium oxide}}{CaO} + \underset{\text{Water}}{H_2O} \longrightarrow \underset{\text{Slaked lime}}{Ca(OH)_2} + \text{Heat}$ [1]
(ii) Silver, gold [1]
(iii) Potassium [1]

13. When solutions of silver nitrate and sodium chloride are mixed, a white precipitate is formed. The ionic equation for the reaction is
$$Ag^+(aq) + Cl^- \longrightarrow AgCl(s)$$
   (i) (a) What is the name of the white precipitate?
   (b) Is it a soluble or insoluble compound?
   (ii) Is the precipitation of silver chloride a decomposition reaction?

Sol. (i) (a) White precipitate of silver chloride (AgCl) is formed. [1]
(b) Silver chloride (AgCl) is an insoluble compound. [1]
(ii) It is not a decomposition reaction. It is infact a double displacement reaction.
$$\underset{\text{Sodium chloride}}{NaCl} + \underset{\text{Silver nitrate}}{AgNO_3(aq)} \longrightarrow \underset{\text{Silver chloride}}{AgCl(s)} + \underset{\text{Sodium nitrate}}{NaNO_3(aq)}$$ [1]
In this reaction, cations Ag^+ and Na^+ have exchanged their anions NO_3^- and Cl^- and a precipitate of AgCl has been formed. [1]

14. In the electrolysis of water,
   (i) name the gas collected at the cathode and at the anode.
   (ii) why is the volume of gas collected at one electrode is double of the other?
   (iii) why are a few drops of dil. H_2SO_4 added to the water?

Sol. (i) Gas collected at cathode – Hydrogen
Gas collected at anode – Oxygen [1]
(ii) On electrolysis, water decomposes according to the following reaction
$$2H_2O \xrightarrow[\text{electric current}]{\text{On passing}} 2H_2(g) + O_2(g)$$
This water decomposes to give hydrogen and oxygen in the ratio 2:1 by volume. So, double volume of the gas collected is hydrogen. [1]
(iii) A few drops of dil. H_2SO_4 are added to water to make it a better conductor of electricity. [1]

c. 4 Marks Questions

15. Write the balanced chemical equation for the following and identify the type of reaction in each case.
   (i) Lead nitrate (aq) + Potassium iodide (aq) $\longrightarrow$ Lead iodide + Potassium nitrate (aq)

(ii) Zinc carbonate $(s) \xrightarrow{\Delta}$ Zinc oxide (s) + Carbon dioxide (g)

(iii) Hydrogen (g) + Chlorine (g) $\longrightarrow$ Hydrogen chloride (g)

(iv) Magnesium(s) + Hydrochloric acid (aq) $\longrightarrow$ Magnesium chloride (aq) + Hydrogen (g)

Sol. (i) $Pb(NO_3)_2(aq) + 2KI(aq) \longrightarrow PbI_2(s) + 2KNO_3(aq)$

Type Double displacement reaction. [1]

(ii) $ZnCO_3(s) \xrightarrow{\Delta} ZnO(s) + CO_2(g)$

Type Thermal decomposition reaction. [1]

(iii) $H_2(g) + Cl_2(g) \longrightarrow 2HCl(g)$

Type Combination reaction. [1]

(iv) $Mg(s) + 2HCl(aq) \longrightarrow MgCl_2(aq) + H_2(g)$

Type Displacement reaction. [1]

16. (i) Classify the following reactions into different types.

(a) $AgNO_3(aq) + NaCl(aq) \longrightarrow AgCl(s) + NaNO_3(aq)$

(b) $CaO(s) + H_2O(l) \longrightarrow Ca(OH)_2(aq)$

(c) $2KClO_3(s) \xrightarrow{\Delta} 2KCl(s) + 3O_2(g)$

(ii) Which of the above reaction(s) is/are precipitation reaction(s)? Why is a reaction called precipitation reaction?

Sol. (i) (a) Double displacement reaction and precipitation reaction

(b) Combination reaction

(c) Thermal decomposition [2]

(ii) Reaction (a) is a precipitation reaction, as white precipitate (insoluble product) of silver chloride (AgCl) is formed in the reaction.

Due to the formation of precipitate (a white coloured solid mass), reaction is called precipitation reaction. [2]

17. Identify the type of chemical reaction taking place in each of the following.

(i) Barium chloride solution is mixed with copper sulphate solution and a white precipitate is observed.

(ii) On heating copper powder in air in a China dish, the surface of copper powder turns black.

(iii) On heating green coloured ferrous sulphate crystals, reddish brown solid is left and small amount of a gas having odour of burning sulphur is experienced.

(iv) Iron nails when left dipped in blue copper sulphate solution become brownish in colour and the blue colour of copper sulphate fades away.

Sol. (i) Double displacement reaction, precipitation reaction. [1]

(ii) Combination reaction, oxidation reaction. [1]

(iii) Thermal decomposition. [1]

(iv) Displacement reaction. [1]

18. You are provided with two containers made up of copper and aluminium. You are also provided with solutions of dilute HCl, dilute HNO_3, $ZnCl_2$ and H_2O. In which of the above containers these solutions can be kept?

Sol. The container made up of copper or aluminium is suitable for storing some solutions. This can be decided by studying their reactions with Cu and Al, based on activity series.

(i) **Reactions of copper with**

(a) **Dilute HCl**

Cu + Dil. HCl $\longrightarrow$ No reaction

So, it can be stored in Cu container.

(b) **Dilute HNO_3** Being a strong oxidising agent, dilute HNO_3 reacts with copper, so it cannot be stored in copper container.

(c) **$ZnCl_2$** Copper is less reactive than zinc so it does not react with $ZnCl_2$ solution. Therefore, it can be stored in copper container.

(d) **H_2O** Copper does not react with water. So, its container can store H_2O in it. [2]

(ii) **Reactions of aluminium with**

(a) **Dilute HCl** Al reacts with dilute HCl, so it cannot be kept in aluminium container.

$$2Al + 6HCl \longrightarrow 2AlCl_3 + 3H_2$$

(b) **Dilute HNO_3** When dil. HNO_3 is kept in Al container, it forms a protective layer of aluminium oxide on it and further reaction is stopped. Therefore, it can be kept in Al container.

(c) **$ZnCl_2$** Al is more reactive than zinc, so, it cannot keep $ZnCl_2$ solution in it.

$$2Al + 3ZnCl_2 \longrightarrow 2AlCl_3 + 3Zn$$

(d) **H_2O** Aluminium does not react with water (hot or cold). Therefore, water can be kept in aluminium container. Aluminium is attacked by steam to form aluminium oxide and hydrogen.

$$2Al(s) + 3H_2O(g) \longrightarrow Al_2O_3(g) + 3H_2(g)$$

[2]

19. Complete the following reactions.

(i) $N_2 + O_2 \longrightarrow$ (ii) $Ca(NO_3)_2 \xrightarrow{\Delta}$

(iii) $PbO_2 \xrightarrow{\Delta}$ (iv) $NO + O_2 \longrightarrow$

Sol. (i) $N_2 + O_2 \longrightarrow 2NO$

(ii) $2Ca(NO_3)_2 \xrightarrow{\Delta} 2CaO + 4NO_2 + O_2$

(iii) $2PbO_2 \xrightarrow{\Delta} 2PbO + O_2$

(iv) $2NO + O_2 \longrightarrow 2NO_2$ [4×1=4]

Chapter Assessment

Section-I

a. Multiple Choice Questions

1. Close contact of reacting substances during a chemical reaction is required for the exchange of
   (a) energy
   (b) neutrons
   (c) protons
   (d) All of the above

2. $AgNO_3(aq) + NaCl(aq) \longrightarrow AgCl(s) + NaNO_3(aq)$
   The above reaction is
   (a) double displacement reaction
   (b) precipitation reaction
   (c) combination reaction
   (d) Both (a) and (b)

3. The process by which we can get sodium and chlorine in elemental state from the common salt is
   (a) photolysis
   (b) thermal decomposition
   (c) electrolysis
   (d) displacement reaction

4. Aluminium metal reacts with sulphuric acid to form
   (a) aluminium sulphate and hydrogen
   (b) aluminium sulphate and oxygen
   (c) aluminium sulphate and water
   (d) aluminium sulphate and sulphur dioxide

5. When dilute hydrochloric acid is added to zinc pieces taken in a test tube
   (a) small bubbles of hydrogen gas appear on the surface of zinc pieces
   (b) the colour of the solution becomes yellow
   (c) a pungent smelling gas gets liberated
   (d) no change takes place

b. Fill in the Blanks

6. The position of copper is .... to that of hydrogen in the activity series. (lower, upper)

7. .... is a pigment, found in plants which helps in photosynthesis by entraping the light energy. (Phloem, Xylem, Chlorophyll)

8. ...... gas is released during respiration. (CO_2, O_2, CO)

9. During endothermic reaction, energy is .... (absorbed, evolved)

10. Magnesium ribbon burns in the environment of .... (O_2 only, N_2 only, O_2 and N_2 both).

c. Give One Word or a Phrase

11. The required conditions for a faster reaction to produce ammonia gas.

12. A chemical process in which a solid of insoluble mass is produced.

13. Chemical reaction that takes place when electric current is passed through fused sodium chloride.

14. The chemical equation for a reaction which can be brought out in laboratory with the help of diffused sunlight.

15. The precipitate formed when sodium sulphate (Na_2SO_4) reacts with barium chloride.

d. Match the Columns

16. Match the following columns.

Column I (Chemical reaction)	**Column II** (Name of reaction)
A. $Cl_2 + 2KBr \longrightarrow 2KCl + Br_2$	1. Double displacement
B. $2HgO \longrightarrow 2Hg + O_2$	2. Synthesis
C. $PbO_2 + SO_2 \longrightarrow PbSO_4$	3. Displacement
D. $KNO_3 + H_2SO_4 \longrightarrow HNO_3 + KHSO_4$	4. Decomposition

e. Balanced Chemical Equation

17. Reaction of sodium with water.

18. Reaction of zinc with dilute hydrochloric acid.

19. Magnesium wire is burnt in air.

20. Reaction of silver nitrate with sodium chloride.

21. Thermal decomposition of potassium chlorate.

Section-II

a. 2 Marks Questions

1. (i) What is displacement reaction?

   (ii) $Zn + CuSO_4(aq) \longrightarrow X + Y$

   What is X and Y in the above reaction?

2. (i) Why molybdenum is used in the manufacture of ammonia?

   (ii) Give an example of each of the following chemical changes.

   (a) Two gases combine to form a white solid.

   (b) Two solids combine to form a liquid.

b. 3 Marks Questions

3. (i) Give an example of a reaction where colour change is noticed.

   (ii) Why we apply paint on iron articles ?

   (iii) What is the difference between displacement and double displacement reactions ?

4. *A*, *B* and *C* are three elements which undergo chemical reaction according to the following equations.

$$A_2O_3 + 2B \longrightarrow B_2O_3 + 2A$$

$$3CSO_4 + 2B \longrightarrow B_2(SO_4)_3 + 3C$$

$$3CO + 2A \longrightarrow A_2O_3 + 3C$$

Answer the following questions with reason.

(i) Which element is the most reactive?

(ii) Which element is the least reactive?

(iii) What is the type of reactions listed above?

c. 4 Marks Questions

5. Give an example of each of the following chemical changes.

   (i) A reaction, where colour change is observed.

   (ii) A reaction involving

   (a) formation of insoluble salt.

   (b) formation of neutral products.

   (iii) An exothermic and endothermic reaction involving carbon as one of the reactants.

6. (i) What will you observe when you put

   (a) some zinc pieces into blue copper sulphate solution ?

   (b) some copper pieces into green ferrous sulphate solution?

   (ii) Write a balance chemical equation when silver metal is added to copper sulphate solution.

   (iii) Write the type of reaction.

   (a) $2H_2O_2 \longrightarrow 2H_2O + O_2$

   (b) $C + O_2 \longrightarrow CO_2$

   (c) $Pb + CuCl_2 \longrightarrow PbCl_2 + Cu$

   (d) $2NH_4NO_3 \xrightarrow{\Delta} 2N_2 + O_2 + 4H_2O$

7. Complete and balance the following equations.

   (i) $CaO + H_2O \longrightarrow$ (ii) $Pb(NO_3)_2 + NaCl \longrightarrow$

   (iii) $BaCl_2 + H_2SO_4 \longrightarrow$ (iv) $P_4 + O_2 \longrightarrow$

For explanations scan the given QR Code

Olympiad Section*

Brain Teasing Questions asked in Previous Olympiads

1. In the balanced chemical equation of the thermal decomposition of lead (II) nitrate to lead (II) oxide, if the coefficient of lead (II) nitrate is 2, then the coefficient of nitrogen dioxide is (INJSO)
   (a) 1 (b) 2 (c) 3 (d) 4

2. In the conversion of compound X into compound Z, it was found that the reaction proceeded by way of Y, which could be isolated. The following steps were involved. (NTSE)
   $X \longrightarrow Y$; endothermic process
   $Y \longrightarrow Z$; exothermic process
   Which is the reaction profile of this conversion from X to Z? (INJSO)

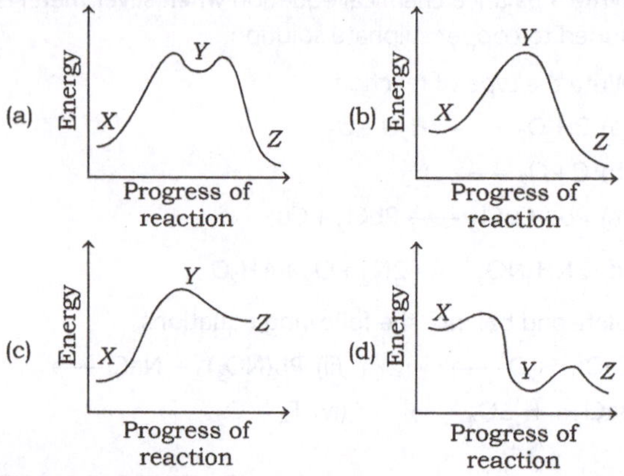

3. Rust is a mixture of (INJSO)
   (a) FeO and $Fe(OH)_3$ (b) FeO and Fe_3O_4
   (c) Fe_2O_3 and $Fe(OH)_3$ (d) $Fe(OH)_3$ and Fe_3O_4

4. All chemical reactions with dissociation can be of following type (NTSE)
   I. Reversible II. Irreversible
   III. Endothermic IV. Exothermic
   (a) I, II, III (b) II, III, IV (c) I, III, IV (d) I, II, IV

5. On thermal decomposition, which of the following substances will give oxygen gas? (NTSE)
   I. NH_4NO_3 II. NH_4ClO_3
   III. $(NH_4)_2Cr_2O_7$ IV. $(NH_4)_2SO_4$
   (a) I and II (b) II and III
   (c) III and IV (d) I and IV

6. Which of the following reaction is displacement reaction? (INJSO)
   (a) $2H_2O_2 \longrightarrow 2H_2O + O_2$
   (b) $Fe_2O_3 + 2Al \longrightarrow Al_2O_3 + 2Fe$
   (c) $P_4 + 3NaOH + 3H_2O \longrightarrow PH_3 + 3NaH_2PO_2$
   (d) $CH_4 + 2O_2 \longrightarrow CO_2 + 2H_2O$

7. Observe the following diagram carefully. Concentration of solution in each test tube is 0.1M. The test tube in which a chemical reaction occurs is (INJSO)

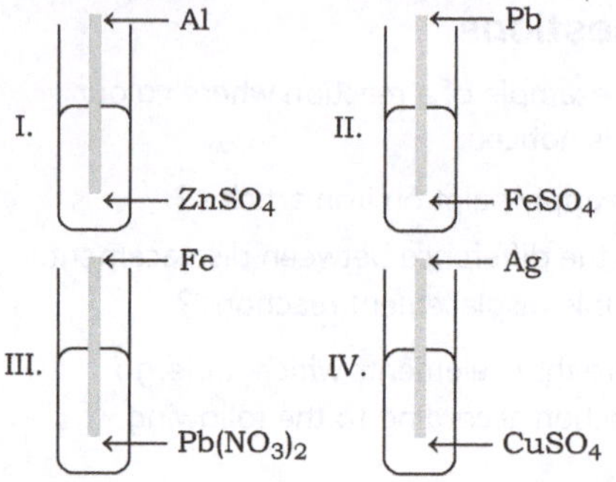

   (a) I and III (b) I and II (c) II and III (d) I and IV

8. Which among the following is/are double displacement reaction(s)? (INJSO)
   I. $Pb + CuCl_2 \longrightarrow PbCl_2 + Cu$
   II. $Na_2SO_4 + BaCl_2 \longrightarrow BaSO_4 + 2NaCl$
   III. $C + O_2 \longrightarrow CO_2$
   IV. $CH_4 + 2O_2 \longrightarrow CO_2 + 2H_2O$
   (a) I and IV (b) Only II (c) I and II (d) III and IV

9. Which of the following are exothermic processes?
   I. Reaction of water with quicklime (NTSE)
   II. Dilution of an acid
   III. Evaporation of water
   IV. Sublimation of camphor (crystals)
   (a) I and III (b) I and II (c) II and IV (d) I and IV

10. Which one of the following process involve chemical reactions? (NTSE)
    (a) Keeping petrol in a China dish in the open.
    (b) Storing of nitrogen gas under pressure in a gas cylinder.
    (c) Evaporation of water.
    (d) Heating copper wire in presence of air at high temperature.

Answers

1. (d) **2.** (b) **3.** (c) **4.** (b) **5.** (a) **6.** (b) **7.** (a) **8.** (b) **9.** (b) **10.** (d)

* *These questions may or may not be asked in the examination, have been given just for additional practice required for olympiads Scholarship Exams etc. For detailed explanations refer Page No. 134.*

CHAPTER

03

Water

CHAPTER OUTLINES

• Water as a Universal Solvent • Solutions • Solubility
• Hydrated and Anhydrous Substances • Drying and Dehydrating Agents • Soft and Hard Water

After the air, water is one of the most common substances on the earth's surface. About 2/3 of earth's surface is covered with water. It is found in the free as well as in combined state.

Occurrence

Water is the most common, abundant and easily obtainable compound as compared to all other known compounds. It is a crucial compound for the survival of life. It can exist in solid (as ice, snow, etc.), liquid (as lake, river, sea, etc.) or gaseous state (as water vapour).

It constitutes a major part of all the living organisms, e.g. it forms about 65% of human body and almost 95% of some plants body. However, its distribution over the earth's surface is not uniform. The fraction of water available for human use is only 0.003% of the total global water availability.

Water as a Universal Solvent

Ancient philosophers thought that water is an element. In 1781, A.L. Lavoisier showed that water is a compound of hydrogen and oxygen atoms combined together in the ratio of 2 : 1. Because of its tendency to dissolve almost all the forms of substances, i.e. solids, gases and other liquids, it is regarded as **universal solvent**.

Ionic compounds (polar compounds) dissolve in it because of its high dielectric constant (78.39), whereas some covalent compounds are soluble in it because of the formation of hydrogen bonds between the water and compound's molecules.

Physical Properties of Water

The important physical properties of water are as follows

(i) **Nature** Pure water is a transparent, colourless, tasteless and odourless substance. It takes the odour of the substance, which is dissolved in it.

(ii) **Freezing point** The term freezing point means the temperature at which a liquid turns into a solid when cooled. Pure water freezes at 0°C under normal pressure.

(iii) **Boiling point** The temperature at which a liquid boils and changes into gaseous state is called its boiling point. Technically, it is defined as the temperature at which vapour pressure of any liquid equalises the atmospheric pressure. Under normal pressure (760 mm Hg) pure water boils at 100°C.

(iv) **Heat of vaporisation** The energy required to change water into its vapour at its boiling point without any change in temperature is called heat of vaporisation. The value of heat of vaporisation of water is 2268 J/g or 540 cal/g.

(v) **Heat of fusion** The energy required to change 1g of solid to a liquid without any change in temperature is called heat of fusion. The heat of fusion of water is 336 J/g or 80 cal/g.

(vi) **Specific heat capacity** The amount of heat needed to raise 1 g of a material by 1°C is known as specific heat capacity. The specific heat capacity of water is 4.186 J/g °C.

(vii) **Density** Water has its maximum density of 1 g cm^{-3} or 10^3 kg m^{-3} at 4°C and minimum volume.

Solutions

A homogeneous mixture of two or more substances is called solution. It is sometimes also called as a **true solution**. Lemonade, soda water, salt solution, sugar solution, etc., all are the examples of solutions.

In a solution, there is homogeneity at the particle level, i.e. the particles of dissolved substances are evenly distributed in the solution and are indistinguishable from one another.

There are two main components of a solution. These are as follows

(i) **Solvent** (Dissolving phase) The component (usually present in larger amount) of the solution that dissolves the other component in it is called the **solvent**.

(ii) **Solute** (Dissolved phase) The component (usually present in lesser quantity) of the solution that is dissolved in the solvent is called the **solute**.

Some common examples of solution are

- In sugar solution, sugar is dissolved in water. Here, sugar is the solute and water is the solvent.
- A solution of iodine in alcohol known as **tincture of iodine**. It has iodine (solid) as the solute and alcohol (liquid) as the solvent.
- Aerated drinks like soda water, etc., are gas in liquid solutions in which CO_2(gas) as solute and water (liquid) as solvent is present.

Properties of a Solution

Some important properties of a solution are as follows

- A solution is a homogeneous mixture.
- The particles of a solution are smaller than 1 nm (10^{-9}m) in diameter. Therefore, they cannot be seen by naked eyes.
- Due to very small particles, they do not scatter the beam of light passing through the solution. So, the path of light is not visible in a solution.
- A solution is stable, i.e. the solute particles do not settle down when left undisturbed.
- The solute particles cannot be separated from the mixture by the process of filtration.

Concentration of a Solution

The concentration of a solution is the amount of solute present in a given amount (mass or volume) of solution, or the amount of solute dissolved in a given mass or volume of the solvent.

Concentration of solution

$$= \frac{\text{Amount of solute}}{\text{Amount of solution}} = \frac{\text{Amount of solute}}{\text{Amount of solvent}}$$

In a solution, the relative proportion of the solute and solvent can be varied and can be categorised in the following ways.

(i) **Depending upon the amount of solute present in comparison to solvent**, it can be classified as

(a) **Dilute solution** The solution in which amount of solute is very less as compared to the amount of solvent.

(b) **Concentrated solution** The solution in which amount of solute is relatively more as compared to the amount of solvent.

(ii) **Depending upon the amount of solute present in a given amount of solvent**, it can be classified as

(a) **Saturated solution** A solution in which no more amount of solute can be dissolved at a given temperature.

(b) **Unsaturated solution** If the amount of solute contained in a solution is less than the saturation level, it is called an unsaturated solution.

(iii) **Solutions based upon physical states**

Types of solutions	Solute	Solvent	Examples
Gaseous solutions	Gas	Gas	Mixture of nitrogen and oxygen gases in air.
	Liquid	Gas	Chloroform mixed with nitrogen gas and humidity.
	Solid	Gas	Camphor in nitrogen gas and dust or smoke.
Liquid solutions	Gas	Liquid	Oxygen in water and carbon dioxide in water.
	Liquid	Liquid	Alcoholic beverages are basically solutions of ethanol in water.
	Solid	Liquid	Sucrose (table sugar) or salt in water.
Solid solutions	Gas	Solid	Hydrogen dissolves in metals, especially in palladium.
	Liquid	Solid	Mercury with sodium forming an amalgam.
	Solid	Solid	Alloys like bronze and many others.

Solubility

It is defined as the maximum amount of a substance that can be dissolved in a specified amount (100 g) of solvent at a specified temperature. It depends on nature of solute, nature of solvent, temperature and pressure.

Solubility of a Gas in a Liquid

The solubility of different gases in the same solvent varies, e.g. gases like hydrogen, oxygen, nitrogen and helium, etc., dissolves in water to a small extent whereas the gases like NH_3, HCl, SO_2, etc., are highly soluble in water.

Effect of Temperature and Pressure

- The solubility of most gases in liquids decreases with increase of temperature.
- An increase in pressure on the surface of water increases the solubility of a gas in water. This is in accordance to Henry's law.
  According to Henry's kaw, the mass of gas dissolved by a fixed volume of liquid is directly proportional to the pressure on the surface of the liquid at any given temperature.

Solubility of a Solid in a Liquid

Solids are soluble in a liquid if their intermolecular interactions are similar.

The solubility of a solid in a liquid at any temperature is defined as the maximum amount of the solid (solute) in gram which can be dissolved in 100 g of the liquid (solvent) to form the saturated solution at that particular temperature.

Effect of Temperature and Pressure

- The solubility of a solid in a liquid is significantly affected by temperature change.
- For most of the solids, solubility in water increases with rise in temperature.
- Pressure does not have any significant effect on solubility of solids in liquids.

Solubility Curves

The graph drawn for the change of solubility of a substance against temperature, (i.e. with the rise of fall) is called solubility curve.

In this curve, solubility is plotted along Y-axis and temperature is plotted along X-axis which is shown below.

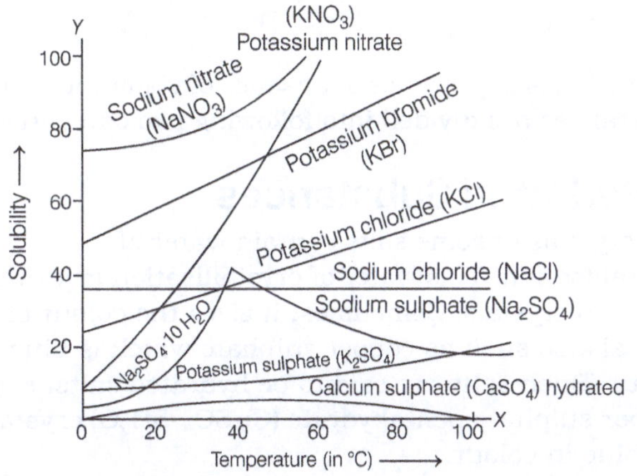

Variation in solubility of some solids with changing temperature

From the solubility curve, it is concluded that the solubilities of some substances varies as follows

- Solubility of sodium chloride increases very little with the increase in temperature.
- Solubility of potassium nitrate and potassium sulphate increases considerably with the increase in temperature.

- Solubility of $CaSO_4$ and $Na_2SO_4 \cdot 10H_2O$ increases with the rise in temperature and then decreases after attaining maximum value.

Applications of Solubility Curves

Solubility curves are used for the following ways

- To calculate the amount of substance which will crystallise out when a hot saturated solution is cooled to a lower temperature.
- To calculate the solubility of a given substance at the specific temperature.
- To compare the solubilities of different substances at the specific temperature.

Check Your LEARNING...

1 Why true solutions are homogeneous in nature?
2 Write any three properties of true solution.
3 What happens when a crystal of solute is introduced into a saturated solution of the solute?
4 Which law helps in studying the effect of increase in the solubility of a gas in liquid?
5 What is the effect of temperature on solubility of a solid in liquid?
6 Mention any two applications of solubility curves.

Hydrated and Anhydrous Substances

On the basis of presence or absence of water molecules, substances are divided into following two categories.

1. Hydrated Substances

The crystals of some salts contain water of crystallisation. This water of crystallisation gives the shape to crystals. Sometimes, it gives the colour of crystal also such as copper sulphate which is blue in colour. Such salts are said to be hydrated salts, e.g. copper sulphate pentahydrate ($CuSO_4 \cdot 5H_2O$) crystals are blue in colour.

Note
- A crystal is a homogeneous solid bounded by the plane surface directed at definite angle and having definite geometrical shape. e.g. NaCl, $CuSO_4$, etc.
- Crystallisation is the process of separating out the crystals from the hot saturated solution on cooling it slowly.

Water of Crystallisation

The fixed amount of water that is associated with hydrated crystals (is an integral part of the crystal), is said to be water of crystallisation. It is also known as water of hydration.

When crystals are heated above 100°C, the water of crystallisation loose their chemical combination. The vapours are produced and condense to form liquid.

Salts Containing Water of Crystallisation

Chemical name	Common name	Chemical formula
Sodium carbonate decahydrate	Washing soda	$Na_2CO_3 \cdot 10H_2O$
Sodium sulphate decahydrate	Glauber's salt	$Na_2SO_4 \cdot 10H_2O$
Magnesium sulphate heptahydrate	Epsom salt	$MgSO_4 \cdot 7H_2O$
Copper (II) sulphate pentahydrate	Blue vitriol	$CuSO_4 \cdot 5H_2O$
Zinc sulphate heptahydrate	White vitriol	$ZnSO_4 \cdot 7H_2O$
Hydrated potassium aluminium sulphate	Potash alum	$K_2SO_4 \cdot Al_2(SO_4)_3 \cdot 24H_2O$
Calcium sulphate semihydrate	Plaster of Paris	$CaSO_4 \cdot \frac{1}{2} H_2O$

2. Anhydrous Substances

When a substance contains no water, then it is said to be anhydrous substance. Such substances lack water of crystallisation.

Some of the examples of anhydrous substances are

- Common salt (NaCl)
- Gaseous HCl
- Potassium nitrate (KNO_3)
- Ammonium chloride (NH_4Cl)
- Sugar ($C_{12}H_{22}O_{11}$)

Anhydrous substance can be obtained from hydrated substances by removing their water of crystallisation through one of the following methods.

- Direct heating.
- By using dehydrating agent (like conc. H_2SO_4).
- Heating under vacuum.
- Heating in hot and dry air.

Properties of Hydrated and Anhydrous Substances

Important properties of hydrated and anhydrous substances are as follows

I. Efflorescence

The phenomenon in which a compound loses its water of crystallisation on exposure to dry air is called efflorescence and such substances are said to be efflorescent substances.

Due to this phenomenon, hydrated salts when left exposed to atmosphere lose their water of crystallisation and crumble down to form powder.

The specific condition required for efflorescence is

Vapour pressure of hydrated crystals > Atmospheric vapour pressure.

Some of the examples of efflorescent substances are

(i) **Washing soda** ($Na_2CO_3 \cdot 10H_2O$) When exposed to dry air, becomes a monohydrate.

$$\underset{\text{Hydrated sodium carbonate}}{Na_2CO_3 \cdot 10H_2O} \xrightarrow{\text{Dry air}} \underset{\text{Monohydrate}}{Na_2CO_3 \cdot H_2O} + 9H_2O$$

(ii) **Epsom salt** ($MgSO_4 \cdot 7H_2O$) When exposed to dry air, becomes a monohydrate.

$$\underset{\text{Magnesium sulphate heptahydrate}}{MgSO_4 \cdot 7H_2O} \xrightarrow{\text{Dry air}} \underset{\text{Monohydrate}}{MgSO_4 \cdot H_2O} + 6H_2O$$

(iii) **Glauber's salt** ($Na_2SO_4 \cdot 10H_2O$) When exposed to dry air, becomes a powdery anhydrous sodium sulphate.

$$\underset{\text{Hydrated sodium sulphate}}{Na_2SO_4 \cdot 10H_2O} \xrightarrow{\text{Dry air}} \underset{\text{Anhydrous}}{Na_2SO_4} + 10H_2O$$

Note The higher the temperature of the air, the higher is the efflorescence. The reason is that the air absorbs more water with increase in temperature and decrease in moisture. It is minimised in the humid conditions.

II. Deliquescence

Some of the water soluble substances, when left exposed to atmosphere at ordinary temperature absorb moisture from atmospheric air, lose their crystalline form and get converted into their saturated solutions. Such a substance is called a **deliquescent substance** and the phenomenon is said to be deliquescency.

The specific condition required for deliquescency is

Vapour pressure inside the crystals << Atmospheric vapour pressure.

Some of the examples of deliquescent substances are

- Caustic soda (NaOH)
- Caustic potash (KOH)
- Calcium chloride ($CaCl_2$)
- Magnesium chloride ($MgCl_2$)

Note During the rainy season, table salt (NaCl) turns moist and forms a solution on exposure to air. But pure NaCl is not deliquescent. The commercial table salt contains impurities such as $MgCl_2$ and $CaCl_2$ which are deliquescent substances.

III. Hygroscopy

The phenomenon where certain substances absorb moisture (water vapour) from the atmosphere when they are exposed to air is called hygroscopy. Such substances are called **hygroscopic substances.**

They have the tendency to take up moisture from the air. In other words, hygroscopy refers to a matter's ability to adsorb and absorb water from the surrounding environment.

Some of the examples of hygroscopic substances are

- Quicklime (CaO)
- Phosphorus pentoxide (P_2O_5)
- Concentrated sulphuric acid (H_2SO_4)

Check Your LEARNING...

1 Give two examples of hydrated substances.
2 What is the chemical formula of epsom salt?
3 What is the colour of anhydrous copper sulphate?
4 Mention the condition for efflorescence.
5 Mention the condition for deliquescence.

Drying and Dehydrating Agents

The substances that can readily absorbs moisture from other substances without chemically reacting with them are called **drying agent**. It is used to absorb water vapour from the air.

Some examples of drying agents are

- Anhydrous zinc chloride ($ZnCl_2$)
- Anhydrous calcium chloride ($CaCl_2$)
- Phosphorus pentaoxide (P_2O_5)
- Dry sodium sulphate (Na_2SO_4)

Almost all hygroscopic substances are drying agents. Drying agents are also known as **desiccants** or **desiccating agents.**

The substances that can remove even the chemically combined water molecules from compound are called **dehydrating agents.**

Some examples of dehydrating agents are

- Concentrated sulphuric acid can remove water molecules from blue vitriol.

$$\underset{\text{(Blue vitriol)}}{CuSO_4 \cdot 5H_2O} \xrightarrow{\text{Conc. } H_2SO_4} \underset{\text{(White)}}{CuSO_4} + 5H_2O$$

- Concentrated phosphoric acid (H_3PO_4)
- Hot aluminium oxide (Al_2O_3)

Soft and Hard Water

(i) **Soft water** Water free from soluble salts of calcium and magnesium is called soft water. It gives lather with soap (sodium or potassium salt of higher fatty acids). It is suitable for use. The most common examples of soft water are distilled water and rain water.

(ii) **Hard water** It contains soluble salt of calcium or magnesium (bicarbonates, sulphates or chlorides). It does not give lather with soap. This is because of the precipitation of the insoluble soap (calcium or magnesium stearate).

$$\underset{\text{Calcium chloride (present in hard water)}}{CaCl_2} + \underset{\text{Sodium stearate (soluble soap)}}{2C_{17}H_{35}CO\bar{O}\overset{+}{Na}} \longrightarrow \underset{\text{Calcium stearate (insoluble soap)}}{(C_{17}H_{35}COO)_2Ca\downarrow} + 2NaCl$$

Cause of Hardness

Water of springs, wells and rivers contains dissolved minerals. When water flows over beds of limestone ($CaCO_3$) and dolomite ($MgCO_3$), carbon dioxide (CO_2) slowly converts some of these into soluble calcium and magnesium bicarbonates. It gets mixed with the water and make it hard.

e.g. $$\underset{\text{(Insoluble)}}{MgCO_3} + CO_2 + H_2O \longrightarrow \underset{\text{Magnesium bicarbonate (soluble)}}{Mg(HCO_3)_2}$$

Chlorides and sulphates of calcium and magnesium are also incorporated in the same way.

Types of Hardness

The hardness of water is of two types

(i) **Temporary hardness** It occurs due to dissolved bicarbonate of calcium and magnesium [$Ca(HCO_3)_2$ and $Mg(HCO_3)_2$], so it is also called **carbonate hardness.** This type of hardness is temporary because it can be easily removed by just boiling and filtering the water.

(ii) **Permanent hardness** It occurs due to dissolved chlorides and sulphates of calcium and magnesium. This type of hardness cannot be removed by simple methods like boiling or filtration, so it is called **permanent hardness.**

Removal of Hardness

The process of removal of hardness from water is called softening of water.

Methods used for removal of hardness are as follows

(i) **Boiling** Temporary hardness of water can be removed by boiling. Due to boiling $Mg(HCO_3)_2$ is converted into insoluble $Mg(CO_3)$, whereas $Ca(HCO_3)_2$ is converted into insoluble $CaCO_3$ and gets precipitated. These precipitates can be removed by filtration or decantation.

$$Mg(HCO_3)_2(aq) \xrightarrow{\Delta} Mg\,(CO_3)_2\downarrow + CO_2\uparrow + H_2O$$

$$Ca(HCO_3)_2(aq) \xrightarrow{\Delta} CaCO_3\downarrow + H_2O + CO_2\uparrow$$

(ii) **Treatment with washing soda** Permanent hardness of water can be removed by adding washing soda. Washing soda reacts with soluble salts in hard water to form insoluble carbonates that can be filtered off.

$$MCl_2 + Na_2CO_3 \longrightarrow MCO_3\downarrow + 2NaCl$$

$$MSO_4 + Na_2CO_3 \longrightarrow MCO_3\downarrow + Na_2SO_4$$

(where, M = Ca and Mg)

Advantages and Disadvantages of Soft Water and Hard Water

Following are advantages and disadvantages of soft water and hard water.

Advantages

- Soft water is used for drinking purpose.
- Soft water is free from dissolved salts and possess pleasant taste.
- The presence of salts in hard water make it tasty, therefore, it is used in the preparation of beverages and wines.
- Calcium and magnesium salts present in hard water are essential for the growth of our bones and teeth.
- To check the poisoning of water in lead pipes, hard water is used. When hard water flows inside the lead pipe, some lead salts get dissolved in water having calcium sulphate. As the result, an insoluble lead sulphate in the form of a layer inside the lead pipe is formed. It checks the lead poisoning.

Disadvantages

- The hard water cannot be used for washing clothes because it contains Ca^{2+} and Mg^{2+} ions, which react with soap (i.e. sodium stearate, $C_{17}H_{35}\overset{-}{CO}\overset{+}{ONa}$ or other sodium or potassium salt of higher, fatty acids) to form scum or precipitate of Ca/Mg stearate.

$$\underset{\text{Sodium stearate (soap)}}{2C_{17}H_{35}COO^-Na^+} + \underset{\text{From hard water}}{M^{2+}} \longrightarrow \underset{\text{Metal stearate (Curdy white ppt.)}}{(C_{17}H_{35}COO)_2M\downarrow} + 2Na^+$$

(where, M = Ca or Mg)

However, after the precipitation of all the Ca^{2+} and Mg^{2+} ions present in the water, the water becomes soft and gives lathers with soap.

Thus, lots of soap get wasted if clothes are washed with hard water. Hence, it is unsuitable for laundry.

- Hard water is also harmful for boiler as the salts present in hard water get deposited in the form of scale and thus, reduce the efficiency of the boilers.
- It cannot be used for domestic purposes as it spoils the utensils lustre and results in scale formation.
- It is also harmful for industries like dying, printing, textiles, sugar, etc., as plenty of water is needed.

Check Your LEARNING...

1 In hard water, salts of which metals are present?

2 Out of soft and hard water, which gives lather with soap?

3 What is the cause of temporary hardness in water?

4 Complete the following.

$$CaCl_2 + 2C_{17}H_{35}CO\overset{-}{O}\,\overset{+}{Na} \longrightarrow$$

5 Which method is best suited for the removal of permanent hardness of water?

6 In hard water, formation of which compound helps in checking the lead poisoning?

7 Write any three disadvantages of hard water.

QUiCK Revision

- Water is most abundant compound. About 80% of earth's surface is covered with water. It can exist in solid, liquid and gaseous states.
- The composition of water is hydrogen and oxygen atoms combined together in the ratio of 2 : 1. Due to high dielectric constant, it is regarded as universal solvent.
- A solution is a homogeneous mixture of two or more substances, whose composition can be varied within certain limits. In such a mixture, a solute dissolved in another substance, known as solvent (present in large quantity). Different types of solution are as follows
  - (i) **Dilute solution** Solute is very less as compared to solvent.
  - (ii) **Concentrated solution** Solute dissolved is relatively more as compared to the amount of solvent.
  - (iii) **Saturated solution** No more solute can be dissolved at the given temperature.
  - (iv) **Unsaturated solution** More solute can be dissolved at the given temperature.
  - (v) **Gaseous solution** Solvent must be gas and solute may be present in any state.
  - (vi) **Liquid solution** Solvent must be liquid and solute may be present in any state.
  - (vii) **Solid solution** Solvent must be solid and solute may be present in any state.
- Solubility of a substance is the maximum amount of solute that can be dissolved in a specified amount of solvent (100 g) at a specified temperature.
- Solubility of a solid in liquid does not have any significant effect of pressure while, it may increase or decrease, with increase in temperature.
- Solubility curves are used to determine the effect of temperature on the solubility.
- Certain substances contain water molecules are called **hydrated substances** while those substances which do not contain any water along with the salts are said to be **anhydrous substances**.
- **Water of crystallisation** It is the fixed amount of water that is associated with hydrated crystal which is an integral part of the crystal.
- **Efflorescence** It is the phenomenon in which a compound loses its water of crystallisation on exposure to dry air.
- **Deliquescency** It is the phenomenon in which substance absorb moisture from atmosphere and get converted into their saturated solution.
- **Hygroscopy** It is the phenomenon in which substance absorb and adsorb moisture from the air.
- **Drying agent** The substance that can readily absorb moisture from other substance without chemically reacting with them is called drying agent.
- **Dehydrating agent** The substance that can remove even the chemically combined water molecules from compound is called dehydrating agent.
- **Soft water** Water free from soluble salts of calcium and magnesium is called soft water.
- **Hard water** contains soluble salt of calcium or magnesium. In the form of bicarbonates, sulphates and chlorides. They are of two types
  - Temporary hardness
  - Permanent hardness

Chapter Practice

Section-I

a. Multiple Choice Questions

1. Consider the following statement regarding true solution.
   I. It is homogeneous and consist of single phase.
   II. The particles of solute do not settle down even after long time.
   III. The size of particle of solute > 1 nm.
   Choose the correct option.
   (a) Only II (b) II and III
   (c) I and III (d) All of these

Sol. (d)

2. Which of the following salt contain water of crystallisation?
   (a) Potash alum (b) Plaster of Paris
   (c) Epsom salt (d) All of these

Sol. (d)

3. The condition of efflorescence is
   (a) Vapour pressure of hydrated crystal < atmospheric vapour pressure
   (b) Vapour pressure of hydrated crystal > atmospheric vapour pressure
   (c) Vapour pressure of hydrated crystal = atmospheric vapour pressure
   (d) Vapour pressure of hydrated crystal ≥ atmospheric vapour pressure

Sol. (d)

4. Hot aluminium oxide (Al_2O_3) is a
   (a) drying agent (b) dehydrating agent
   (c) hygroscopic substance (d) deliquescent substance

Sol. (b)

5. Hardness of water is due to
   (a) chloride of calcium
   (b) bicarbonate of magnesium
   (c) sulphate of aluminium
   (d) Both (a) and (b)

Sol. (d)

6. $CaSO_4 + Na_2CO_3 \longrightarrow X + Y$
   What is the X and Y in the above reaction?
   (a) $X = CaCO_3; Y = H_2SO_4$ (b) $X = H_2SO_4, Y = CaCl_2$
   (c) $X = CaCO_3; Y = Na_2SO_4$ (d) $X = CaCl_2; Y = NaCl$

Sol. (c)

7. A salt whose solubility decreases with increase in temperature.
   (a) $CaCO_3$ (b) $CaCl_2$ (c) $CaSO_4$ (d) $Ca(HCO_3)_2$

Sol. (c)

b. Fill in the Blanks

8. Water forms about ...... of human body and almost ...... of some plant bodies. (65%, 95%, 89%, 75%).

Sol. 65%, 95%

9. If the amount of solute is very less, the solution is known as ... solution (dilute, concentrated).

Sol. dilute

10. A solution of iodine in alcohol is known as .... (tincture of iodine, amalgam).

Sol. tincture of iodine

11. Air is the example of .... solution (liquid, gaseous, solid).

Sol. gaseous

12. Washing soda contains .... molecules of water of crystallisation (ten, eleven, twelve).

Sol. ten

13. Anhydrous substance lack their ....(water of crystallisation, sulphate ion).

Sol. water of crystallisation

14. Higher the temperature of the air, the .... is the efflorescence (higher, lower).

Sol. higher

15. Concentrated .... remove water of molecules from blue vitriol (sulphuric acid, hydrochloric acid).

Sol. sulphuric acid

16. .... is used for drinking purpose (Soft water, Hard water).

Sol. Soft water

17. .... is a soap (Sodium stearate, Calcium stearate).

Sol. Sodium stearate

c. Give One Word or a Phrase

18. Size of the particle of solution.

Sol. 10^{-19}nm

19. Solution in which both solute and solvent are solid.

Sol. Alloys

20. The type of hardness that can be removed simply by boiling.

Sol. Temporary hardness

21. The property which reduces force of attraction between the existing ions.

Sol. High dielectric constant

22. The temperature at which water has a maximum density of 1g/cc.

Sol. 4°C

d. Match the Columns

23. Match the following columns.

Column I (Occurrence of water)	Column II (Examples)
A. Hydrated salt	1. Mist and fog
B. Solid state	2. $CuSO_4 \cdot 5H_2O$
C. Liquid state	3. Ice, frost
D. Gaseous state	4. Well water, sea water

Sol. A →(2), B →(3), C →(4), D →(1)

24. Match the following columns.

Column I (Common name)	Column II (Formula)
A. Epsom salt	1. $Na_2SO_4 \cdot 10H_2O$
B. Potash alum	2. $Na_2CO_3 \cdot 10H_2O$
C. Glauber's salt	3. $CuSO_4 \cdot 5H_2O$
D. Blue vitriol	4. $K_2SO_4 \cdot Al_2(SO_4)_3 \cdot 24H_2O$
E. Washing soda	5. $MgSO_4 \cdot 7H_2O$

Sol. A →(5), B →(4), C →(1), D →(3), E →(2)

e. State One Relevant Reason

25. Ice floats on water.

Sol. Ice floats on water because ice has lower density than water.

26. In carbonated cold drinks gas rapidly bubbles out on opening the bottle.

Sol. At high pressure, the solubility of gas is more. As the bottle opened, pressure decreases which results in the decrease of solubility of carbon dioxide, hence the gas bubbles out.

27. The solute cannot be separated from a solution by filtration method.

Sol. The solute cannot be separated from a solution by filtration because solute particles get dissolved into the intermolecular space present in water.

28. Copper and lead are used for making water pipes.

Sol. Copper and lead are used for making pipes because they do not react with water at any temperature.

29. A solution is always clear and transparent.

Sol. Water soluble substances dissolve completely in water and remain disappeared, after this water retains its property, hence solution remains clear and transparent.

30. Define dilute and concentrated solutions.

Sol. The solution in which amount of solute is very less as compared to the amount of solvent is called **dilute solution**.

The solution in which amount of solute is relatively more as compared to the amount of solvent is called **concentrated solution.**

31. Give one example of each of gaseous and solid solution.

Sol. The example of gaseous solution is mixture of nitrogen and oxygen gases in air and solid solution is alloys.

32. Why efflorescence increase with increase in temperature ?

Sol. The higher the temperature of the air, the higher is the efflorescence. This is because at higher temperature air to dry and absorbs more water due to decrease in moisture.

33. Write two examples of deliquescent substance.

Sol. Caustic soda (NaOH) and calcium chloride ($CaCl_2$) are two examples of deliquescent substance.

34. What is the cause of hardness of water?

Sol. The cause of hardness of water is the presence of bicarbonates, sulphates and chlorides of calcium and magnesium.

Section-II

a. 2 Marks Questions

1. What is the effect of temperature on the solubility of the following compounds in water?

(i) $CaSO_4$ (ii) KNO_3

Sol. (i) The solubility of $CaSO_4$ in water decreases with the increase in temperature. [1]

(ii) The solubility of KNO_3 in water increases with the increase in temperature. [1]

2. Write any two differences between deliquescent substance and hygroscopic substance.

Sol.

Deliquescent substance	Hygroscopic substance
These are crystalline and solid in nature.	These may be crystalline solids or liquids. [1]
These substances absorb moisture from the atmosphere and form saturated solution.	These substances also absorb moisture from the atmosphere and become wet but do not form saturated solution. [1]

b. 3 Marks Questions

3. (i) Why water is called universal solvent?

(ii) What is the particle size of solution?

(iii) What is the maximum density of water?

Sol. (i) Water has tendency to dissolve almost all the substances.

Its high dielectric constant (78.39) enables it to dissolve all ionic compounds and some covalent compounds as well. [1]

(ii) The particles of a solution are smaller than 1 nm (10^{-9} m) in diameter. Therefore, they cannot be seen by naked eyes. [1]

(iii) Water has its maximum density at 4°C. [1]

4. Write the name of two compounds whose solubility
(i) decreases with the rise in temperature.
(ii) increases with the rise in temperature.
(iii) slightly affected with the rise in temperature.

Sol. (i) Calcium sulphate : $CaSO_4$
Sodium sulphate decahydrate : $Na_2SO_4 \cdot 10H_2O$ [1]
(ii) Potassium bromide : KBr
Potassium sulphate : K_2SO_4 [1]
(iii) Potassium chloride : KCl
Sodium chloride : NaCl [1]

5. What is water of crystallisation? Among the following, choose the salt containing water of crystallisation.
Epsom salt, potash alum, blue vitriol, white vitriol, dolomite, quicklime, phosphorus pentaoxide.

Sol. The fixed amount of water that is associated with hydrated crystals which is an integral part of the crystal is said to be water of crystallisation.

The salts containing water of crystallisation are
Epsom salt - $MgSO_4 \cdot 7H_2O$
Potash alum - $K_2SO_4 \cdot Al_2(SO_4)_3 \cdot 24H_2O$
White vitriol - $ZnSO_4 \cdot 7H_2O$
Blue vitriol - $CuSO_4 \cdot 5H_2O$ [3]

6. Answer the following.
(i) What are desiccating agents? Mention atleast three examples.
(ii) How can you remove permanent hardness by using washing soda?

Sol. (i) Drying agents are also called desiccating agents. These substances can remove even the chemically combined water molecules. e.g. Conc. H_2SO_4, H_3PO_4, Al_2O_3, $CaCl_2$. [1½]
(ii) Permanent hardness can be removed by adding washing soda. In this method, washing soda reacts with soluble salts in hard water to form insoluble carbonates. [1½]

C. 4 Marks Questions

7. Write the name of one substance whose solubility
(i) increases slightly with rise of temperature.
(ii) decreases with rise of temperature.
(iii) increases gradually with rise of temperature.
(iv) increases rapidly with rise of temperature.

Sol. (i) **Sodium chloride** (NaCl) Solubility increases slightly with rise of temperature. [1]
(ii) **Calcium sulphate** ($CaSO_4$) Solubility decreases with rise of temperature. [1]
(iii) **Potassium chloride** (KCl) Solubility increases gradually with rise of temperature. [1]
(iv) **Potassium nitrate** (KNO_3) Solubility increases rapidly with rise of temperature. [1]

8. Explain the following with suitable reason.
(i) The level of conc. H_2SO_4 in the jar increases when exposed to atmosphere.
(ii) Common salt becomes wet during rainy season.
(iii) Ferric chloride is stored in airtight bottles.
(iv) Washing soda loses its weight when exposed to atmosphere.

Sol (i) Conc. sulphuric acid (H_2SO_4) is hygroscopic in nature. Hence, when exposed to atmosphere it absorbs moisture and the level of sulphuric acid in the jar increases. [1]
(ii) Common salt (NaCl) contains the impurities of magnesium chloride which is deliquescent in nature.
Thus, common salt becomes wet during rainy season. Sodium chloride is not deliquescent in nature. [1]
(iii) Ferric chloride is highly deliquescent in nature and form saturated solution. Hence, it should be stored in airtight bottles. [1]
(iv) Washing soda is an efflorescent salt and it loses weight when exposed to atmosphere. [1]

9. Among the following salts, write which increases in weight, decrease in weight or remain same when exposed to atmosphere.
(i) Green vitriol (ii) Soda ash
(iii) Magnesium chloride (iv) Conc. sulphuric acid
(v) Sodium hydroxide (vi) Washing soda
(vii) Glauber's salt (viii) Common salt

Sol. (i) Decreases (ii) Remain same
(iii) Increases (iv) Increases
(v) Increases (vi) Decreases
(vii) Decreases (viii) Increases

$[8 \times \frac{1}{2} = 4]$

Chapter Assessment

Section-I

a. Multiple Choice Questions

1. The factors affecting solubility of a solid in a liquid is/are
   I. Nature of solute   II. Nature of solvent
   III. Temperature   IV. Pressure

   Choose the correct option.
   (a) Only III   (b) Only IV   (c) I, II and IV   (d) All of these
2. Which of the following is drying agent?
   (a) Anhydrous $ZnCl_2$ (b) Phosphorus pentaoxide
   (c) Dry sodium sulphate   (d) All of these
3. Hardness of water is expressed in equivalents of
   (a) $CaCO_3$ (b) $Ca(HCO_3)_2$ (c) $MgCO_3$ (d) $Mg(HCO_3)_2$
4. Which of the following is not a dehydrating agent?
   (a) P_2O_5 (b) CaO   (c) $CaCl_2$ (d) Conc. H_2SO_4
5. Hardness of water is measured in
   (a) degree clarke   (b) degree french
   (c) ppm   (d) mg/L

b. Fill in the Blanks

6. The homogeneous mixture of solute in a solvent is known as ...... (solute, solvent, solution).
7. The component present in large amount in solution is known as ...... (solvent, solute).
8. Soft water is free from .... (dissolved salts, oxygen).
9. Hardness of water is caused due to the presence of ... (dissolved salts of Ca^{2+} and Mg^{2+}, undissolved $CaCO_3$).
10. Permanent hardness is removed by adding .... (Na_2CO_3, $NaHCO_3$, NaOH).
11. Water is the only substance that expands on .... (cooling, heating, mixing).

c. Give One Word or a Phrase

12. Water which occur in nature in the form of free state.
13. A solvent for chlorophyll.
14. A solution in which large amount of solute can dissolve.
15. The vapours are condense to form which state.
16. The chemical formula of soap.

d. Match the Columns

17. Match the following columns.

	Column I (Chemical name)		Column II (Chemical formula)
A.	Caustic potash	1.	CaO
B.	Quicklime	2.	$MgCO_3$
C.	Limestone	3.	$CaCO_3$
D.	Dolomite	4.	$CaSO_4 \cdot \frac{1}{2} H_2O$
E.	Plaster of Paris	5.	KOH

e. State One Relevant Reason

18. Write the effect of increasing and decreasing temperature on the solubility of the gas in a liquid.
19. Explain with equation, when permanent hard water is treated with washing soda.
20. The molecular formula of water is H_2O. Write the information do you get from this formula.

Section-II

a. 2 Marks Questions

1. What are the cause of
   (i) temporary hardness ? (ii) permanent hardness ?
2. State two disadvantages of using hard water.

b. 3 Marks Questions

3. Why hard water is not fit for industrial use ?
4. (i) What is the dielectric constant of water?
   (ii) Name the substance which do not contain any water along with it?
   (iii) Write one method by which anhydrous substance is obtained.

c. 4 Marks Questions

5. Define the following.
   (i) Dilute solution   (ii) Saturated solution
   (iii) Unsaturated solution   (iv) Concentrated solution
6. (i) Why hard water is not suitable for washing clothes? Explain with equation.
   (ii) How the permanent hardness is removed?
7. Explain in brief the advantages and disadvantages of soft water and hard water.

For explanations scan the given QR Code

Olympiad Section*

Brain Teasing Questions asked in Previous Olympiads

1. Maximum amount of a solid solute that can be dissolved in a specified amount of a given liquid solvent does not depend upon .... (NTSE)
   (a) temperature
   (b) nature of solute
   (c) pressure
   (d) nature of solvent

2. If water turns into ice at a pressure of atmosphere at 0°C, then the temperature of this system in this process. (NTSE)
   (a) decreases
   (b) increases
   (c) remains same
   (d) None of the above

3. Physical state of water at 0°C is (INJSO)
   (a) solid (b) liquid
   (c) gas (d) All of these

4. A solution contains 50 g of common salt in 450 g of water. The concentration of the solution is
   (a) 50% (b) 10% (NTSE)
   (c) 20% (d) 5%

5. What are the percentages of water present in human body and plants, respectively? (INJSO)
   (a) 95 and 65
   (b) 65 and 95
   (c) 90 and 70
   (d) 30 and 70

6. Temporary hardness of water is due to the presence of (NTSE)
   (a) calcium and magnesium chlorides
   (b) calcium and magnesium sulphates
   (c) calcium and magnesium phosphate
   (d) calcium and magnesium hydrogen carbonates

7. Which of the following is a dehydrating agent?
   (a) Hot aluminium oxide (INJSO)
   (b) Potassium nitrate
   (c) Caustic soda
   (d) Quicklime

8. What is the chemical name of white vitriol? (NTSE)
   (a) Copper (II) sulphate pentahydrate
   (b) Iron sulphate heptahydrate
   (c) Cobalt sulphate heptahydrate
   (d) Zinc sulphate heptahydrate

9. Glauber's salt is an example of (NTSE)
   (a) hygroscopy
   (b) deliquescence
   (c) hydrated substances
   (d) efflorescence

10. The solution in which the amount of solute contained in a solution is less than the saturation level is called (INJSO)
    (a) unsaturated solution
    (b) concentrated solution
    (c) dilute solution
    (d) saturated solution

Answers

1. (c) **2.** (c) **3.** (d) **4.** (b) **5.** (b) **6.** (d) **7.** (a) **8.** (d) **9.** (d) **10.** (a)

* *These questions may or may not be asked in the examination, have been given just for additional practice required for olympiads Scholarship Exams etc. For detailed explanations refer Page No. 134.*

CHAPTER 04

Atomic Structure and Chemical Bonding

CHAPTER OUTLINES

• Atom • Structure of an Atom • Atomic Number (Z) • Mass Number (A) • Distribution of Electrons in Different Orbits (Shells) • Valency • Different Atomic Species • Chemical Bonding • Electrovalent or Ionic Bond • Covalent Bond

We have learnt that atoms and molecules are the fundamental building blocks of matter. The existence of different kinds of matter around us is due to different types of atoms and molecules present in them.

John Dalton assumed that atom is indivisible, i.e. it has no constituent particles. But a series of experimental evidences revealed that an atom is not the smallest particle. Some other particles smaller than the atom are also present, which are called **subatomic particles**, i.e. electrons, protons and neutrons.

In this chapter, we will describe how electrons, protons and neutrons were discovered and the various models that have been proposed to explain how these particles are arranged within the atom.

Atom

An atom is the smallest particle of an element that exhibit all the properties of that element. This means that all the atoms of an element are similar to each other in every aspect and different from the atoms of different element.

The atoms of different elements differ in the number of electrons, protons and neutrons.

Constituents of an Atom

An atom consist of three fundamental particles; electron, proton and neutron. Various experiments that lead to the discovery of these fundamental particles are as follows

1. Discovery of Electrons

It was known by 1900, that the atom was not a simple, indivisible particle. It contained atleast one subatomic particle—the electron, which was identified by **J. J. Thomson**, while performing his cathode ray experiment using a discharge tube.

In the experiment, a gas at low pressure was taken in the discharge tube made up of glass. At its ends, two electrodes (metal plates) were placed. These electrodes were connected to a battery for high voltage supply. Out of these, the electrode connected to the negative end was called cathode and that to the positive as anode.

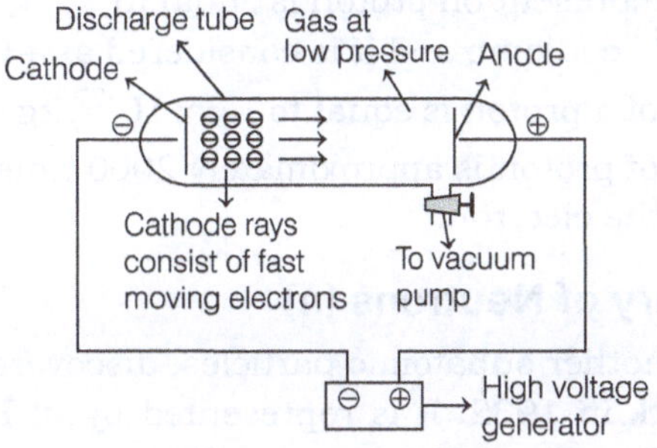

Cathode ray experiment

During this experiment, he found a beam of negatively charged particles, called **cathode rays**. They were so named as they were originated from the cathode and moved towards anode.

These cathode rays were consisted of negatively charged particles, called as **electrons**.

Properties of Electrons

- Electrons are negatively charged particles and are denoted by 'e^-'.
- The charge present on an electron is equal to -1.6×10^{-19} coulomb. Since, this charge is considered to be the smallest, therefore, charge on e^- is taken as -1.
- The mass of an electron is equal to 9.1×10^{-31} kg.

2. Discovery of Protons

Before the identification of electron, **E. Goldstein** in 1886, discovered the presence of new radiations known as **canal rays** or **anode rays**. These were the positively charged rays which were seen moving from the anode towards cathode in a specially designed discharge tube (with a porous cathode). When a high voltage is applied across the electrodes, porous cathode is used to provide the path for passing anode rays.

The name proton has given by **Ernest Rutherford**. He identified that the nucleus of the hydrogen atom (i.e. proton) is present in the nuclei of all other atoms in the year 1917.

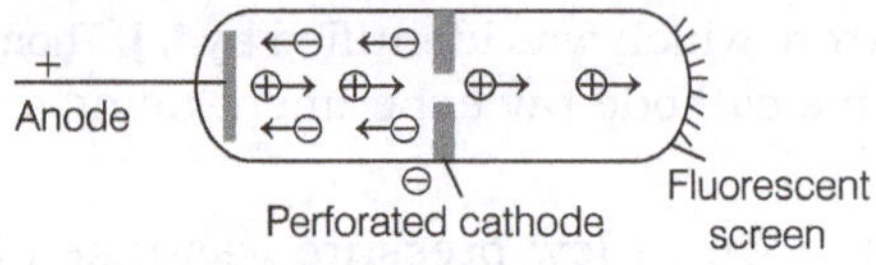

Production of canal rays

Properties of Protons

- Protons are positively charged particles and are denoted as 'p^+'.
- The charge present on proton is equal to $+1.6 \times 10^{-19}$ coulomb and it is considered as +1.
- The mass of a proton is equal to 1.6×10^{-27} kg.
- The mass of proton is approximately 2000 times as that of the electron.

3. Discovery of Neutrons (n)

These are another subatomic particles, discovered by **J. Chadwick** in 1932. It is represented by n. He bombarded beryllium (Be) or boron (B) sheet with high speed alpha particles and noticed the emission of neutral particles.

$$_4Be^9 + {}_2He^4 \longrightarrow {}_6C^{12} + \underset{\text{Neutron}}{{}_0n^1}$$

Properties of Neutrons

- Neutrons are electrically neutral particles and as heavy as protons (i.e. their mass is 1.67493×10^{-27}kg).
- Neutrons are present in the nucleus of all atoms except hydrogen.

Properties of the Electron, Proton and Neutron

Properties	Proton (p)	Neutron (n)	Electron (e^-)
Mass	1.67262×10^{-27} kg	1.67495×10^{-27} kg	9.1094×10^{-31} kg
Charge	1.6022×10^{-19}C	0	-1.6022×10^{-19}C
Mass relative to the electron	1836	1839	1
Spin	$\frac{1}{2}$	$\frac{1}{2}$	$\frac{1}{2}$
Charge relative to the proton	+1	0	−1
Discovery	E. Goldstein	J. Chadwick	J.J. Thomson

Structure of an Atom

According to **Dalton's atomic theory**, atom was indivisible and indestructible. But, the discovery of two fundamental particles (electrons and protons) inside the atom, led to the failure of this aspect of Dalton's theory. To know the arrangement of electrons and protons within an atom, many scientists proposed various atomic models.

These are discussed below

Thomson's Model of an Atom

J.J. Thomson was the first scientist to propose a model for the structure of an atom. He proposed that in an atom the electrons are present as embedded in a sphere of positive charge, just like currants (dry fruits) in a spherical Christmas pudding. It can also be compared to a watermelon, in which the positive charge of an atom is spread all over like the red edible part, while the electrons studded in the positively charged sphere, like the seeds in watermelon.

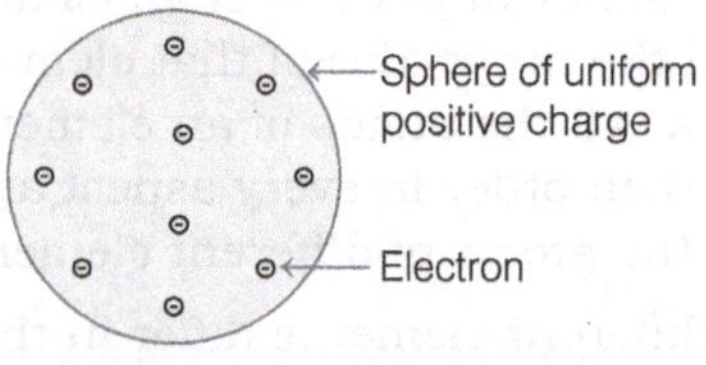

Thomson's model of an atom

Following are the postulates of this model

- Electrons are embedded in a sphere of positive charge.
- The negative and positive charges are equal in magnitude. Therefore, the atom as a whole is electrically neutral.
- The mass of an atom is assumed to be uniformly distributed throughout the atom.

Limitations of Thomson's Model of an Atom

Limitations of J.J. Thomson's model of an atom were

- J.J. Thomson's model could not explain the experiments and the results of other scientists such as Rutherford, as there is no nucleus in the atomic model proposed by Thomson.
- It could not explain the stability of an atom, i.e. how positive and negative charges could remain, so close together.
- Thomson's atomic model failed to explain how the positive charge holds on the electrons inside the atom.

Rutherford's Model of an Atom

Ernest Rutherford, with the help of Geiger and Marsden designed an experiment to know how the electrons are arranged within an atom.

He bombarded thin sheets of gold foil with fast moving α-particles (these are doubly charged helium ions having a mass of 4u).

He selected a gold foil because he wanted a layer as thin as possible (most malleable). This gold foil was about 1000 atoms thick.

The following observations were made by Rutherford

- Most of the fast moving α-particles passed straight through the gold foil.
- Some of the α-particles were deflected by the foil with small angles.
- Very few α-particles (one out of 12000) appeared to rebound.

On the basis of his experiment, Rutherford concluded that

- Most of the space inside the atom is empty because most of the α-particles passed through the gold foil without getting deflected.
- Very few particles were deflected from their path, indicating that the positive charge of the atom occupies very little space.
- A very small fraction of α-particles were deflected by 180° (i.e. they rebound), indicating that all the positive charge and mass of atom were concentrated in a very small volume within the atom.

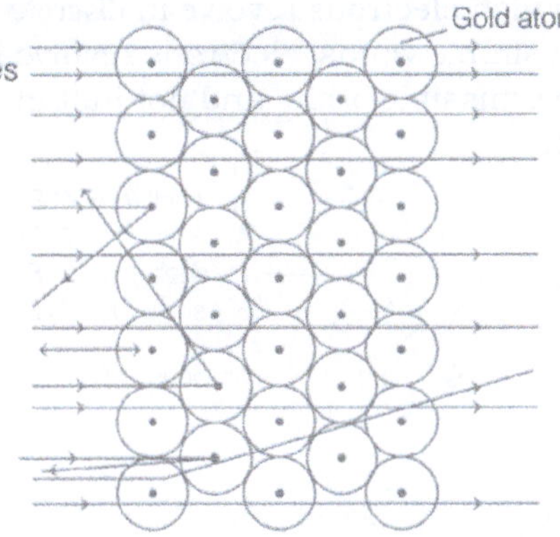

Scattering of α-particles by a gold foil

On the basis of his experiment, Rutherford put forward the nuclear model of an atom, having the following features

- There is a positively charged, highly densed centre in an atom, called **nucleus**. Nearly, the whole mass of the atom resides in the nucleus.
- The electrons revolve around the nucleus in circular path. He named these circular paths as orbits.
- The size of the nucleus (10^{-15}m) is very small as compared to the size of the atom (10^{-10}m).

Note Rutherford suggested that his model of atom was similar to that of our solar system. In the solar system, the different planets are revolving around the Sun. In the same manner, in an atom the electrons are revolving around the nucleus. So, these electrons are also called **planetary electrons**.

Limitations of Rutherford's Model of an Atom

Any charged particle when accelerated is expected to radiate energy. To remain in a circular orbit, the electron would need to undergo acceleration. Therefore, it would radiate energy.

Thus, the revolving electron would lose energy and finally fall into the nucleus. If this were so, the atom should be highly unstable. Therefore, matter would not exist, but we know matter exists. It means that atoms are quite stable.

Thus, it could not explain the stability of an atom when charged electrons are moving under the attractive force of positively charged nucleus.

Bohr's Model of an Atom

To overcome the objections raised against Rutherford's model of the atom, **Neils Bohr** put forward the following postulates about the model of an atom.

- Atom consists of positively charged nucleus around which electrons revolve in **discrete orbit** shells. In simple words, electrons revolve in certain permissible orbits and not just in any orbit.

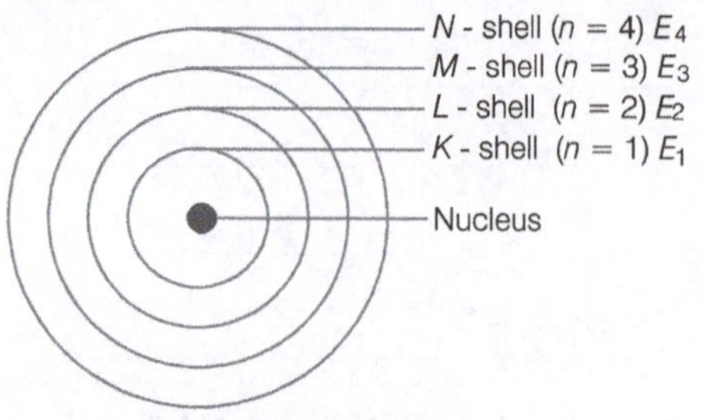

A few energy levels in an atom

- Each of these orbits are associated with certain value of energy. Hence, these orbits are called **energy shells** or **energy levels.**
- As the energy of an orbit is fixed (stationary), orbit is also called **stationary state** or **stationary orbit.**
- Starting from nucleus, energy levels (orbits) are represented by numbers (1, 2, 3, 4, etc.) or by alphabets (*K, L, M, N*, etc.).
- Normally, the electrons present in first energy level (E_1) have lowest energy. Their energies increase on moving towards outer energy levels.
- Energy of an electron remains same as long as it remains in certain discrete orbit and it does not radiate energy while revolving.
- When energy is supplied to an electron, it can go to higher energy levels. While an electron falls to lower energy level, after radiating energy.

Limitations of Bohr's Model

- It could not explain the spectra obtained from larger atoms.
- It considers electrons to have a known exact radius and orbit which is impossible according to Heisenberg.

Check Your LEARNING...

1 Name all the fundamental particles of atom.
2 Write the name of discoveror of electrons, protons and neutrons.
3 What conclusion would be drawn by Rutherford when he observed that most of the fast moving α-particles passed straight through the gold foil?
4 Nucleus of an atom is positively charged and electrons around it are negatively charged, then why do electrons not just fall to the nucleus out of attraction?
5 What do you understand by the term 'discrete orbit'?
6 What are the names given to first 4 discrete shells?

Atomic Number (Z)

It is defined as the number of protons present in the nucleus of an atom. It is also equal to the number of electrons in the neutral atom.

It is denoted by *Z* and written as a subscript towards the left of the symbol. Atomic number is unique for atoms of each element.

Atomic number (*Z*) = Number of protons in the nucleus
= Number of electrons

e.g. $^{4}_{2}He$, $^{7}_{3}Li$; $Z = 2$ and 3 for He and Li respectively.

Mass Number (A)

It is defined as the sum of number of protons and neutrons present in the nucleus of an atom. Protons and neutrons together called as nucleons. Mass number is denoted by '*A*'.

Mass number (*A*) = Number of protons + Number of neutrons.

Number of neutrons = Mass number − Atomic number

Mass number is written as a superscript towards the left of the symbol. In the notation for an atom, the atomic number, mass number and symbol of the element are to be written as

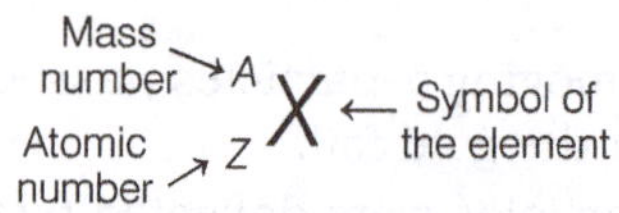

e.g. For nitrogen, the notation is $^{14}_{7}N$, i.e. its atomic number is 7 and mass number is 14.

Note

- If number of electrons < number of protons, the atom carries positive charge and called **cation.**
- If number of electrons > number of protons, the atom carries negative charge and called **anion.**
- If number of electrons is equal to number of protons, the atom carries no charge, i.e. it is **neutral.**

Distribution of Electrons in Different Orbits (Shells)

The distribution of electrons into different orbits of an atom was suggested by **Bohr** and **Bury**.

For writing the number of electrons in different energy levels or shells, some rules are followed.

- The maximum number of electrons present in a shell is given by the formula $2n^2$, where n is the orbit number or energy level, 1, 2, 3, ...

Therefore, the maximum number of electrons in different shells are as follows

First orbit or *K*-shell $= 2 \times (1)^2 = 2$
Second orbit or *L*-shell $= 2 \times (2)^2 = 8$
Third orbit or *M*-shell $= 2 \times (3)^2 = 18$
Fourth orbit or *N*-shell $= 2 \times (4)^2 = 32$ and so on.

- The maximum number of electrons that can be accommodated in the outermost orbit is 8.
- Electrons are not accommodated in a given shell, unless the inner shells are filled (i.e. the shells are filled in a stepwise manner).

Representation of Atomic Structure (First Twenty Elements)

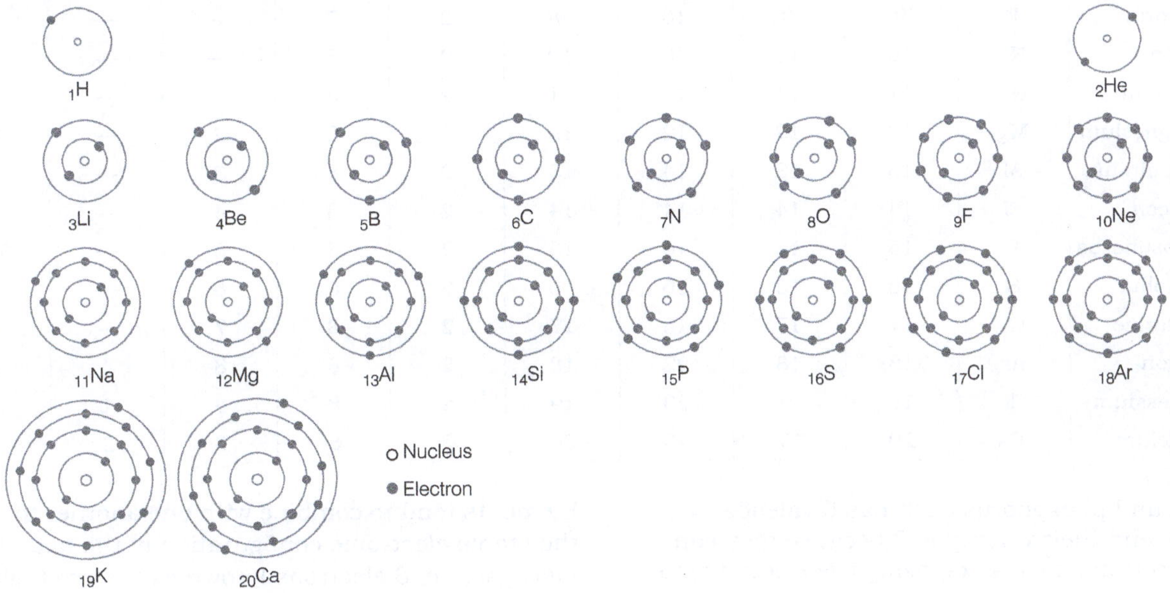

Atomic structures of elements with atomic numbers in the range $Z = 1$ (Hydrogen) to $X = 20$ (Calcium).

Valency

The electrons present in the outermost shell of an atom are known as **valence electrons.** They govern the chemical properties of elements as they take part in chemical reactions.

The elements with same number of electrons in the valence shell show similar properties and with different number of valence electrons show different chemical properties. An outermost shell, which had eight electrons is called an **octet**.

The tendency to react with atoms of the same or different elements to form molecules is an attempt to attain fully-filled outermost shell. This can be achieved by sharing, gaining or the loss of electrons.

The number of electrons lost or gained or shared by an atom to become stable or to achieve an octet in the outermost shell. This is known as **octet rule**. The number of electrons gained, lost or shared is known as valency of that element.

In other words, valency is the combining capacity of the atom of an element with the atom(s) of other element(s) in order to complete its octet.

e.g. Hydrogen, lithium, sodium and potassium atoms contain one electron each in their outermost shell, therefore each one of them can lose one electron to become stable.
Hence, their valency is 1.

Composition of Atoms of the First Twenty Elements with Electron Distribution in Various Shells

S. no.	Name of elements	Symbol	Atomic number	Number of protons	Number of neutrons	Number of electrons	Distribution of electrons				Valency
							K	*L*	*M*	*N*	
1.	Hydrogen	H	1	1	—	1	1	—	—	—	1
2.	Helium	He	2	2	2	2	2	—	—	—	0
3.	Lithium	Li	3	3	4	3	2	1	—	—	1
4.	Beryllium	Be	4	4	5	4	2	2	—	—	2
5.	Boron	B	5	5	6	5	2	3	—	—	3
6.	Carbon	C	6	6	6	6	2	4	—	—	4
7.	Nitrogen	N	7	7	7	7	2	5	—	—	3
8.	Oxygen	O	8	8	8	8	2	6	—	—	2
9.	Fluorine	F	9	9	10	9	2	7	—	—	1
10.	Neon	Ne	10	10	10	10	2	8	—	—	0
11.	Sodium	Na	11	11	12	11	2	8	1	—	1
12.	Magnesium	Mg	12	12	12	12	2	8	2	—	2
13.	Aluminium	Al	13	13	14	13	2	8	3	—	3
14.	Silicon	Si	14	14	14	14	2	8	4	—	4
15.	Phosphorus	P	15	15	16	15	2	8	5	—	3, 5
16.	Sulphur	S	16	16	16	16	2	8	6	—	2
17.	Chlorine	Cl	17	17	18	17	2	8	7	—	1
18.	Argon	Ar	18	18	22	18	2	8	8		0
19.	Potassium	K	19	19	20	19	2	8	8	1	1
20.	Calcium	Ca	20	20	20	20	2	8	8	2	2

Nitrogen and phosphorus each has 5 valence electrons and their valency is 3 because they can gain 3 electrons (instead of losing five electrons) to become stable.

All the inert elements, i.e. He, Ne, Ar, etc., have completely filled outermost shells.

They do not combine with other atoms or among themselves to form molecules. Therefore, their valency is zero.

Note For metals, valency = number of valence electrons and for non-metals, valency = 8 − number of valence electrons.

Reason for Chemical Activity of an Atom

The chemical activity of an atom depends upon the number of electrons in the valence shell of its atom.

Chemically active atoms have an incomplete octet, i.e. less than 8 electrons or less than 2 electrons in their valence shell. The valence electrons of atoms contribute to the formation of molecules.

Elements tend to combine with one another to attain the stable electronic configuration of the nearest inert gas, i.e. 8 electrons known as the **octet rule**.

Note All the six inert gases namely, helium (He), neon (Ne), argon (Ar), krypton (Kr), xenon (Xe) and radon (Rn). These all are non-reactive, i.e. inert. They do not combine with other atoms to form molecules. So, their combining capacity is zero.

Check Your LEARNING...

1 How can you denote the atomic number of any element?

2 What do you understand by mass number?

3 What can be the maximum number of electrons in the outermost orbit?

4 Find out the number of electrons present in last shell of an atom having atomic number 15.

5 In an atom first four shells (*K*, *L*, *M* and *N*) are completely filled, then what is the total number of electrons in that atom?

6 A non-metal has six electrons in its outermost shell. Predict its valency.

Different Atomic Species

Different atomic species are as given below

Isotopes

Isotopes are defined as the atoms of the same element, having the same atomic number but different mass numbers. In other words, it can be said that isotopes have same number of protons but differ in the number of neutrons.

Each isotope of an element is a pure substance. They have same chemical properties but different physical properties and occupy same position in the periodic table. e.g.

(i) **Hydrogen** It has three isotopes all having atomic number equal to one but mass numbers as 1, 2 and 3.

Isotopes	Atomic number	Mass number	No. of electrons	No. of protons	No. of neutrons
Protium $_1^1H$	1	1	1	1	0
Deuterium $_1^2H$ or $_1^2D$	1	2	1	1	1
Tritium $_1^3H$ or $_1^3T$	1	3	1	1	2

(ii) **Carbon** It has three isotopes as listed below.

Isotopes	Atomic number	Mass number	No. of electrons	No. of protons	No. of neutrons
C-12 or $_6^{12}C$	6	12	6	6	6
C-13 or $_6^{13}C$	6	13	6	6	7
C-14 or $_6^{14}C$	6	14	6	6	8

(iii) **Chlorine** It has many isotopes found in traces. Two major isotopes of it are listed below.

Isotopes	Atomic number	Mass number	No. of electrons	No. of protons	No. of neutrons
Cl-35 or $_{17}^{35}Cl$	17	35	17	17	18
Cl-37 or $_{17}^{37}Cl$	17	37	17	17	20

Properties of Isotopes

- Isotopes have similar chemical properties.
- However, they differ in physical properties that depend on the atomic mass such as density, boiling point, light scattering, etc.

Applications of Isotopes

- An isotope of uranium (U-235) is used as a fuel for the production of electricity in nuclear reactors.
- U-238 is used to determine the age of very old rocks and even the age of the earth.
- An isotope of cobalt (Co-60) is used in the treatment of cancer.
- An isotope of carbon (C-14) is used to determine the age of old specimens of wood or old bones of living organisms.
- An isotope of iodine (I-131) is used in the treatment of goitre.
- P-32 is used in agricultural research.
- Na-24 is used to detect blood clots.

Isobars

Atoms of different elements with different atomic numbers but same mass number are known as **isobars**. In other words, isobars are the atoms of different elements that have same number of nucleons (protons + neutrons) but differ in the number of protons.

e.g. $_{18}^{40}Ar$ and $_{20}^{40}Ca$ are **isobars**.

Since, isobars have different atomic number as well as different electronic configuration. Thus, they also have both different physical and chemical properties.

Check Your LEARNING...

1 Identify the isotopic pair(s) out of the following species.
$_8C^{16}, _6C^{14}, _7N^{14}, _8O^{18}, _7N^{16}$

2 Which isotope of hydrogen contain same number of electrons, protons and neutrons?

3 How many isotopes of carbon found in nature?

4 Name the isotope used as a fuel in nuclear reactors.

5 Write any two uses of isotopes.

6 Give an example of isobars.

Chemical Bonding

A chemical bond is a kind of attraction which holds two or more constituents (atoms, molecules or ions) together. The process of their combination is called **chemical bonding**. There are mainly two types of chemical bond which are as follows

- Electrovalent bond or ionic bond
- Covalent bond or molecular bond

Electrovalent Bond or Ionic Bond

The bond formed as a result of electrostatic force of attraction which holds the array of oppositely charged ions, i.e. positive and negative ions together is termed as the **electrovalent** or **ionic bond**.

The compounds in which ionic bond is present are called **electrovalent** or **ionic compounds**.

This type of bond is formed between an electropositive (metal) element and an electronegative (non-metal) element. It is formed by the complete transfer of electrons from one atom to another, such, that all the combining atoms complete their octet (or duplet in case of H, Li, etc.).

Properties of Ionic Bonds

- Due to the presence of a strong electrostatic force of attraction between cations and anions, the ionic bonds are the strongest of all the bonds.
- The ionic bond has charge separation, so they are the most reactive of all the bonds in the proper medium.
- The ionic bonded molecules have high melting and boiling points.
- The ionic bonded molecules in their aqueous solution are good conductors of electricity.

Important Terms to Understand the Formation of Electrovalent Bonds

(i) **Electrovalency** The number of electrons lost or gained by the valence shell of an atom of any element to achieve the stable electronic configuration is called its electrovalency.

(ii) **Electropositive elements** Atoms with tendency to lose electron are called electropositive elements.

On losing an electron, these atoms becomes positively charged because number of protons exceeds the number of electrons, i.e. cation is formed.

e.g. Na^+, K^+, Ca^{2+}, Mg^{2+}, Al^{3+}, etc.

$$\underset{}{Na} \longrightarrow \underset{\text{(Cation)}}{Na^+} + e^-$$

(iii) **Electronegative elements** Atoms with tendency to gain electrons are called electronegative. When such an atom gains an electron, the number of electrons exceed the number of protons and thus, atom becomes negatively charged anion, i.e. is formed e.g. Cl^-, Br^-, I^-, F^-, O^{2-}, S^{2-}, N^{3-}, etc.

Note Group 1 elements are most electropositive. In same way, group 17 elements are most electronegative. Therefore, CsF is ionic in nature.

Formation of Electrovalent Bonds

Electrovalent bond is formed only when one of an atom can easily lose electron(s) while other can easily gain to acquire the stable electronic configuration (or arrangement) of nearest noble gas. e.g. Formation of sodium chloride.

$$\underset{(2,\,8,\,1)}{Na\cdot} + \underset{(2,\,8,\,7)}{:\!\ddot{\underset{\cdot\cdot}{Cl}}\!:} \longrightarrow \underset{(2,\,8)}{Na^+} \; \underset{(2,\,8,\,8)}{:\!\ddot{\underset{\cdot\cdot}{Cl}}\!:^-}$$

Structure of Some Electrovalent Compounds

The structure of some electrovalent compounds are as follows

1. Sodium Chloride (NaCl)

The electronic configuration of sodium (atomic number is 11) is 2, 8, 1. It loses one electron from its outermost shell and acquires the inert gas configuration of nearest noble gas (i.e. neon [Ne] = 2, 8), thus cation is formed.

$$\underset{(2,8,1)}{Na} \longrightarrow \underset{(2,8)}{Na^+} + e^-$$

The electronic configuration of chlorine (atomic number is 17) is 2, 8, 7. It can accept one electron (which was released by sodium) and, thus anion is formed.

$$\underset{(2,\,8,\,7)}{:\!\ddot{\underset{\cdot\cdot}{Cl}}\cdot} + e^- \longrightarrow \underset{(2,\,8,\,8)}{\left[:\!\ddot{\underset{\cdot\cdot}{Cl}}\!:\right]^-}$$

The above two oppositely charged ions (i.e. chloride and sodium ions) approach each other.

They are held together by the strong electrostatic force of attraction. In this way, formation of sodium chloride takes place.

Orbit structure of NaCl

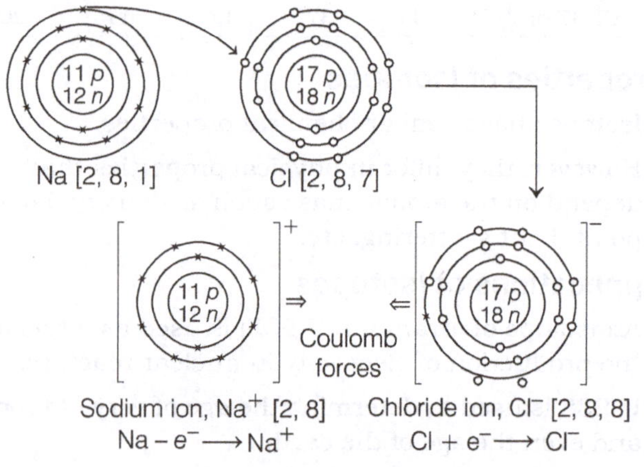

Electron dot structure of NaCl

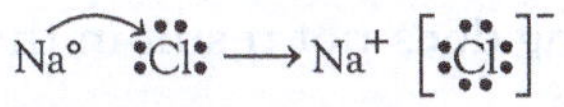

2. Magnesium Chloride ($MgCl_2$)

The number of valence electrons in magnesium atom (atomic number is 12) and chlorine atom (atomic number is 17) are 2 and 7, respectively.

Therefore, magnesium atom loses its two electrons, acquire a stable noble gas configuration (2, 8) and attains +2 charge (cation).

Each chlorine atom containing seven electrons in its valence shell can accept one-one electron of the two electrons that are donated by the magnesium atom. Therefore, two chloride ions will combine with one magnesium ion (Mg^{2+}) to form magnesium chloride molecule ($MgCl_2$).

Orbit structure of $MgCl_2$

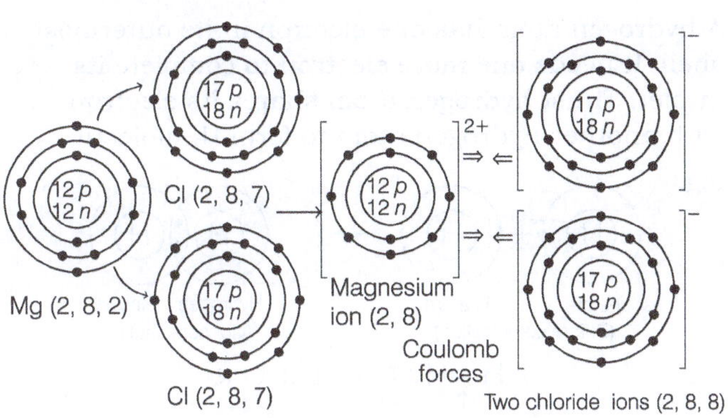

Electron dot structure of $MgCl_2$

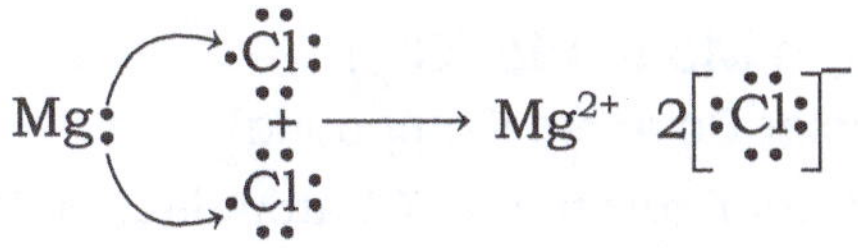

3. Calcium Oxide (CaO)

Calcium (atomic number is 20, electronic configuration = 2, 8, 8, 2) loses two electrons and attains +2 charge by forming calcium ion and acquires stable noble gas electronic configuration (i.e. argon [Ar] = 2, 8, 8).

On the other hand, oxygen (atomic number is 8, electronic configuration = 2, 6) gain two electrons to forms oxide ion and acquires stable configuration of nearest noble gas (i.e. neon).

Orbit structure of CaO

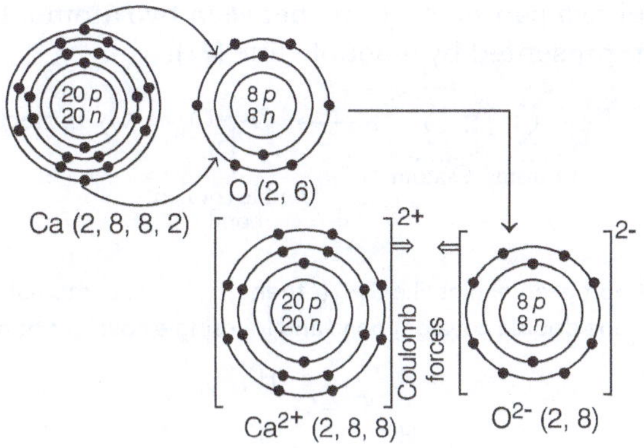

Electron dot structure of CaO

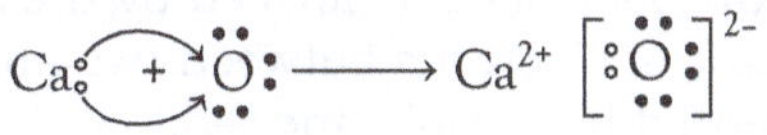

Covalent Bond or Molecular Bond

A chemical bond formed by the mutual sharing of electrons between the combining atoms of the same or different elements is called the **covalent bond.** This bond is generally formed between two electronegative, i.e. non-metallic elements.

The number of electrons shared by an atom in order to complete its octet is called the **covalency** of that atom.

e.g. Formation of chlorine molecule.

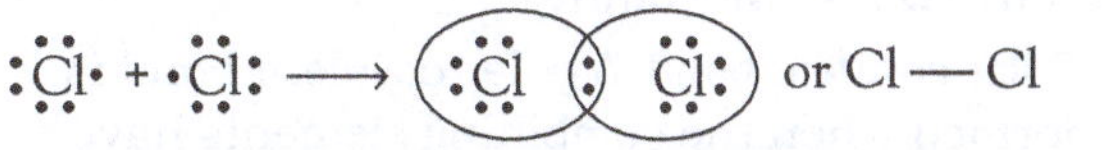

Covalent bond between two Cl-atoms

Note Number of covalent bonds formed depend upon the number of shared pair of electrons between the two atoms.

Types of Covalent Bonds

Covalent bonds are broadly classified into following types

1. On the Basis of Sharing of Electrons

(i) **Single covalent bond** It is formed by the sharing of one pair of electrons between two atoms. It is represented by a single line (—).

e.g.

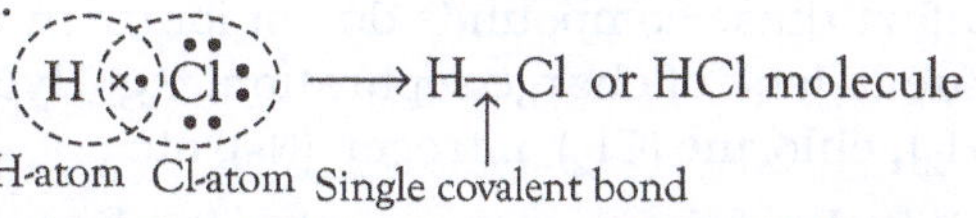

(ii) **Double covalent bond** It is formed by the sharing of two pair of electrons between two atoms. It is represented by a double line (=).

e.g.

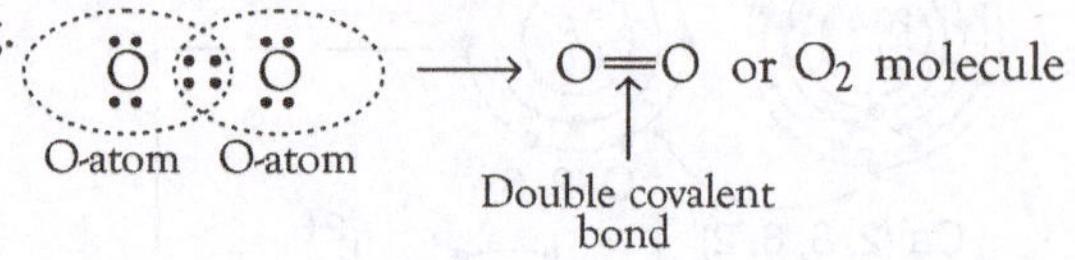

Note Some molecules like C_2H_4 (ethene) have the combination of one double covalent bond and four single covalent bonds.

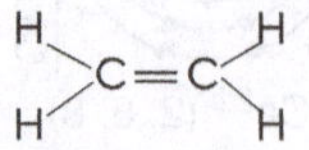

Ethene (C_2H_4)

(iii) **Triple covalent bond** It is formed by the sharing of three pair of electrons between two atoms. It is represented by a triple line (≡).

e.g.

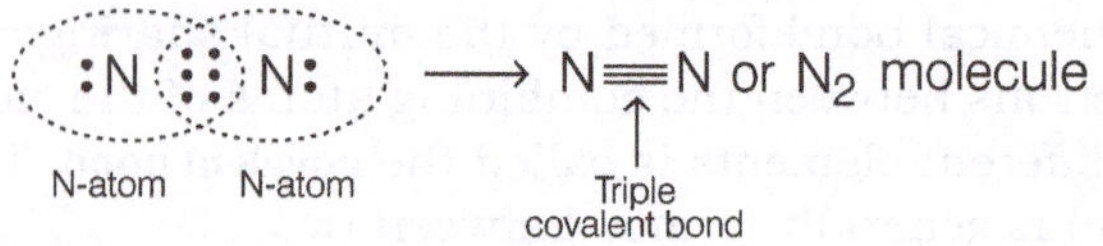

Note Some molecules like C_2H_2 (ethyne) have the combination of one triple and two single covalent bonds.

H—C≡C—H

Ethyne (C_2H_2)

2. On the Basis of Polarity

(i) **Polar covalent bond** A polar covalent bond is formed when the combining elements have significant difference in their electronegativity. They are generally gases, liquids or soft solids. These compounds have high melting and boiling point. Infact, these compounds have free ions therefore, these are soluble in polar solvents. e.g. Water (H_2O) and ammonia (NH_3).

(ii) **Non-polar covalent bond** A covalent bond is formed when the combining elements have no or very slight difference in their electronegativity. They are generally gases, liquids or solids. These compounds have low melting and boiling points.

Infact these compounds do not ionise in water due to lack of charge separation. e.g. Hydrogen (H_2), chlorine (Cl_2), nitrogen (N_2), etc.

All hydrocarbons are non-polar covalent compounds because their electronegativity difference is little and pair of electrons are equally shared by the linked atoms.

Properties of Covalent Bond

- Covalent bonding does not result in the formation of new electrons.
- Covalent bonds rarely break spontaneously.
- These bonds are directional whereas the atoms that are bonded showcase specific orientations relative to one another.
- Most compounds having covalent bonds exhibit relatively low melting points and boiling points.
- Covalent compounds are not soluble in water.

Atomic Orbital Structure of Some Covalent Compounds

The structures of some covalent compounds are as follows

1. Hydrogen Molecule (H_2) (Non-polar Covalent Compound)

A hydrogen atom has one electron in its outermost shell. It needs one more electron to complete its duplet. Thus, hydrogen atom shares its electron with another hydrogen atom to form H_2 molecule.

e.g.

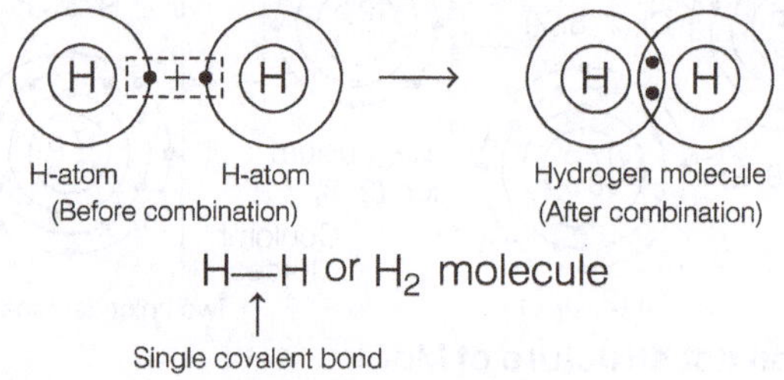

2. Chlorine Molecule (Cl_2) (Non-polar Covalent Compound)

Electronic configuration of Cl-atom is 2, 8, 7. So, it needs one electron to complete its octet. Hence, it shares one electron with another Cl-atom to form Cl_2 molecule.

e.g.

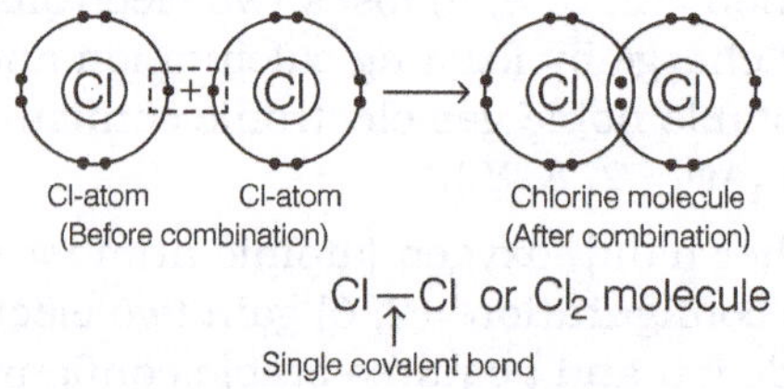

3. Nitrogen Molecule (N_2) (Non-polar Covalent Compound)

Electronic configuration of N is 2, 5. To complete its octet, nitrogen needs three electrons. Hence, two

N-atoms share three pair of electrons to form N_2 molecule.

e.g.

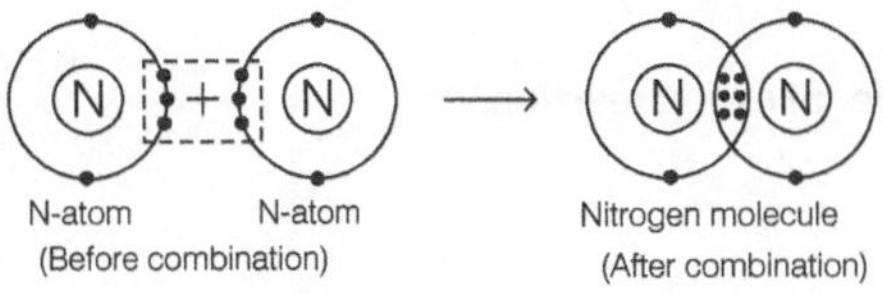

N≡N or N_2 molecule

Triple covalent bond

4. **Ammonia Molecule** (NH_3) (Polar Compound)

Electronic configuration of N is 2, 5 and that of H is 1. Nitrogen needs three electrons to complete its octet while hydrogen needs one electron to complete its duplet. Number of covalent bonds involved in NH_3 = 3

e.g.

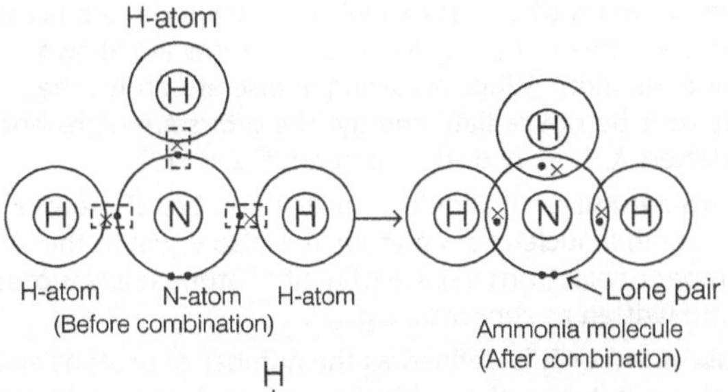

H—N̈—H (with H above N) or N̈H_3 molecule

3 single covalent bonds

5. **Water Molecule** (H_2O) (Polar Compound)

Electronic configuration of H is 1 and O is 2, 6. Hydrogen needs one electron to complete its duplet while oxygen needs two electrons to complete its octet. Hence, one O-atom shares its two electrons with two H-atoms.

e.g.

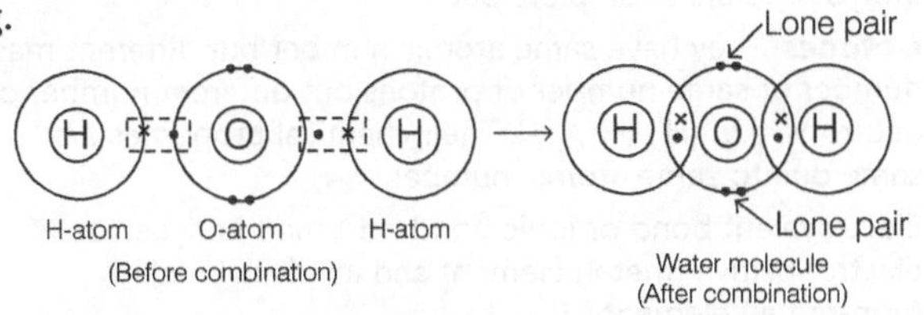

H—Ö—H or H_2Ö: molecule

Two single covalent bonds

6. **Oxygen Molecule** (O_2) (Non-polar Covalent Compound)

Electronic configuration of O is 2,6. To complete its octet, oxygen needs two electrons. Hence, two O-atoms share two pair of electrons to form O_2 molecule.

e.g.

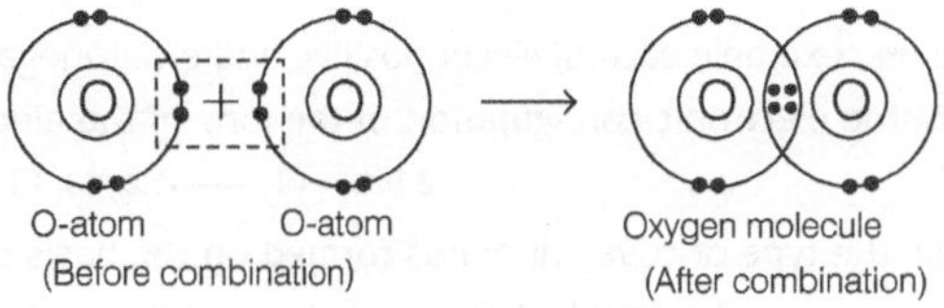

O=O or O_2 molecule

Double covalent bond

7. **Methane** (CH_4) (Non-polar Compound)

Carbon atom has four electrons in its valence shell. In order to complete octet, it shares four electrons, one each with four hydrogen atoms.

e.g.

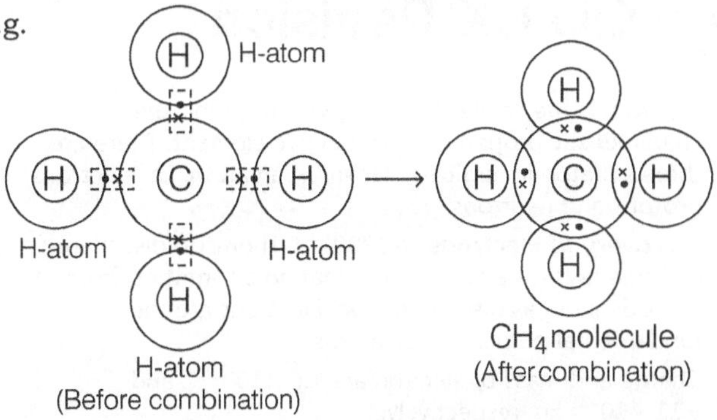

8. **Carbon Tetrachloride Molecule** (CCl_4) (Non-polar Covalent Compound)

Electronic configuration of C = 2, 4 and Cl = 2, 8, 7.

Carbon needs 4 electrons while Cl requires one more electron to attain the stable electronic configuration of nearest noble gas by completing their octet.

e.g.

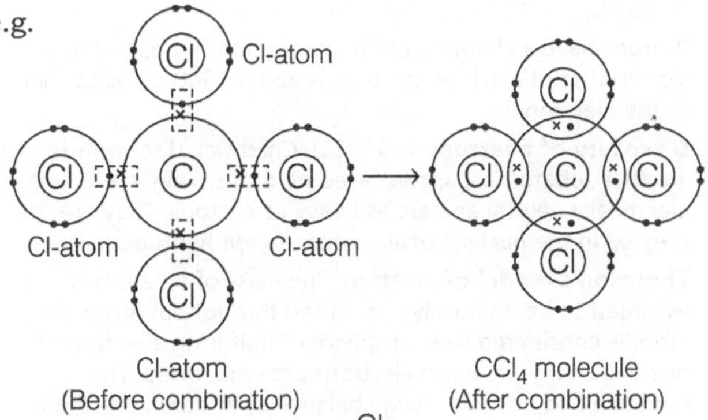

Cl—C(Cl)(Cl)—Cl or CCl_4 molecule

4-single covalent bonds

Check Your LEARNING...

1 Give one example each of electropositive and electronegative elements.
2 Write the electronic configuration of the ions of the electrovalent products of the following reaction.

$$2\,Na + Cl_2 \longrightarrow 2\,Na^+Cl^-$$

3 Name the type of covalent bonds formed on the basis of sharing of electrons.
4 Name a non-polar covalent compound containing two pair of electrons.
5 Give the orbit structure of $MgCl_2$.
6 How many covalent bonds are formed during the formation of water molecule?

QUiCK Revision

- An atom is the smallest particle, which exhibit the characteristic properties of respective element. There are three subatomic particles present in an atom, i.e. electrons, protons and neutrons.
- **Discovery of electrons** In 1990, J.J. Thomson discovered cathode rays (or electrons) originating or emitting from the cathode in a gas discharge tube. Electrons are the fundamental particles of all atoms.
- Charge and mass of electron are 1.6×10^{-19} C and 9.11×10^{-31} kg, respectively.
- **Discovery of protons** In 1886, E. Goldstein discovered the presence of new radiations known as canal rays or anode rays passing through holes or 'canals' of cathode and moving towards cathode in a discharge tube.
- After this experiment, Ernest Rutherford identified that the nucleus of the hydrogen atom (i.e. proton) is present in the nuclei of all other atoms in the year 1917.
- Anode rays consist of positively charged particles, known as protons.
- Protons have a charge equal in magnitude but opposite in sign to that of electron. Its mass is about 1840 times to that of the electron.
- **Discovery of neutrons** In 1932, J. Chadwick discovered another subatomic particle called neutrons. They are electrically neutral and are as heavy as protons. They are present in the nucleus of all atoms, except hydrogen.
- **Thomson's model of an atom** The mass of an atom is assumed to be uniformly distributed throughout atom. An atom is considered to be a sphere of uniformly distributed positive charge in which electrons are embedded. The negative and positive charge balance each other, therefore atom as a whole is neutral.
- **Rutherford's model of an atom** After performing α-particle experiment, he suggested that: There is a positively charged, highly densed centre in an atom, called the **nucleus**. Nearly the whole mass of atom resides on it. The electrons revolve around the nucleus in well defined orbits.
- **Bohr's model of an atom** Only certain special orbits called discrete orbits or energy levels of electrons are allowed inside the atom. While revolving in discrete orbits, the electrons do not radiate energy. The orbits are represented by letters *K, L, M, N* or the numbers 1, 2, 3, 4.
- **Atomic number** It is defined as the number of protons present in a nucleus of an atom. It is also equal to the number of electrons in case of neutral atom. It is denoted by *Z* and written as subscript, e.g. ${}_6C$
- **Mass number** It is defined as the number of protons and neutrons in the nucleus. It is denoted by *A* and written as superscript, e.g. ${}^{14}N$.
- **Bohr and Bury scheme for distribution of electrons in different energy levels** The maximum number of electrons in an energy level is equal to $2n^2$, where *n* is the energy level or orbits or shells.
- **Valency** It is the combining capacity of an element with the atom(s) of other element(s) in order to complete its octet.
- **Chemical activity of an atom** It depends upon the number of electrons in the valence shell of its atom. Chemically active atoms have an incomplete octet.
- **Isotopes** They have same atomic number but different mass number or same number of protons but different number of neutrons. e.g. ${}_1H^1$, ${}_1H^2$, ${}_1H^3$. Their chemical properties are same due to same atomic number.
- Electrovalent bond or ionic bond is formed between an electropositive (metal) element and an electronegative (non-metal) element.
- Ionic bonds are the strongest due to presence of strong electrostatic force of attraction between cations and anions.
- Covalent bond is generally formed between two electronegative, i.e. non-metallic elements.
- Covalent compounds are of two types : polar and non-polar.

Chapter Practice

Section-I

a. Multiple Choice Questions

1. A pure substance, constituted of only one type of particles is called a/an
(a) atom (b) element
(c) compound (d) None of these

Sol. (a)

2. Name of the smallest particle which can take part in a chemical reaction independently is
(a) atom (b) proton
(c) neutron (d) electron

Sol. (a)

3. The constituent particle of an element showing almost all the properties of element is
(a) electron (b) proton
(c) atom (d) molecule

Sol. (c)

4. Cathode rays are composed of
(a) proton (b) neutron
(c) electron (d) nucleus

Sol. (c)

5. J.J. Thomson, in his atomic model, assigned positive charge to
(a) electron
(b) proton
(c) neutron
(d) atomic sphere

Sol. (d)

6. In Christmas pudding model, the currants were compared with
(a) electrons (b) protons
(c) neutrons (d) atoms

Sol. (a)

7. Who discovered that positive charge in an atom is concentrated at nucleus?
(a) Thomson (b) Rutherford
(c) Goldstein (d) Chadwick

Sol. (b)

8. Which scientist proposed that electrons revolve in distinct energy level, around nucleus?
(a) Rutherford (b) Bohr
(c) Chadwick (d) Thomson

Sol. (b)

9. Number of valence electrons in Cl^- ion are
(a) 16 (b) 8 (c) 17 (d) 18

Sol. (b)

10. Which one of the following is a correct electronic configuration of magnesium (Mg)?
(a) 2, 8 (b) 8, 2, 1
(c) 2, 1, 8 (d) 2, 8, 2

Sol. (d)

11. How many energy levels are present in sodium atom?
(a) 1 (b) 2
(c) 3 (d) 4

Sol. (c)

12. The valency of fluorine atom is
(a) 1 (b) 2
(c) 3 (d) 0

Sol. (a)

13. Isobars don't have
(a) the same physical properties
(b) different chemical properties
(c) different number of neutrons
(d) different atomic numbers

Sol. (a)

14. Which of the following is not an isotope of hydrogen?
(a) ${}^{1}_{1}H$ (b) ${}^{2}_{1}H$
(c) ${}^{3}_{1}H$ (d) ${}^{4}_{1}H$

Sol. (d)

15. The bond formed between nitrogen atoms in a molecule is
(a) single covalent bond (b) double covalent bond
(c) ionic bond (d) triple covalent bond

Sol. (d)

b. Fill in the Blanks

16. The size of an atom is decided by the number of .... (electrons, protons, neutrons)

Sol. electrons

17. Neutron has mass roughly equal to ...... (proton, electron, positron)

Sol. proton

18. Almost all the mass of an atom is concentrated in a small region, called .... (proton, neutron, nucleus)

Sol. nucleus

19. Rutherford's α-particle scattering experiment was responsible for the discovery of .... (neutron, electron, nucleus)

Sol. nucleus

20. According to Bohr's model, an atom has discrete ...... levels. (energy, valence)

Sol. energy

21. ...... is an element with atomic number three. (Lithium, Helium, Sodium)

Sol. Lithium

22. Mass number is the sum of number of ...... and ...... (proton, electron; proton, neutron; electron, neutron)

Sol. proton, neutron

23. First energy level can have maximum .... electrons. (2, 3, 4)

Sol. 2

24. Electronic configuration of neon atom is .... (2, 8), (2, 8, 1), (2, 8, 2)

Sol. 2, 8

25. Maximum number of electrons occupied by *L*-shell is .... (8, 9, 10)

Sol. 8

26. An element having atomic number 13 has valency equal to .... (3, 4, 5)

Sol. 3

27. Isotopes has same .... numbers but has different .... numbers. (atomic, mass; atomic, neutron; mass, electron)

Sol. atomic, mass

28. Isotope of .... is used to determine the age of old specimens of wood. (carbon, chlorine hydrogen)

Sol. carbon

29. In covalent compounds, the bond is formed due to the .... of electrons. (sharing, attach, gaining)

Sol. sharing

c. Give One Word or a Phrase

30. Beam of negatively charged particles.

Sol. Cathode rays

31. Proton name is given by

Sol. Ernest Rutherford

32. Scientist who discovered electrons.

Sol. J. J. Thomson

33. Circular path around nucleus in which electrons revolve ?

Sol. Orbits

34. Elements having 1, 2 or 3 valence electrons.

Sol. Metals

35. Elements having 4, 5, 6, 7 or 8 valence electrons.

Sol. Non-metals

36. The subatomic particles of an atom are responsible for mass number.

Sol. Protons, neutrons

37. The maximum number of electrons present in a shell.

Sol. $2n^2$

38. Combining capacity of an atom.

Sol. Valency

39. Elements having same atomic number but different mass numbers.

Sol. Isotopes

d. Match the Columns

40. Match the following columns.

	Column I (Experiments)		Column II (Conducted by)
A.	Cathode rays experiment	1.	Mulliken
B.	Gold foil experiment	2.	Goldstein
C.	Anode rays experiment	3.	Thomson
		4.	Rutherford
		5.	Neils Bohr

Sol. A → (3), B → (4), C → (2)

41. Match the following columns.

Column I (Discoverer or scientist)	Column II (Related discovery or theory)
A. John Dalton	1. Nucleus
B. E. Goldstein	2. Electron
C. J. Chadwick	3. Proton
D. J.J. Thomson	4. Neutron
	5. Indivisiblity of atom

Sol. A → (5), B → (3), C → (4), D → (2)

42. Match the following columns.

	Column I (Element)	Column II (Valency)
A.	Oxygen	1. 1
B.	Potassium	2. 2
C.	Nitrogen	3. 3
D.	Silicon	4. 4

Sol. A → (2), B → (1), C → (3), D → (4)

e. State One Relevant Reason

43. In Rutherford's experiment most of the α-particles passed straight.

Sol. Because most of space in atom is empty.

44. Potassium chloride is an electrovalent compounds. While hydrogen chloride is a covalent compound. However, both conduct electricity in their aqueous solution.

Sol. Because both have free mobile ions in their aqueous solution.

45. Isobars have different physical and chemical properties.

Sol. Because isobars have different atomic number as well as different electronic configuration.

46. Isotopes occupy the same position in the periodic table.

Sol. Because isotopes have same atomic number.

47. Atoms are found to be electrically neutral.

Sol. Because in them negative charged particles (electrons) is equal to the positive charged particles (protons).

Section-II

a. 2 Marks Questions

1. Write the mass number of neon and argon from the data given below.

Element	Number of protons	Number of neutrons
Neon	10	10
Argon	18	22

Sol. Mass number = Number of protons + Number of neutrons

For neon, mass number = 10 + 10 = 20

For argon, mass number = 18 + 22 = 40 [2]

2. Which of the two would be chemically more reactive: element *A* with atomic number 18 or element *D* with atomic number 16 and why?

Sol. Electronic configuration of $_{18}A = 2, 8, 8$

It would be chemically inert due to its complete octet.

Electronic configuration of $_{16}D = 2, 8, 6$

To complete its octet, it will gain 2 electrons, therefore it will be more reactive. [2]

3. (i) Write the name of an element whose atom has same number of sub-atomic particles. Draw the atomic structure of the atom.

(ii) Draw atomic structure of an atom with same number of electrons in *L* and *M*-shells.

Sol. (i) Name of element: Oxygen ($^{16}_{8}O$)

Number of electrons = 8

Number of protons = 8

Number of neutrons = 16 − 8 = 8

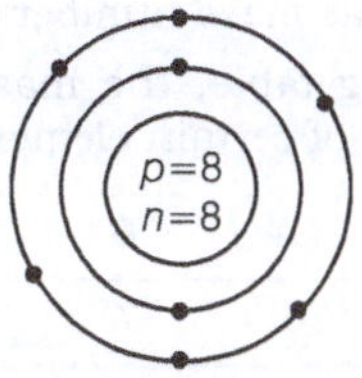

[1]

(ii) Name of element : Argon

Atomic number (18) = 2, 8, 8 (K L M)

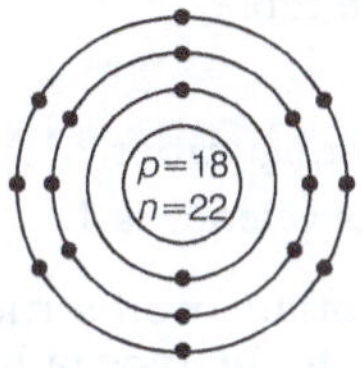

Number of electrons in *L*-shell = 8

Number of electrons in *M*-shell = 8 [1]

b. 3 Marks Questions

4. Elements from *A* to *F* have the distribution of electrons, protons and neutrons in the following way.

Atom/Ion	Number of electrons	Number of protons	Number of neutrons
A	4	3	4
B	10	11	12
C	17	17	18
D	17	17	20
E	18	18	22
F	19	19	21

From the table, find

(i) a pair of ions. (ii) a pair of isobars.

(iii) a pair of isotopes.

Sol. (i) *A* and *B*, because number of electrons and protons are different for these elements. [1]

(ii) *E* and *F*, because these have same mass number (number of protons + number of neutrons) but different atomic number. [1]

(iii) *C* and *D*, because these have same atomic number (number of protons) but different mass number. [1]

5. Answer the following questions.

(i) The electronic configuration of an element is 2(*K*), 8(*L*), 2(*M*). Predict its valency.

(ii) Name of the element.

(iii) Determine the number of protons and neutrons in the element.

Sol. (i) *M*-shell has 2 electrons therefore, its valency is 2. [1]

(ii) The element has atomic number = 2 + 8 + 2 = 12

∴ The element is magnesium. [1]

(iii) Number of protons = Number of electrons = 12
Number of neutrons = $A - Z = 24 - 12 = 12$ [1]
(as mass number of magnesium is 24)

6. In the following table, the mass number and the atomic number of certain elements are given below.

Elements	A	B	C	D	E
Mass number	1	7	14	40	40
Atomic number	1	3	7	18	20

(i) Select a pair of isobars from the above table.
(ii) What would be the valency of element *B* listed in the above table?

Sol. (i) *D* and *E* [1]
(ii) Electronic configuration of the element *B* is 2, 1. Therefore, its valency is 1. [2]

7. Draw an appropriate orbit structure of sodium chloride and state the type of bond present in it.

Sol.

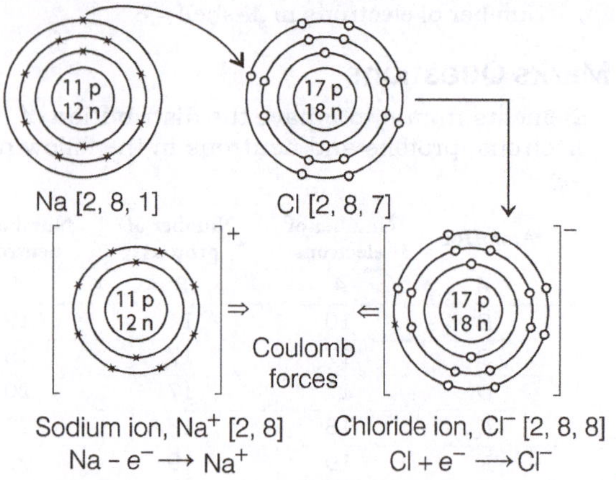

[2]

The above two oppositely charged ions are held together by electrovalent bond or ionic bond. [1]

8. Answer the following questions.
(i) What was Thomson's model of an atom?
(ii) Write any two observations of Rutherford's model of an atom.
(iii) Draw the sketch of Bohr's model of an atom with three shells.

Sol. (i) Thomson's model of an atom was compared to Christmas pudding. The electrons in a sphere of positive charge were like currants (dry fruits) in a spherical Christmas pudding. [1]
(ii) Observations based on Rutherford's model are
(a) Most of the fast moving α-particles passed straight through the gold foil.
(b) Some of the α-particles were deflected by the foil at small angles. [1]
(iii)

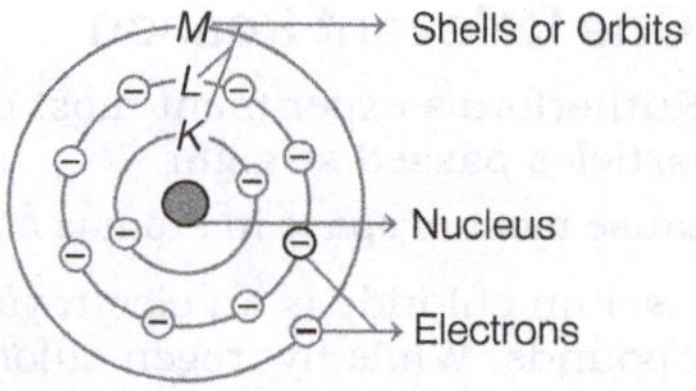

[1]

Bohr's model for sodium atom (Na) [$_{11}$Na = 2, 8, 1]

9. Answer the following questions.
(i) What is the number of electrons in Cl^- ion? (Cl = 17)
(ii) What is the electronic configuration of sodium? (Na = 11)
(iii) Which isotope of uranium is used in nuclear fuel?

Sol. (i) Cl^- ion, 17 + 1 (gained) = 18 electrons (because negative charge shows gain of electrons.) [1]
(ii) Atomic number of sodium = 11
K L M
Electronic configuration = 2, 8, 1 [1]
(iii) Uranium-235 isotope. [1]

C. 4 Marks Questions

10. Answer the following questions.
(i) What is an octet? How do elements reach an octet?
(ii) Make a schematic atomic structure of magnesium and phosphorus.
(Given number of protons of magnesium = 12 and that of phosphorus = 15)

Sol. (i) An outermost shell, which has eight electrons is said to possess an octet.
Elements reach their octet by sharing, gaining or losing electrons. [2]
(ii) **Atomic structure of Mg**

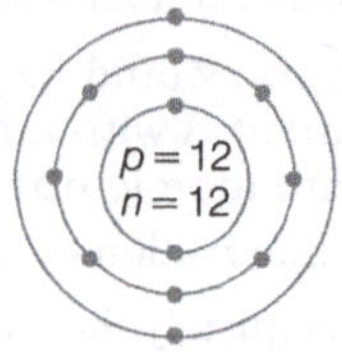

K L M
$_{12}$Mg = 2, 8, 2 [1]

Atomic structure of P

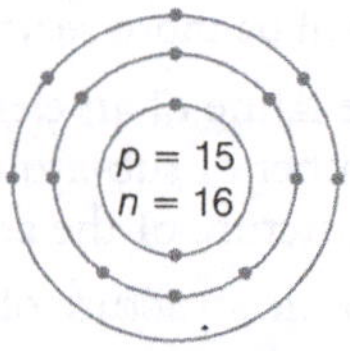

K L M
$_{15}$P = 2, 8, 5 [1]

11. Write down the electronic configuration of first four elements in the periodic table mentioning their energy levels.

Sol. (i) Hydrogen, atomic number = 1
Outermost shell K
Electronic configuration = 1 [1]

(ii) Helium, atomic number = 2
Outermost shell K
Electronic configuration = 2 [1]

(iii) Lithium, atomic number = 3
Outermost shells K L
Electronic configuration = 2, 1 [1]

(iv) Beryllium, atomic number = 4
Outermost shells K L
Electronic configuration = 2, 2 [1]

12. Answer the following questions.
(i) State the three observations made by Rutherford on his α-particle scattering experiment.
(ii) Write the electronic configuration of an element whose mass number is 31 and atomic number is 15. What is its valency?

Sol. (i) The three observations made by Rutherford are
(a) Most of the α-particles passed undeviated, which shows that 'most part of an atom is hollow'. [1]
(b) Some α-particles were scattered with large angular deviations which shows that 'the centre of an atom is positively charged'. [1]
(c) A few of these particles were reflected back, which shows that they had direct collision with the entire mass and the whole mass of the atom is concentrated in the nucleus. [1]

(ii) Electronic configuration of an element (15) = 2, 8, 5
Valency = 8 − 5 = 3 [1]

13. How are the electrons distributed in different orbits (shells)?

Sol. The electrons are distributed in different orbits in the following ways
(i) The maximum number of electrons present in a shell is given by the formula $2n^2$, where n is the orbit number or energy level, 1, 2, 3...... .
Therefore, the maximum number of electrons in different shells are as follows
First orbit or K-shell $= 2 \times 1^2 = 2$
Second orbit or L-shell $= 2 \times 2^2 = 8$
Third orbit or M-shell $= 2 \times 3^2 = 18$
Fourth orbit or N-shell $= 2 \times 4^2 = 32$ and so on. [2]
(ii) The maximum number of electrons that can be accommodated in the outermost orbit is 8. [1/2]
(iii) The penultimate shell (i.e. the second last shell) cannot accommodate more than 18 electrons. [1/2]
(iv) The anti-penultimate shell (i.e. the third last shell) can have a maximum of 32 electrons. [1/2]
(v) Electrons are not accommodated in a given shell, unless the inner shells are filled, i.e. the shells are filled in a stepwise manner. [1/2]

14. Write four properties of covalent bond.

Sol. (i) Covalent bonds are formed by the sharing of electrons. [1]
(ii) Covalent bonds rarely break spontaneously after it is formed. [1]
(iii) Covalent bonds are directional where the atoms that are bonded showcase specific orientations relative to one another. [1]
(iv) Most compounds having covalent bonds exhibit relatively low melting points and boiling points. Covalent compounds are not soluble in water. [1]

Chapter Assessment

Section-I

a. Multiple Choice Questions

1. Which of the following rays is deflected under electric field?
   (a) X-rays (b) Cathode rays (c) γ-rays (d) UV-rays
2. Thomson's atomic model is also called
   (a) Christmas pudding model
   (b) plum pudding model
   (c) Both (a) and (b)
   (d) None of the above
3. Distribution of electrons into different shells of an atom was suggested by
   (a) J.J. Thomson (b) Rutherford
   (c) Bohr and Bury (d) Neil Bohr
4. The formula used to represent the maximum number of electrons present in a shell
   (a) $2n^2$ (b) n^2 (c) $2n$ (d) n
5. Which isotope of hydrogen is used in making heavy water ?
   (a) Protium (b) Deuterium (c) Tritium (d) Both (b) and (c)
6. The atomic mass of chlorine is
   (a) 37 (b) 34 (c) 35.5 (d) 33

b. Fill in the Blanks

7. Electrons revolve around the .... in well defined orbits. (nucleus, shell, orbit)
8. The extranuclear part of the atom in which electrons are revolving, is known as .... (orbits, nucleus, valencies)
9. In a neutral atom, the atomic number is equal to the number of .... (proton, atomic mass)
10. Helium has .... valence electrons. (two, three, four)
11. Deuterium and tritium are .... of hydrogen. (isotopes, isobar, isotone)
12. .... bond is formed by the mutual sharing of electrons between the combining atoms of the same or different elements. (Ionic, Covalent, Electrovalent)

c. Give One Word or a Phrase

13. Atoms of the same element having different masses.
14. The electrons present in the inner shells.
15. The outermost electrons of an atom.
16. Scientist who discovered proton.
17. Elements having same mass number.

d. Match the Columns

18. Match the following columns.

Column I (Properties of chlorine)	Column II (Value)
A. Atomic number	1. 1
B. Total number of shells	2. 3
C. Atomic mass (approx.)	3. 7
D. Valency	4. 17
E. Number of valence electrons	5. 35.5

Section-II

a. 2 Marks Questions

1. An ion M^{3-} contains 10 electrons and 7 neutrons. What is the atomic number and mass number of the element M ? Name the element.
2. The atom of an element has 9 protons, 9 electrons and 10 neutrons.
   (i) What is the atomic number and atomic mass of the element?
   (ii) Predict the valency of the element.

b. 3 Marks Questions

3. Compare the properties of electrons, protons and neutrons.
4. Give any three applications of radioisotopes.
5. The electronic configuration of some elements is given below. Name the elements.
   (i) 2, 8, 5 (ii) 2, 8, 8, 2 (iii) 2, 8, 1
6. Explain the formation of calcium oxide and magnesium chloride with the help of orbit diagram.
   (Atomic number : Ca = 20, O = 8, Mg = 12, Cl = 17)

c. 4 Marks Questions

7. Write four characteristics of cathode rays.
8. Write the rules suggested by Bohr and Bury for the distribution of electrons in an atom giving suitable examples.
9. Write four properties of ionic bonds.

For explanations scan the given QR Code

Olympiad Section*

Brain Teasing Questions asked in Previous Olympiads

1. Arrange the following elements in the increasing order of their atomic raddi. **(INJSO)**
   (a) Na < Li < Rb < C < K (b) Cs < Rb < K < Na < Li
   (c) K < Rb < Cs < Na < Li (d) Li < Na < K < Rb < Cs

2. Metal react with oxygen to form metal oxides. If the metals considered are K, Cs, Mg and Sr, the correct order of the basic character of their oxides is
   (a) $MgO > SrO > K_2O > Cs_2O$ **(INJSO)**
   (b) $Cs_2O > K_2O > MgO > SrO$
   (c) $MgO < SrO < K_2O < Cs_2O$
   (d) $K_2O < MgO < SrO < Cs_2O$

3. What charge would be attained by the ion of the element P below during a reaction? **(NSO Odisha)**

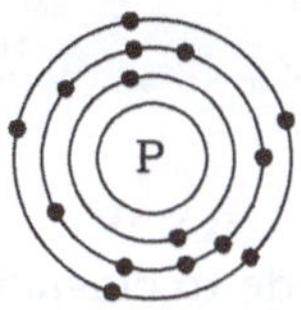

   (a) + 3 (b) – 3 (c) + 5 (d) – 5

4. An element *X* combines with hydrogen to form a compound XH_3. The element *X* is placed on the right side of the periodic table. Which of the following statement is correct for element *X*?
   I. Has three valence electrons.
   II. Is a metal and is solid.
   III. Is a non-metal and is a gas.
   IV. Has five valence electrons.
   V. XH_3 reacts with water to form a basic compound.
   (a) I, II and III (b) II, III and IV **(NTSE)**
   (c) III, IV and V (d) V, I and II

5. An element *X* belongs to group 2 and period 3 of the periodic table. The chemical formulae of its nitrate, sulphate and phosphate respectively will be
   (a) $X(NO_3)_3$, $X_2(SO_4)_3$, $X_2(PO_4)_3$ **(NTSE)**
   (b) $X_3(NO_3)_3$, $X_2(SO_4)_2$, $X_2(PO_4)_3$
   (c) XNO_3, XSO_4, XPO_4
   (d) $X(NO_3)_2$, XSO_4, $X_3(PO_4)_2$

6. An element belongs to group 17. It is present in third period and its atomic number is 17. What is the atomic number of the element belonging to same group and present in fifth period? **(NTSE)**
   (a) 25 (b) 33
   (c) 35 (d) 53

7. Powdered beryllium burns in order to give .... **(INJSO)**
   (a) beryllium nitride
   (b) beryllium chloride
   (c) beryllium sulphate
   (d) beryllium hydride

8. Which group of elements are highly reactive?
   (a) Group 13 **(NTSE)**
   (b) Group 17
   (c) Group 18
   (d) Group 12

9. Noble gases are inert and do not form compounds like other elements because of their **(NTSE)**
   (a) low ionisation energy
   (b) high electron affinities
   (c) close shell electronic configuration
   (d) high density

10. The melting point of alkali metals is ....
   (a) high **(INJSO)**
   (b) low
   (c) zero
   (d) depends on the atmosphere

11. The flame of caesium is of .... colour.
   (a) red violet (b) yellow **(INJSO)**
   (c) white (d) blue

12. The nature of normal oxide formed by the element present on extreme left in the periodic table is
   (a) most acidic **(INJSO)**
   (b) most basic
   (c) amphoteric
   (d) neutral

Answers

1. (d) **2.** (c) **3.** (b) **4.** (d) **5.** (d) **6.** (d) **7.** (a) **8.** (b) **9.** (c) **10.** (b) **11.** (d) **12.** (b)

* *These questions may or may not be asked in the examination, have been given just for additional practice required for olympiads Scholarship Exams etc. For detailed explanations refer Page No. 134.*

CHAPTER

05

The Periodic Table

CHAPTER OUTLINES

- Earlier Attempts to Classify Elements
- Mendeleev's Periodic Table
- Atomic Number as the Basis for Modern Periodic Law
- Modern and Long Form of Periodic Table
- Trends in the Modern Periodic Table
- Study of Some Specific Groups

Elements are the building blocks of all substances. There are 118 elements known at present, out of which 98 are naturally occurring. In order to study the properties of all these elements separately, scientists felt the necessity to group elements having similar characteristics together.

So, all the elements are divided into a few groups in such a way that elements in the same group have similar properties.

In this chapter, we will study various attempts which have been made to classify the elements from time to time and finally we will study the present form classification.

Reasons for Classification of Elements

There are many reasons for the classification of these elements, some of them are as follows

- It helps to predicts the properties of the elements and their compounds.
- It helps in correlating the properties of elements with the fundamental properties of all states of matter.
- It helps in defining the relationship of one element with another element.

Earlier Attempts to Classify Elements

Several attempts were made to classify the elements according to their properties.
Some important of them are discussed below.

Lavoisier's Classification (1789)

It is one of the earliest attempt to classify elements. Lavoisier divided elements into two main groups, called **metals** and **non-metals**.

Limitations

- The number of elements falling in a particular group were so large that it did not serve the purpose of generalisation.
- Certain elements showed both metallic as well as non-metallic characteristics.

Dobereiner's Triads (1817)

In the year 1817, Johann Wolfgang Dobereiner, a German chemist, had made an attempt to arrange the elements with similar properties into groups having three elements each. He called these groups as **triads**.

Dobereiner showed that when the three elements in a triad were arranged in the order of increasing atomic masses, the atomic mass of the middle element was roughly the average of the atomic masses of the other two elements.

Dobereiner's Triads

Elements	Atomic mass	Average atomic mass of first and third elements
Li Na K	7 23 39	$\frac{7+39}{2}=23$
Cl Br I	35.5 80 127	$\frac{35.5+127}{2}=81.25$
Ca Sr Ba	40 88 137	$\frac{40+137}{2}=88.5$

The given classification of elements into triads had a great significance in predicting atomic mass and properties of middle element.

Limitations

- All the elements discovered at that time were not able to be classified into triads. Dobereiner could identify only three triads from the elements known at that time. These are
  Li, Na, K; Ca, Sr, Ba; Cl, Br, I
- The law did not fully apply even within the same family.
  e.g. In halogens, the first three members, fluorine (19), chlorine (35.5) and bromine (80). It was observed that the mean of the atomic masses of fluorine and bromine is $\frac{1}{2}(19+80)=49.5$, not 35.5. So, Dobereiner's scheme of classification of elements was not successfull.

Newlands' Law of Octaves (1866)

In 1866, **John Newlands'**, an English scientist, arranged the known elements in the order of increasing atomic masses and found that every eighth element had properties similar to that of the first.

He compared this to the octaves found in music, i.e. sa, re, ga, ma, pa, da, ni. Whereas in the west, they use the notations – do, re, mi, fa, so, la, ti. Therefore, he called it the **law of octaves.** In chemistry this is known as Newlands' law of octaves. A part of the original form of Newlands' octaves is given in table below.

Notes of Music

sa (do)	**re** (re)	**ga** (mi)	**ma** (fa)	**pa** (so)	**da** (la)	**ni** (ti)
H	Li	Be	B	C	N	O
F	Na	Mg	Al	Si	P	S
Cl	K	Ca	Cr	Ti	Mn	Fe
Co and Ni	Cu	Zn	Y	In	As	Se
Br	Rb	Sr	Ce and La	Zr	–	–

Merits of Newlands' Classification

This classification relate the properties of the elements with their atomic masses.

Through this, distinct periodicity in the properties of elements were shown for the first time.

Limitations

- This law was applicable only upto calcium. After calcium, every eighth element do not possess the same properties to that of the first.
- Newland assumed that there were only 56 elements existed in nature and no more elements would be discovered in the future. But, later on, several new elements were discovered, whose properties did not fit into the law of octaves.
- One more drawback is that, in order to fit elements into his table, Newlands' adjusted two elements in the same slot and also put some unlike elements under the same column.
  e.g. Cobalt and nickel were kept in the same slot and these are placed in the same column as fluorine, chlorine and bromine which have very different properties than these elements. Iron, which resembles cobalt and nickel in properties, has been placed far away from these elements.

Mendeleev's Periodic Table (1834-1907)

Dmitri Ivanovich Mendeleev, a Russian chemist, arranged the elements on the basis of their fundamental property (atomic mass) and also on the similarity in their chemical properties.

On this basis, he organised the elements in a table, known as **periodic table.**

He arranged 63 elements (known at that time) in the increasing order of their atomic masses and found that the elements with similar and chemical properties occur at regular intervals.

He observed that elements with similar properties fall in the same vertical column. These vertical columns are called **groups** and horizontal rows of elements are called **periods.**

On this basis, Mendeleev gave a periodic law, which states that "physical and chemical properties of elements are a periodic function of their atomic masses".

Mendeleev's Periodic Table (Published in a German Journal in 1872)

Group	I		II		III		IV		V		VI		VII		VIII
Oxide Hydride	R_2O RH		RO RH_2		R_2O_3 RH_3		RO_2 RH_4		R_2O_5 RH_3		RO_3 RH_2		R_2O_7 RH		RO_4
Periods	A	B	A	B	A	B	A	B	A	B	A	B	A	B	Transition series
1	H 1.008														
2	Li 6.939		Be 9.012		B 10.81		C 12.011		N 14.007		O 15.999		F 18.998		
3	Na 22.99		Mg 24.31		Al 29.98		Si 28.09		P 30.974		S 32.06		Cl 35.453		
4 **First series**	K 39.102		Ca 40.08			Sc 44.96		Ti 47.90		V 50.94		Cr 50.20		Mn 54.94	Fe 55.85 Co 58.93 Ni 58.71
Second series		Cu 63.54		Zn 65.37	Ga 69.72		Ge 72.59		As 74.92		Se 78.96		Br 79.909		
5 **First series**	Rb 85.47		Sr 87.62			Y 88.41		Zr 91.22		Nb 92.91		Mo 95.94		Tc 99	Ru 101.07 Rh 102.91 Pd 106.4
Second series		Ag 107.87		Cd 112.40	In 114.82		Sn 118.69		Sb 121.75		Te 127.60		I 126.90		
6 **First series**	Cs 132.90		Ba 137.34			La 138.91		Hf 178.49		Ta 180.95		W 183.85			Os 190.2 Ir 192.2 Pt 195.09
Second series		Au 196.97		Hg 200.59	Tl 204.37		Pb 207.19		Bi 208.98						

Note In the formula of oxides and hydrides at the top of the columns, the letter '*R*' is used to represent any of the elements in the group.

Features of Mendeleev's Periodic Table

The important features of this table are

- This table contains 8 vertical columns, called **groups** and 6 horizontal rows, called **periods.**
- All the groups were divided in two sub groups *A* and *B*, except the group VIII.
- All the elements of a sub group or group VIII, that had no sub-group were showing similar properties and same valency.
- Out of the 6 periods, period 4 to 6 had elements placed in 2 series.
- In a period, on moving from left to right across the horizontal row, the metallic character was decreasing.

Merits of Mendeleev's Table

- In the table, Mendeleev's left gaps for the elements which was not discovered at that time. He named such elements by prefixing a Sanskrit numeral *Eka* (one), *divi* (two), *tri* (three) etc., to the name of the preceding similar (analogous) element in the same group. e.g. Eka-boron, eka-aluminium, eka-silicon, which after their discovery were named as scandium, gallium and germanium, respectively.
- He also predicted the atomic masses and properties of several elements that were not known at that time. Elements like scandium, gallium and germanium have properties similar to those predicted by Mendeleev.
- **Noble gases** like helium (He), neon (Ne), argon (Ar), etc., were discovered very late because they are very inert and present in extremely low concentrations in our atmosphere.
- One of the strengths of **Mendeleev's periodic table** was that, when these gases were discovered, they could be placed in a new group without disturbing the existing order.

Limitations of Mendeleev's Periodic Table

Although this table was greatly helpful for the study of elements but a few anomalies could not be explained on the basis of this table. These anomalies are

(i) **Position of hydrogen** The electronic configuration of hydrogen resembles with alkali metals.

It combines with halogen, oxygen and sulphur to give similar type of compounds as given by alkali metals, e.g. (HCl, NaCl), (H_2O, Na_2O) and (H_2S, Na_2S). However, just like halogen, it exists in diatomic form and combines with metals and non-metals to form covalent compounds.

Thus, its position was not fixed in the Mendeleev's periodic table but it was kept with alkali metals.

(ii) **Position of isotopes** All isotopes of an element, have similar chemical properties but different atomic masses. In Mendeleev's periodic table, no place was given to these elements.

e.g. The element chlorine has two isotopes, Cl-35 and Cl-37, having atomic masses of 35 and 37, respectively.

The placing of these two isotopes of chlorine (having different atomic masses) in the same group of periodic table could not be explained by Mendeleev's periodic law.

(iii) **Uncertainty in atomic masses** Another problem was that the atomic masses do not increase in a regular manner on moving from one element to the next. So, it was not possible to predict how many elements could be discovered between two elements especially when we consider the heavier elements.

(iv) **Placing of heavier element before the lighter one** In order to group the elements with similar properties together, at some places,

Mendeleev had to place an element with a slightly greater atomic mass before an element with a slightly lower atomic mass.

e.g. Argon (39.9) was placed before potassium (39.1), cobalt (58.9) before nickel (58.6), tellurium (127.60) before iodine (126.9).

(v) **Electron arrangement** It does not explain the electron arrangement of elements.

(vi) **Grouping of chemically dissimilar elements** Some elements like those which are chemically similar (copper and silver) bear no resemblance to alkali metals (lithium, sodium etc.), but they have been placed together in first group.

Check Your LEARNING...

1 Write an example of Dobereiner's triad.
2 What is the basis of Newlands' law of octaves?
3 What was the reason for the failure of Newlands' law of octaves?
4 How many periods and groups are there in Mendeleev periodic table?
5 Write any one limitation of Mendeleev's periodic table.

Atomic Number as the Basis for Modern Periodic Law

In 1913, Henry Moseley measured the frequencies of X-rays emitted by different elements when bombarded with high speed electrons.

He observed that the square root of the frequency of X-rays emitted by an element was proportional to its atomic number and not the atomic mass of an element.

Hence, **Henry Moseley** showed that the atomic number of an element is a better fundamental property and on the basis of this, he modified **Mendeleev's periodic law** as "physical and chemical properties of the elements are a periodic function of their atomic number". This is called **modern periodic law**.

Modern and Long Form of Periodic Table

When the elements were arranged in the increasing order of their atomic number, the obtained table was called **modern periodic table**.

The long form of periodic table was drawn as an extension of modern periodic table. It was developed by group of scientists with major ones as Bohr-Bury, Werner etc. This table is based upon the electronic configuration of elements as it was concluded that electronic configuration of element is also a periodic function. Due to the contributions of Bohr and Bury, this table is also called Bohr's periodic table.

Features of Modern Periodic Table

This table has 18 vertical columns, known as **groups** and 7 horizontal rows, known as **periods.**

Features of Groups

Important features of the elements present in groups are as follows

- The modern periodic table contains eighteen vertical columns, comprising of groups.
- These groups are named as I to VIII. Out of these group I to VII are further divisible into sub groups *A* and *B*. At the end a separate zero (0) group is also present.
- Elements of group III B to II B are called as **transition elements.**
- Elements of group zero are called **inert gas** or **noble gases** due to their stable electronic configuration.
- The elements present in a group have the same number of valence or similar electrons.
- The elements present in a group have the same valency.
- The number of shells increases as we go down the group.
- The physical properties of the elements such as melting point, boiling point, density in a group vary gradually.
- The elements present in a group have identical chemical properties.

Features of Periods

Important features of the elements present in period are as follows

- Elements of a period do not have the same number of valence electrons but they contain the same number of shells.
- The number of valence shell electrons increases by one unit as the atomic number increases by one unit on moving from left to right in a period. Therefore, the atoms of different elements with same number of shells are placed in the same period.
- As the number of valence shell electrons changes, the chemical properties of the elements also change.
- **The 1st period** contains only two elements, atomic number 1 and 2. It is the shortest period.
- **The 2nd and 3rd periods** contain eight elements each. Elements with atomic number 3-10 placed in 2nd period and 11-18 in 3rd period. These are short periods.
- **The 4th and 5th periods** contain eighteen elements each (i.e. from atomic number 19 to 36 in the fourth and from atomic number 37 to 54 in the fifth period). These are **long periods.**
- **The 6th period** contain 32 elements (from atomic number 55 to 86). It is the longest period.
- **The 7th period** contains 32 elements (from atomic number 87 to 118). It is also a longest period.
- **In group III B** (Group number 3) of the **sixth period**, there is a set of elements with atomic number 57 to 71. (La-Lu), beginning with lanthanum (La-57). These elements are called lanthanoids.
- **In group III B** (Group number 3) of the **7th period**, there is a set of elements with atomic number 89 to 103 (Ac-Lr) beginning with actinium (Ac-89). These elements are called as **actinoides** (radioactive elements).

Note Actinoids and lanthanoids are shown at the bottom of the periodic table as they cannot be accommodated within the one box of group IIIB and their respective periods.

Explanation of the Anomalies of Mendeleev's Periodic Table

Different anomalies of Mendeleev's periodic table can be explained with the help of modern periodic table as

- The fundamental basis for modern periodic table is atomic number, not atomic mass, hence it is more accurate.
- Since, the table is based on atomic number and isotopes have same atomic number and chemical properties, so they can be put at one place in the same group of the periodic table.
- In this periodic table, a unique position has been given to hydrogen. It is kept at the top left corner because of its unique characteristics.
- The position of cobalt and nickel is justified itself because atomic number of cobalt is less than atomic number of nickel.

Long Form of Periodic Table

Metals | Metalloids | Non-metals

The *zig-zag* line separates the metals from the non-metals.

s-block or representative elements: Groups 1, 2
d-block or transition elements: Groups 3–12
p-block or representative elements: Groups 13–18

PERIODS	1	2	3	4	5	6	7	8	9	10	11	12	13	14	15	16	17	18
1	1 H Hydrogen 1.0																	2 He Helium 4.0
2	3 Li Lithium 6.9	4 Be Beryllium 9.0											5 B Boron 10.8	6 C Carbon 12.0	7 N Nitrogen 14.0	8 O Oxygen 16.0	9 F Fluorine 19.0	10 Ne Neon 20.2
3	11 Na Sodium 23.0	12 Mg Magnesium 24.3											13 Al Aluminium 27.0	14 Si Silicon 28.1	15 P Phosphorus 31.0	16 S Sulphur 32.1	17 Cl Chlorine 35.5	18 Ar Argon 39.9
4	19 K Potassium 39.1	20 Ca Calcium 40.1	21 Sc Scandium 45.0	22 Ti Titanium 47.8	23 V Vanadium 50.9	24 Cr Chromium 52.0	25 Mn Manganese 54.9	26 Fe Iron 55.9	27 Co Cobalt 58.9	28 Ni Nickel 58.7	29 Cu Copper 63.5	30 Zn Zinc 65.4	31 Ga Gallium 69.7	32 Ge Germanium 72.6	33 As Arsenic 74.9	34 Se Selenium 79.0	35 Br Bromine 79.9	36 Kr Krypton 83.8
5	37 Rb Rubidium 85.5	38 Sr Strontium 87.6	39 Y Yttrium 88.9	40 Zr Zirconium 91.2	41 Nb Niobium 92.9	42 Mo Molybdenum 95.9	43 Tc Technetium (99)	44 Ru Ruthenium 101.1	45 Rh Rhodium 102.3	46 Pd Palladium 106.4	47 Ag Silver 107.9	48 Cd Cadmium 112.4	49 In Indium 114.8	50 Sn Tin 118.7	51 Sb Antimony 121.8	52 Te Tellurium 127.6	53 I Iodine 126.9	54 Xe Xenon 131.3
6	55 Cs Caesium 132.9	56 Ba Barium 137.3	57 La* Lanthanum 138.9	72 Hf Hafnium 178.5	73 Ta Tantalum 181.0	74 W Tungsten 183.9	75 Re Rhenium 186.2	76 Os Osmium 190.2	77 Ir Iridium 192. 2	78 Pt Platinum 195.1	79 Au Gold 197.0	80 Hg Mercury 200.6	81 Tl Thallium 204.4	82 Pb Lead 207.2	83 Bi Bismuth 209.0	84 Po Polonium (210)	85 At Astatine (210)	86 Rn Radon (222)
7	87 Fr Francium (223)	88 Ra Radium (226)	89 Ac** Actinium (227)	104 Rf Rutherfordium (267)	105 Db Dubnium (268)	106 Sg Seaborgium (271)	107 Bh Bohrium (272)	108 Hs Hassium (277)	109 Mt Meitnerium (276)	110 Ds Darmstadium (281)	111 Rg Roentgenium (280)	112 Cn Copernicium (285)	113 Nh Nihonium (—)	114 Fl Flerovium (287)	115 Mc Moscovium (—)	116 Lv Livermorium (291)	117 Ts Tennessine (—)	118 Og Oganesson (—)

f-block or inner-transition elements

*Lanthanoids	58 Ce Cerium 140.1	59 Pr Praseodymium 140.9	60 Nd Neodymium 144.2	61 Pm Promethium (145)	62 Sm Samarium 150.4	63 Eu Europium 152.0	64 Gd Gadolinium 157.3	65 Tb Terbium 158.9	66 Dy Dysprosium 162.5	67 Ho Holmium 164.9	68 Er Erbium 167.3	69 Tm Thulium 168.9	70 Yb Ytterbium 173.0	71 Lu Leutetium 175.5
**Actinoids	90 Th Thorium 232.0	91 Pa Protactinium (231)	92 U Uranium 238.1	93 Np Neptunium (237)	94 Pu Plutonium (242)	95 Am Americium (243)	96 Cm Curium (247)	97 Bk Berkelium (245)	98 Cf Californium (251)	99 Es Einsteinium (254)	100 Fm Fermium (253)	101 Md Mendelevium (256)	102 No Nobelium (254)	103 Lr Lawrencium (257)

Difference Between Modern and Long Form of Periodic Table

Both modern and long forms of periodic table are more or less similar in appearance.However, following minor differences helps in identifying them

1. In modern form the groups are numbered in subgroups A and B. e.g. I A, I B, IIA, IIB etc. While in long form, groups are numbered 1 to 18.
2. Zero group of modern periodic table does not seen in long form. In long form, the group of inert gases is named as 18th group.
3. Group VIII of modern periodic table is divided into groups 8, 9 and 10 in long form.
4. The long form periodic table is divided into four blocks
   (i) ***s*-block elements** It includes group 1 (alkali metals) and group 2 (alkaline earth metals) elements.
   (ii) ***p*-block elements** It includes group 13 to 18 elements.
   (iii) ***d*-block elements** It includes group 3 to group 12. These are also called transition elements (in between *s*-block and *p*-block elements).
   (iv) ***f*-block elements** It includes 14 elements after lanthanum (La, 57), called lanthanoides and 14 elements after actinium (Ac, 89), called actinoides.

   Representative elements Together *s* and *p*-block elements are called as representative elements.

Position of the Elements in the Long Form of Periodic Table

In order to find the position of an element in the periodic table, first write its electronic configuration and then find period and group number from its electronic configuration in the following ways

- The **period number** of an element is equal to the number of electron shells in its atom.
  e.g. If the atom of an element has 2 electron shells (K and L), then it belongs to 2nd period.
- If two (or more) elements have the same number of valence shells, then they belong to the same period of the periodic table.
- The **group number** of an element is equal to the number of valence electrons (for elements upto 2 valence electrons).
- The group number of an element having more than 2 valence electrons is equal to the number of valence electrons plus 10.
  e.g. If an element has 1 valence electron, it belongs to group 1 while element with 3 valence electrons has group number 3 + 10 = 13.
- If two (or more) elements have the same number of valence electrons then they belong to the same group of the periodic table.

Note
- Position of elements in the periodic table also tell us about their **chemical reactivity**. If they are present at extreme left or extreme right, they are highly reactive metals and non-metals, respectively.
- These metals and non-metals prone to form ionic bond between them.
- Other elements (of the middle or even non-metals are prone to form bond with sharing of electrons. Such bonds are called covalent bonds.

Check Your LEARNING...

1 What is the basis of modern periodic table?
2 Write other name of long form of periodic table.
3 What is the position of hydrogen in modern periodic table?
4 Why lanthanides and actinides are kept at the bottom of the periodic table?
5 Give the terms which are used for horizontal rows and vertical columns of the periodic table, respectively.

Trends in the Modern Periodic Table

In the periodic table, properties show a regular trend when we move along a period from left to right or in a group from top to bottom. Some of these properties and their variation in periodic table are as follows

1. Valency

It is the combining capacity of an atom of an element to acquire noble gas configuration. It depends upon the number of valence electrons, i.e. the electrons present in the outermost shell of its atom.

(i) For the elements of group 1, 2, 13 and 14, valency = number of valence electron(s).

(ii) For the elements of group 15 onwards, valency = 8 – valence electron(s).

Thus, the valencies of elements of different groups are as follows

- Valency of group 1 elements is 1.
- Valency of group 2 elements is 2.
- Valency of group 13 elements is 3.
- Valency of group 14 elements is 4.
- Valency of group 15 elements is 3.
- Valency of group 16 elements is 2.
- Valency of group 17 elements is 1.
- Valency of group 18 elements is 0.

Variation Along a Group

In a group, outer electronic configuration is same for all the elements, so all have the same number of valence electrons and the valency. e.g. All the elements of group 1 have valency = 1.

Group 1 element	Symbol	Electronic configuration	No. of valence electron
Lithium (3)	Li	2, 1	1
Sodium (11)	Na	2, 8, 1	1
Potassium (19)	K	2, 8, 8, 1	1

Similarly, for the elements of group 17, valency = 8 − 7 = 1

Group 17 element	Symbol	Electronic configuration	No. of valence electrons
Fluorine (9)	F	2, 7	7
Chlorine (17)	Cl	2, 8, 7	7
Bromine (35)	Br	2, 8, 18, 7	7
Iodine (53)	I	2, 8, 18, 18, 7	7

Variation Along a Period

The valency increases from 1 to 4 (till group 14) and then decreases to zero from group 15 to 18.

Group	1	2	13	14	15	16	17	18
Valency	1	2	3	4	3	2	1	0

2. Atomic Size

It refers to the radius of an atom. It may be visualised as the distance between the centre of the nucleus and the outermost shell of an isolated atom. It is measured in picometres.

[1 pm (picometre) = 10^{-12} m].

e.g. Atomic radius of hydrogen atom is 53 pm (or 53×10^{-12} m).

Variation Along a Group

The atomic size increases down the group. This is because new shells are being added as we go down the group. This increases the distance between the outermost electrons and the nucleus such that the atomic size increases inspite of the increase in nuclear charge.

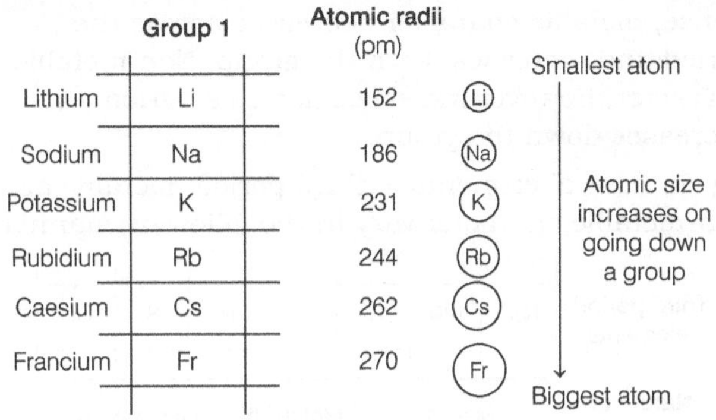

Variation Along a Period

The atomic radius decreases on moving from left to right along a period. This is due to an increase in nuclear charge which tends to pull the valence electrons closer to the nucleus and reduces the size of the atom.

e.g.

Third period elements	Na	Mg	Al	Si	P	S	Cl
Atomic radii (pm)	186	160	143	118	110	104	99

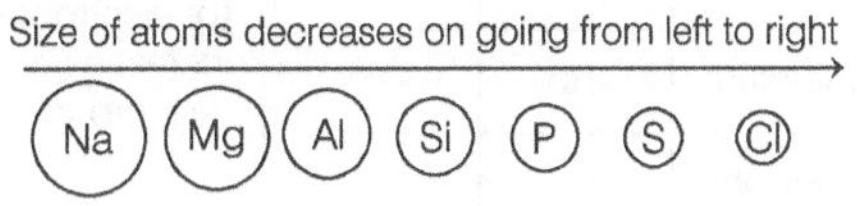

3. Metallic and Non-metallic Properties

The tendency of elements to lose electron(s) is called their **metallic character**. Because of the formation of positive ions these are also called **electropositive elements**.

Non-metals are the elements which have a tendency to gain one or more electron(s) to form negative ions. Thus, these are **electronegative elements**. These are present on the right side in the periodic table. There are some elements which exhibit the properties of both metals and non-metals. These are called **metalloids**. In the modern periodic table, a *zig-zag* line separates metals from non-metals.

The borderline elements—boron, silicon, germanium, arsenic, antimony, tellurium and polonium are intermediate in properties, so they are called **metalloids** or **semi-metals**.

Variation Along a Period and a Group

As the effective nuclear charge acting on the valence shell electrons increases across a period, the tendency to lose electrons will decrease. Down the group, the effective nuclear charge experienced by valence electrons decreases because the outermost electrons are farther away from the nucleus.

Hence, metallic character decreases across the period and increases down the group. Non-metallic character, however increases across a period and decreases down the group.

e.g. In case of elements of third period, metallic and non-metallic character vary in the following manner.

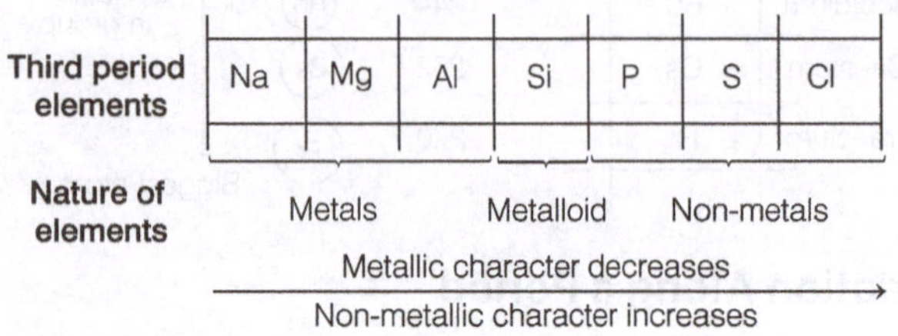

However, in groups, the order of variation of metallic and non-metallic character is as follows

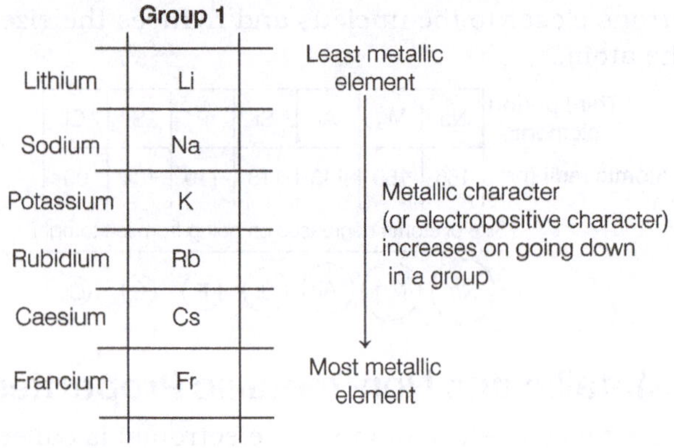

4. Nature of Oxides

Oxides of the metals are of basic nature while those of non-metals are acidic. Hence, nature of oxides also vary in accordance with the variation in metallic and non-metallic characters.

Variation Along a Period and a Group

Along a period, the basic character of the oxides of the elements decreases while their acidic character increases.

On going down in a group of the periodic table, the order is reversed, i.e. basic character of oxides increases and acidic character of oxides decreases.

e.g. In case of oxides of elements of group 2, the nature varies as

Oxide	Nature
MgO	Least basic
CaO	↓
SrO	
BaO	Most basic

5. Electronegativity

It may be defined as the relative electron attracting tendency of an atom for a shared electron pair in a covalent bond with other atom.

Variation Along a Period and a Group

The electronegativity of the elements increases along a period since the non-metallic character increases. Similarly, it decreases down the group, since the non-metallic character decreases.

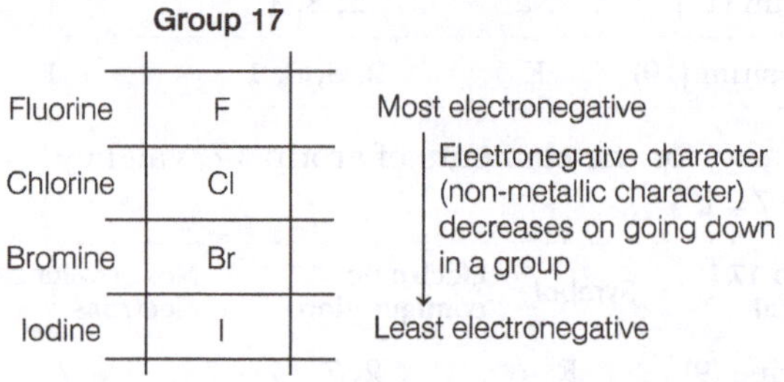

4 elements with maximum electronegativity in periodic table are F > O > N ≈ Cl.

Example 1. A group of elements in the periodic table are given below among which boron is the first member of the group and thallium is the last.

(Boron, aluminium, gallium, indium, thallium)

Answer the following questions in relation to the above group of elements.

(i) Which element has the most metallic character?

(ii) Which element would be expected to have the highest electronegativity?

(iii) Will the elements in the group to the right of boron be more metallic or less metallic in character? Justify your answer.

Sol. (i) Thallium has the most metallic character. Metallic character increases down in a group.

(ii) Boron has the highest electronegativity because electronegativity decreases down a group.

(iii) Less metallic in character because on moving across a period, metallic nature decreases.

Example 2. An element X (atomic number = 17) reacts with an element Y (atomic number = 20) to form a divalent halide.

(i) Where does the elements X and Y placed in the periodic table?

(ii) Classify X and Y as metal(s), non-metal(s) or metalloid(s).

(iii) What will be the nature of oxide of element Y?

Sol. (i) The electronic configuration of element X with atomic number 17 is 2, 8, 7. Since, it has 7 valence electrons.

Therefore, it lies in group 17 (10 + 7). Further, since in element X, third shell is being filled, it lies in third period. In other words, X is chlorine.

The electronic configuration of element Y with atomic number 20 is 2, 8, 8, 2. Since, it has 2 valence electrons, it lies in group 2.

Further, since in element Y, fourth shell is being filled, it lies in 4th period. In other words, Y is calcium.

(ii) Since, element X (i.e. Cl) has seven electrons in the valence shell and needs one more electron to complete its octet. Therefore, it is a **non-metal**.

Further, the element Y has two electrons in the valence shell which it can easily lose to achieve the stable electronic configuration of the nearest inert gas, therefore, it is a **metal**.

(iii) Since, element Y (i.e. Ca) is a metal, therefore its oxide (i.e. CaO) must be basic in nature.

Check Your LEARNING...

1 What is the most important cause of periodicity?

2 What is the valency of group 13 elements?

3 Arrange F, Cl, Br and I in increasing order of their atomic size down the group.

4 Write the name of any two metalloids.

5 Define electronegativity and how it vary along the period?

Study of Some Specific Groups

The elements present in a group exhibit similar properties, as they have same number of valence electrons and same electronic configuration.

The properties of some groups, group 1 (alkali metals), group 2 (alkaline earth metals), group 17 (halogens) and group 18 (zero group) are discussed below.

Alkali Metals (Group 1)

The elements which belong to the group 1 of the periodic table are called as **alkali metals**. These are lithium (Li), sodium (Na), potassium (K), rubidium (Rb), caesium (Cs) and francium (Fr).

They have one electron in their outermost orbit and show one valency. So, they are placed in group 1 of the periodic table.

General Characteristics

(i) **Electronic configuration**

Element	K	L	M	N	O	P	Q
$_{3}Li$	2	1					
$_{11}Na$	2	8	1				
$_{19}K$	2	8	8	1			
$_{37}Rb$	2	8	18	8	1		
$_{55}Cs$	2	8	18	18	8	1	
$_{87}Fr$	2	8	18	32	18	8	1

(ii) **Occurrence** These are highly reactive elements and occur in the combined state only.

(iii) **Nature** Soft in nature (can be cut with a knife) and have low melting and boiling points.

(iv) They are generally soft when freshly cut, show typical silvery white metallic lustre but on exposure to the air, they turn into dull black colour.

(v) They have very low ionisation energy which means that they can easily form unipositive ions.

$$M(g) - e^- \longrightarrow M^+(g)$$

(vi) **Bonding** Alkali metals have one electron in the valence shell, i.e. their valency is 1, so they form ionic bond by loosing electrons.

$$M - e^- \longrightarrow M^+$$

(vii) They are strong reducing agents.

(viii) **Action of air** On exposure to moist air, they react rapidly with oxygen and form metal oxide. Hence, these metals (Na and K) are kept immersed in kerosene.

$4M + O_2 \longrightarrow 2M_2O$ (where, M = any alkali metal)

The reactivity increases on moving down the group.

(ix) **Action of water** React violently with water to produce alkali and hydrogen gas.

$$2M + 2H_2O \longrightarrow \underset{\text{Alkali}}{2MOH} + H_2\uparrow$$

(where, M = any alkali metal)

(x) **Action of acids** React violently with dil. HCl and dil. H_2SO_4 and produce H_2 gas.

$$2M + \underset{\text{Dil.}}{2HCl} \longrightarrow 2MCl + H_2\uparrow$$

$$2M + \underset{\text{Dil.}}{H_2SO_4} \longrightarrow M_2SO_4 + H_2\uparrow$$

(where, M = any alkali metals)

(xi) They impart colour to the flame, e.g. lithium (crimson red), sodium (golden yellow), potassium (pale violet).

(xii) Alkali metals are obtained by the electrolysis of their molten salts, e.g. Na metal can be easily obtained from NaCl salt.

$$NaCl \rightleftharpoons Na^+ + Cl^-$$

At cathode $Na - e^- \longrightarrow Na^+$

At anode $Cl + e^- \longrightarrow Cl^-$

Alkaline Earth Metals (Group 2)

The oxides of group 2 elements are earthen (i.e. soil like) and occurs in the earth's crust. Their hydroxides are alkaline in nature that's why they are known as alkaline earth metals.

The elements belongs to this group are beryllium (Be), magnesium (Mg), calcium (Ca), strontium (Sr), barium (Ba) and radium (Ra).

General Characteristics Alkaline Earth Metals

(i) **Electronic configuration**

Element	K	L	M	N	O	P	Q
$_4Be$	2	2					
$_{12}Mg$	2	8	2				
$_{20}Ca$	2	8	8	2			
$_{38}Sr$	2	8	18	8	2		
$_{56}Ba$	2	8	18	18	8	2	
$_{88}Ra$	2	8	18	32	18	8	2

(ii) **Occurrence** They are reactive elements thus, occur in the combined state only.

(iii) **Nature** They are slightly harder than alkali metals. These can also be out with a sharp knife.

(iv) Melting and boiling points are comparatively low but higher than the alkali metals.

(v) They have low ionisation energy (higher than alkali metals) and forms dipositive ion.

$$M - 2e^- \longrightarrow M^{2+}$$

(where, M = any alkaline earth metal)

(vi) **Bonding** They possess two electrons in the valence shell hence form dipositive cations and shows ionic bonding.

$$M - 2e^- \longrightarrow M^{2+}$$

(where, M = any alkaline earth metals)

(vii) They also act as reducing agents.

(viii) **Action of air** On exposure to moist air, they react slowly. Upon heating in the presence of air they form oxide and nitrides.

e.g. $2M + O_2 \longrightarrow 2MO$

$3M + N_2 \longrightarrow M_3N_2$

(where, M = any alkaline earth metals)

(ix) **Action of water** They react with water to produce alkali and hydrogen gas.

$$\underset{\text{Alkaline earth metal}}{M} + 2H_2O \longrightarrow \underset{\text{Alkali}}{M(OH)_2} + H_2\uparrow$$

(x) **Action of acids** They react with dil. HCl and dil. H_2SO_4, respectively to produce hydrogen gas.

$$\underset{\text{Alkaline earth metal}}{M} + 2HCl \longrightarrow MCl_2 + H_2\uparrow$$

$$\underset{\text{Alkaline earth metal}}{M} + H_2SO_4 \longrightarrow MSO_4 + H_2\uparrow$$

(xi) Generally, all the alkaline earth metals impart colour to the flame (except beryllium and magnesium), e.g. Ca (Brick red), Sr (Crimson), Ba (Apple green), Ra (Crimson).

(xii) They are also obtained by the electrolysis of their molten salts.

e.g. $MgCl_2 \rightleftharpoons Mg^{2+} + 2Cl^-$

At cathode, $Mg^{2+} + 2e^- \longrightarrow Mg$

At anode, $2Cl^- - 2e^- \longrightarrow 2[Cl]$

$2[Cl] \longrightarrow Cl_2$

Halogens (Group 17)

Fluorine (F), Chlorine (Cl), Bromine (Br), Iodine (I) and Astatine (At) belongs to group 17 and are collectively known as **halogens.**

The name halogens greek is derived from word 'halo' means 'salt' and 'genes' means 'born', i.e. salt producers. The elements of group 17 show great similarity amongst themselves, like group 1 and 2 elements.

General Characteristics of Halogens

(i) **Electronic configuration**

Element	K	L	M	N	O	P
$_{9}F$	2	7				
$_{17}Cl$	2	8	7			
$_{35}Br$	2	8	18	7		
$_{53}I$	2	8	18	18	7	
$_{85}At$	2	8	18	32	18	7

(ii) **Occurrence** They are highly reactive non-metallic elements.

(iii) **Nature** Fluorine and chlorine are gases, bromine is liquid and iodine is solid.

(iv) All these halogens are coloured. F_2 is yellow, Cl_2 is greenish yellow, Br_2 is reddish brown and I_2 is violet in colour.

(v) Halogen having high electron affinity and low bond enthalpy. These can react with most of elements in the periodic table. However, the order of reactivity of the group members decreases down the group as

$$F > Cl > Br > I$$

(vi) **Bonding** Halogens due to the presence of seven electrons in their valence shell, are highly reactive and form ionic compounds with highly electropositive metals, readily. However, with weakly electropositive metals and non-metals, they form covalent bonds.

(vii) Most of the metals react with halogens to form metal halides as

$$2M + nX_2 \longrightarrow 2MX_n$$

(Here, M = metal, n = oxidation state of metal X = F, Cl, Br or I)

Noble Gases (Group 18 or Zero Group)

Helium (He), Neon (Ne), Argon (Ar), Krypton (Kr), Xenon (Xe) and Radon (Rn). So, belong to group 18. These are collectively known as noble gases. These are inert or less reactive in nature.

Due to their inertness these gases were discovered on the basis of study of their physical properties such as density.

Note W. Ramsay was awarded the noble prize in chemistry for the discovery of the inert gases in air.

General Characteristics of Noble Gases

(i) **Electronic configuration**

Element	K	L	M	N	O	P
$_{2}He$	2					
$_{10}Ne$	2	8				
$_{18}Ar$	2	8	8			
$_{36}Kr$	2	8	18	8		
$_{54}Xe$	2	8	18	18	8	
$_{86}Rn$	2	8	18	32	18	8

(ii) **Occurrence** Due to inert nature of these gases, they always occur in free state.

(iii) **Nature** These are colourless, odourless and tasteless gases.

(iv) These are monoatomic gases and are sparingly soluble in water.

(v) They have low melting and boiling points due to weak dispersion forces. Helium has the lowest boiling point of any known substance.

(vi) Helium is a *s*-block element but has been placed in group 18, at the top, as its chemical inertness is similar to the rest of the members of group 18.

(vii) Helium is used in filling balloons for meteorological observations as it is a non-inflammable and light gas. Neon is used in discharge tubes. Neon bulbs are used in botanical gardens and in greenhouses.

Argon because of its inert nature is used to provide an inert atmosphere in high temperature metallurgical process.

Check Your LEARNING...

1 What happens when alkali metals are exposed to the air?

2 How do alkali metals and alkaline earth metals differ from each other with respect to the formation of metallic ions?

3 Arrange the halogens in increasing order of reactivity towards other group members.

4 Why do noble gases have low melting and boiling point?

5 Name the noble gas which is used in bulbs.

QUiCK Revision

- **Dobereiner** grouped the three elements in a triad which were written in the order of increasing atomic masses; the atomic mass of the middle element was roughly the average of the atomic masses of the other two elements.
- **In Newlands' law of octaves**, elements are arranged in increasing order of atomic masses and found that every eighth element had properties similar to that of the first. This law is based on the octaves found in music.
- **Periodic table** It is a chart of elements in which the elements having similar physical and chemical properties occur in the same vertical column (group).
- **Mendeleev's periodic** table (1834-1907) is based on Mendeleev's periodic law, which states that the properties of the elements are the periodic functions of their atomic masses. This table contains 8 groups and 6 periods and containing gaps for the elements which were not discovered at that time.
- **Mendeleev** predicted the atomic masses and properties of several elements that were not known at that time. He also corrected the atomic mass of some elements such as Be from 13 to 9.
- There are some limitations of Mendeleev's periodic table such as
  - Position of hydrogen was not fixed.
  - No place was given to isotopes.
  - Atomic masses do not increase in a regular manner.
  - Heavier element were placed before the lighter one.
- **Modern periodic table or Long form of periodic table** (1913) is based on modern periodic law which states that the properties of the elements are the periodic function of their atomic numbers. This table contains 18 groups and 7 periods
- The long form of periodic table is created on the basis of electronic configuration. This periodic table is divided into four blocks as follows
  - ***s*-block** Group 1 (alkali metals) and 2 (alkaline earth metals) elements
  - ***p*-block** Group 13 to 18 elements
  - ***d*-block** (Transition elements) Group 3 to group 12 elements
  - ***f*-block** 14 elements after lanthanum (lanthanoids) and 14 elements after actinium (actinoids)
- Properties showing regular gradation along the period and group. These can be properties like valency, atomic size, metallic and non-metallic properties, electronegativity and nature of oxides, etc.
- The elements present in a group exhibit similar properties as they have same number of valence electrons and same electronic configuration.
- Alkali (group 1) and alkaline earth metals (group 2) are reactive elements and occur in combined state only.
- Alkali metals have one electron in their outermost orbit while alkaline earth metals have 2 electrons in their valence shell.
- Both alkali and alkaline earth metals are good reducing agents and produce hydrogen while reacting with water.
- Alkaline earth metals are less reactive than alkali metals.
- Alkali metals and alkaline earth metals both are obtained by electrolysis of their molten salts.
- Halogens (group 17) are highly reactive non-metallic elements and are placed in group 17 of the periodic table.
- All halogens form diatomic molecules like F_2, Cl_2, Br_2, etc.
- Fluorine and chlorine exist as a gas, bromine as a liquid and iodine as a solid.
- Halogens can react directly with metals to form metal halides (or salts).
- Group 18 elements because of their inert nature is known as **inert gases.**
- Noble gases are monoatomic because of their fully-filled octet.
- When electrical discharge is passed through the noble gases, they emit coloured light.
- Noble gases can be liquified with great difficulty.

Chapter Practice

Section-I

a. Multiple Choice Questions

1. Which of the following is the correct set of elements to Dobereiner's triads?

(a) Li Na K
7 23 39

(b) Br Cl I
80 35.5 127

(c) Fe Ni Co
55.85 58.71 58.93

(d) Data is insufficient

Sol. (a)

2. Which of the following is correct?
   (a) Law of triads seemed to work only for large elements
   (b) John Newlands' (law of octaves) arranged the elements in the increasing order of their atomic weights
   (c) Dobereiner arranged elements by the help of triads method
   (d) Both (b) and (c)

Sol. (d)

3. Which of the following statement(s) about the modern periodic table is correct?
   (a) The elements in the modern periodic table are arranged on the basis of their decreasing atomic number.
   (b) The elements in the modern periodic table are arranged on the basis of their increasing atomic masses.
   (c) Isotopes are placed in adjoining group(s) in the periodic table.
   (d) The elements in the modern periodic table are arranged on the basis of their increasing atomic number.

Sol. (d)

4. Which of the elements *A, B, C, D* and *E* with atomic number 2, 3, 7, 10 and 30, respectively belong to the same period?
   (a) *A, B, C*
   (b) *B, C, D*
   (c) *A, D, E*
   (d) *B, D, E*

Sol. (b) *B, C, D* elements belong to 2nd period.

5. Two elements *M* and *N* belong to group 2 and 3, respectively in the same period. The formulae of their oxides are
   (a) MO, N_2O_3 (b) M_3O_2, N_3O_2
   (c) M_2O_3, N_3O_2 (d) M_3O_2, N_2O_3

Sol. (a)

6. Which one among the following is an alkaline earth metal ?
   (a) Potassium (b) Calcium
   (c) Lead (d) Copper

Sol. (b)

b. Fill in the Blanks

7. Dobereiner's relationship referred to as the .... (law of triads, law of octaves, periodic law).

Sol. law of triads

8. Newland in 1866 arranged the elements in increasing order of their .... (atomic number, atomic masses, electronic configuration).

Sol. atomic weight

9. In Newlands' octave law every eighth element has properties similar to the .... element (first, second, third).

Sol. first

10. Mendeleev arranged elements in horizontal rows and .... (horizontal columns, vertical column, vertical rows).

Sol. vertical columns

11. In Mendeleev's periodic table, eka-silicon and eka-aluminium were germanium and .... respectively. (lead, indium, gallium)

Sol. gallium

12. Strontium belongs to second group and .... (fifth, sixth, seventh) period.

Sol. fifth

13. The number of valence shell electrons increases by one unit as the .... increases (basicity, atomic mass, atomic number).

Sol. atomic number

14. Boron is .... (smaller, larger, equal) than beryllium in size.

Sol. smaller

15. Elements having a tendency to lose one or more electrons and form positive ions are called .... (metals, non-metals, metalloids).

Sol. metals

16. Elements of group 17 are called as .... (alkali metals, alkaline earth metals, halogens).

Sol. halogen

17. The inert gas with least weight is .... (helium, neon, argon).

Sol. helium

c. Match the Columns

18. Match the following columns.

Column I (Scientist)		Column II (Laws)
A.	Doberiener's	1. Modern periodic law
B.	Newland	2. Law of triads
C.	Mendeleev	3. Law of octaves
D.	Henry Moseley	4. Periodic law

Sol. A → (2), B → (3) C → (4) D → (1)

19. Match the following columns.

Column I (Group)		Column II (Block)
A.	1 and 2	1. *p*-block
B.	3 to 12	2. *d*-block
C.	13 to 18	3. *s*-block
		4. *f*-block

Sol. A → (3), B → (2), C → (1)

d. Give One Word or a Phrase

20. Write the name of latest table in which elements are arranged in periods and groups.

Sol. Long form of periodic table

21. Name of the classification in which elements are grouped in a group of three.

Sol. Dobereiner's triad

22. Name of classification in which first and eighth elements had similar properties.

Sol. Newlands' law of octaves

23. Which law states that "properties of elements are a periodic function of their atomic masses"?

Sol. Mendeleev's periodic table

24. Vertical column and horizontal rows of periodic table.

Sol. Groups and periods respectively.

25. Another name of group 1 elements.

Sol. Alkali metals

26. Nature of metal oxides of group 1 and element.

Sol. Basic nature

27. Another name of group 2 elements.

Sol. Alkaline earth metals

28. Number of elements in 2nd period.

Sol. 8 (eight)

29. Longest period of periodic table.

Sol. 6th (sixth)

30. A group in which inert gases elements are present.

Sol. Zero group

31. Inner transition elements placed in sixth period.

Sol. Lanthanoids

32. Number of elements in lanthanoids and actinoids series each.

Sol. Fourteen

33. An element *X* is present at the left corner of modern periodic table. State whether it would be a metal or a non-metal.

Sol. It would be a metal.

34. Elements which are placed at the bottom of long form of periodic table.

Sol. Lanthanoids and actinoids

35. Another name of eka-boron.

Sol. Scandium

36. An element whose weight was corrected by Mendeleev.

Sol. Gold or Platinum

37. An element used in atomic clock.

Sol. Caesium

38. A halogen which is liquid at room temperature.

Sol. Bromine

39. Collectively name given to *s* and *p*-block elements.

Sol. Representative elements

40. Another name of second period elements ?

Sol. Bridge elements

e. State One Relevant Reason

41. Lithium, sodium and potassium were placed in one triad.

Sol. Lithium, sodium and potassium are placed in one triad because atomic mass of sodium is approximately mean of lithium and potassium.

42. Position of hydrogen was not fixed in Mendeleev's periodic table.

Sol. The electronic configuration of hydrogen resembles with alkali metals. It combines with halogen, oxygen to give similar type of compounds as given by alkali metals.

However, just like halogen, it exists in diatomic form and combine with metals and non-metals to form covalent compound.

Hence, position of hydrogen was not fixed in the Mendeleev's periodic table but it was kept with alkali metals.

43. The valency of alkali metals is 1.

Sol. Alkali metals have only one electron in their outermost shell. So, they can easily lose that electron to attain octet. Hence, the valency of alkali metals is 1.

44. Sodium and potassium element are kept immersed in kerosene.

Sol. Sodium and potassium react with oxygen and water vapour present in the air to form oxide and hydroxides.

$$4Na + O_2 \longrightarrow 2Na_2O$$
$$Na_2O + H_2O \longrightarrow 2NaOH$$

Thus, due to their reactive nature they are kept in kerosene.

45. Helium is used in filling balloons.

Sol. Helium is used in filling balloons because it is lighter than air, due to which balloon rises.

Section-II

a. 2 Marks Questions

1. Define
(i) Modern periodic law
(ii) Valency

Sol. (i) According to modern periodic law, physical and chemical properties of elements are the periodic function of their atomic numbers. [1]
(ii) Valency can be defined as the combining capacity of an atom of any element to acquire noble gas configuration. It depends upon the number of valence electrons. [1]

2. Give reason for the following.
(i) Why did Mendeleev left gaps in his periodic table?
(ii) Why did metallic character increases down the group ?

Sol. (i) Mendeleev left gaps in his periodic table for the undiscovered elements which were not discovered at that time. [1]
(ii) As we move down the group, the number of shells increases. The effective nuclear charge experienced by valence electrons decreases because the outermost electrons move away from the nucleus. Hence, metallic character increases. [1]

3. Given reason.
(i) Atomic radius increase down the group.
(ii) Non-metallic character increases from left to right in a period.

Sol. (i) The atomic size increase down the group because new shells are being added as we go down the group. This increases the distance between the outermost electrons and the nucleus. Thus, the atomic size increases inspite of the increase in nuclear charge. [1]
(ii) As the effective nuclear charge acting on the valence shell electrons increases across a period, the tendency to lose electrons will decrease. Non-metallic character, thus, increase across a period. [1]

4. What is the number of elements in the
(i) first group, and
(ii) second period, of the modern periodic table?

Sol. (i) Seven elements are present in first group. [1]
(ii) Eight elements are present in the modern periodic table. [1]

b. 3 Marks Questions

5. What were the reasons for classification of elements?

Sol. (i) It helps to systematise the study of elements.
(ii) It makes the study of elements simple and easy.
(iii) It helps to correlate the properties of elements with the fundamental properties of elements.
(iv) It reveals the relationship between the different elements.
(v) To forecast existence of other elements. [3]

6. Can the following groups of elements be classified as Dobereiner's triad?
(i) Na, Si, Cl (ii) Be, Mg, Ca
(iii) Cl, Br, I
(Atomic mass of Be-9, Na-23, Mg-24, Si-28, Cl-35.5, Ca-40, Br-80, I-127.)
Explain by giving reason.

Sol. (i) No, because Si have approx an average atomic mass than that of Na and Cl but they do not resemble in their properties. Na (23); Si (28); Cl (35.5)

$$\text{Atomic mass of Si} = \frac{23 + 35.5}{2} = \frac{58.5}{2} = 29.25$$ [1]

(ii) Yes, Be (9); Mg (24); Ca (40)

$$\text{Atomic mass of Mg} = \frac{9 + 40}{2} = \frac{49}{2} = 24.5$$

It can be classified as Dobereiner's triads because the middle element of the triad had both atomic mass and properties similar to average of the two other elements of the triad. [1]

(iii) Yes, Cl(35.5), Br(80) and I(127)

$$\text{Atomic mass of Br} = \frac{35.5 + 127}{2} = 81.25$$

So, it can be classified as Dobereiner's triads because the middle element of the triad has both atomic mass and properties similar to average of the two other elements of the triad. [1]

7. The three elements *A*, *B* and *C* with similar properties have atomic masses *X*, *Y*, and *Z* respectively. The mass of *Y* is approximately equal to the average mass of *X* and *Z*. What is such an arrangement of elements called as? Give one example of such a set of elements. Also give the reason why this arrangement was rejected?

Sol. The arrangement of elements in which the atomic mass of middle element is almost the mean of atomic masses of first and third element is known as triads.

This arrangement was given by scientist named Dobereiner.

e.g. Ca (40), Sr (88), Ba (137)

$$Sr = \frac{40 + 137}{2} = 88.5$$ [2]

Here, we can see that atomic mass middle element has mean of other two elements.

The reason for rejection of this arrangement was that the classification was applicable only upto a limited number of elements. Also the law did not fully apply even with in the same family. [1]

8. Consider the part of periodic table given below and answer the following questions.

Period \ Group	1	2	13	14	15	16	17	18
I	*a*							*j*
II	*b*	*e*				*g*	*h*	*k*
III	*c*			*f*			*i*	*l*
IV	*d*							

(i) Among '*e*' and '*h*' atom of which element are smaller in size.

(ii) Which element is most electropositive in nature?

(iii) Which element has only one proton in its atom?

(iv) What is the valency of '*g*'?

(v) How many valence electrons does '*g*' have?

(vi) Name the element which is a metalloid.

Sol. (i) '*h*' is smaller in size because atomic size decreases as one moves from left to right in a period.

(ii) '*d*'

(iii) '*a*'

(iv) valency of *g* is $= 8 - 6 = 2$

(v) 6 electrons

(vi) *f* [3]

9. Elements have been arranged in the following sequence on the basis of their increasing atomic masses.

F, Na, Mg, Al, Si, P, S, Cl, K

(i) Pick two sets of elements which have similar properties.

(ii) The given sequence represents which law of classification of elements?

(iii) What are the limitations of this law?

Sol. (i) Here, the elements are arranged in the order of increasing atomic masses, so according to Newlands' law of octaves there is a repetition of properties in every eighth element as compared to the given element.

The two sets of elements which have similar properties are

Set I → F, Cl Set II → Na, K [1]

(ii) The given sequence represents Newlands' law of octaves. [1]

(iii) Limitations of this law are

- This classification fails for the heavier elements beyond calcium.
- After discovery of noble gases the idea of octaves failed.
- It does not provide specific position for hydrogen. [1]

10. An element *X* (atomic number 17) reacts with an element *Y* (atomic number 20) to form a divalent halide.

(i) What is the position of elements *X* and *Y* in the periodic table?

(ii) What will be the nature of oxide of element *Y*? Identify the nature of bonding in the compound formed.

(iii) Also write valencies of these elements.

Sol. *X* is the non-metal while *Y* is the metal.

Divalent halide $= YX_2$

(i) Position of *X* (2, 8, 7) - Group - 17, Period - 3
Position of *Y* (2,8, 8, 2)- Group - 2, Period - 4 [1]

(ii) Oxide of element *Y* (*YO*) is basic in nature as it is found in 2nd group of periodic table that forms basic oxides. It forms ionic bond. [1]

(iii) *X* belongs to group 17 so, valency is $8 - 7 = 1$.
and *Y* belongs to group 2. So, valency is 2. [1]

11. Mention any three characteristics of halogens.

Sol. (i) They are highly reactive non-metallic elements. [1]

(ii) All the halogens are coloured. F_2 is yellow, Cl_2 is greenish yellow, Br_2 is reddish brown and I_2 is violet in colour. [1]

(iii) Most of the metals react with halogens to form metal halides as

$$2M + nX_2 \longrightarrow 2MX_n$$

(Here, M = metal, n = oxidation state of metal, X = F, Cl, Br or I) [1]

C. 4 Marks Questions

12. (i) State Mendeleev's periodic law.

(ii) Which group of elements could be placed in Mendeleev's periodic table without disturbing the original order? Give reason.

(iii) How was the study of elements made simpler and systematic with respect to Mendeleev's periodic law?

(iv) Why did he left gaps in his periodic table?

Sol. (i) Mendeleev's Periodic law states that physical and chemical properties of elements are a periodic function of their atomic masses. [1]

(ii) The noble gases could be placed in a new group without disturbing the existing order because they were very inert and present in extremely low concentrations in our atmosphere. [1]

(iii) The study of elements was made simpler and systematic by adopting a more fundamental property, i.e. atomic mass. [1]

(iv) Some gaps were left in the periodic table for undiscovered elements but the properties were predicted before. [1]

13. Mendeleev predicted the existence of certain elements not known at that time and named two of them as eka-silicon and eka-aluminium.

(i) Name the elements which have taken the place of these elements.

(ii) Mention the group and the period of these elements in the long form periodic table.

(iii) Classify these elements as metals or non-metals or metalloids.

(iv) How many valence electrons are present in each one of them?

Sol. (i) Germanium and gallium have taken the place of these elements. [1]

(ii) Germanium - Group 14, Period 4

Gallium - Group 13, Period 4 [1]

(iii) They are metalloids. [1]

(iv) In germanium, the number of valence electrons is 4 and in gallium it is 3. [1]

14. A part of the periodic table has been shown below.

Group / Period	1	2			13	14	15	16	17	18
1										
2	*A*	*C*							*E*	*G*
3	*B*					*D*			*F*	

Answer the following questions on the basis of position of elements in the given table.

(i) Which element is a noble gas? Give reason.

(ii) Which element is most electronegative? Give reason.

(iii) Write the electronic configuration of (a) *B* and (b) *E*.

Sol. (i) *G* is a noble gas because it is present in group 18 and has zero valency. [1]

(ii) *E* is the most electronegative element due to its smallest atomic size and more electron affinity. [1]

(iii) (a) Electronic configuration of *B* – *K L M*
2, 8, 1 [2]

(b) Electronic configuration of *E* – *K L*
2, 7 [2]

15. The position of three elements *A*, *B* and *C* in the periodic table are shown below.

Group 16	Group 17
—	—
—	*A*
—	—
B	*C*

(i) State whether *A* is a metal or non-metal.

(ii) State whether *C* is more reactive or less reactive than *A*.

(iii) Will *C* be larger or smaller in size than *B*?

(iv) Which type of ion, cation or anion, will be formed by *A*?

Sol. (i) Since, *A* belongs to group 17 and has 7 valence electrons so, it is a non-metal because it will gain electrons to complete its octet. [1]

(ii) *C* lies below *A* and in the same group. As we move down in a group, the size increases and electronegative character decreases.
With the increase in electronegative character, the electron adapting tendency and hence the reactivity decreases, so *C* is less reactive than *A*. [1]

(iii) *C* is smaller than *B* in size because as when we move from left to right in a period, atomic size decreases due to increased effective nuclear charge. [1]

(iv) As discussed in part (i) that element *A* has a tendency to gain electron to complete its octet. It needs to take up one electron, so it will form anion (A^-). [1]

16. Properties of the elements are given below. Where would you locate the following elements in the periodic table?

(i) A soft metal stored in kerosene.

(ii) An element with variable (more than one) valency stored in water.

(iii) An element which is tetravalent (valency 4) and forms the basis of organic chemistry.

(iv) An element which is an inert gas with atomic number 2.

Sol. (i) Group 1, Period 3 (Na) [1]

(ii) Group 15, Period 3 (P) [1]

(iii) Group 14, Period 2 (C) [1]

(iv) Group 18, Period 1 (He) [1]

17. Atomic number of a few elements are given below.
10, 20, 7, 14

(i) Identify the elements.

(ii) Identify the group number of these elements in the periodic table.

(iii) Identify the periods of these elements in the periodic table.

(iv) What would be the electronic configuration for each of these elements?

Sol. (i) The elements are 10 – Neon
20 – Calcium
7 – Nitrogen
14 – Silicon [1]

(ii) Group number of Neon – 18
Calcium – 2
Nitrogen – 15
Silicon – 14 [1]

(iii) The periods are 2, 4, 2, 3 respectively. [1]

(iv) Electronic configuration of neon – K L
2, 8

Electronic configuration of calcium – K L M N
2, 8, 8, 2

Electronic configuration of nitrogen – K, L
2, 5

Electronic configuration of silicon – K, L, M
2, 8, 4 [1]

18. (i) A metal M forms an oxide having the formula MO. It belongs to 2nd period in the modern periodic table. Write its atomic number and valency.

(ii) Write the reaction of alkaline earth metal with (a) oxygen (b) water.

Sol. (i) Since, the metal form MO type oxide, it belongs to second group and have configuration 2, 2 because have two shells. Thus, atomic number of the element is 4 and its valency is 2. [2]

(ii) (a) Alkaline earth metals reacts with oxygen to form respective oxides

$$2M + O_2 \longrightarrow 2MO$$

(where, M = any alkaline earth metals) [1]

(b) They reacts with water to produce alkali and hydrogen gas

$$\underset{\text{Alkaline earth metal}}{M} + 2H_2O \longrightarrow \underset{\text{Alkali}}{M(OH)_2} + H_2\uparrow$$ [1]

19. (i) "Hydrogen occupies a unique position in the modern periodic table". Justify the statement.

(ii) Give one use of

(a) Argon gas (b) Neon gas

Sol. (i) In electronic configuration, hydrogen (1) resembles with alkali metals. Moreover, it combines with halogen, oxygen and sulphur to give similar type of compounds as given by alkali metals. e.g. (HCl, NaCl), (H_2O, Na_2O), (H_2S, Na_2S).

But just like halogens, it exists in diatomic form and combines with metals and non-metals to form covalent compounds. In this periodic table, a unique position has been given to the hydrogen. It is kept at the top left corner because of its unique characteristic. [2]

(ii) (a) Argon gas is used to provide an inert atmosphere in high temperature metallurgical process. [1]

(b) Neon gas is used in discharge tubes. [1]

Chapter Assessment

Section-I

a. Multiple Choice Questions

1. Newlands' law of octaves seemed to be true for upto which element.
   (a) Calcium (b) Argon (c) Potassium (d) Zinc
2. Which of the following is incorrect explanation about Mendeleev's periodic law?
   (a) Mendeleev arranged elements in horizontal rows only
   (b) Mendeleev arranged elements with increasing atomic mass
   (c) Mendeleev's system of classifying elements was more elaborated
   (d) Both (a) and (b)
3. The element with atomic number 14 is hard and forms acidic oxide and a covalent halide. To which of the following categories does the element belong?
   (a) Metal
   (b) Metalloid
   (c) Non-metal
   (d) None of the above
4. Which one of the following depicts the correct representation of atomic radius (r) of an atom?

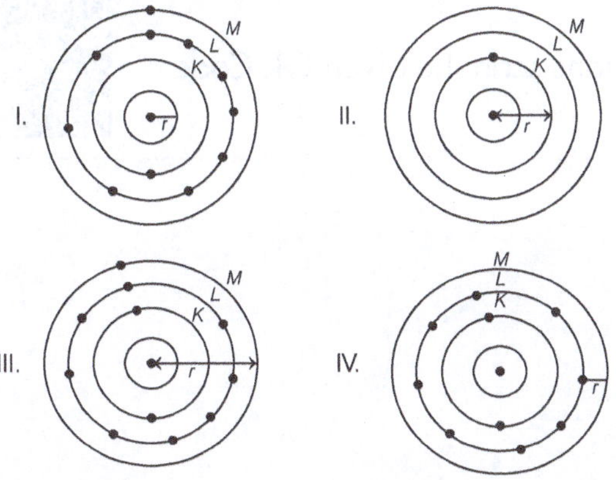

   (a) I and II (b) II and III
   (c) III and IV (d) I and IV
5. How many elements have been discovered till now?
   (a) 120 (b) 118
   (c) 116 (d) 114

b. Fill in the Blanks

6. The physical and chemical properties of elements are the periodic function of their atomic masses is known as .... (Mendeleev's periodic law, Dobereiner's triad, law of octaves).
7. Modern periodic table has .... (16, 17,18) groups and .... (6, 7, 8) periods.
8. According to modern periodic law physical and chemical properties of elements are periodic function of their .... (atomic number, atomic mass, ionisation enthalpy).
9. .... (Metallic, Non-metallic, Metalloids) character of an element is the tendency of its atom to lose electrons.
10. Metals form .... (acidic, basic, neutral) oxides.
11. There are .... (8, 14, 18) elements in lanthanide series.

c. Match the Columns

12. Match the following columns.

	Column I (Characteristics)		Column II (Trends in the modern periodic table)
A.	Valency	1.	Decreases in group, increase in period.
B.	Atomic size	2.	First decrease upto 14 group then increases
C.	Electronegativity	3.	Same in group, increase in period
D.	Reactivity	4.	Increase in group decrease in period

d. Give One Word or a Phrase

13. A law which states that atomic mass of the middle element was approximately equal to average of atomic mass of other two elements.
14. Law in which properties of first element were similar to that of eight element.
15. Total number of groups present in modern periodic table.
16. The incomplete period of modern periodic table.
17. The inner transition series that starts from lanthanum.

e. State One Relevant Reason

18. Given reason for classification of elements.
19. Why did Mendeleev left gaps in his periodic table?
20. Why reactivity of alkali metals increases down the group?
21. Alkali metals and halogens do not occur free in nature.
22. Most of the alkali metal are kept in their solvent.

Section-II

a. 2 Marks Questions

1. Define
   (i) Mendeleev periodic law
   (ii) Atomic number
2. State the relevant reason for the following.
   Chlorine, bromine and iodine with atomic mass 35.5, 80 and 127 respectively, can make Dobereiner's triad.

b. 3 Marks Questions

3. The atomic number of an element is 19.
   (i) Write the electronic configuration of the element.
   (ii) Determine the valency of the element.
   (iii) Write the formula of the oxide of the element.
4. Answer the following questions.
   (i) Why is it necessary to classify the elements?
   (ii) Give an example of Dobereiner's triad.
   (iii) On what basis Newland proposed his classification?
5. Name or state the following with reference to the elements of the first three periods of the periodic table.
   (i) Noble gas with duplet arrangement of electrons.
   (ii) Metalloid in 3rd period.
   (iii) Noble gas having electronic configuration 2, 8, 8.
6. Arrange the following.
   (i) Elements of group 1, in increasing order of reactivity.
   (ii) Elements of group 17, in decreasing order of reactivity.
   (iii) Al, Na, Mg increasing order of valency.

c. 4 Marks Questions

7. Name the gas used in following
   (i) filling balloons
   (ii) light bulbs
   (iii) bright coloured advertising light works
   (iv) provide inert atmosphere in high temperature metallurgical process.
8. Write short notes on the following.
   (i) Atomic radius
   (ii) Electronegativity
   (iii) Valency
   (iv) Metallic character

For explanations scan the given QR Code

Olympiad Section*

Brain Teasing Questions asked in Previous Olympiads

1. Consider a hypothetical situation where the mass of neutron in argon is made half and the mass of electron in argon is doubled with respect to their actual masses. In this case, the atomic mass of $_{18}Ar^{40}$ will approximately **(INJSO)**
   (a) remain the same (b) become half
   (c) increase by 45% (d) reduce by 27%

2. Haemoglobin is composed of four pyrrole groups bound to Fe^{2+} (ferrous ion). Fe (iron) is a transition metal, with atomic number 26 and mass number 56. The ion of Fe (iron) above mentioned, will have **(INJSO)**
   (a) 26 protons, 26 electrons and 30 neutrons
   (b) 26 protons, 24 electrons and 30 neutrons
   (c) 26 protons, 24 electrons and 24 neutrons
   (d) 26 protons, 26 electrons and 32 neutrons

3. Hydrogen contains three types of atoms ($_1H^1$ protium, $_1H^2$ deuterium and $_1H^3$ tritium) these atoms are **(NTSE)**
   (a) isotopic
   (b) isobaric
   (c) isotopic and isobaric
   (d) None of the above

4. What is the maximum number of electrons that an be accommodated in the outermost orbit? **(NTSE)**
   (a) 2 (b) 8 (c) 3 (d) 18

5. Which of the following radioactive isotope is used in the treatment of cancer? **(NTSE)**
   (a) Iodine-131 (b) Uranium-235
   (c) Sodium-24 (d) Cobalt-60

6. The ion of an element has 3 positive charge, 27 mass number and 14 neutrons. Which of the number of electrons in this ion? **(NTSE)**
   (a) 13 (b) 10
   (c) 14 (d) 16

7. Which of the following elements does not consist isotopes? **(NTSE)**
   (a) Carbon (b) Neon
   (c) Chlorine (d) Iodine

8. Pick out the isobar pair **(NTSE)**
   (a) $_1H^1$, $_1H^2$, (b) $_6Cl^{13}$, $_7N^{14}$
   (c) $_{17}Cl^{35}$, $_{17}H^{37}$ (d) $_{18}Ar^{40}$, $_{20}Ca^{40}$

9. Number of neutrons in isotope of hydrogen, tritium is **(NTSE)**
   (a) 0 (b) 1
   (c) 2 (d) 3

10. Isotopes of an element contains **(INJSO)**
    (a) similar physical properties
    (b) different chemical properties
    (c) different number of neutrons
    (d) different atomic number

11. Valence electron in Cl^- ion is **(INJSO)**
    (a) 16 (b) 8
    (c) 17 (d) 18

12. Which one of the following is correct electronic configuration of sodium? **(INJSO)**
    (a) 2, 8 (b) 8, 2, 1
    (c) 2, 1, 8 (d) 2, 8, 1

13. Electron is discovered by **(INJSO)**
    (a) J.J. Thomson
    (b) Dalton
    (c) Niels Bohr
    (d) None of the above

14. Distribution of electrons in carbon is as follow **(INJSO)**
    (a) 2, 4
    (b) 2, 2, 2
    (c) 4, 2
    (d) None of the above

Answers

1. (d)	**2.** (b)	**3.** (a)	**4.** (b)	**5.** (d)	**6.** (b)	**7.** (b)	**8.** (d)	**9.** (c)	**10.** (c)
11. (b)	**12.** (d)	**13.** (a)	**14.** (a)						

* *These questions may or may not be asked in the examination, have been given just for additional practice required for olympiads Scholarship Exams etc. For detailed explanations refer Page No. 135.*

CHAPTER

06

Study of First Element-Hydrogen

CHAPTER OUTLINES

- Position of Hydrogen in the Periodic Table
- General Methods of Preparation of Hydrogen Gas
- Laboratory Preparation of Hydrogen Gas
- Industrial Preparation of Hydrogen Gas by Bosch Process
- Tests for Hydrogen
- Uses of Hydrogen Gas

Hydrogen is the lightest element known to us, it is thus placed at the first position in the periodic table. The atomic number of hydrogen is one (1) and it is the only element, which occurs without a neutron in its nucleus. It is represented by the symbol H.

Discovery

Hydrogen was discovered by **Henry Cavendish** in 1766 by the action of an acid on the metal.

Although **Robert Boyle** had prepared the gas in 1672. Cavendish also established its elementary nature and showed that water is formed when this gas burns in air. He called it inflammable air because of its combustible nature. The name hydrogen was given by **Antoine Lavoisier,** which means water producer (Greek word: *Hydro*- water, *gen*-to produce).

Occurrence

In nature, hydrogen occurs in free as well as in combined state. In elemental form, it exists as a diatomic (H_2) molecule and forms 90% of Sun's atmosphere.

Combined state Most of the hydrogen on earth occurs in combined state as in water, living masses, fossil fuels and many organic and inorganic compounds. In water, hydrogen is 11.1% by weight.

Physical Properties

- Hydrogen is colourless and odourless.
- It is flavourless and non-toxic in nature.
- Hydrogen is slightly soluble in water.
- It liquefies below −240°C under pressure of about 20 atmosphere.

Isotopes of Hydrogen

Hydrogen is known to exist in three isotopes, which are listed below in the table.

Isotopes	Protium (^1_1H)	Deuterium (^2_1D or ^2_1H)	Tritium (^3_1T or ^3_1H)
Atomic number	1	1	1
Mass number	1	2	3
Number of electron	1	1	1
Number of proton	1	1	1
Number of neutron(s)	0	1	2
Natural abundance (%)	99.98	0.01	Traces

Note Heavy water (D_2O) consist of deuterium. Tritium ^3_1H is known to be radioactive.

Position of Hydrogen in the Periodic Table

Hydrogen resembles with alkali metals (group 1) and halogens (group 17). It also differs from them as well. Thus, it is unique in behaviour and is, therefore best placed separately in the periodic table.

Hydrogen shows *dual nature* since it resembles the alkali metals of group IA(1) and the halogens of group VII A (17).

1. Resemblance with Alkali Metals

Hydrogen resembles with alkali metals in the following ways

(i) **Electronic configuration** Hydrogen has only one electron in its outermost shell which is similar to alkali metal.

(Shells)

Alkali metals		K	L	M	N	O	P	Q
	H(1)	1						
	Li(3)	2	1					
	Na(11)	2	8	1				
	K(19)	2	8	8	1			
	Rb(37)	2	8	18	8	1		
	Cs(55)	2	8	18	18	8	1	
	Fr(87)	2	8	18	32	18	8	1

(ii) **Ion formation** (Electropositive nature) Just like alkali metals, hydrogen readily loses its one electron to form unipositive hydrogen ion, i.e. H^+ which is also called proton. It shows that it is an electropositive element.

$$H \longrightarrow H^+ + e^-$$

$$Na \longrightarrow Na^+ + e^-$$

(iii) **Valency** All alkali metals, including hydrogen, have 1 valency.

(iv) **Oxidation state** Hydrogen exhibits +1 oxidation state in its compounds just like alkali metals.

(v) **Burning** Hydrogen burns in oxygen with a pop sound to form neutral oxide (water).

$$\underset{\text{Hydrogen}}{2H_2} + \underset{\text{Oxygen}}{O_2} \longrightarrow \underset{\text{Water}}{2H_2O}$$

Alkali metals also burn vigorously when heated in oxygen to form their respective oxides.

$$\underset{\text{Lithium}}{4\,Li} + O_2 \longrightarrow \underset{\text{Lithium oxide}}{2Li_2O}$$

Hydrogen also form peroxide like sodium.

$$H_2 + O_2 \longrightarrow \underset{\text{Hydrogen peroxide}}{H_2O_2}$$

$$\underset{\text{(Sodium)}}{2Na} + O_2 \longrightarrow \underset{\text{Sodium peroxide}}{Na_2O_2}$$

(Peroxides are those compounds which have *R*—O—O—*R* type structure.)

(vi) **Reducing power** Both the alkali metals and hydrogen act as reducing agents.

$$\underset{\text{Copper oxide}}{\overset{2+}{CuO}} + \overset{0}{H_2} \longrightarrow \overset{0}{Cu} + \overset{+1}{H_2O}$$

$$\overset{2+}{CuO} + \overset{0}{2Na} \longrightarrow \overset{0}{Cu} + \underset{\text{Sodium oxide}}{\overset{+1}{Na_2O}}$$

(vii) **Combination with non-metals** Hydrogen as well as alkali metals react with non-metals like oxygen, sulphur and chlorine to form respective compounds. e.g.

Hydrogen forms - H_2O, H_2S, HCl.

Sodium forms - Na_2O, Na_2S, NaCl.

2. Resemblance with Halogens

Hydrogen resembles with halogens in the following ways

(i) **Electronic configuration** Like halogens, hydrogen requires only one electron to achieve the nearest inert or noble gas configuration.

	K	L	M	(Nearest noble gas)
H :	1			[He = 2]
F :	2	7		[Ne = 2, 8]
Cl :	2	8	7	[Ar = 2, 8, 8]

(ii) **Ion formation** (Electronegative character) Like halogens, hydrogen also have a tendency to accept one electron to form uninegative, hydride ion (H^-).

$$H + e^- \longrightarrow H^-, \quad Cl + e^- \longrightarrow Cl^-$$

(iii) **Valency** Both halogens and hydrogen have valency 1. They both can accept one electron to attain the nearest noble gas configuration.

(iv) **Atomicity and non-metallic character** Hydrogen exists as a diatomic molecule (H_2) like halogens (F_2, Cl_2, Br_2 and I_2).

Further, it shows the tendency of non-metals like halogens.

(v) **Physical state** Like halogens (fluorine and chlorine only), hydrogen is also a gas at room temperature.

Properties different from Alkali Metals as well as Halogens

These characteristics are as follows

- Hydrogen is less electropositive than alkali metals and less electronegative than halogens.
- The shell present in hydrogen atom is only one, while in alkali metals and halogens, there are more than one shell.
- Oxides of alkali metals are generally basic, while those of halogens are generally acidic. Oxide of hydrogen, i.e. water (H_2O) is, however, neutral.

Conclusion

As we have studied that hydrogen resembles with both the alkali metal and the halogen group. This leads to confusion about the placing of it in the periodic table. But considering its electronic configuration and fact that it has 1 valence electron like alkali metals, it has been placed in the group 1 of the periodic table.

Check Your LEARNING...

1. Write the name of scientist, who discovered hydrogen?
2. Which isotope of hydrogen is radioactive?
3. Write the name of that isotope of hydrogen, which has no neutron.
4. In which form hydrogen molecule exist?
5. Why hydrogen has been placed in the group 1 of the periodic table?

General Methods of Preparation of Hydrogen Gas

Some of the methods for the preparation of hydrogen gas are as follows

1. Preparation of Hydrogen from Water

Action of metals on water in different states or at different temperature produces hydrogen gas. The reactions of different metals, in different conditions with water are as follows

(i) Action of Active Metals with Cold Water

Active metals like sodium, potassium and calcium being highly reactive, react with cold water producing bases (hydroxides of metals) and releasing hydrogen gas.

$$\underset{\text{Sodium}}{2Na} + \underset{\text{Water}}{2H_2O} \longrightarrow \underset{\text{Sodium hydroxide}}{2NaOH} + \underset{\text{Hydrogen}}{H_2\uparrow}$$

$$\underset{\text{Potassium}}{2K} + \underset{\text{Water}}{2H_2O} \longrightarrow \underset{\text{Potassium hydroxide}}{2KOH} + \underset{\text{Hydrogen}}{H_2\uparrow}$$

$$\underset{\text{Calcium}}{Ca} + \underset{\text{Water}}{2H_2O} \longrightarrow \underset{\text{Calcium hydroxide}}{Ca(OH)_2} + \underset{\text{Hydrogen}}{H_2\uparrow}$$

The above reactions are exothermic and the reactions of sodium and potassium is violent and may result in explosion.

Action of Cold Water on Potassium, Sodium and Calcium in Laboratory

1. **Action of cold water on potassium**

   Bubbles of hydrogen gas are seen and the solution formed is colourless, soapy and alkaline.

   Although pure hydrogen burns with a pale blue flame, the colour of the flame is lilac due to presence of traces of potassium vapour.

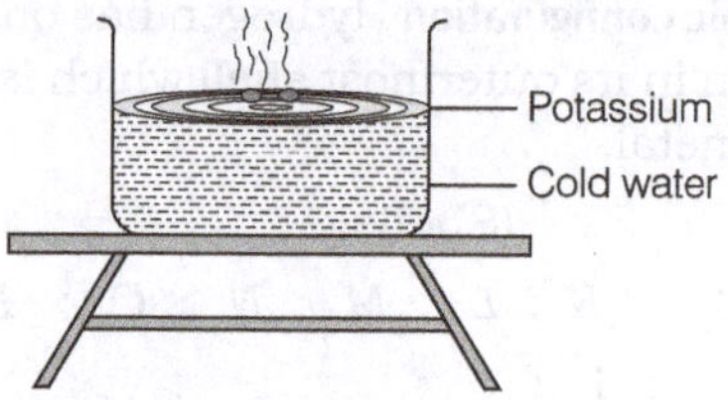

Action of cold water on potassium

2. **Action of cold water on sodium**

   Bubbles of hydrogen gas are produced and the solution formed is colourless, soapy, slightly warm and alkaline.

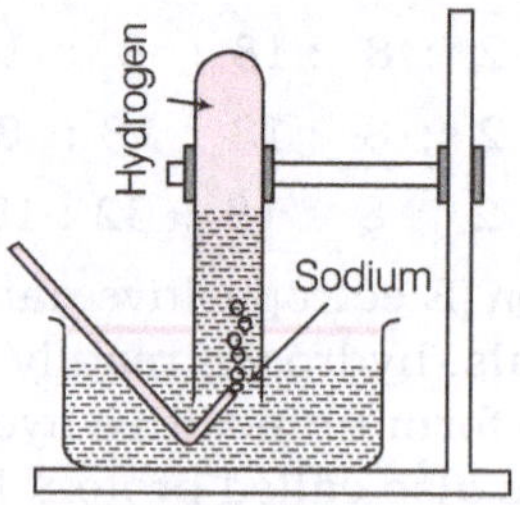

Action of cold water on sodium

3. **Action of cold water on calcium**

   Bubbles of hydrogen are liberated and the solution turns milky, turbid and alkaline. If red litmus is introduced in solution, it turns blue.

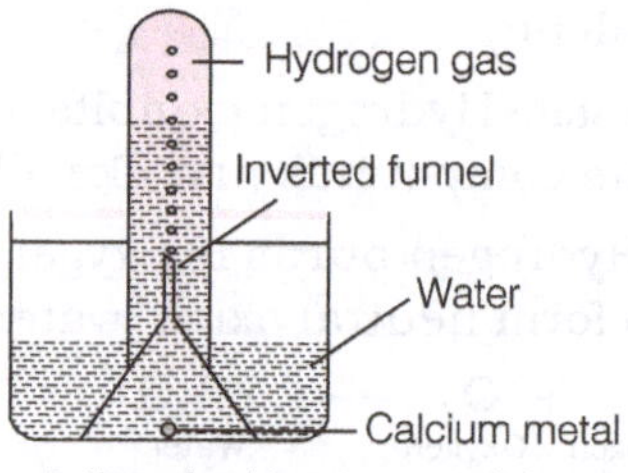

Action of cold water on calcium

(ii) Action of Hot Water on Magnesium

Magnesium react with hot water slowly to produce magnesium hydroxide and evolving hydrogen gas.

$$\underset{\text{Magnesium}}{Mg} + \underset{\text{Water}}{2H_2O} \xrightarrow{\Delta} \underset{\text{Magnesium hydroxide}}{Mg(OH)_2} + \underset{\text{Hydrogen}}{H_2\uparrow}$$

Magnesium burns in steam with an intense white light, liberating hydrogen gas and white ash, i.e. magnesium oxide.

$$Mg + \underset{\text{(Steam)}}{H_2O} \longrightarrow MgO + H_2\uparrow$$

Magnesium oxide crumbles down due to heating. Further on exposing magnesium to steam, results in catenation of hydrogen gas.

(iii) Action of Steam on Metals

Metals like magnesium, aluminium, iron and zinc react with steam to form oxides of metals and evolve hydrogen gas.

$$\underset{\text{Magnesium}}{Mg} + \underset{\text{Steam}}{H_2O(g)} \xrightarrow{\Delta} \underset{\text{Magnesium oxide}}{MgO} + \underset{\text{Hydrogen}}{H_2\uparrow}$$

$$\underset{\text{Aluminium}}{2Al} + \underset{\text{Steam}}{3H_2O(g)} \xrightarrow{800^\circ C} \underset{\text{Aluminium oxide}}{Al_2O_3} + \underset{\text{Hydrogen}}{3H_2\uparrow}$$

$$\underset{\text{Zinc}}{Zn} + \underset{\text{Water}}{H_2O(g)} \xrightarrow{\Delta} \underset{\text{Zinc oxide}}{ZnO} + \underset{\text{Hydrogen}}{H_2\uparrow}$$

$$\underset{\text{Iron}}{3Fe} + \underset{\text{Steam}}{4H_2O(g)} \rightleftharpoons \underset{\text{Iron oxide}}{Fe_3O_4} + \underset{\text{Hydrogen}}{4H_2\uparrow}$$

The reaction between iron and water is reversible. If the hydrogen formed is not removed, the iron oxide formed is reduced back to iron.

Whereas in case of magnesium, aluminium and zinc, the reaction stops after sometime. As these newly formed metal oxides stick to the surfaces of the respective metals. Thus, they interfere with the further contact of steam and metal.

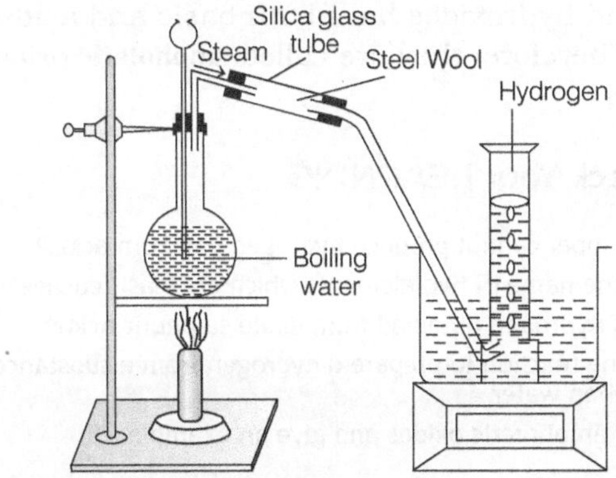

Action of steam of iron

(iv) Action of Steam on Non-metals

When steam is passed over red hot coke, water gas ($CO + H_2$) is formed.

$$\underset{\substack{\text{Carbon}\\\text{(Red hot coke)}}}{C} + \underset{\text{Steam}}{H_2O(g)} \longrightarrow \underbrace{CO + H_2}_{\text{Water gas}}$$

Application of Activity Series in the Preparation of Hydrogen

In activity series, metals are arranged in decreasing order of their relative tendency to lose electron and their reactive nature. Reactivity series of metals with respect to hydrogen is given below

K	—	Potassium	Highly reactive ↑
Na	—	Sodium	
Ca	—	Calcium	
Mg	—	Magnesium	
Al	—	Aluminium	
Zn	—	Zinc	
Fe	—	Iron	
Sn	—	Tin	
Pb	—	Lead	
H	—	Hydrogen	
Cu	—	Copper	
Hg	—	Mercury	
Ag	—	Silver	
Au	—	Gold	
Pt	—	Platinum	Less reactive

Metal present on the top of the series are active metals. The ability of metals to reduce water to hydrogen decreases on going down the series.

$$K > Na > Ca > Mg > Al > Zn \ldots\ldots$$

The highly reactive metal, potassium is placed at the top of this series and the least reactive metal gold is placed at the bottom of this series.

Features of Activity Series

- The tendency of any metal to get oxidised decreases down the series. So, potassium is most readily oxidised.
- Electropositive character decreases down the series.
- Reducing power of metals decreases down the series.
- Metals placed above hydrogen displaces hydrogen from water and dilute acid, but metals placed below it, do not displace it.

i.e. $2Na + H_2O \longrightarrow 2NaOH + H_2$

$Cu + H_2O \longrightarrow$ No reaction

- A metal higher up in the series displaces a metal below it from the salt solution of latter and *vice-versa* does not takes place.
  i.e. $CuSO_4(aq) + Zn \longrightarrow ZnSO_4(aq) + Cu$
- Oxides of metals K, Na, Ca, Mg and Al cannot be reduced by common reducing agents like H_2, CO or C. They can be reduced only by electrolysis.
- Since, the reactivity series lists metals in decreasing order of electropositivity, it is expected that those at the top will combine with more electronegative elements to form ionic compounds.

2. Displacement of Hydrogen from Acids

Few metals which are more active than hydrogen in activity series (or reactivity series) displace hydrogen from acids.

Metals such as Zn, Fe, Al and Mg (above hydrogen in the activity series) react with dil. H_2SO_4 or HCl at room temperature liberating hydrogen and forming their respective salts.

$$\underset{\text{Zinc}}{Zn} + \underset{\text{Sulphuric acid}}{H_2SO_4} \longrightarrow \underset{\text{Zinc sulphate}}{ZnSO_4} + H_2\uparrow$$

$$Zn + \underset{\text{Hydrochloric acid}}{2HCl} \longrightarrow \underset{\text{Zinc chloride}}{ZnCl_2} + H_2\uparrow$$

$$\underset{\text{Iron}}{Fe} + H_2SO_4 \longrightarrow \underset{\text{Iron sulphate}}{FeSO_4} + H_2\uparrow$$

$$Fe + 2HCl \longrightarrow \underset{\text{Iron chloride}}{FeCl_2} + H_2\uparrow$$

$$\underset{\text{Magnesium}}{Mg} + 2HCl \longrightarrow \underset{\text{Magnesium chloride}}{MgCl_2} + H_2\uparrow$$

$$Mg + H_2SO_4 \longrightarrow \underset{\text{Magnesium sulphate}}{MgSO_4} + H_2\uparrow$$

$$\underset{\text{Aluminium}}{2Al} + 3H_2SO_4 \longrightarrow \underset{\text{Aluminium sulphate}}{Al_2(SO_4)_3} + 3H_2$$

$$2Al + 6HCl \longrightarrow \underset{\text{Aluminium chloride}}{2AlCl_3} + 3H_2$$

On the other hand, metals which are less reactive than hydrogen like copper and silver (below hydrogen in the activity series) has no effect on acid.

$$Cu + H_2SO_4 \longrightarrow \text{No reaction}$$

$$Cu + HCl \longrightarrow \text{No reaction}$$

Potassium, sodium and calcium react with dilute H_2SO_4 and dilute HCl but the reaction is explosive and thus not feasible.

$$2Na + 2HCl \longrightarrow \underset{\text{Sodium chloride}}{2NaCl} + H_2\uparrow$$

$$2K + 2HCl \longrightarrow \underset{\text{Potassium chloride}}{2KCl} + H_2\uparrow$$

$$Ca + 2HCl \longrightarrow \underset{\text{Calcium chloride}}{CaCl_2} + H_2\uparrow$$

Nitric acid should not be used to form hydrogen because nitric acid reacts with only magnesium and manganese to liberate hydrogen.

$$Mg + 2HNO_3 \longrightarrow \underset{\text{Magnesium nitrate}}{Mg(NO_3)_2} + H_2\uparrow$$

$$Mn + 2HNO_3 \longrightarrow \underset{\text{Manganese nitrate}}{Mn(NO_3)_2} + H_2\uparrow$$

If it reacts with rest of the metals, it produces oxides of nitrogen or ammonium nitrate and not hydrogen as it is an oxidising agent.

3. Displacement of Hydrogen from Alkalies

Powdered form of active metals like aluminium, zinc and lead, when boiled with alkalies (like NaOH , KOH) evolve hydrogen gas.

$$\underset{\text{Aluminium}}{2Al} + \underset{\text{Sodium hydroxide}}{2NaOH} + \underset{\text{Water}}{2H_2O} \longrightarrow \underset{\text{Sodium meta-aluminate}}{2NaAlO_2} + 3H_2\uparrow$$

$$\underset{\text{Aluminium}}{2Al} + \underset{\text{Potassium hydroxide}}{2KOH} + \underset{\text{Water}}{2H_2O} \longrightarrow \underset{\text{Potassium meta-aluminate}}{2KAlO_2} + 3H_2\uparrow$$

$$\underset{\text{Zinc}}{Zn} + \underset{\text{Sodium hydroxide}}{2NaOH} \longrightarrow \underset{\text{Sodium zincate}}{Na_2ZnO_2} + H_2\uparrow$$

$$\underset{\text{Zinc}}{Zn} + \underset{\text{Potassium hydroxide}}{2KOH} \longrightarrow \underset{\text{Potassium zincate}}{K_2ZnO_2} + H_2\uparrow$$

$$\underset{\text{Lead}}{Pb} + \underset{\text{Sodium hydroxide}}{2NaOH} \longrightarrow \underset{\text{Sodium plumbate}}{Na_2PbO_2} + H_2\uparrow$$

Metals like zinc, lead and aluminium react with both acids and alkalies to produce hydrogen and salts. This is unique nature of these metals. Their oxides and hydroxides have both basic and acidic nature. Therefore, they are called **amphoteric oxides** or **hydroxides.**

Check Your LEARNING...

1 Why copper cannot produce hydrogen gas from acids?
2 Write the name of two elements which are least reactive.
3 How is hydrogen obtained from dilute sulphuric acid?
4 Give one reaction to prepare dihydrogen from a substance other than water.
5 Define amphoteric oxides and give an example.

Laboratory Preparation of Hydrogen Gas

In laboratory, hydrogen is mainly prepared by treating zinc granules either with dilute sulphuric acid or with aqueous alkali (NaOH).

$$\underset{\text{Zinc}}{Zn} + \underset{\substack{\text{Dil.}\\ \text{Sulphuric acid}}}{H_2SO_4} \longrightarrow \underset{\text{Zinc sulphate}}{ZnSO_4} + \underset{\text{Hydrogen}}{H_2\uparrow}$$

$$\underset{\text{Zinc}}{Zn} + \underset{\text{Sodium hydroxide}}{2NaOH} \longrightarrow \underset{\text{Sodium zincate}}{Na_2ZnO_2} + \underset{\text{Hydrogen}}{H_2\uparrow}$$

Zinc metal is preferred over other active metals as hydrogen gas produced slowly and hence, easy to collect in this case.

Procedure

Take few granules of zinc metal in a round bottom flask fixed with air tight cork having two holes. Through one hole, pass a thistle funnel with a long stem which allow dil. H_2SO_4 to pass in round bottom flask, and through the other, a long delivery tube.

The same setup is shown below in the figure.

Reactions

$$Zn + \underset{\text{(Dil.)}}{2HCl} \longrightarrow \underset{\text{Zinc chloride}}{ZnCl_2} + H_2\uparrow$$

or $$Zn + \underset{\text{(Dil.)}}{H_2SO_4} \longrightarrow \underset{\text{Zinc sulphate}}{ZnSO_4} + H_2\uparrow$$

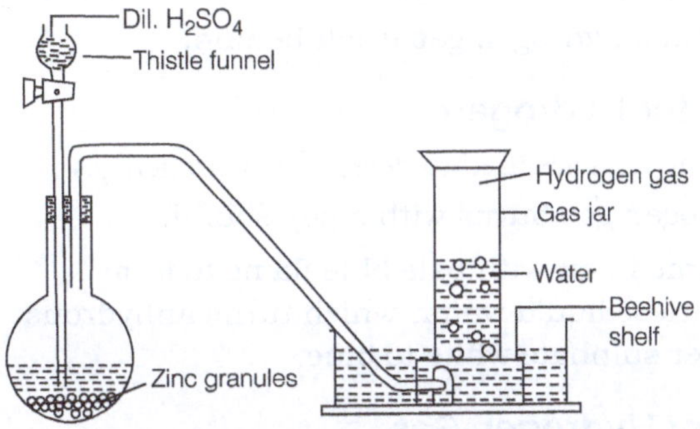

Laboratory preparation of hydrogen

Observation

A brisk effervescence is produced and hydrogen gas is collected over water. Wait until all the air from the setup is expelled and finally hydrogen gas is collected in the jar.

Collection of Hydrogen

Hydrogen is collected by **downward displacement of water** because

- it is virtually insoluble in water.
- it forms an explosive mixture with air and hence, cannot be collected by downward displacement of air even though it is lighter than air.

Impurities Present in Hydrogen Gas

Presence of impurities in the zinc granules (like As, P, S, C, etc.) and air inside the setup results in the formation of many other gases as impurities.

Main impurities that usually found are phosphine (PH_3), arsine (AsH_3), hydrogen sulphide (H_2S), sulphur dioxide (SO_2), oxides of nitrogen, carbon dioxide (CO_2), water vapour (H_2O), etc.

Note Some of the impurities that are present in zinc granules speed up the rate of reaction. That's why, zinc granules are preferred over pure zinc metal.

Removal of Impurities

To remove the impurities, hydrogen gas is treated with following compounds or reagents.

Reagents/Compounds	Impurities removed
Silver nitrate solution (*aq.* $AgNO_3$) e.g. $\underset{\text{Arsine}}{AsH_3} + 6AgNO_3 \longrightarrow \underset{\text{Silver arsenide}}{Ag_3As} + 3AgNO_3 + 3HNO_3$ $\underset{\text{Phosphene}}{PH_3} + 6AgNO_3 \longrightarrow \underset{\text{Silver phosphide}}{Ag_3P} + 3AgNO_3 + 3HNO_3$	PH_3, AsH_3
Lead nitrate solution (*aq.* $Pb(NO_3)_2$) e.g. $Pb(NO_3)_2 + \underset{\text{Hydrogen sulphide}}{H_2S} \longrightarrow \underset{\text{Lead sulphide}}{PbS} + 2HNO_3$	H_2S
Potassium hydroxide solution (*aq.* KOH) e.g. $\underset{\text{Sulphur dioxide}}{SO_2} + 2KOH \longrightarrow \underset{\text{Potassium sulphite}}{K_2SO_3} + H_2O$ $\underset{\text{Carbon dioxide}}{CO_2} + 2KOH \longrightarrow \underset{\text{Potassium carbonate}}{K_2CO_3} + H_2O$ $\underset{\text{Nitrogen dioxide}}{2NO_2} + 2KOH \longrightarrow \underset{\text{Potassium nitrite}}{KNO_2} + KNO_3 + H_2O$	SO_2, CO_2 and oxides of nitrogen
Anhydrous calcium chloride ($CaCl_2$) as a water vapours drying agent.	

The complete setup looks like

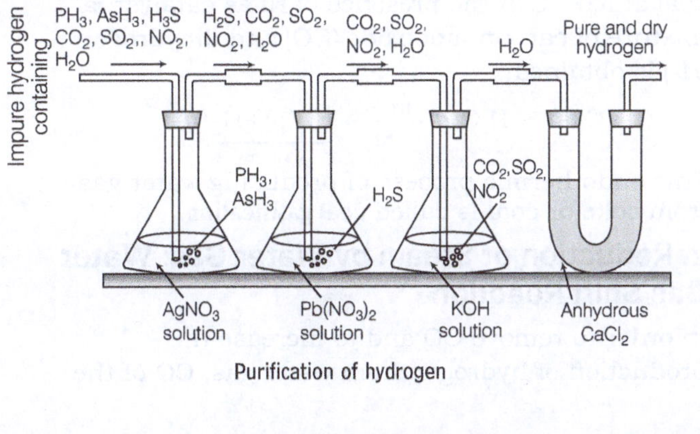

Purification of hydrogen

Concentrated sulphuric acid is a good drying agent but it is not used to dry hydrogen as it reacts with hydrogen, thus defeating the purpose of the reaction.

$$H_2SO_4 + H_2 \longrightarrow 2H_2O + SO_2$$

Precautions

Following precautions must be taken while preparing the gas

- The apparatus used should be airtight, otherwise gas will leak from the set up.
- Hydrogen gas being highly inflammable should be devoid of any flame or lighting object.
- Make sure all the air has been escaped from the setup as the mixture of hydrogen gas and air is highly explosive.
- The end of the thistle funnel must be dipped in sulphuric acid, otherwise gas will also escape through the thistle funnel.

Note

- Nitric acid even in its dilute form, is not used in the preparation of hydrogen from metals because it is powerful oxidising agent and the oxygen formed due to its decomposition oxidises the hydrogen to give water, thus not fulfil the purpose of the reaction.
- Also concentrated sulphuric acid is not used in the preparation of hydrogen gas because it is a good oxidising agent and will produce SO_2 on reaction with zinc.

$$Zn + 2H_2SO_4 \longrightarrow \underset{\text{Zinc sulphate}}{ZnSO_4} + SO_2\uparrow + 2H_2O$$

Industrial Preparation of Hydrogen Gas By Bosch Process

Various steps involved in this process are as follows

1. Production of Water Gas: Coal Gasification

On passing super-heated steam over red hot coke or coal at 1000° C in the presence of Ni as catalyst, a mixture of carbon monoxide (CO) and dihydrogen (H_2) is obtained.

$$C(s) + H_2O(g) \xrightarrow[\text{Ni}]{1000^\circ C} \underbrace{CO(g) + H_2(g)}_{\text{Water gas}}$$

This endothermic process of producing water gas from coke or coal is called **coal gasification.**

2. Reduction of Steam by Water Gas: Water Gas Shift Reaction

In order to remove CO and to increase the production of hydrogen from water gas, CO of the water gas is oxidised to CO_2 by mixing it with more steam at 673 K in the presence of iron chromate or ferric oxide and little chromium oxide (at 450°C) as catalyst.

$$\underbrace{CO(g) + H_2(g)}_{\text{Water gas}} + \underset{\text{Steam}}{H_2O(g)} \xrightarrow[Fe_2O_3,\ Cr_2O_3]{450^\circ C} CO_2(g) + 2H_2(g)$$

This exothermic chemical reaction in which carbon monoxide of the water gas reacts with steam to give carbon dioxide and more hydrogen gas is called **water gas shift reaction.**

3. Separation of Carbon Dioxide (CO_2) and Carbon Monoxide (CO)

(i) **Carbon dioxide** can be removed either by passing the mixture, (i.e. $CO + H_2$), through cold water under high pressure. As the result most of the CO_2 is dissolved in cold water leaving behind hydrogen.

It can also be removed by passing the mixture ($CO + H_2$) through potassium hydroxide solution, which removes carbon dioxide by reacting with it and hydrogen remain unreactive.

(ii) **Carbon monoxide** is removed by passing hydrogen gas into ammoniacal solution of cuprous chloride.

$$CuCl + CO + 2H_2O \longrightarrow CuCl\cdot CO\cdot 2H_2O$$

Thus, hydrogen gas is left behind.

Tests for Hydrogen

Following tests are used to detect the hydrogen gas

- Hydrogen gas burns with a pop sound.
- It burns in air with pale blue flame to form colourless liquid water, which turns anhydrous copper sulphate white to blue.

Uses of Hydrogen Gas

Some of the important applications of hydrogen gas are as follows

- It is used in the manufacture of ammonia (by Haber's process).
- It is used for hardening of oil and in the synthesis of many important compounds like metallic hydrides, hydrogen chloride, methanol (an organic compound), etc.

$$\underset{\text{Carbon monoxide}}{CO(g)} + \underset{\text{Dihydrogen}}{2H_2(g)} \xrightarrow[\text{Catalyst}]{\text{Cobalt}} \underset{\text{Methanol}}{CH_3OH(l)}$$

- It is used in oxy-hydrogen and oxy-atomic hydrogen torches for cutting and welding.
- It has very high heat of combustion, thus, it is used as a fuel in the form of
  - coal gas
  - water gas ($CO + H_2$)
  - liquid hydrogen (non-polluting)
- In self lighting gas jets and automatic lighters.
- For hydrogenation of vegetable oil.
- For producing artificial petrol from coal.
- In extraction of metals, hydrogen reduces heated metallic oxide to metals, i.e.

$$\underset{\text{Iron oxide}}{Fe_2O_3} + 3H_2 \longrightarrow 2Fe + 3H_2O$$

$$\underset{\substack{\text{(Black)}\\\text{Copper oxide}}}{CuO} + H_2 \longrightarrow \underset{\text{(Red brown)}}{Cu} + H_2O$$

Oxidation and Reduction Reactions

The process of oxidation and reduction; and various related reactions are as follows

Oxidation

It is defined as a chemical process which involves either the addition of oxygen or electronegative element to the substance or removal of hydrogen or electropositive element from the substance.

(i) **Addition of oxygen**

$$2Mg + O_2 \longrightarrow 2MgO$$
$$2CO + O_2 \longrightarrow 2CO_2$$

(ii) **Addition of electronegative element**

$$2FeCl_2 + Cl_2 \longrightarrow 2FeCl_3$$

(iii) **Removal of hydrogen**

$$H_2S + Cl_2 \longrightarrow 2HCl + S$$

(iv) **Removal of electropositive element**

$$2KI + H_2O_2 \longrightarrow 2KOH + I_2$$

Note If a substance gains oxygen or loses hydrogen during reaction, it is said to be oxidised.

Reducing agents Those substances that reduces other substances either by providing electrons, or by providing hydrogen or an electropositive ion, or by removing oxygen or an electronegative ion in a chemical process are known as reducing agents. They itself gets oxidised.

Some of the common examples are, carbon, hydrogen peroxide, hydrogen iodide (HI), hydrogen bromide (HBr), hydrogen sulphide (H_2S), carbon monoxide (CO), sulphur dioxide (SO_2), ammonia (NH_3), some metals (like Zn, Al, Cu, Na) etc.

Reduction

It is defined as a chemical process which involves either the addition of hydrogen or electropositive element to the substance or removal of oxygen or electronegative element from the substance.

(i) **Addition of hydrogen**

$$2Na + H_2 \longrightarrow 2NaH$$

(ii) **Addition of electropositive element**

$$HgCl_2 + Hg \longrightarrow Hg_2Cl_2$$

(iii) **Removal of oxygen**

$$2KClO_3(s) \xrightarrow{\Delta} 2KCl(s) + 3O_2(g)$$

(iv) **Removal of electronegative element**

$$2FeCl_3 + H_2S \longrightarrow 2FeCl_2 + 2HCl + S$$

Note If a substance loses oxygen or gains hydrogen during a reaction, it is said to be reduced.

Oxidising agents Those substances that oxidises other substances either by accepting electrons or by providing oxygen or an electronegative ion, or by removing hydrogen or an electropositive ion in a chemical process are known as oxidising agents. They itself gets reduced.

Some examples of oxidising agents are lead dioxide (PbO_2), Ozone (O_3), chlorine (Cl_2), hydrogen peroxide (H_2O_2), bromine (Br_2).

Differences Between Oxidation and Reduction

Oxidation involves	Reduction involves
1. Addition of oxygen	Removal of oxygen
2. Removal of hydrogen	Addition of hydrogen
3. Addition of electronegative ion or atom	Removal of electronegative ion or atom
4. Removal of electropositive atom or ion	Addition of electropositive atom or ion
5. Loss of electron(s)	Gain of electron(s)

Check Your LEARNING...

1 Give the equation of laboratory preparation of hydrogen gas.
2 Name the constituents of water gas.
3 Write the reaction to prepare hydrogen using Bosch process.
4 Write the use of oxy-hydrogen torch.
5 Identify the substances that are oxidised and substance that are reduced in the following reactions.
(i) $4Na(s) + O_2(g) \longrightarrow 2Na_2O(s)$
(ii) $CuO(s) + H_2(g) \longrightarrow Cu(s) + H_2O(l)$

QUiCK Revision

- Hydrogen is the lightest element known and placed separately due to its resemblance with elements of group 1 and 17 both.
- It was discovered by Henry Cavendish in 1766.
- Hydrogen occurs in free state (minerals, rocks, sun and many other stars) as well in combined state (water, living masses and fossil fuels).
- Hydrogen is the only element which does not have neutrons in its nucleus. It exists in three isotopes such as protium ($_1H^1$), deuterium ($_1H^2$ or $_1D^2$) and tritium ($_1H^3$ or $_1T^3$).
- **General methods of preparation of hydrogen gas**

  (i) **Reaction with water**

$$2Na + 2H_2O\text{ (cold water)} \longrightarrow 2NaOH + H_2\uparrow$$

$$Mg + 2H_2O\text{ (boiling water)} \xrightarrow{\Delta} Mg(OH)_2 + H_2\uparrow$$

$$Mg + H_2O(g,\text{ steam}) \xrightarrow{\Delta} MgO + H_2\uparrow$$

  (ii) **Reaction with acid**

  There are few metals (such as Zn, Fe and Mg) which are more reactive than hydrogen in reactivity series and hence, displace hydrogen from acids.

$$Zn + H_2SO_4 \longrightarrow ZnSO_4 + H_2\uparrow$$

$$Zn + 2HCl \longrightarrow ZnCl_2 + H_2\uparrow$$

  (iii) **Reaction with alkalies**

$$2Al + 2NaOH + 2H_2O \longrightarrow 2NaAlO_2 + 3H_2\uparrow$$

$$Zn + 2NaOH \longrightarrow Na_2ZnO_2 + H_2\uparrow$$

- **Laboratory preparation of hydrogen gas**
  Hydrogen is mainly prepared by treating zinc granules either with dilute sulphuric acid or with aqueous alkali (NaOH).
- **Industrial preparation of hydrogen gas** (Bosch process)
  The four steps involved in this process are

  (i) Production of water gas,

$$C(s) + H_2O(g) \xrightarrow{1000°C} \underbrace{CO + H_2}_{\text{Water gas}}\uparrow$$

  (ii) Reduction of steam to hydrogen

$$\underbrace{CO + H_2}_{\text{Water gas}} + H_2O(g) \xrightarrow[450°C]{Fe_2O_3/Cr_2O_3} CO_2(g) + 2H_2(g)$$

  (iii) Separation of CO_2 by passing through KOH

$$CO_2 + 2KOH \longrightarrow K_2CO_3 + H_2O$$

  (iv) Separation of carbon monoxide.

$$CuCl + CO + 2H_2O \longrightarrow \underset{\text{(Addition compound)}}{CuCl\cdot CO\cdot 2H_2O}$$

- **Uses of hydrogen gas** Hydrogen gas is used as/in
  (i) Haber's process
  (ii) hardening of oil
  (iii) reducing agent
  (iv) atomic hydrogen torch and oxy-hydrogen torch
  (v) rocket fuel in space research
- **Oxidation** It is defined as a chemical process which involves.
  (i) Addition of oxygen
  (ii) Addition of electronegative elements
  (iii) Removal of hydrogen
  (iv) Removal of electropositive elements
- **Reduction** It is defined as a chemical process which involves.
  (i) Addition of hydrogen
  (ii) Addition of electropositive element
  (iii) Removal of oxygen
  (iv) Removal of electronegative element
- **Redox reaction** Those reactions in which oxidation and reduction takes place simultaneously are called redox reactions.
- **Oxidising agents** are those substance that oxidises other substances either by accepting electrons or by providing oxygen or by removing hydrogen or an electropositive ion in a chemical process. They themselves gets reduced.
- **Reducing agents** Those substances that reduces other substances either by providing electrons, or by providing hydrogen or an electropositive ion, or by removing oxygen or an electronegative ion in a chemical process is known as reducing agents. They themselves gets oxidised.

Chapter Practice

Section-I

a. Multiple Choice Questions

1. Which of the following isotope(s) make heavy water?
   (a) ${}^{1}_{1}H$ (b) ${}^{1}_{2}H$
   (c) ${}^{3}_{1}H$ (d) Both (b) and (c)

Sol. (b)

2. Which of the following metal oxide would reduced by hydrogen?
   (a) MgO (b) Na_2O
   (c) CuO (d) CaO

Sol. (c)

3. Which of the following would displace hydrogen from acid?
   (a) Copper (b) Mercury
   (c) Platinum (d) None of these

Sol. (d)

4. Water upon reaction with sodium metal produce
   (a) acidic solution
   (b) basic solution
   (c) amphoteric solution
   (d) neutral solution

Sol. (b)

5. Zinc metal reacts with sulphuric acid
   (a) explosively (b) fast
   (c) slowly (d) does not react

Sol. (c)

6. Carbon dioxide in Bosch process is separated as
   (a) $CaCO_3$ (b) $NaHCO_3$
   (c) Na_2CO_3 (d) H_2CO_3

Sol. (d)

7. Hydrogen is collected through
   (a) air displacement method
   (b) water displacement method
   (c) Both (a) and (b)
   (d) Neither (a) nor (b)

Sol. (b)

8. Solubility of hydrogen in water is
   (a) very low
   (b) moderate
   (c) high
   (d) cannot be determined

Sol. (a)

9. Which of the statement about the reaction below is incorrect?
   $2PbO(s) + C(s) \longrightarrow 2Pb(s) + CO_2(g)$
   (a) Lead is getting reduced
   (b) Carbon is getting oxidised
   (c) Lead oxide is getting reduced
   (d) Cannot be predicted

Sol. (a)

10. A gas used with hydrogen for filling of balloons and airships.
    (a) Helium (b) Neon (c) Argon (d) Krypton

Sol. (a)

11. Hardening of vegetable oils use the ...... catalyst
    (a) zinc (b) aluminium
    (c) iron (d) nickel

Sol. (d)

12. The gas released when hydrogen gas is bubbled in molten sulphur is
    (a) sulphur dioxide (b) sulphur dioxide
    (c) hydrogen sulphide (d) None of these

Sol. (c)

13. Conc. H_2SO_4 reacts with hydrogen to release
    (a) hydrogen sulphide (b) sulphur trioxide
    (c) sulphur trioxide (d) None of these

Sol. (b)

14. Which of the following solution is used to remove arsine impurity from hydrogen gas?
    (a) Lead nitrate (b) Silver nitrate
    (c) Lead chloride (d) Silver chloride

Sol. (b)

15. Granulated zinc contains impurity of
    (a) lead (b) aluminium
    (c) sodium (d) copper

Sol. (d)

16. Reaction of which metal with water is violent and exothermic
    (a) copper (b) calcium
    (c) potassium (d) iron

Sol. (c)

17. A drying agent used to remove moisture
    (a) anhydrous calcium chloride
    (b) anhydrous copper sulphate
    (c) anhydrous magnesium chloride
    (d) anhydrous copper chloride

Sol. (a)

b. Fill in the Blanks

18. Hydrogen literally means .... producer. (acid, base, water)

Sol. water

19. Heavy water is made up of .... isotope of hydrogen. (protium, deuterium, tritium)

Sol. deuterium

20. Hydrogen is placed in same group as the .... (alkali, alkaline earth, noble gas) metals.

Sol. alkali

21. .... is the least reactive metal. (Potassium, Iron, Gold)

Sol. Gold

22. .... burns with a pop sound and is absorbed by metals like palladium. (Hydrogen, Ammonia, Carbon dioxide)

Sol. Hydrogen

23. Water gas is a mixture of .... and hydrogen. (carbon, carbon dioxide, carbon monoxide)

Sol. carbon monoxide

24. Hydrogen alongwith .... is used in flame for welding metals. (carbon, nitrogen, oxygen)

Sol. oxygen

25. Hydrogen in .... state alongwith oxygen is used as rocket fuel. (solid, liquid, gaseous)

Sol. liquid

26. Carbon dioxide present as impurity in hydrogen gas is removed using .... solution. (aqueous KOH, alkaline KOH)

Sol. aqueous KOH

d. Give One Word or a Phrase

27. A gas is formed when steam is passed over red hot coke.

Sol. Water gas ($CO + H_2$)

28. A compound formed, when zinc reacts with KOH.

Sol. Potassium zincate (K_2ZnO_2)

29. A gas is prepared by reacting active metal with water.

Sol. Hydrogen gas

30. A metal that react reversibly with steam.

Sol. Iron

31. A form of zinc contain copper as impurity.

Sol. Amalgamated zinc

32. A solution that absorbs hydrogen sulphide.

Sol. Lead nitrate

33. A solution by which arsine and phosphine can be removed.

Sol. Silver nitrate solution.

34. A method used to collect hydrogen.

Sol. Downward displacement of water.

35. Some unique metals that produce hydrogen by reacting with acids as well as alkalies.

Sol. Zinc, lead and aluminium.

36. Two metals that can reacts with very dilute nitric acids to produce hydrogen.

Sol. Magnesium and manganese.

d. Match the Columns

37. Match the following columns.

Column I (Properties)	Column II (Element)
A. An isotope of hydrogen	1. Aluminium
B. Less reactive metal than hydrogen	2. Potassium
C. Form amphoteric oxides	3. Tritium
D. Form alkali	4. Platinum

Sol. A → (3), B → (4), C → (1), D → (2)

38. Match the following columns.

Column I (Element)	Column II (Properties)
A. Aluminium	1. does not displace hydrogen
B. Copper	2. used in laboratory preparation of hydrogen
C. Potassium	3. form amphoteric oxide
D. Zinc	4. most reactive metal

Sol. A → (3), B → (1), C → (4), D → (2)

39. Match the following columns.

Column I (Properties)	Column II (Gases)
A. Rotten egg smell	1. NH_3
B. Greenish yellow gas	2. H_2S
C. Water gas	3. Cl_2
D. Haber's process	4. $CO + H_2$

Sol. A → (2), B → (3), C → (4), D → (1)

e. State One Relevant Reason

40. Potassium should not be used for preparation of hydrogen.

Sol. Potassium is not used for preparation of hydrogen because the reaction of water with potassium is explosive.

41. Hydrogen is lightest element, but it is not used in weather forecasting balloons.

Sol. Hydrogen is not used in weather forecasting balloons because of its inflammable nature.

42. When a mixture of hydrogen and chlorine is exposed to sunlight, the greenish yellow colour of chlorine disappears.

Sol. The greenish yellow colour of chlorine disappears because chlorine reacts with hydrogen to form hydrogen chloride, which is a colourless gas.

43. When hydrogen is bubbled through boiling sulphur, smell of rotten eggs is observed.

Sol. The smell of rotten eggs is observed, when hydrogen is bubbled through boiling sulphur because hydrogen combines with molten sulphur to form hydrogen sulphide gas which has peculiar rotten egg smell.

$$H_2(g) + S \xrightarrow{\text{High temperature}} \underset{\text{Hydrogen sulphide}}{H_2S}$$

44. Why the end of the thistle funnel should be dipped under acid during the preparation of H_2 gas ?

Sol. To prevent the hydrogen gas from escaping from the thistle funnel.

f. Balanced Chemical Equation

45. Water gas is mixed with excess steam and passed over heated ferric oxide.

Sol. $$\underbrace{CO + H_2}_{\text{Water gas}} + \underset{\text{Excess steam}}{H_2O} \xrightarrow[450°C]{\text{Heated } Fe_2O_3} \underset{\text{Carbon dioxide}}{CO_2} + \underset{\text{Hydrogen}}{2H_2} + \text{Heat}$$

46. Reaction of nitric acid with zinc.

Sol. $$\underset{\text{Zinc}}{3Zn} + \underset{\text{Nitric acid}}{8HNO_3} \longrightarrow \underset{\text{Zinc nitrate}}{3Zn(NO_3)_2} + 4H_2O + \underset{\text{Nitric oxide}}{2NO}\uparrow$$

47. Reaction of lead nitrate solution with hydrogen sulphide.

Sol. $$\underset{\text{Lead nitrate solution}}{Pb(NO_3)_2} + \underset{\text{Hydrogen sulphide}}{H_2S} \longrightarrow \underset{\text{Lead sulphide}}{PbS} + \underset{\text{Nitric acid}}{2HNO_3}$$

48. Reaction of nitrogen with hydrogen in the presence of iron and molybdenum catalyst.

Sol. $$N_2 + 3H_2 \underset{450°C\ /200\ \text{atm}}{\overset{Fe\ /Mo}{\rightleftharpoons}} 2NH_3$$

49. Reaction of calcium with water.

Sol. $$\underset{\text{Calcium}}{Ca} + \underset{\text{Cold water}}{2H_2O} \longrightarrow \underset{\text{Calcium hydroxide}}{Ca(OH)_2} + \underset{\text{Hydrogen}}{H_2}\uparrow$$

50. Reaction of magnesium with steam.

Sol. $$\underset{\text{Magnesium}}{Mg} + \underset{\text{Steam}}{H_2O} \longrightarrow \underset{\text{Magnesium oxide}}{MgO} + \underset{\text{Hydrogen}}{H_2}\uparrow$$

51. Reaction of aluminium with steam.

Sol. $$\underset{\text{Aluminium}}{2Al} + \underset{\text{Steam}}{3H_2O} \xrightarrow{800°C} \underset{\text{Aluminium oxide}}{Al_2O_3} + \underset{\text{Hydrogen}}{3H_2}\uparrow$$

52. Reaction of iron with steam.

Sol. $$\underset{\text{Iron}}{3Fe} + \underset{\text{Steam}}{4H_2O} \rightleftharpoons \underset{\text{Iron oxide (magnetite)}}{Fe_3O_4} + \underset{\text{Hydrogen}}{4H_2}\uparrow$$

Section-II

a. 2 Marks Questions

1. Define

(i) Redox reaction (ii) Isotopes

Sol. (i) A redox reaction can be defined as a chemical reaction in which oxidation and reduction takes place simultaneously. [1]

(ii) Isotopes are defined as an element with same atomic number (number of protons in their nuclei) but they differ in mass number (different number of nucleons). [1]

2. How can production of hydrogen from water gas be increased by using water gas shift reaction?

Sol. In order to remove CO and to increase the production of hydrogen from water gas, CO of the water gas is oxidised to CO_2 by mixing it with more steam at 673 K in the presence of iron chromate or ferric oxide and little chromium oxide (at 450°C) as catalyst. [1]

$$\underbrace{CO(g) + H_2(g)}_{\text{Water gas}} + \underset{\text{Steam}}{H_2O(g)} \xrightarrow[FeCrO_4 \text{ or } Fe_2O_3 + Cr_2O_3]{450°C} CO_2(g) + 2H_2(g)$$ [1]

3. How does the atomic hydrogen or oxy-hydrogen torch function for cutting and welding purposes? Explain.

Sol. Atomic hydrogen atoms, produced by dissociation of hydrogen with the help of an electric arc, are allowed to recombine on the surface to be welded. In this process, a large amount of energy is liberated, which is used to generate a temperature of 4000 K for cutting and welding purpose in the form of atomic hydrogen or oxy-hydrogen torches. [2]

4. Give an example each of oxidation and reduction reaction on the basis of electronegative and electropositive element.

Sol. Oxidation

$$Zn + 2HCl \longrightarrow ZnCl_2 + H_2$$

(addition of electronegative Cl element)

$$2KI + H_2O_2 \longrightarrow 2KOH + I_2$$

(removal of electropositive K element) [1]

Reduction

$$HgCl_2 + Hg \longrightarrow Hg_2Cl_2$$

(addition of electropositive Hg element)

$$2FeCl_3 + H_2S \longrightarrow 2FeCl_2 + 2HCl + S$$

(removal of electronegative Cl element) [1]

5. (i) Given an example of metal which is preferred for preparing hydrogen from (i) cold water and (ii) hot water.
(ii) Write the balance equation for each case.

Sol. (i) (a) Potassium (b) Magnesium [1]

(ii) • Potassium react with water to give potassium hydroxide and hydrogen (gas).

$$2K + 2H_2O \longrightarrow 2KOH + H_2\uparrow$$

• Magnesium reacts slowly with boiling water and forms a base, (magnesium hydroxide) liberating hydrogen gas.

$$Mg + 2H_2O \longrightarrow Mg(OH)_2 + H_2\uparrow$$ [1]

6. Identify the substance that are oxidised and the substances that are reduced in the following reactions.
(i) $4Na(s) + O_2(g) \longrightarrow 2Na_2O(s)$
(ii) $CuO(s) + H_2(g) \longrightarrow Cu(s) + H_2O(l)$

Sol. (i) $Na(s) + O_2(g) \longrightarrow 2Na_2O$

So, Na is oxidised and O_2 is reduced. [1]

(ii) $CuO(s) + H_2(g) \longrightarrow Cu(s) + H_2O(l)$

CuO has lost oxygen and forms Cu.

So, Cu is reduced while H_2 has gained oxygen hence, it is oxidised. [1]

b. 3 Marks Questions

7. Justify the position of hydrogen in the periodic table on the basis of its electronic configuration. Also write the isotope of hydrogen which has same number of protons and neutrons.

Sol. The electronic configuration of hydrogen can be compared as follows

(i) The electronic configuration of hydrogen is similar to the outer electronic configuration of alkali metals.

	K	L	M
Hydrogen (H) :	1		
Lithium (Li) :	2,	1	
Sodium (Na) :	2,	8,	1

It forms H^+ ion just like alkali metals. [1]

(ii) Like halogens, hydrogen requires only one electron to achieve the nearest inert or noble gas configuration. e.g.

H$\binom{K}{1}$ has one electron less than He$\binom{K}{2}$

F$\binom{K\,L}{2\,7}$ has one electron less than Ne$\binom{K\,L}{2\,8}$

Cl$\binom{K\,L\,M}{2\,8\,7}$ has one electron less than Ar$\binom{K\,L\,M}{2\,8\,8}$

As we can see hydrogen resembles with both the alkali metal group and the halogen group.

Their arises confusion about the placing of it in the periodic table. But considering its electronic configuration and fact that it has one valence electron like alkali metals, it has been placed in the group 1 of the periodic table.

The isotope of hydrogen that has same number of protons and neutrons is deuterium ^2_1D or ^2_1H. [2]

8. Why is it safe to store acid in a copper container but not to store in an iron container?

Sol. Iron lies above hydrogen in the activity series, hence, it displaces hydrogen from an acid when the acid is kept in an iron container.

$$\underset{\text{Iron}}{Fe} + \underset{\text{Sulphuric acid}}{H_2SO_4} \longrightarrow \underset{\text{Iron sulphate}}{FeSO_4} + \underset{\text{Hydrogen}}{H_2\uparrow}$$

In this process iron corrodes and hence, wall of container deplete. [1½]

On the other side, copper is less reactive than hydrogen, hence it cannot react with acid to displace hydrogen. And thus, the copper container remains harmless and can be used as container to store acid.

$$\underset{\text{Copper}}{Cu} + \underset{\text{Sulphuric acid}}{H_2SO_4} \longrightarrow \text{No reaction}$$ [1½]

9. How is hydrogen obtained from
(i) dilute sulphuric acid
(ii) sodium hydroxide
(iii) water?
Give one equation in each case.

Sol. (i) When metal reacts with dilute sulphuric acid, hydrogen is obtained along with metal salts.

$$\underset{\text{Magnesium}}{Mg(s)} + \underset{\text{Dil. sulphuric acid}}{H_2SO_4(aq)} \longrightarrow \underset{\text{Magnesium sulphate}}{MgSO_4(aq)} + H_2(g)\uparrow$$ [1]

(ii) When zinc reacts with sodium hydroxide, sodium zincate is formed and hydrogen gas is evolved.

$$\underset{\text{Zinc}}{Zn(s)} + \underset{\text{Sodium hydroxide}}{2NaOH(aq)} \longrightarrow \underset{\text{Sodium zincate}}{Na_2ZnO_2(aq)} + H_2(g)\uparrow$$ [1]

(iii) When acidified water is electrolysed using platinum electrodes, hydrogen gas is evolved at cathode.

$$\underset{\text{(Acidified water)}}{H_2O} \xrightarrow{\text{Electrolysis}} H^+(aq) + OH^-(aq)$$

At cathode, $2H^+ + 2e^- \longrightarrow 2H \longrightarrow H_2\uparrow$

At anode, $OH^-(aq) \longrightarrow OH + e^-$

$$4OH + 4e^- \longrightarrow 2H_2O + O_2\uparrow$$ [1]

10. (i) Describe the industrial applications of hydrogen dependent on the heat liberated when its atoms are made to combine on the surface of a metal.
(ii) Give the difference between oxidation and reduction with examples.

Sol. (i) Due to given property, hydrogen is used in atomic hydrogen torch for welding/cutting. [1]

(ii) Oxidation is defined as a chemical process which involves either the addition of oxygen to the substance or loss of hydrogen from the substance.

e.g. Oxidation ($H_2S \rightarrow S$)

(a) $$\underset{\text{Hydrogen sulphide}}{H_2S} + Cl_2 \longrightarrow \underset{\text{Hydrogen chloride}}{2HCl} + \underset{\text{Sulphur}}{S}$$

(b) $\underset{\text{Copper}}{2Cu} + \underset{\text{Oxygen}}{O_2} \longrightarrow \underset{\text{Copper oxide}}{2CuO}$ (Oxidation) [1]

Reduction is defined as a chemical process which involves either the addition of hydrogen to the substance or loss of oxygen from the substance.

e.g. $\underset{\text{Sodium}}{2\overset{0}{Na}} + \underset{\text{Hydrogen}}{H_2} \longrightarrow \underset{\text{Sodium hydride}}{2\overset{+1}{Na}H}$ (Reduction)

$\underset{\text{Zinc oxide}}{\overset{2+}{Zn}O} + \underset{\text{Hydrogen}}{H_2} \longrightarrow \underset{\text{Zinc}}{\overset{0}{Zn}} + \underset{\text{Water}}{H_2O}$ (Reduction) [1]

C. 4 Marks Questions

11. (i) (a) How would you prepare dihydrogen from water by using a reducing agent?

(b) How would you prepare dihydrogen from a substance other than water?

(ii) Write the names of isotopes of hydrogen. What is the mass ratio of these isotopes?

Sol. (i) (a) Sodium metal is a good reducing agent. It reduces water to hydrogen (or dihydrogen).

$\underset{\text{Water}}{2\overset{+1}{H_2}O} + \underset{\text{Sodium (Reducing agent)}}{2\overset{0}{Na}} \longrightarrow \underset{\text{Sodium hydroxide}}{2\overset{+1}{Na}OH} + \underset{\text{Hydrogen}}{\overset{0}{H_2}(g)}$ [1]

(b) Dihydrogen can be obtained by treating zinc with dilute HCl.

$\underset{\text{Zinc}}{Zn(s)} + \underset{\text{Hydrochloric acid}}{2HCl\,(aq)} \longrightarrow \underset{\text{Zinc chloride}}{ZnCl_2(aq)} + \underset{\text{Hydrogen}}{H_2(g)}$ [1]

(ii) Protium ${}^1_1H$, deuterium ${}^2_1H$ or D, tritium ${}^3_1H$ or T are the isotopes of hydrogen. The mass ratio of protium: deuterium : tritium = 1 : 2 : 3. [2]

12. (i) Complete the following reactions:

(a) $H_2(g) + Al_2O_3(s) \xrightarrow{\Delta}$

(b) $C(s) + H_2O(g) \xrightarrow{Ni,\ \Delta}$

(c) $Zn(s) + NaOH\,(aq) \xrightarrow{Heat}$

(ii) What do you understand by the term 'water gas'?

Sol. (i) (a) $\underset{\text{Hydrogen}}{3H_2(g)} + \underset{\text{Aluminium oxide}}{Al_2O_3\,(s)} \xrightarrow{\Delta} \underset{\text{Aluminium}}{2Al(s)} + \underset{\text{Water}}{3H_2O(l)}$ [1]

(b) $\underset{\text{Carbon}}{C(s)} + \underset{\text{Water}}{H_2O(g)} \xrightarrow{Ni,\ 1270\ K} \underbrace{CO\,(g) + H_2(g)}_{\text{Water gas}}$ [1]

(c) $\underset{\text{Zinc}}{Zn(s)} + \underset{\text{Sodium hydroxide}}{2NaOH(aq)} \xrightarrow{Heat} \underset{\text{Sodium zincate}}{Na_2ZnO_2(aq)} + H_2(g)$ [1]

(ii) **Water gas** Mixture of CO and H_2 is known as synthesis gas or water gas. Reaction of steam on hydrocarbons or coke at high temperatures in the presence of catalyst yields water gas.

e.g. $\underset{\text{Methane}}{CH_4(g)} + \underset{\text{Steam}}{H_2O(g)} \xrightarrow[Ni]{1270\ K} \underbrace{CO\,(g) + 3H_2(g)}_{\text{Water gas}}$ [1]

13. When a neutral gas *A* which burns with popping sound is passed through boiling yellow non-metal *B'* it forms gas *C*.

(i) Identify *A*, *B* and *C*.

(ii) Give balanced chemical equation for the reaction.

(iii) Give equation for the preparation of water gas.

(iv) Write a balanced chemical equations for the reaction of hydrogen with oxygen.

Sol. (i) *A* = Hydrogen *B* = Sulphur

C = Hydrogen sulphide [1]

(ii) $\underset{\text{'A'}}{H_2} + \underset{\text{Boiling yellow non-metal 'B'}}{S} \longrightarrow \underset{\text{Hydrogen sulphide 'C'}}{H_2S}$ [1]

(iii) $\underset{\text{Hot charcoal}}{C} + \underset{\text{Super heated steam}}{H_2O} \xrightarrow{170°\ C} \underbrace{CO + H_2}_{\text{Equivolume mixture of CO and H}_2\text{ (water gas)}}$ [1]

(iv) $\underset{\text{Hydrogen}}{2H_2} + \underset{\text{Oxygen}}{O_2} \longrightarrow \underset{\text{Water}}{2H_2O}$ [1]

14. Answer the following questions with regard to laboratory preparation of hydrogen.

(i) Name the reactant taken for the preparation of hydrogen in round bottom flask.

(ii) Which chemical is added through thistle funnel?

(iii) How is hydrogen collected?

(iv) Why is hydrogen collected by the above stated method ?

Sol. (i) Reactant used for the preparation of hydrogen in round bottom flask is granulated zinc. [1]

(ii) Concentrated sulphuric acid is added through thistle funnel. [1]

(iii) Hydrogen is collected by downward displacement of air. [1]

(iv) It is collected by above stated method because

(a) it is almost insoluble in water.

(a) it forms an explosive mixture with air. [1]

Chapter Assessment

Section-I

a. Multiple Choice Questions

1. The radioactive isotope of hydrogen has *l*... neutron(s) in the nucleus of its atom. Here, *l* refers to
(a) 1 (b) 2 (c) 3 (d) 0

2. Which of the following differs in terms of valency as that of hydrogen?
(a) Na (b) Mg (c) Cl (d) K

3. Which one of the following is least reactive?
(a) Zinc (b) Iron (c) Copper (d) Tin

4. Which of the following is not amphoteric?
(a) Mg (b) Pb (c) Al (d) Zn

5. Which of the following impurity is removed by $Pb(NO_3)_2$ solution?
(a) PH_3 (b) AsH_3 (c) SO_2 (d) H_2S

b. Fill in the Blanks

6. Both alkali metals and hydrogen act as .... (reducing agent, dehydrating agent, oxidising agent).

7. The reaction of calcium and water is .... (more, less, not) vigorous.

8. .... metal lies below hydrogen but above mercury in the activity series. (Copper, Gold, Sodium)

9. Main products of water gas shift reaction are .... and .... ($SO_2 + H_2$, $CO + H_2$, $CO_2 + SO_2$).

c. Match the Columns

10. Match the following columns.

Column I (Properties)	Column II (Description)
A. Amphoteric nature	1. Removal of electronegative atom or ion.
B. Lead nitrate solution	2. Oxides of zinc
C. Oxidation	3. Remove H_2S
D. Reduction	4. Addition of electronegative atom or ion.

d. Give One Word or a Phrase

11. An oxidising agent that does not contain oxygen.

12. A substance that oxidise concentrated HCl to chlorine.

13. A liquid that can act as an oxidising as well as reducing agent.

e. Balanced Chemical Equation

14. Reaction of manganese dioxide and hydrogen chloride.

15. Reaction of hydrogen sulphide with chlorine.

16. Reaction of sodium and hydrochloric acid.

f. State One Relevant Reason

17. Oxides and hydroxides of zinc are amphoteric in nature.

18. Concentrated sulphuric acid is not used in preparation of hydrogen gas.

19. H^+ ion is known as proton.

Section-II

a. 2 Marks Questions

1. Give two properties in which hydrogen neither resembles with alkali metals nor with halogens.

2. Give four uses of hydrogen gas.

b. 3 Marks Questions

3. How do active metals like sodium, potassium and calcium react with water? Explain your observations.

4. (i) Why zinc granules are preferred over pure zinc for the preparation of hydrogen in labs ?
(ii) Under what condition iron reacts with water.
(iii) Arrange the following metals in increasing order of their reactivity toward water : sodium, magnesium, zinc, calcium, iron.

c. 4 Marks Questions

5. Answer the following questions with respect to Bosch's process.
(i) Give the first step for the production of hydrogen.
(ii) How is water gas used to reduce steam?
(iii) How is carbon dioxide separated from the mixture of CO_2 and H_2?
(iv) How is carbon monoxide separated from the mixture ?

For explanations scan the given QR Code

Olympiad Section*

Brain Teasing Questions asked in Previous Olympiads

1. In which of the following respect, electronic configuration of hydrogen has resemblance to alkali metals and halogens respectively? **(NTSE)**
   (a) It lose one electron to form unipositive ion and gain one electron to form uninegative ion
   (b) It gain one electron to form uninegative ion and lose one electron to form unipositive ion
   (c) It has the ability only to gain one electron
   (d) None of the above

2. The number of proton and electron in atomic form of hydrogen respectively are **(INJSO)**
   (a) 2 and 1 (b) 1 and 2
   (c) 1 and 1 (d) 2 and 2

3. Hydrogen has three isotopes–protium (^1_1H), deuterium (^2_1H) and tritium (^3_1H). These isotopes differ from one another in respect of the presence of **(NTSE)**
   (a) neutrons (b) electrons
   (c) protons (d) neutrons and protons

4. How many neutrons are present in protium, deuterium and tritium respectively? **(INJSO)**
   (a) 1, 0 and 2 (b) 0, 2 and 1
   (c) 0, 1 and 2 (d) 2, 1 and 0

5. Which of the following isotopes of hydrogen is radioactive? **(NTSE)**
   (a) Protium (b) Deuterium
   (c) Tritium (d) *Ortho* and *para* hydrogens

6. Oxides are acidic, basic or amphoteric based on their metallic or non-metallic character. Which one of the following oxides reacts with both HCl and NaOH? **(INJSO)**
   (a) CaO (b) ZnO (c) SO_2 (d) CO_2

7. Helium is preferred over hydrogen for filling balloons because it is **(NTSE)**
   (a) lighter than air
   (b) almost as light as hydrogen
   (c) non-combustible
   (d) inflammable

8. An active metal on reaction with water produces **(INJSO)**
   (a) oxygen
   (b) nitric acid
   (c) a base
   (d) None of the above

9. Choose the incorrect statements about hydrogen. **(NTSE)**
   (a) It is an inflammable gas.
   (b) It is the lightest gas.
   (c) It is not easily liquefied.
   (d) It is a strong oxidising agent.

10. For the reation $PbO + H_2 \longrightarrow Pb + H_2O$, which of the following statements is wrong? **(INJSO)**
    (a) H_2 is the reducing agent.
    (b) PbO is the oxidising agent.
    (c) PbO is oxidised to Pb
    (d) H_2 is oxidised to H_2O

11. Which metal gives hydrogen with all of the following : water, acids, alkalies? **(NTSE)**
    (a) Fe (b) Zn
    (c) Mg (d) Pb

12. Which of the following metals does not give hydrogen with acids? **(INJSO)**
    (a) Iron
    (b) Copper
    (c) Magnesium
    (d) Zinc

Answers

1. (a) **2.** (c) **3.** (a) **4.** (c) **5.** (c) **6.** (b) **7.** (c) **8.** (c) **9.** (d) **10.** (c)
11. (b) **12.** (b)

* *These questions may or may not be asked in the examination, have been given just for additional practice required for olympiads Scholarship Exams etc. For detailed explanations refer Page No. 135.*

CHAPTER 07

Study of Gas Laws

CHAPTER OUTLINES

- Gaseous State
- Molecular Motion : Relationship with Temperature, Pressure and Volume
- Standard Temperature and Pressure (STP)
- Gas Laws
- Absolute Zero
- Ideal Gas

Matter generally exists in solid, liquid and gaseous states. In these states, the chemical composition and chemical properties of a substance remains the same but their rate to undergo a chemical reaction is different.

Gaseous State

It is the simplest state of matter. Only eleven elements, out of the total 118 elements known until today which exist in gaseous state under normal conditions of temperature and pressure. These eleven elements are H, He, N, O, F, Ne, Cl, Ar, Kr, Xe and Rn.

The state of matter is decided by the net effect of intermolecular forces, (i.e. forces present in between the particles), molecular interactions and thermal energy. These are the characteristic parameters which constitute the concept of kinetic molecular theory of gases.

Kinetic Molecular Theory of Gases

The molecular details about the gases can be visualised with the help of a theory, called the kinetic molecular theory of gases. This theory provides a microscopic model of gases to explain their behaviour.

The main assumptions of this theory are as follows

(i) **Composition of gases** Gases are aggregation of large number of identical tiny particles (i.e. atoms or molecules), which are so far apart that their combined volume is almost negligible as compared to empty space present between them.

(ii) **Gases are highly expandable** The intermolecular forces of attraction between the particles of a gas at ordinary temperature and pressure are negligible. That's why, gases expand and occupy all the available space.

(iii) **Gases neither have definite shape nor a fixed volume** Particles of the gases are always in a state of constant and random motion. That's why, shape and volume of gases are not definite or fixed.

(iv) **Gases exert same pressure in all directions** The particles of the gas move in all possible directions in straight lines, collide with each other and also with the walls of the container. Thus, they exert same pressure on the walls of the container.

(v) **Gases are highly compressible** There are large intermolecular (interparticle) spaces between gas molecules. On applying the pressure, the intermolecular space between the molecules is very much decreased. Thus, the gases are highly compressible.

(vi) **Gases have low density** Gases have large intermolecular space between their molecules, so that the number of molecules per unit volume in a gas is very small. Thus, gases have very low density.

(vii) **Gases show diffusion** Diffusion is the process in which gradual mixing of two substances occurs. When two gases are brought in contact with each other, their molecules move into intermolecular space of each other forming homogeneous mixture.

(viii) **Gases can be liquefied** Upon cooling and applying pressure on a cooled gas, the intermolecular space gets reduced and there is an increase in the molecules per unit volume. Thus, the gas liquefies.

(ix) **Average K.E. of gases depends upon absolute temperature** Because of their different speeds, the kinetic energy of gas particles is called the average kinetic energy (E). It is directly proportional to the absolute temperature (T).

Measurable Properties of Gases

The physical behaviour of gases can be explained on the basis of four measurable variables called standard variables. These variables are as follows

1. Mass

Gases have definite masses. It can be expressed in grams or moles.

$$\text{Number of moles of a gas} = \frac{\text{Mass of the gas in grams}}{\text{Molecular mass of the gas}}$$

2. Volume

It is measurable space occupied by a gas. The space occupied by a gas is equal to volume of its container.

It can be expressed in mL or cc and dm^3 or L.

1 L = 1000 cc = 1000 mL

1 mL (millilitre) = $1 cm^3$ or cc (cubic centimetre)

1 L or 1 (litre) = $1 dm^3$ (cubic decimetre)

3. Temperature

It is defined as the degree of hotness or coldness. Several scales are used to measure temperature. Common three scales are °C (degree Celsius), K (Kelvin) and °F (degree Fahrenheit).

Kelvin (K) = °C + 273

4. Pressure

Force exerted by the gas per unit area on the walls of container is called pressure. It can be expressed in mm of Hg, cm of Hg, atmosphere or kPa.

1 atmosphere (atm) = 76 cm of Hg
= 760 mm of Hg
= 760 torr of Hg
= 101.325 kPa

Molecular Motion : Relationship with Temperature, Pressure and Volume

According to the kinetic molecular theory of gases, molecules of gases are in constant random motion and thus, they possess kinetic energy.

The effect of temperature, pressure and volume on this molecular motion is as follows

1. Temperature

The average kinetic energy of a particle (molecule) is directly proportional to the absolute temperature. In other words, molecular motion of a particle increases with increase in temperature and decreases with decrease in temperature.

The temperature at which the molecular motion completely ceases (theoretically), on Kelvin scale, is called absolute zero.

2. Pressure

A gas enclosed in a vessel, exerts uniform pressure on the walls of the vessel. This is because inside the vessel large number of particles of gas collide with the walls and hence an appreciable force act on the walls. The force exerted on a unit area of the wall of the vessel is equal to the pressure of the gas, i.e.

Pressure = Force per unit area

3. Volume

On increasing the temperature of a gas, the force exerted on the walls of the vessel also increases, which causes the increase in the pressure exerted by the gas. If one of the walls of the vessel is flexible, then the gas expands, which also causes increase in volume with the increase in molecular motion.

Standard Temperature and Pressure (STP)

Changes in volume of a gas takes place with respect to change in the temperature and pressure. Thus, it becomes necessary to choose standard values of temperature and pressure. The abbreviation of standard temperature and standard pressure is STP, whereas for normal temperature and normal pressure, it is NTP.

Standard or normal temperature = 0°C = 273 K

Standard or normal pressure = 760 mm of Hg
= 76 cm of Hg = 1 atm

Any change in pressure or temperature is likely to change the volume of a gas. Thus, while expressing the specific volume of a gas, it is necessary to specify both, its pressure and its temperature.

Note By increasing the pressure on an enclosed gas, its volume decreases, whereas by increasing the temperature, its volume increases. Thus, by keeping equilibrium between an increase in pressure and an increase in temperature, it is possible to keep the volume constant.

Significance

For comparing the masses or densities of the gases, their temperatures and pressures are taken at STP or NTP. This is because the volume of a given mass of a gas depends upon pressure as well as temperature.

At STP, one mole of any gas occupies 22.4 L (22400 mL) of volume. This is called molar volume of a gas at STP.

Check Your LEARNING...

1. Out of 118 elements known how many elements are found is gaseous state under normal conditions of temperature and pressure?
2. What are the measurable properties of gases?
3. How is molecular motion related with pressure?
4. What happens to volume, if one of the walls of container is flexible and temperature in on increase?
5. What is the molar volume of a gas at STP condition?

Gas Laws

Gas laws are actually the relationships between measurable properties of gases. These relationships are of great importance as they describe the state of the gas and give quantitative relationships between any two variables when others are kept constant.

Boyle's Law

(Pressure-Volume Relationship)

This law was given by Robert Boyle in 1662 which states that at constant temperature, the pressure of a fixed amount (i.e. number of moles, n) of a gas varies inversely with its volume.

Mathematical Expression of Boyle's Law

Suppose a gas occupies volume V at temperature T and pressure p, then

$$p \propto 1/V \quad \text{or} \quad p = k_1\ (1/V)$$

Here, k_1 = proportionality constant, value of which depends upon the amount of the gas, temperature of the gas and units of pressure and volume.

Another form of the expression is $pV = k_1$.

Thus, the law can also be given as, at **constant temperature, the product of pressure and volume of a fixed amount of a gas is constant**. Let V_1 be the volume of a given mass of gas at pressure p_1 and at a given temperature T.

When the pressure is changed to p_2 at the same temperature, let the volume becomes V_2. According to Boyle's law,

$$p_1V_1 = k \quad \text{...(i)}$$

$$p_2V_2 = k \quad \text{...(ii)}$$

From Eqs. (i) and (ii), we get,

$$p_1V_1 = p_2V_2 = \text{constant (at constant temperature)}$$

or

$$\frac{p_1}{p_2} = \frac{V_2}{V_1}$$

Graphical Representation of Boyle's Law

Following are the conventional ways to show Boyle's law graphically.

1. Pressure (p) *versus* Volume (V) Graph

When volume of a given mass of a gas is plotted against pressure at different constant temperatures, the equilateral hyperbola is obtained for each temperature as shown in figure.

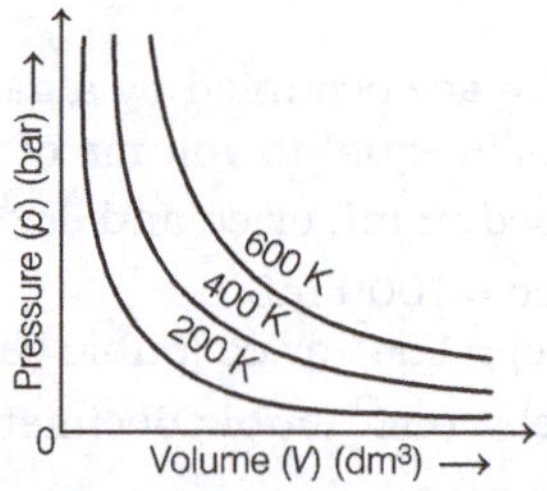

Graph of pressure, p *versus* volume, V of a gas at different constant temperatures

Note The term isotherm (meaning at constant temperature) is used to describe such graphs.

2. Pressure (p) *versus* (1/V) Volume Graph

On plotting the reciprocal of volumes of a fixed mass of a gas against pressure, we get straight line passing through the origin as shown in figure.

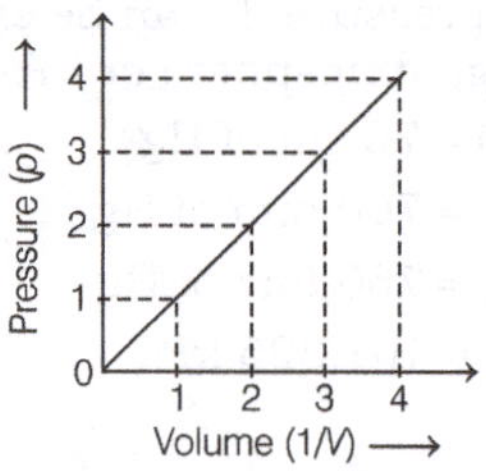

Graph of pressure p *versus* 1/V at constant temperature

3. Pressure Volume (pV) *versus* p Graph

When the product of pressure and volume (i.e. pV) is plotted against pressure, at different fixed temperatures, the straight line parallel to pressure axis (X-axis) is obtained as shown in figure.

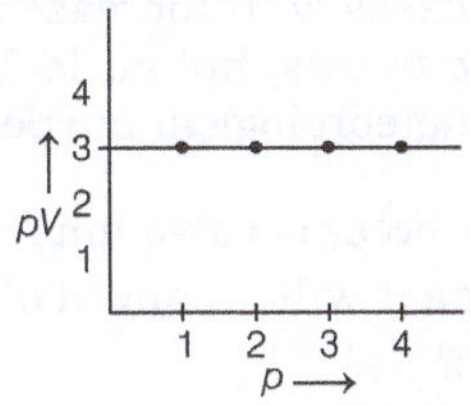

Graph of pV *versus* p at constant temperature

Explanation of Boyle's Law Based upon Kinetic Molecular Theory of Gases

According to the kinetic theory of gases, number of particles (molecules) present in a given mass and the average kinetic energy possessed by the particles is constant.

It has been observed that, if the volume of gas is reduced to one-half at constant temperature, the number of molecules striking per unit area of the walls of the vessel become doubled, thus, pressure is doubled, i.e. it becomes $2p$.

The reverse process also happens when volume is doubled. Hence, it is seen that if pressure increases, the volume of a given mass of gas decreases at constant temperature (Boyle's law).

Significance of Boyle's Law

It correlates pressure and volume and thus, proves that the gases are compressible. As we know,

$$\text{Pressure} \propto \frac{1}{\text{Volume}}$$

On increasing pressure, volume decreases. The gas becomes denser. Thus, at constant temperature the density of a gas is directly proportional to its pressure.

Density $\propto$ Pressure (at constant temperature)

At high altitudes, the atmospheric pressure is low thus, air is less denser. This result in less availability of oxygen for breathing. Therefore, a mountaineer has to carry oxygen cylinders with them.

Example 1. A gas occupies 1500 cm^3 at pressure of 720 mm of Hg. Find the pressure at which its volume will be 1000 cm^3. Assume that temperature remains constant.

Sol. Initial pressure, p_1 = 720 mm of Hg

Initial volume, V_1 = 1500 cm^3

Final volume, V_2 = 1000 cm^3

Final pressure, p_2 = ?

According to Boyle's law, $p_1V_1 = p_2V_2$

$$720 \times 1500 = p_2 \times 1000$$

$$\Rightarrow \quad p_2 = \frac{720 \times 1500}{1000} = 1080 \text{ mm of Hg}$$

Example 2. A gas occupies a volume of 250 mL at 745 mm Hg and 25°C. What additional pressure is required to reduce the gas volume to 200 mL at the same temperature?

Sol. Given, initial volume, V_1 = 250 mL

Initial pressure, p_1 = 745 mm Hg

Final volume, V_2 = 200 mL

Final pressure, p_2 = ?

Additional pressure p = ?

$$\therefore \quad p_1V_1 = p_2V_2$$

$$745 \text{ mm Hg} \times 250 \text{ mL} = p_2 \times 200 \text{ mL}$$

$$p_2 = \frac{745 \text{ mm Hg} \times 250 \text{ mL}}{200 \text{ mL}} = 931.25 \text{ mm Hg}$$

Additional pressure $= p_2 - p_1$

$= 931.25 - 745 = 186.25$ mm Hg

Note Always write the units along with the value in calculations as the remaining units help us to find out the correctness of our results.

Charles' Law

(Temperature-Volume Relationship)

Jacques charles observed that at a fixed pressure, the volume of a given mass of a gas increases or decreases by 1/273 of its volume at 0°C for each one degree rise or fall in temperature, respectively.

Mathematical Expression of Charles' Law

If at 0°C, the volume of a gas is V_0 and at t°C, it becomes V_t, then according to Charles' law.

$$V_t = V_0\left[1 + \frac{t}{273}\right] \quad \text{(at constant } p\text{)}$$

or

$$V_t = V_0\left(\frac{273 + t}{273}\right) \quad \ldots\text{(i)}$$

At this condition, a new scale of temperature called the Kelvin temperature scale or absolute temperature scale or thermodynamic scale is used.

On this scale, $273 + t = T$.

Thus, if temperature is 0°C, then T_0 = 273 K or we can say that, 0°C on the Celsius scale is equal to 273 K at the Kelvin scale.

If temperature on the Celsius scale is t°C, then

$$T = 273 + t°\text{C} = T_t \text{ (K)}$$

On replacing $273 + t$ and 273 in the equation (i) by T_t and T_0, respectively, we get

$$V_t = V_0\left(\frac{T_t}{T_0}\right) \quad \text{or} \quad \frac{V_t}{V_0} = \frac{T_t}{T_0}$$

Thus, the general form of the equation can be written as,

$$\frac{V_2}{V_1} = \frac{T_2}{T_1} \text{ or } \frac{V_1}{T_1} = \frac{V_2}{T_2} \text{ or } \frac{V}{T} = \text{constant} = k_2$$

Thus, $$V = k_2 T \quad \text{...(ii)}$$

Here, k_2 is a constant, value of which depends upon the pressure of the gas, its amount and the units in which volume V is expressed. Eq. (ii) is the mathematical expression for **Charles' law**, according to which **at a constant pressure, the volume of a given mass of a gas is directly proportional to its absolute temperature.** At very low pressure and high temperature, this law is obeyed by all gases. According to this equation,

- if the temperature is doubled, the volume would be doubled.
- if it is reduced by half, the volume would be reduced by half.

Graphical Representation of Charles' Law

The plot of volume *vs* temperature at constant pressure are called **isobars** or **isoplestics**. When volume of fixed mass of a gas is plotted with temperature at different constant pressures, we get straight line in each case.

$$p_1 < p_2 < p_3 < p_4$$

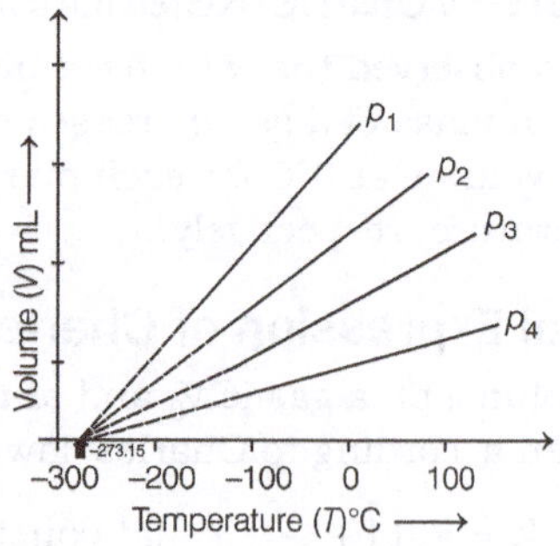

Graph of volume (*V*) *versus* temperature (*T*) at different constant pressure

Explanation of Charles' Law Based upon Kinetic Molecular Theory of Gases

As, average kinetic energy ∝ temperature

When the temperature of a gas is increased at constant pressure, the molecules will move with higher velocities and hence, with greater momentum and so volume must increase in order to keep pressure constant.

Hence, at constant pressure, volume of a given mass of a gas is directly proportional to its temperature (Charles' law).

Significance of Charles' Law

As we know that,

volume of given mass of gas ∝ temperature

Hence, $$\text{Density} \propto \frac{1}{\text{Temperature}}$$

Thus, density decreases with increase in temperature and *vice-versa*. Due to this, hot air is filled into balloons used for meteorological purposes.

Example 3. A gas occupies a volume of 120 cm^3 at 27.3 K. What volume it will occupy at 0°C; pressure remaining constant?

Sol. Given, initial volume, $V_1 = 120 \text{cm}^3$

Initial temperature, $T_1 = 27.3$ K

Final volume, $V_2 = ?$

Final temperature, $T_2 = 0°\text{C} = 273\text{K}$

By Charles' law, $\frac{V_1}{T_1} = \frac{V_2}{T_2} \Rightarrow \frac{120}{27.3} = \frac{V_2}{273}$

$$\Rightarrow \quad V_2 = \frac{120 \times 273}{27.3} = 1200 \text{ cm}^3$$

Example 4. At what temperature in centigrade will the volume of a gas at 0°C double itself with pressure remains constant?

Sol. Let the volume of the gas at $0°\text{C} = V$ mL

Thus, we have $V_1 = V$ mL, $V_2 = 2V$ mL

$T_1 = 0 + 273 = 273$ K, $T_2 = ?$

By Charles' law, $\frac{V_1}{V_2} = \frac{T_1}{T_2} \Rightarrow \frac{V_1}{T_1} = \frac{V_2}{T_2}$

On substituting the corresponding values, we get

$$\frac{V}{273} = \frac{2V}{T_2} \Rightarrow T_2 = \frac{2V \times 273}{V} = 546 \text{ K}$$

$$\therefore \quad T_2 = 546 - 273 = 273°\text{C}$$

Absolute Zero

The temperature at which all molecular motions ceases in a gas is called absolute zero. It is a hypothetical concept. It is also known as zero Kelvin. It is equal to –273.15° C. It is the lowest temperature at which the gases are supposed to occupy zero volume.

Note Temperature below –273.15°C is not possible because it corresponds to negative volume which is meaningless.

We know that, $V = V_0\left(\frac{273 + t}{273}\right)$

Volume at $-273°\text{C} = V_0\left(\frac{273 - 273}{273}\right) = 0$

Thus, it can be concluded that the volume of a gas would be reduced to zero at – 273° C.

According to Lord Kelvin, if the temperature of an enclosed gas at 0°C is lowered to – 273° C, its volume becomes zero.

However, this is not possible, because gas is one of the states of matter and hence, must have some definite mass and volume.

Absolute Zero Kelvin Scale of Temperature

With –273° C as its zero, a new scale of temperature has been built up, which is called Kelvin scale or absolute scale of temperature.

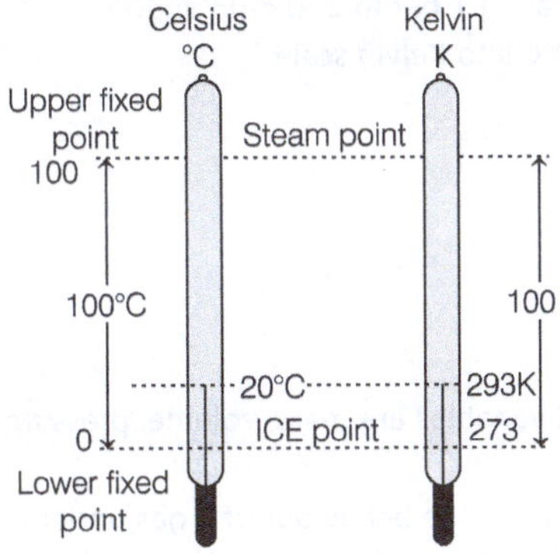

Celsius and Kelvin thermometers

Important Facts of Kelvin Scale of Temperature

- It starts with –273° C as its zero.
- All temperatures on Kelvin scale are positive.
- The magnitude of each degree on Kelvin scale is same as on centrigrade scale.
- No degree sign is written for absolute temperature values.
- The unit size of the temperature on Kelvin scale (i.e. 1 K) is equal to the unit size on celsius scale (i.e. 1°C).

  ∴ 1 K = 1°C

Conversion of Temperature from Celsius Scale to Kelvin Scale and *Vice-Versa*

- The value of temperature present on the Celsius scale can be converted to Kelvin scale by adding 273 to it. e.g. 25°C = 25 + 273 = 298 K.
- The value of temperature present on the Kelvin scale can be converted to Celsius scale by subtracting 273 from it.

  e.g. 25 K = 25 – 273 = –248°C

Example 5. Convert the following.

(a) 37 K to °C (b) 27°C to K

(c) –27°C to K (d) 0°C to K

Sol. (a) 37 K = 37 – 273 = –236° C

(b) 27°C = 27 + 273 = 300 K

(c) –27° C = –27 + 273 = 246K

(d) 0°C = 0 + 273 = 273 K

Ideal Gas

A gas which follows Boyle's law and Charles' law in all conditions of temperatures and pressures is called an **ideal gas**. In actual practice, such gas is only hypothetical.

Ideal Gas Equation

On combining Boyle's law and Charles' law, we get a single equation, which is called **ideal gas equation**. This equation gives the simultaneous effect of pressure and temperature on the volume of a gas.

Mathematical Expression of Ideal Gas Equation

At constant T and n; $V \propto 1/p$ (Boyle's law)

At constant p and n; $V \propto T$ (Charles' law)

On combining the above two relations, we get

$$V \propto (T/p) \text{ or } V = R(T/p)$$

(here, R = proportionality constant or gas constant whose value in SI unit is 8.314 $JK^{-1}mol^{-1}$).

On rearranging the above equation, we get

$$pV = RT$$

This equation is called **ideal gas equation** and is applicable for all gases that behave ideally with n number of moles it is written as $pV = nRT$. It describes the state of any gas, so it is also called **equation of state**. In this equation, if we know any three variable then we can calculate the value of remaining fourth variable.

Let the volume of a certain mass of a gas changes from V_1 to V_2 when the pressure is changed from p_1 to p_2 and temperature from T_1 to T_2.

Then, for initial condition, ideal gas equation is

$$p_1V_1 = RT_1 \text{ or } (p_1V_1/T_1) = R \quad \text{...(i)}$$

For final condition, ideal gas equation is

$$p_2V_2 = RT_2 \text{ or } p_2V_2/T_2 = R \quad \text{...(ii)}$$

From Eqs. (i) and (ii), we get

$$\boxed{p_1V_1/T_1 = p_2V_2/T_2}$$

This equation is called **combined gas law.** In this relation, if out of six, the values of five variables are known, the value of remaining variable can be calculated.

Example 6. At 25°C and 760 mm of Hg pressure, a gas occupies 600 mL volume. What will be its pressure at a height where temperature is 10°C and volume of the gas is 640 mL?

Sol. Given, $p_1 = 760\,\text{mm Hg}, V_1 = 600\,\text{mL}, T_1 = 25 + 273 = 298\,\text{K}$

$$V_2 = 640\,\text{mL} \text{ and } T_2 = 10 + 273 = 283\text{ K}$$

According to combined gas law,

$$\frac{p_1V_1}{T_1} = \frac{p_2V_2}{T_2} \Rightarrow p_2 = \frac{p_1V_1T_2}{T_1V_2}$$

On substituting the corresponding values, we get

$$p_2 = \frac{(760\text{ mm Hg}) \times (600\text{ mL}) \times (283\text{ K})}{(640\text{ mL}) \times (298\text{ K})} = 676.6\,\text{mm Hg}$$

Check Your LEARNING...

1 What type of graph is obtain when pressure is plotted against volume at constant temperature?

2 In terms of Charles' law, explain why – 273°C is considered as which temperature?

3 How is the pressure of a gas related to its density at a particular temperature?

4 What will be the minimum pressure required to compress 500 dm^3 of air at 1 bar to 200 dm^3 at 30°C?

5 Convert −38°C into Kelvin scale.

QUiCK Revision

- Matter generally exists in solid, liquid and gaseous states.
- The states of matter is decided by intermolecular forces and thermal energy.
- The molecular details about the gases can be visualised with the help of kinetic molecular theory of gases, which states that gases
  - (i) are highly expandible.
  - (ii) don't have definite shape.
  - (iii) exert same pressure in all directions.
  - (iv) are highly compressible.
  - (v) have low density.
  - (vi) show diffusion.
  - (vii) can be liquefied.
- The average K.E. of gases depend upon absolute temperature.
- The physical behaviour of gases can be explained on the basis of four measurable variables called standard variables.
- The standard variables are mass, volume, pressure and temperature.
- **Gas laws** describe the behaviour of a gas under the conditions of pressure, volume and temperature.
  - (i) **Boyle's law** $p \propto (1/V)$ (at constant T and n)
  - (ii) **Charles' law** $V \propto T$ (at constant p and n)
- **Ideal gas equation**

$$pV = nRT$$

  where, p = pressure, V = volume, R = gas constant, n = no. of moles, T = temperature.
- At standard temperature and pressure (STP), i.e. at 273K (0°C) and 1 atm (76 cm of Hg) of pressure, one mole of any gas occupies 22.4 L of volume.
- Absolute zero is the lowest hypothetical temperature at which the gases are supposed to occupy zero volume.

Chapter Practice

Section I

a. Multiple Choice Questions

1. The theory that attempts to elucidate the behaviour of gases is known as ...... of gases.
(a) valence bond theory
(b) kinetic molecular theory
(c) Both (a) and (b)
(d) None of the above

Sol. (b)

2. Gases expand and occupy all the space available to them. Which of the following assumption explain this behaviour correctly?
(a) There is no force of attraction between gas molecules
(b) Gas molecules are considered as negligible masses
(c) Collisions of the gas molecules are perfectly elastic
(d) All of the above

Sol. (a)

3. On applying the pressure, the intermolecular spaces can be reduced. This assumption explains the
(a) fixed volume of gases
(b) partial pressure exerted by the gases
(c) compressibility of gases
(d) All of the above

Sol. (c)

4. The pressure exerted by the gas is due to
(a) the repulsion between gas molecules
(b) the attraction between gas molecules
(c) collision of the particles with the wall of the container
(d) Both (a) and (b)

Sol. (c)

5. In kinetic molecular theory, it is assumed that average kinetic energy of the gas molecules is directly proportional to the ...*A*... . Here, *A* refers to
(a) absolute pressure (b) absolute volume
(c) absolute temperature (d) None of these

Sol. (c)

6. 6 atmosphere = ...*X*... torr of Hg. Here, *X* is
(a) 5760 (b) 3876
(c) 2769 (d) 4560

Sol. (d) 1 atmosphere = 760 torr of Hg
So, 6 atmosphere = 6×760
= 4560 torr of Hg

7. The first reliable measurement on the properties of gases was made by ....
(a) Dalton
(b) Robert Brown
(c) Robert Boyle
(d) Jacques Charles'

Sol. (c)

8. Which of the expression represent the Boyle's law?
(a) $p \propto \frac{1}{V}$ (at constant T and n)
(b) $p \propto \frac{1}{T}$ (at constant V and n)
(c) $p \propto V$ (at constant T and n)
(d) All of the above

Sol. (a)

9. "At constant temperature, the pressure of a fixed amount of gas varies inversely with its volume". This law is known as ... *A*... . Here, *A* refers to
(a) Charles' law
(b) Boyle's law
(c) Newton's law
(d) Dalton's law

Sol. (b)

10. Boyle's law is valid for
(i) $pV = \text{constant}$ (ii) $\frac{p_1}{V_2} = \frac{p_2}{V_1}$

(iii) 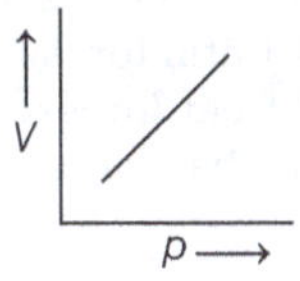

Which of the following is the correct option?
(a) (i) and (iii) (b) (i) and (ii)
(c) (ii) and (iii) (d) (i), (ii) and (iii)

Sol. (b)

11. Volume-temperature relationship is given by
(a) Gay-Lussac's law
(b) Boyle's law
(c) Charles' law
(d) Dalton's law

Sol. (c)

12. The graph of pV *vs* p for a gas is
(a) straight line passing through origin
(b) straight line parallel to *X*-axis
(c) hyperbolic
(d) parabolic

Sol. (b)

13. When the temperature is raised through 1°C, the volume is increased by $\frac{1}{273}$ th times of the original volume. This is

(a) Boyle's law (b) Charles' law
(c) Avogadro's law (d) Graham's law

Sol. (b)

14. Charles' law is represented mathematically as

(a) $pV = \text{constant}$ (b) $V_t = V_0\left(1 + \frac{273}{t}\right)$
(c) $V_t = V_0\left(1 + \frac{t}{273}\right)$ (d) $\frac{V_t}{V_0} = \frac{T_0}{T_t}$

Sol. (c)

15. If the pressure is doubled for a fixed mass of a gas, its volume will become

(a) 2 times (b) $\frac{1}{2}$ times
(c) 4 times (d) No change

Sol. (b) $\because p \propto \frac{1}{V}$ so if p doubles then V will become half.

16. Point out the correct relationship regarding ideal gas law

(a) $\frac{pV}{T} = \text{constant}$ (b) $\frac{p_1V_1}{T_1} = \frac{p_2V_2}{T_2}$
(c) Both (a) and (b) (d) None of these

Sol. (c)

17. The STP (standard temperature and pressure) condition stands for

(a) 273°C (temperature) and 1 atm (pressure)
(b) 273 K (temperature) and 1 atm (pressure)
(c) 273 K (temperature) and 1 bar (pressure)
(d) 273°C (temperature) and 1 bar (pressure)

Sol. (b)

18. What will be the minimum pressure required to compress 2 L of gas at 1 bar to 1 L at 25°C ?

(a) 1 bar (b) 2 bar
(c) 4 bar (d) 6 bar

Sol. (b)

19. Which of the following options represent an ideal gas equation?

(a) $pV = RT$ (b) $p = VRT$
(c) $pRT = V$ (d) $pVT = R$

Sol. (a)

20. An ideal gas equation is also called the ...*I*... . Here, *I* refers to

(a) equation of state
(b) equation of variable
(c) equation of parabola
(d) either (a), (b) or (c)

Sol. (a)

21. On the basis of theoretical concept, the temperature at which the molecular motion completely stop is

(a) 273°C (b) absolute zero
(c) 273 K (d) – 173 K

Sol. (b)

22. The Kelvin temperature scale is also known as

(i) absolute temperature scale
(ii) thermodynamic scale

Choose the correct option.

(a) Only (i)
(b) Only (ii)
(c) Both (i) and (ii)
(d) Neither (i) nor (ii)

Sol. (c)

b. Fill in the Blanks

23. The average kinetic energy of the molecules of a gas is directly proportional to the .... (absolute pressure, absolute temperature, volume).

Sol. absolute temperature

24. The force exerted on a unit area of the wall of the vessel is equal to the .... (temperature, volume, pressure) of the gas.

Sol. pressure

25. The SI unit of pressure is .... (Pascal, Newton, Dyne).

Sol. Pascal

26. If the temperature is reduced to half, the volume would also reduce to .... (double, constant, half).

Sol. half

27. If the pressure is doubled, the volume would be .... (half, constant, doubled).

Sol. half

28. The different molecules possess different velocities and hence different .... (energies, moles, volumes).

Sol. energies

29. The melting point of ice is .... (0 K, 100 K, 273 K).

Sol. 273 K

30. Standard temperature is .... (0°C, 100°C, 4°C).

Sol. 0°C

31. Kelvin zero is equal to .... (0°C, – 100° C, – 273° C).

Sol. –273°C

32. All temperature on Kelvin scale are .... (negative, positive, integer).

Sol. positive

33. The magnitude of each degree on Kelvin scale is same as on ...... (Fahrenheit, Centigrade, STP) scale.

Sol. Centigrade

34. The temperature on the Kelvin scale at which molecular motion completely stop is called .... (Charles' law, Boyle's law, absolute zero).

Sol. absolute zero

c. Match the Columns

35. Match the following columns.

Column I	Column II
A. Boyle's law	1. $-273°$ C
B. Charles' law	2. $\frac{V_1}{T_1} = \frac{V_2}{T_2}$
C. Ideal gas equation	3. $p_1V_1 = p_2V_2$
D. Absolute zero	4. $\frac{p_1V_1}{T_1} = \frac{p_2V_2}{T_2}$

Sol. A → (3), B → (2), C → (4), D → (1)

36. Match the following columns.

Column I (Graphical representation)	Column II (*X* and *Y* coordinates)
A. 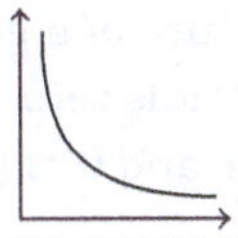	1. pV *vs* V
B. 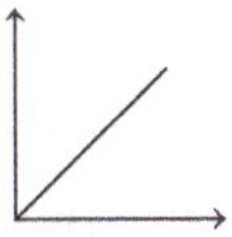	2. p *vs* V
C. 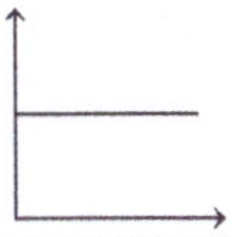	3. p *vs* $\frac{1}{V}$
D. 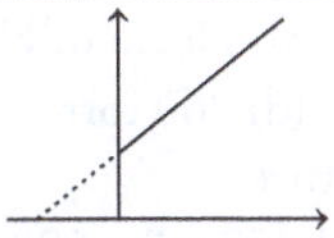	4. V *vs* T

Sol. A → (2), B → (3), C → (1), D → (4)

37. Match the following columns.

Column I (Temperature in Celsius)	Column II (Temperature in Kelvin)
A. 17°C	1. 273 K
B. 20°C	2. 0 K
C. –273°C	3. 290 K
D. 0°C	4. 293 K

Sol. A → (3), B → (4), C → (2), D → (1).

d. Give One word or a Phrase

38. Measure of kinetic energy possessed by the gas molecules.

Sol. Temperature

39. Spaces occupied by a gas is called.

Sol. Volume

40. Movement of one gas molecule into another gas.

Sol. Diffusion

41. Coming closer to molecules of a gas.

Sol. Compression

42. Molecules strike against each other

Sol. Collision, pressure

e. State One Relevant Reason

43. Gases are highly compressible, why?

Sol. As there are large intermolecular spaces between the molecules. On applying pressure, the vacant spaces between the molecules decreases, the molecules come closer and occupy less space. Thus, we say gases can be compressed.

44. Gases show diffusion, why?

Sol. There are large intermolecular spaces between the molecules of a gas. When two gases are brought in contact, the molecules of one gas move into the vacant spaces of the other, therefore gases show the property of diffusion.

Section II

a. 2 Marks Questions

1. Define

(i) Boyle's law (ii) Charles' law

Sol. (i) Boyle's law states that at constant temperature, the pressure of a fixed amount (i.e. number of moles, *n*) of a gas varies inversely with its volume. [1]

(ii) Charles' law states that at constant pressure, the volume of a given mass of a gas is directly proportional to its absolute temperature. At very low pressure and high temperature. [1]

2. The molecular theory accounts for the pressure exerted by a gas in a closed vessel as a result of the gas molecules striking on the walls of the vessel. How will the pressure changes, if

(i) the volume is made half of original value, maintaining the temperature constant?

(ii) temperature is doubled maintaining the volume constant?

Sol. (i) When the volume is halved, the number of gas molecules striking per unit area of the walls of the vessel is doubled. Thus, the pressure is doubled as per the Boyle's law. [1]

(ii) When the temperature is doubled, the average kinetic energy of the gas molecules is doubled. Thus, the pressure is doubled. [1]

3. Explain, why

(i) temperature – 273°C is a theoretical temperature, but cannot be achieved?

(ii) Kelvin temperature is always positive?

Sol. (i) At –273°C, volume of a gas becomes zero. But it is not possible because gas is a state of matter and cannot have zero volume. Thus, –273°C is a theoretical temperature, which cannot be achieved. [1]

(ii) Kelvin scale of temperature starts from zero, which is equal to –273°C. Temperature below –273°C is not possible.

Thus, Kelvin temperature is always positive. [1]

4. (i) What does STP or NTP denotes?

(ii) Why is it necessary to compare gases at STP?

Sol. (i) STP stands for standard temperature and standard pressure. NTP denotes normal temperature and normal pressure. [1]

(ii) The volume of a fixed mass of dry enclosed gas depends upon the pressure of the gas and temperature of the gas in Kelvin, hence to express the volume of the gases, we need to compare these to STP. [1]

b. 3 Marks Questions

5. Write important characteristics of a gas based upon kinetic theory of gases.

Sol. (i) Gases have neither fixed shape nor fixed volume.

(ii) Gases have negligible attractive forces between the molecules of a gas.

(iii) Gases exert pressure in all the direction.

(iv) Gases have low density.

(v) Gases have high compressibility.

(vi) Gases easily undergo diffusion. [6 × ½ = 3]

6. Mention an experiment to show the pressure-volume relationship of gas.

Sol. Take a 10 mL syringe fitted with a piston and move the piston upward to mark 10 mL.

Cover the adhesive tape over its nozzle. Fit this nozzle tightly into a hole in the rubber stopper as shown in given figure.

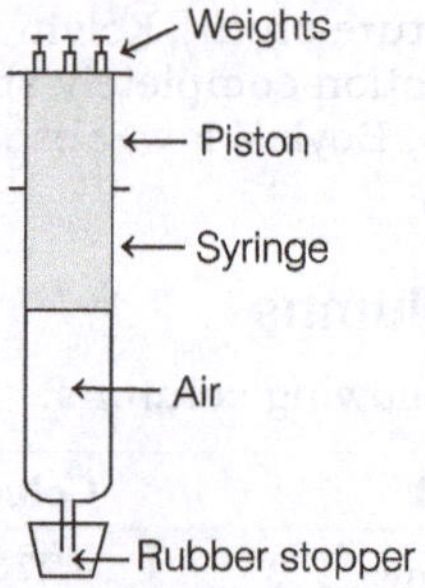

On putting some weight on the piston (pressure increases), the piston moves downward and volume of the air in the syringe decreases.

Then put some more weight, the piston moves further downwards and the volume of the air is further reduced. Similarly, if the weights on the piston are gradually decreased, the piston moves upwards and volume of air starts increasing. [3]

7. State the following.

(i) The volume of a gas at 0 K.

(ii) The STP conditions

(iii) The absolute temperature of a gas at 7°C

Sol. (i) The volume of a gas at 0 K is zero. [1]

(ii) 1 atmospheric pressure and 0°C (273 K) temperature. [1]

(iii) 7°C + 273 = 280 K. [1]

8. Write the value of

(i) standard pressure in

(a) mm of Hg (b) cm of Hg

(c) atm (d) torr

(ii) Standard temperature in

(a) °C (b) K

Sol. (i) Standard pressure

(a) 760 mm of Hg (b) 76 cm of Hg

(c) 1 atmosphere (d) 760 torr [2]

(ii) Standard temperature

(a) 0°C (b) 273 + 0 = 273 K [1]

9. The product of pressure and volume of an enclosed dry gas at a given temperature is always a constant quantity. Explain it.

Sol. According to Boyle's law, temperature remaining constant, volume of a fixed mass of a dry gas is inversely proportional to the pressure exerted on it.

Mathematically, $V \propto \frac{1}{p}$ (T is kept constant)

where, V is the volume of a certain mass of a gas at pressure p and temperatue T.

$\therefore$ $V = \frac{k}{p}$

(where, k is a constant of proportionality)

$\therefore$ $pV = k$

Thus, the product of pressure and volume of an enclosed dry gas at a given temperature is always a constant quantity. [3]

10. How did Charles' law state the concept of absolute scale of temperature?

Sol. From the Charles' law, at constant pressure, the volume of a given mass of a gas increases or decreases by $\frac{1}{273}$ of its volume at 0°C for each 1°C rise or fall in temperature.

Suppose V_0 be the volume of a fixed mass of a gas at 0°C and its pressure is p.

$\therefore$ At constant pressure, volume of gas (V) at t° C is

$$V = V_0 + \frac{1}{273} \times V_0 t$$

Volume of a gas at −273° C (at constant pressure),

$$V_{-273°C} = V_0 + \frac{1}{273} \times V_0(-273)$$
$$= V_0 - V_0 = 0$$

The temperature, −273° C is called absolute zero. [3]

11. State the laws which are represented by the given graphs.

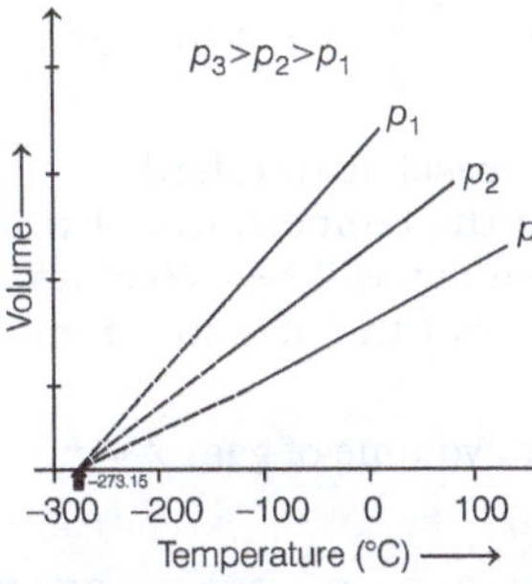

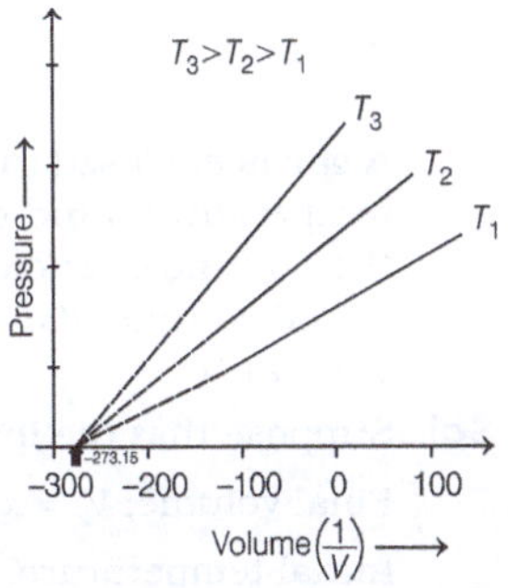

Sol. (i) The first graph represents the Charles' law, i.e. graph of volume *versus* temperature, at constant pressure which states that volume of a given mass of a dry gas is directly proportional to its absolute temperature.

(ii) The second graph represent the Boyle's law, i.e. graph of pressure *vs* reciprocal of volume, at constant temperature. This states that volume of a given mass of a dry gas is inversely proportional to its pressure at constant temperature. [3]

C. 4 Marks Questions

12. Give reason for the following statements.

(i) It is necessary to specify its temperature and pressure while stating volume of a gas.

(ii) Gas fills the vessel completely in which it is kept.

(iii) Inflating a balloon seems to violate Boyle's law.

(iv) Mountaineers carry oxygen cylinders with them.

Sol. (i) This is due to the fact that volume of a gas changes with the change in temperature or pressure.

The relation it follows is

$$\frac{p_1V_1}{T_1} = \frac{p_2V_2}{T_2}$$ [1]

(ii) The molecules in a gas are far apart and are in a state of rapid motion in all possible directions with greater speeds. They move throughout the vessel in which they are kept. Therefore, a gas fills the vessel completely. [1]

(iii) Because of inflation of a balloon though the volume and pressure inside the balloon is increased while Boyle's law is valid for a definite mass of a gas in a closed container. Thus, in this case the mass of the balloon is also rapidly increased as the air is blown into the balloon. Hence, it is not violating the Boyle's law. [1]

(iv) This is because at higher altitudes (at mountains) the density of oxygen is less. Thus, lesser volume of oxygen is available for breathing.

Hence, mountaineers carry oxygen cylinders with them. [1]

13. Give one line/one word to answer the following:

(i) Volume of a gas compared to the solid state.

(ii) Standard temperature of a gas in Kelvin.

(iii) Standard pressure of a gas in mm of Hg.

(iv) Celsius temperature of a gas at 300 K.

Sol. (i) Volume of a gas is very large as compared to the volume of solid.

(ii) 273 K

(iii) 760 mm of Hg

(iv) 300 − 273 = 27° C [4]

14. (i) State one difference and similarity between the Celsius scale and Kelvin scale.

(ii) What are the two fixed points normally used to calibrate the instrument used to measure temperature? Write its value on absolute scale.

(iii) What are STP and NTP? Write its significance.

Sol. (i) The difference is that the temperature on Kelvin scale is always positive while temperature on Celsius scale may be negative, zero or positive. The similarity is that, the magnitude of each degree on Celsius scale is same as on Kelvin scale. [1]

(ii) The two fixed points to calibrate the instrument to measure temperature are
freezing point of water = 0° C = 273 K.
boiling point of water = 100°C
= 273 + 100 = 373 K. [1]

(iii) STP stands for (standard temperature and standard pressure). It is equal to 0°C to 273 K. NTP stands for normal temperature and normal pressure. It is equal to 760 mm or 76 cm of Hg or 1 atm.

Significance For comparing the masses or densities of the gases, their temperature and pressure are taken at STP or NTP. This is because the volume of a given mass of a gas depends upon pressure as well as temperature. [2]

d. Numerical Based Questions

15. What will be the minimum pressure required to compress 500 dm^3 of air at 1 bar to 200 dm^3 at 30°C?

Sol. Given, $p_1 = 1\,\text{bar}$, $p_2 = ?$, $V_1 = 500\,dm^3$, $V_2 = 200\,dm^3$

$$\therefore\ p_1V_1 = p_2V_2$$

$$\Rightarrow\ p_2 = \frac{p_1V_1}{V_2} = \frac{1\,\text{bar} \times 500\,dm^3}{200\,dm^3} = 2.5\,\text{bar}$$ [2]

16. A balloon filled with an ideal gas is taken from the surface of the sea to a depth of 100 m. What will be its volume in terms of its original volume?

Sol. Pressure at the surface = 76 cm = 76 × 13.6 cm Hg
= 1033.6 cm of Hg
= 10.3 m of Hg

∴ Pressure at 100 m depth = 100 + 10.3 m
= 110.3 m

Applying, $p_1V_{1,\,(\text{at surface})} = p_2V_{2,\,(\text{at 100 m depth})}$

$$10.3 \times V = 110.3 \times V_2$$

or $V_2 = 0.093\,V = 9.3\,\%$ of V [2]

17. Calculate the temperature of 4.0 moles of a gas occupying 5 dm^3 at 3.32 bar.
(Take, $R = 0.083$ bar dm^3 K^{-1} mol^{-1}).
Given : n = 4 moles]
$V = 5\,dm^3$
p = 3.32 bar
$R = 0.083$ bar dm^3 $K^{-1}mol^{-1}$

Sol. Apply ideal gas equation, $pV = nRT$

$$\Rightarrow\ T = \frac{pV}{Rn} = \frac{3.32\,\text{bar} \times 5\,dm^3}{0.083\,\text{bar}\,dm^3\,K^{-1}\,mol^{-1} \times 4\,\text{mol}}$$

T = 50 K [2]

18. Determine the pressure of a gas, when its volume is 250 mL initially, the gas is expanded to volume of 1000 mL and the pressure of 0.4 atmosphere. Assume that temperature during the reaction remains constant.

Sol. Given, initial volume, V_1 = 250 mL
Final volume, V_2 = 1000 mL
Initial pressure, p_1 = ?
Final pressure, p_2 = 0.4 atm
Applying Boyle's law,

$$p_1V_1 = p_2V_2$$

$$p_1 \times 250 = 0.4 \times 1000$$

$$\Rightarrow\ p_1 = \frac{0.4 \times 1000}{250} = 1.6\,\text{atm}$$ [2]

19. The volume occupied by a given gas was 5.6 dm^3 when the pressure was 2 atmosphere. If the pressure is increased by 20%, calculate the new volume of the gas.

Sol. Initial volume of gas, $V_1 = 5.6\,dm^3$
Initial pressure of gas, p_1 = 2 atm

20% of initial pressure $= 2 \times \frac{20}{100}$
$= \frac{4}{10} = 0.4$

Final pressure, p_2 = 0.4 + 2 = 2.4 atm
Final volume, V_2 = ?
Applying Boyle's law, $p_1V_1 = p_2V_2$

$$2 \times 5.6 = 2.4 \times V_2$$

$$\Rightarrow\ V_2 = \frac{5.6 \times 2}{2.4} = 4.67\,dm^3$$ [2]

20. A gas is enclosed in a vessel at standard temperature. Find out the temperature at which the volume of enclosed gas will be 1/6 of its initial volume. (Given that the pressure remain constant)

Sol. Suppose that the initial volume of gas, $V_1 = x$
Final volume, $V_2 = x/6$
Initial temperature, T_1 = 0° C = 0 + 273 K = 273 K
Final temperature, T_2 = ?
Applying Charles' law,

$$\frac{V_1}{T_1} = \frac{V_2}{T_2}$$

$$\Rightarrow\ \frac{x}{273} = \frac{x}{6 \times T_2}$$

$$T_2 = \frac{273x}{6 \times x} = 45.5\,K$$ [2]

21. 6 dm^3 of dry gas is present at temperature of 27°C and pressure of 700 mm of Hg. Determine the volume of gas at STP.

Sol. Initial volume, $V_1 = 6\ dm^3$

Final volume, $V_2 = ?$

Initial pressure, $p_1 = 700$ mm of Hg

Final pressure, $p_2 = 760$ mm of Hg

Initial temperature, $T_1 = 27 + 273 = 300$ K

Final temperature, $T_2 = 273$ K

Applying ideal gas equation,

$$\frac{p_1V_1}{T_1} = \frac{p_2V_2}{T_2}$$

$$\frac{700 \times 6}{300} = \frac{760 \times V_2}{273}$$

or $$V_2 = \frac{700 \times 6 \times 273}{300 \times 760}$$

$$= 5.02\ dm^3$$ [3]

22. Moist nitrogen at a pressure of 700 mm of Hg and temperature of 300 K is found to occupy a volume of 100 cm^3. Determine the volume of dry nitrogen gas at STP. (Take, aqueous tension at 27°C is 15 mm of Hg)

Sol. Initial pressure, $p_1 = 700 - 15 = 685$ mm of Hg

Final pressure, $p_2 = 760$ mm of Hg

Initial volume, $V_1 = 100\ cm^3$

Final volume, $V_2 = ?$

Initial temperature, $T_1 = 300$ K

Final temperature, $T_2 = 273$ K

Applying ideal gas equation,

$$\frac{p_1V_1}{T_1} = \frac{p_2V_2}{T_2}$$

$$\frac{685 \times 100}{300} = \frac{760 \times V_2}{273}$$

or $$V_2 = \frac{685 \times 100 \times 273}{300 \times 760}$$

$$= 82.01\ cm^3$$ [3]

23. A certain mass of a gas occupies 4 L at 27°C and 200 Pascal. Calculate the temperature when the volume and pressure become half of their initial value.

Sol. Given,

$p_1 = 200$ Pascal, $p_2 = 100$ Pascal

$V_1 = 4$ L $\quad V_2 = 2$ L

$T_1 = 300$ K $\quad T_2 = ?$

Using gas equation,

$$\frac{p_1V_1}{T_1} = \frac{p_2V_2}{T_2} \Rightarrow \frac{200 \times 4}{300} = \frac{100 \times 2}{T_2}$$

$$T_2 = \frac{100 \times 2 \times 300}{4 \times 200} = 75\ \text{K}$$

$$\therefore \quad T_2 = 75\ \text{K}$$ [3]

24. 150 cm^3 of hydrogen is collected over water at 27°C and 750 mm pressure. Find the volume of dry gas at STP if the vapour pressure at 27°C is 48 mm.

Sol. $V_1 = 150\ cm^3 \quad V_2 = ?$

$T_1 = 300$ K $\quad T_2 = 273$ K

$p_1 = 750 - 48 \quad p_2 = 760$ mm of Hg

$= 702$ mm of Hg

Using gas equation,

$$\frac{p_1V_1}{T_1} = \frac{p_2V_2}{T_2} \Rightarrow V_2 = \frac{p_1V_1T_2}{p_2T_1}$$

$$V_2 = \frac{702 \times 150 \times 273}{760 \times 300} = 126.08\ cm^3$$ [3]

25. 370 cc of moist hydrogen measured at 19°C and 859 mm pressure. Calculate the volume of dry hydrogen at NTP. The vapour pressure of water at 19°C is 9 mm.

Sol. $V_1 = 370$ cc, $V_2 = ?$

$T_1 = 19°\text{C} = 19 + 273 = 292$ K, $T_2 = 292$ K

$p_1 = 859 - 9 = 850$ mm $\quad p_2 = 760$ mm

Using gas equation, $\frac{p_1V_1}{T_1} = \frac{p_2V_2}{T_2}$

$$\Rightarrow \quad V_2 = \frac{p_1V_1T_2}{p_2T_1}$$

$$V_2 = \frac{850 \times 370 \times 273}{760 \times 292}$$

$$V_2 = 386.88\ \text{cc}$$ [3]

Chapter Assessment

Section I

a. Multiple Choice Questions

1. At any particular time different particles in the gas have ...I... speed and hence ...II... kinetic energies.

   Here, I and II refer to
   (a) I → same, II → same
   (b) I → different, II → same
   (c) I → different, II → different
   (d) I → same, II → different

2. According to the Boyle's law, as the pressure increases volume
   (a) decreases
   (b) increases
   (c) remains same
   (d) first increases then decreases

3. The absolute temperature value that corresponds to 27°C is
   (a) 273 K (b) 300 K
   (c) 373 K (d) 246 K

4. The values of Celsius scale can be converted to Kelvin scale by
   (a) subtracting 273 (b) adding 273
   (c) subtracting 373 (d) adding 373

5. On converting 25°C, 38°C and 66°C to Kelvin scale, the correct sequence of temperature will be
   (a) 273 K, 278 K and 543 K
   (b)298 K, 310 K and 338 K
   (c) 298 K, 300 K and 543 K
   (d) 298 K, 311 K and 339 K

6. The Kelvin scale of temperature is always
   (a) negative
   (b) positive
   (c) sometimes positive sometimes negative
   (d) None of the above

7. The pressure, volume and temperature relationship is
   (a) $\frac{T_1}{p_1V_1} = \frac{T_2}{p_2V_2}$ (b) $\frac{p_1V_1}{T_1} = \frac{p_2V_2}{T_2}$
   (c) $\frac{p_1T_1}{V_1} = \frac{p_2T_2}{V_2}$ (d) $p_1V_1T_1 = p_2V_2T_2$

b. Fill in the Blanks

8. There are large vacant space between the molecules known as ....(volume, intermolecular space, intermolecular force).

9. All gases are made up of large number of identical .... particles. (tiny, large, mixed).

10. Charles' law states that at constant pressure, volume of a given mass of a gas is directly proportional to its .... (temperature, kinetic energy, moles).

11. The melting point of ice is .... on Kelvin scale. (273 K, 0 K, 373 K).

12. 1 litre = ... cm^3 = 1000 mL. (1, 10, 1000).

c. Match the Columns

13. Match the following columns.

	Column I (Property)		Column II (Status with ref. to gases)
A.	Intermolecular spaces	1.	Not definite
B.	Volume	2.	Fast rate
C.	Attractive forces	3.	More
D.	Diffusion	4.	Least or negligible

d. Give One Word or a Phrase

14. This quantity is usually expressed in terms of mm of Hg or cm of Hg.

15. At constant temperature, the product of pressure and volume of a given mass of gas is constant. This law is

16. At constant pressure, volume of a given mass of a gas is directly proportional to its Kelvin temperature. This law is

e. State One Relevant Reason

17. When volume of gas decreased, then pressure increases. Explain.

18. Why mountaineers carry oxygen cylinders with them?

Section II

a. 2 Marks Questions

1. Explain, why
   (i) gases have neither definite shape nor definite volume ?
   (ii) gases can be liquefied?

2. Give reason for the following statement.
   (i) It is necessary to specify pressure and temperature of a gas while stating its volume.
   (ii) It is necessary to choose the standard values of temperature and pressure.

b. 3 Marks Questions

3. Explain the following.
   (i) Gases have low densities.
   (ii) Gases are highly expandable.
   (iii) Gases exert same pressure in all directions.

4. Mention whether the volume of a given mass of a gas increases or decreases if
   (i) pressure increases, while temperature remain constant.
   (ii) temperature decreases and pressure remains constant.

5. Convert the following temperature from Kelvin scale to the Celsius scale.
   (i) 426 K (ii) 105 K
   (iii) 250 K (iv) 338 K
   (v) 285 K (vi) 728 K

c. 4 Marks Questions

6. Give one word for the following.
   (i) Theory that help in explaining the relationship between *p*, *V* and *T*.
   (ii) Process used for gradual mixing of two substances.
   (iii) Term used for degree of hotness of gas.
   (iv) Theoretical concept of temperature at which the molecular motion completely ceases.

7. Write the observable properties or variable of gases and explain it.

d. Numerical Based Questions

8. The volume of a certain mass of a gas was found to be 800 cc when pressure was 760 mm of Hg. If the pressure increases by 50%. Calculate the new volume of the gas, assuming that temperature remains constant.

9. At constant temperature, a gas is at a pressure of 570 mm of mercury. At what pressure its volume will decrease by 25%?

10. 2 L of a gas is enclosed in a vessel when the pressure is 760 mm. If the temperature remains constant, find the pressure, if
    (i) the volume changes to 4 dm^3.
    (ii) the volume is increased by one and half time.

11. At constant pressure, a gas at $-27°C$ is heated to 127°C. Find the percentage increase in the volume of the gas.

For explanations scan the given QR Code

Olympiad Section*

Brain Teasing Questions asked in Previous Olympiads

1. All gases obey Charles' law at **(NTSE)**

(a) low temperature and high pressure
(b) low temperature and low pressure
(c) high temperature and high pressure
(d) high temperature and low pressure

2. Which of the following expression is true for an ideal gas? **(INJSO)**

(a) $\frac{p_1V_1}{p_2V_2} = \frac{T_1}{T_2}$
(b) $\frac{V_1V_2}{p_1p_2} = T_1T_2$
(c) $\frac{p_1T_1}{p_2T_2} = \frac{V_1}{V_2}$
(d) $p_1V_1T_1 = p_2V_2T_2$

3. When gases expand, the volume of gases **(NTSE)**

(a) increases
(b) decreases
(c) remain same
(d) None of the above

4. The force exerted by gas molecules when they strike on the wall of container is known as **(NTSE)**

(a) force
(b) thrust
(c) pressure
(d) temperature

5. Kinetic energy of the molecules of a gas is directly proportional to **(INJSO)**

(a) pressure
(b) volume
(c) temperature
(d) potential energy

6. The conversion of 58°C in Kelvin is equal to **(INJSO)**

(a) 334 K
(b) 332 K
(c) 331 K
(d) 330 K

7. The unit of pressure is .... **(NTSE)**

(a) kilogram
(b) atmosphere
(c) cubic centimetre
(d) litre

8. The relationship $p_1V_1 = p_2V_2$ is called **(INJSO)**

(a) Boyle's law
(b) Charles' law
(c) Ideal gas equation
(d) None of these

9. What is the lowest hypothetical temperature at which all molecular motion ceases ? **(INJSO)**

(a) 273°C
(b) 273 K
(c) −273°C
(d) −273 K

10. If pressure is increased by 4 times for a fixed mass of a gas, it's volume will become **(INJSO)**

(a) 2 times
(b) 1/4 time
(c) 6 times
(d) No change

Answers

1. (d) **2.** (a) **3.** (a) **4.** (c) **5.** (c) **6.** (c) **7.** (b) **8.** (a) **9.** (c) **10.** (b)

* *These questions may or may not be asked in the examination, have been given just for additional practice required for olympiads Scholarship Exams etc. For detailed explanations refer Page No. 136.*

CHAPTER 08

Atmospheric Pollution

CHAPTER OUTLINES

• Acid Rain • Global Warming • Ozone Depletion

Earth is surrounded by a covering of various gases (air), called atmosphere, which extends to a height of about 1600 km above the earth surface.

Dry air contains roughly (by volume) nitrogen (78.08%), oxygen (20.95)%, argon (0.93%), carbon dioxide (0.033%) and trace amount of other gases such as Ne (18 ppm), He (5.2 ppm), methane (1.3 ppm), Kr (1 ppm), H_2 (0.5 ppm), CO (0.10 ppm), O_3 (0.02 ppm), SO_2 (0.001 ppm) etc.

Addition of some undesirable substances into the atmosphere (either due to some natural phenomenon or due to human activity), which have adverse effect on plants and animals including human being is called **atmospheric pollution.** These undesirable substances are called pollutants.

On the basis of origin or sources, pollutants are of two types, i.e. natural and man-made.

Natural Sources of Air Pollutants

- **Volcanoes** Large amount of air pollutants like carbon monoxide, sulphur dioxide, hydrogen sulphide etc., are released by volcanoes.
- **Decaying vegetations** Microbial action on organic matter in soil releases pollutant-nitrous oxide.
- Forest fires releases the poisonous gas, i.e. carbon monoxide.
- Winds and dust storms carry particulate matter like sand and dust.

Man-made Sources of Air Pollutants

Some man-made sources of air pollutants are as follows

- **Automobiles** uses diesel or petrol as fuel. Their incomplete combustion releases carbon monoxides, hydrocarbons, nitrogen oxides and particulates like lead.
- **Factories** releases carbon dioxide, sulphur dioxide, nitrogen monoxide and particulates.
- **Industrial processes** releases different types of air pollutants depending upon the type of process involved, i.e. coal power plants releases, sulphur dioxide, carbon monoxide etc.
- Burning of plastic produces carbon monoxide and other harmful gases.

These pollutants are responsible for producing many undesirable phenomenons to affect human life. e.g. Acid rains, global warming, ozone layer depletion on etc.

Acid Rain

In simple words, the rain water (pH = 5.6) which is acidic in nature due to presence of certain pollutants in the air is called **acid rain** (pH = below 5.6).

It is the deposition of wet acidic solutions or dry acidic particles in the water droplets present in the air. Rain, snow, fog or dew is made acidic by the presence of certain acids that results when sulphur and nitrogen oxides combine with O_2 and H_2O in the atmosphere.

These oxides are formed in bulk from burning of fossil fuels, electrical power generation and other industrial activities. Combustion engines of automobiles also contribute in increasing the amount of these oxides in atmosphere.

Note The term acid rain was put forth by **Robert Augus.**

Composition

Acid rain results from acids such as sulphuric acid (H_2SO_4) and nitric acid (HNO_3) present in polluted air. These acids are formed when oxides of sulphur and nitrogen, respectively come into contact with rain water and oxygen.

Causes

Acid rain is caused by a chemical reaction that starts when compounds like sulphur dioxide and nitrogen oxides are released into the air. They are formed due to combustion of fuels. These substances can rise very high into the atmosphere where they mix and react with water, oxygen and other chemicals to form more acidic pollutants.

The main cause of acid rain is due the formation of mineral acids like nitric acid, carbonic acid and sulphuric acid during rains.

$$\underset{(SO_2)}{\text{Sulphur dioxide}} + \underset{(NO_x)}{\text{Nitrogen oxides}} + \underset{\text{(clouds)}}{\text{Water vapours}} \longrightarrow \text{Acid rain}$$

Formation of Nitric Acid

Oxides of nitrogen are introduced into the atmosphere by the burning of the fossil fuels in internal combustion engines which results in the production of a very high temperature. Thus, nitrogen and oxygen of air combine to form nitrogen monooxide.

$$\underset{\text{Nitrogen}}{N_2} + \underset{\text{Oxygen}}{O_2} \xrightarrow[3000^\circ C]{\text{High temperature}} \underset{\text{Nitrogen monooxide}}{2NO}$$

Nitrogen monoxide or nitric oxide combines with more of oxygen to form nitrogen dioxide.

$$\underset{\text{Nitric oxide}}{2NO} + \underset{\text{Oxygen}}{O_2} \longrightarrow \underset{\text{Nitrogen dioxide}}{2NO_2}$$

Further, nitrogen dioxide (NO_2) dissolves with rain water to form a mixture of nitric acid and nitrous acid.

$$\underset{\text{Nitrogen dioxide}}{2NO_2} + H_2O \longrightarrow \underset{\text{Nitric acid}}{HNO_3} + \underset{\text{Nitrous acid}}{HNO_2}$$

$$\underset{\text{Nitrogen dioxide}}{4NO_2} + 2H_2O + \underset{\text{Oxygen}}{O_2} \longrightarrow \underset{\text{Nitric acid}}{4HNO_3}$$

Formation of Sulphuric Acid

Sulphur is a non-metallic element found in coal and fuel oil. When these fuels are burned, sulphur combines with oxygen in presence of air to form sulphur dioxide.

$$S + O_2 \longrightarrow SO_2$$

Sulphur dioxide is oxidised by atmospheric oxygen to form sulphur trioxide.

$$2SO_2 + O_2 \longrightarrow 2SO_3$$

Further, SO_2 and SO_3 combines with water to form sulphuric acid which is the main cause of acid rain.

$$\underset{\text{Sulphur trioxide}}{SO_3} + \underset{\text{Water}}{H_2O} \longrightarrow \underset{\text{Sulphuric acid}}{H_2SO_4}$$

$$\underset{\text{Sulphur dioxide}}{2SO_2} + \underset{\text{Oxygen}}{O_2} + \underset{\text{Water}}{2H_2O} \longrightarrow \underset{\text{Sulphuric acid}}{2H_2SO_4}$$

Harmful Effects of Acid Rain

Acid rain causes the following adverse effects

- **Acid rain affects soil chemistry** Acid rain causes harmful effects to the soil such as nutrient leaching, accumulation of toxic metals and the release of toxic aluminium.

  When acid rain adds hydrogen ions to the soil which interact chemically with existing minerals causes nutrient leaching.

  It displaces important minerals such as Ca, Mg and K from soil particles and deprives nutrition of trees. It washes a number of essential minerals from soil and the later depletion of these minerals cause harmful effect on the growth of plants.

  Due to acid rain, damage of trees at large number and loss of leaves occur (brown and fall off). Acid rain increases the acidity of the soil, causes adverse effect on the plants.

- Acid rain damages the **buildings** and other structures made up of limestone or marble, i.e. $CaCO_3$.

  Sulphuric acid and nitric acid dissolve calcium carbonate to form calcium sulphate and calcium nitrate, respectively.

$$CaCO_3 + H_2SO_4 \longrightarrow CaSO_4 + CO_2\uparrow + H_2O$$

$$CaCO_3 + 2HNO_3 \longrightarrow Ca(NO_3)_2 + CO_2\uparrow + H_2O$$

  The Taj Mahal is facing this serious problem.

- In human beings and animals, it causes several respiratory diseases. Sulphur dioxide irritates the upper respiratory tract, the part of our body that serves to expel soot particles and dust from inhaled air. In lower concentration, it affects lung tissues.
- When acid rain water is mixed with river or lakes, it affects the aquatic life adversely. The acids dissolved the heavy metals such as Al, Mn, Pb, Zn, etc., that are present on the lake. These metal salts are extremely harmful to fish and the other animals living under the water.
- Acid rain increases corrosion of metals.
For example, formation of rust on structure like iron gates and iron frames increases due to acid rain.

Taj Mahal and Acid Rain

In the city of Agra, the air is highly contaminated with oxides of nitrogen and sulphur since a large number of industries and power plants are present around it. Along with coal, kerosene and fire wood of poor quality are widely used as fuel for domestic purposes. This leads to acid rain, due to which the marble of a wonderful monument Taj Mahal, situated in Agra, is getting discoloured and lustreless.

$$\underset{\text{Calcium carbonate (Marble)}}{CaCO_3} + \underset{\text{(From acid rain)}}{H_2SO_4} \longrightarrow \underset{\text{Calcium sulphate}}{CaSO_4} + H_2O + \underset{\text{Carbon dioxide}}{CO_2 \uparrow}$$

Methods to Reduce Formation of Acid Rain

Acid rain occurs because of the oxides of nitrogen and sulphur, so the methods by which these oxides can be removed is used to reduce the formation of acid rain.

Some such methods are as follows

- By using less vehicles working on fossil fuels.
- By using fossil fuels having less sulphur content for power plants and industries, i.e. using natural gas which is a better fuel as compared to coal or using coal with less sulphur content.
- By using catalytic converters in cars to reduce the effect of exhaust on the atmosphere, e.g. NO_x and CO present in the exhaust gases are converted into N_2 and CO_2 respectively at 573 K. The main component of the converter is ceramic honey-comb coated with precious metals like Pt, Pd and Rh.

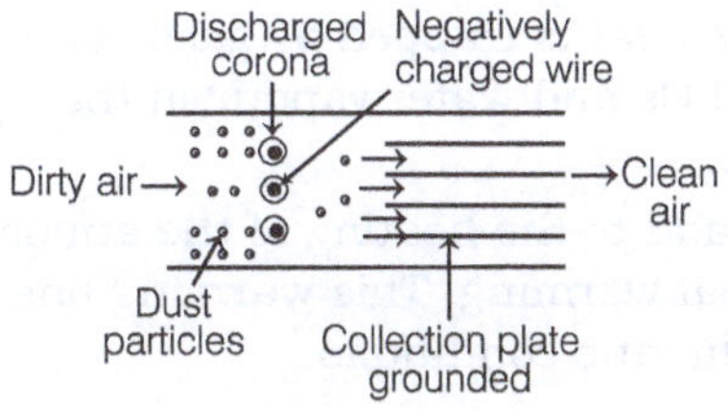

Electrostatic precipitator

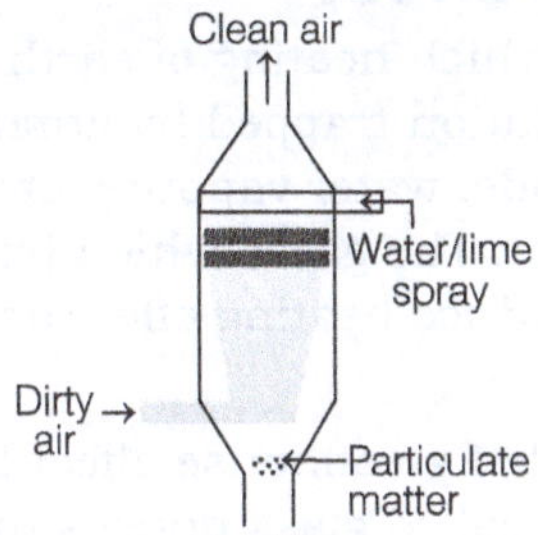

Scrubber

- By adding powdered limestone to neutralise the acidic soil.
- By spreading information about the harmful effects of oxides of N and S.
- By using scrubber that removes SO_2 from a smoke stack.

Check Your LEARNING...

1. Define atmospheric pollution.
2. Who discovered the term acid rain?
3. Mention the balanced chemical equation for the formation of acid rain.
4. Write only the chemical reaction for the formation of sulphuric acid.
5. How the acid rain damages the building made up of marble?
6. Write the names of any two methods to reduce the formation of acid rain.

Global Warming

When concentration of green house gases increases (e.g. if CO_2 concentration crosses delicate proportion of 0.03%), these trap excess radiation and increases the temperature of earth too much, i.e. increases the green house effect, which is termed as **global warming**.

About three-fourth of the solar energy reaching the earth is absorbed by the earth's surface due to which the temperature of earth increases. The rest of the heat radiates back to atmosphere.

Some of this heat is trapped by gases such as CO_2, CH_4, CFCs and water vapour in the atmosphere.

Thus, they add to the heating of the atmosphere and caused global warming. This warming has drastic effects on climatic conditions.

Greenhouse Effect

The process by which heating of earth takes place due to solar radiation trapped by atmospheric gases like carbon dioxide, water vapours, etc., is called greenhouse effect. The gases which trap solar radiations to produce heating effect are called green house gases.

This effect is called greenhouse effect because of glass structures called glass houses that are used to grow green plants in colder regions. The glass houses allow sunlight to enter but does not allow the radiated heat to escape, results in heating up of the green houses.

Mechanism

Sunlight containing UV rays, IR rays and visible rays falls on earth. The UV rays are absorbed by ozone. Visible and IR rays reach on the earth. IR rays having heating effect, thus, heat up the earth and its various objects. As a result, the earth and its objects also begin to emit heat radiation or IR rays of higher wavelength.

The CO_2 present in the air traps most of these radiations and does not allow them to go out of the earth's atmosphere. Consequently, earth and its atmosphere remains warm.

Green house effect

Green house Gases and their Sources

As discussed earlier, the gases that contribute to green house effect like carbon dioxide, water vapour, oxides of nitrogen etc., are called **green house gases.**

Their relative contributions toward green house effect are CO_2(50%), CH_4(19%), CFCs(17%), O_3(8%), N_2O(4%) and H_2O(2%). Various green house gases and their sources are given below

(i) **Water vapours** The main sources of water vapour are industrial exhaust, vehicular exhaust, burning of fuels and volcanic eruptions.

$$\text{Hydrocarbon} + \text{Oxygen} \longrightarrow \text{Carbon dioxide} + \text{Water vapour}$$

(ii) **Carbon dioxide** (CO_2) Respiration, burning of fossil fuels for energy, decomposition of limestone for cement manufacturing, volcanic eruptions etc. all processes proceed with the liberation of carbon dioxide into the atmosphere.

Thus, a large amount of carbon dioxide is released into the atmosphere which is removed by green plants on account of photosynthesis and in turn they release oxygen and maintain an appropriate level of CO_2 (i.e. 0.03%) in the troposphere (or atmosphere).

Source Deforestation and excessive burning of fossil fuels increase the level of CO_2 and disturb the atmospheric balance.

(iii) **Hydrocarbons** (Methane, CH_4) These are the compounds of carbon (C) and hydrogen (H) only. Among various hydrocarbons, methane (CH_4) or **marsh gas** is the most abundant hydrocarbon pollutant.

Source These are obtained by the incomplete combustion of fossil fuels in automobile engines and by anaerobic decomposition of organic matter or vegetation. From paddy fields, coal mines and rotting garbage dumps, large amounts of methane are released.

(iv) **Oxides of nitrogen** Among the various oxides of nitrogen, nitrogen monooxide (NO), a colourless, odourless gas and nitrogen dioxide (NO_2), a brown gas with pungent odour, are the two oxides that act as tropospheric pollutants.

Source At high altitudes when lightening strikes or thunderstorm, the two major constituents of air, i.e. dinitrogen and dioxygen which do not react with each other at normal temperature combine to give these oxides. Other sources of these oxides are combustion of fossil fuels such as coal, oil, gasoline etc., in automobile engines, (at high temperature as given by the reaction below), tobacco smoke, denitrifying bacteria and many industrial processes.

$$N_2(g) + O_2(g) \xrightarrow{1483\,K} 2NO(g)$$

Actually NO, itself is not a strong pollutant but reacts readily with oxygen in the troposphere to give NO_2. The reaction with ozone (O_3) is much faster in stratosphere than the reaction with oxygen.

$$2\,NO(g) + O_2(g) \longrightarrow 2NO_2(g)$$

$$NO\,(g) + O_3(g) \longrightarrow NO_2(g) + O_2(g)$$

NO_2 gets further oxidised to nitrate ion, NO_3^- which is washed into the soil, where it acts as a fertilizer.

Effects or Consequences of Global Warming

Global warming is the main consequence of disturbance of green house effect. Global warming had a drastic effect on climatic conditions. It may cause melting of polar ice caps and glaciers which result in floods of low lying areas.

Moreover, global warming also increases the incidence of several infectious diseases such as malaria, sleeping sickness, dengue, yellow fever etc.

Methods of Reducing Global Warming

Following are the methods of reducing global warming

- Use of solar energy, hydrogen or atomic energy, hydroelectricity can help in reducing greenhouse effect.
- Deforestation must be stop and afforestation should be made to develop new forests by encouraging tree planting programmes as it act as CO_2 sinks.
- Educating the masses to use cleaner fuels, not the coal, fire wood, etc.
- Use of precipitators, wet scrubbers made obligatory for the factories to remedial measures.
- Advanced technologies are used in the automobiles to initiate complete combustion of fuels.
- Use public transport where possible, as well as pooling of cars can be practised. A lot of pollutants are released by the automobiles.

Check Your LEARNING...

1. What is the role of CO_2 in the 'greenhouse effect'?
2. What is the percent (%) composition of CO_2 in the pure dry air?
3. List gases which are responsible for greenhouse effect.
4. What is the main constituent of green house gas?
5. State one source and effect of carbon dioxide and methane in the atmosphere.
6. Write any method by which global warming can reduced.

Ozone Depletion

Ozone (O_3) is a light bluish gas and an allotropic form of oxygen which is found in the upper layer of atmosphere about 20 km away from the surface of earth. It is formed from oxygen in the presence of sunlight. It protects earth's surface from UV radiations.

Formation

It is prepared by subjecting pure and dry oxygen to silent electric discharge in Siemen's ozoniser. 10-15% of O_2 is converted to O_3. The product so formed is called **ionised oxygen**.

$$3O_2(g) \longrightarrow 2O_3(g);\ \Delta H = +142\,kJ\,mol^{-1}$$

The structure of ozone is given below

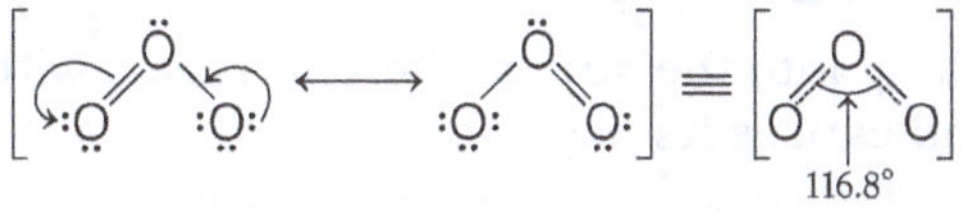

Resonance hybrid

Function of Ozone in the Atmosphere

The upper stratosphere consists of considerable amount of ozone (O_3) which protect us from the harmful ultraviolet (UV) radiations coming from the sun. These radiations cause skin cancer in humans. Therefore, it is important to maintain the ozone shield.

When UV rays interact with dioxygen molecule (O_2), it gets split up into free oxygen atoms (O), which combine with molecular oxygen to give ozone.

$$O_2(g) \xrightarrow{UV} O(g) + O(g)$$

(Nascent oxygen)

$$O(g) + O_2(g) \overset{UV}{\rightleftharpoons} O_3(g)$$

$$\text{Net reaction } 3O_2 + UV \longrightarrow 2O_3$$

The obtained ozone absorbs UV radiations of comparatively longer wavelength which, decomposes to give molecular oxygen back.

$$O_3 \longrightarrow O_2 + \underset{\text{(Nascent oxygen)}}{O}$$

Thus, there is a dynamic equilibrium between the formation and decomposition of ozone layer.

Depletion or Destruction of Ozone Layer

Decrease in quantity of ozone in the upper layer of atmosphere (stratosphere) is called depletion of ozone layer or destruction of the ozone layer.

Depletion of ozone layer is being caused by certain compounds such as chlorofluorocarbon compounds (CFCs), oxides of nitrogen, etc., obtained from various human activities. Effect of ozone hole is maximum in Australia.

Chemicals Responsible for Destruction of Ozone layer

The various chemicals responsible for destruction of ozone layer are as follows

Nitric Oxide

It is released into upper atmosphere from engine of supersonic transport planes.

On reaching into the stratosphere, it reacts with ozone and causes its depletion.

Chlorofluorocarbon Compounds

(CFCs), i.e. freons being non–reactive, non–inflammable, non–toxic organic molecules, are widely used in air conditioners, refrigerators, in electronic industry for cleaning computer parts etc.

Due to very long life time (CF_2Cl_2 or CFC-12 has life time of 139 yr and $CFCl_3$ or CFC-11 has life time of 77 yr), these compounds ultimately reach the stratosphere where they get broken down by powerful UV radiations and release chlorine free radical.

The reaction, once start, continues for a long time. Thus, a single chlorine free radical is able to convert about one lakh ozone molecules into oxygen and hence, it may lead to massive ozone depletion.

Note Now-a-days, some chlorine free substituted CFCs such as hydrofluorocarbons (HFC-1349), hydrochlorofluorocarbons (HCFCs), methyl cyclohexane (MCH) are widely used, in place of CFCs.

Ozone Hole

A large scale depletion in the concentration of O_3 was observed over Antarctica. This is called **ozone hole.**

It was found that for the depletion of ozone layer, unique set of conditions was responsible.

During summer season, there exists nitrogen dioxide and methane which act as sink for chlorine free radicals and prevent much ozone depletion.

$$Cl\dot{O}(g) + NO_2(g) \longrightarrow \underset{\text{Chlorine nitrate}}{ClONO_2(g)}$$

$$\dot{C}l(g) + CH_4(g) \longrightarrow \underset{\text{Methyl free radical}}{\dot{C}H_3(g)} + \underset{\text{Hydrogen chloride}}{HCl(g)}$$

While in winters, there exist special type of clouds, called **polar stratospheric clouds** (PSCs) over Antarctica.

These clouds convert chlorine nitrate ($ClONO_2$) and hydrochloric acid (HCl) formed in the above reactions, into HOCl and Cl_2.

$$ClONO_2(g) + H_2O(g) \longrightarrow HOCl(g) + HNO_3(g)$$

$$ClONO_2(g) + HCl(g) \longrightarrow Cl_2(g) + HNO_3(g)$$

PSCs also result in the formation of **polar vortex** (a tight whirlpool of wind) which unables the ozone rich air of the non-polar regions to reach in Antarctica.

Thus, ozone hole remains unfilled. During spring season, the sunlight returns to the Antarctica and breaks up the clouds and cause photolysis of HOCl and Cl_2.

$$HOCl(g) \xrightarrow{h\nu} \dot{O}H(g) + \dot{C}l(g)$$

$$Cl_2(g) \xrightarrow{h\nu} 2\dot{C}l(g)$$

The chlorine free radicals, thus formed, again start the chain reaction for ozone depletion. However, after spring, the high intensity sunlight breaks down these vortex and ozone rich air from surroundings rushes in and replenishes the ozone hole.

Effects of Depletion of the Ozone Layer

Following problems are caused by the depletion of the ozone layer

- Depletion of ozone layer results in entering of ultraviolet rays into the atmosphere causing skin cancer.

- Ultraviolet rays causes weakening of eye-sight and finally lead to blindness. It has been estimated that decrease in 1% ozone concentration in stratosphere will lead to blindness of almost 1 lakh people.
- Ultraviolet radiations lead to weakening of the human immune system (immuno suppression).
- Several of the world's major crop species are particularly vulnerable to increased UV-radiations resulting in reduced growth, photosynthesis and flowering.

List of Major Air Pollutants : Their Origin and Health Impact

	Pollutants	Origin	Health impact
(i)	Carbon monoxide (CO)	Produced due to incomplete burning of petrol, diesel and wood.	Reduces oxygen in blood resulting into retardation dizziness and death at last.
(ii)	Carbon dioxide (CO_2)	Produced on burning of coal, oil and natural gases.	Reduces oxygen levels.
(iii)	Chloro - fluorocarbons (CFCs)	Released from refrigerators and air-conditioning systems.	Reduces ozone layer that protects us from the harmful ultraviolet radiations of the Sun.
(iv)	Ozone (O_3)	Emitted from vehicles and industries.	Burning, itching, watery eyes and lowered resistance to respiratory diseases.
(v)	Lead (Pb)	Present in petrol, diesel, paints and batteries.	Damages the nervous and digestive systems and can cause cancer.
(vi)	Sulphur dioxide (SO_2)	Produced from burning of coal, petrol and diesel.	Smog and acid rain containing sulphuric acid make children more susceptible to respiratory diseases.
(vii)	Oxides of nitrogen (NO_x)	Produced on burning of petrol, diesel and coal.	Smog (combination of fog and smoke), produces acid rain that makes children more susceptible to respiratory diseases.
(viii)	Suspended particulate matter (SPM)	Solids suspended in smoke, dust and vapour.	Small particles get lodged in the lungs and gradually damage the functioning of lungs.

Bhopal Gas Tragedy

On December 1984, in which about 3000 people were killed and about 50,000 are still suffering from respiratory, lung and eye diseases, was due to leakage of methyl isocyanate (MIC) vapours.

Check Your LEARNING...

1. Write the chemical equation for the formation of ozone in the atmosphere.
2. Draw the resonating structure of ozone.
3. Name the chemical responsible for ozone layer destruction ?
4. Which disease is caused due to hole in the ozone layer and why?
5. How many percent (%) decrease in ozone concentration in stratosphere cause blindness?
6. Name the gas that caused the Bhopal Gas Tragedy.

QUiCK Revision

- Pollution may be defined as contamination of air, water or soil by undesirable amounts of materials or heat and is caused by the concentration of substances that have harmful effects.
- **Atmospheric pollution** is alteration in the composition of air due to the addition of foreign harmful materials (i.e. pollutants).
- Atmospheric pollution is mainly concerned with **pollution of troposphere** (lowest portion of earth's atmosphere) and stratosphere (second major portion of earth's atmosphere).
- Acid rain is defined as the deposition of wet and dry acidic components. Its pH is less then 5.6.
- Acid rain results from acids like nitric acid and sulphuric acid present in polluted air.
- Formation of nitric acid

$$N_2 + 2O_2 \longrightarrow 2NO + O_2 \longrightarrow 2NO_2,$$

$$4NO_2 + 2H_2O + O_2 \longrightarrow 4HNO_3$$

- Formation of sulphuric acid

$$S + O_2 \longrightarrow SO_2$$

$$2SO_2 + O_2 \longrightarrow 2SO_3$$

$$SO_3 + H_2O \longrightarrow H_2SO_4$$

- Acid rain has many adverse effects on soil chemistry, water bodies, damages the buildings, corrodes metal pipes, nutrients leaching and also causes respiratory diseases.
- Methods to reduce formation of acid rain is by using less vehicles, fossil fuels having less sulphur content, catalytic converters in cars to reduce the effect of exhaust.
- **Green house effect** is heating up of earth due to trapping of IR radiation (thermal radiations) by CO_2, CH_4, O_3, NO, CFCs, water vapour, etc.
- **Global warming** is increase in the temperature of earth due to increased concentration of green-house gases. It may cause melting of ice-caps and glaciers, several infectious disease like malaria, sleeping sickness, etc.
- Green house gases and their sources are
  - Water vapours (main source-industrial exhaust, vehicular exhaust, burning of fuel, volcano eruption).
  - CO_2 (main source -deforestation and excessive burning of fossil fuel).
  - Hydrocarbons (main source - automobile engines and vegetation).
  - NO and NO_2 (main source - lightening strikes, automobile engines, etc).
- Green house gases are useful in keeping the earth warm with an average temperature of about 15°C. In their absence, average surface temperature will fall to about –18°C. This temperature will freeze all water and destroy most of the living beings.
- Methods for reducing **global warming** is the use of solar energy, afforestation, use of precipitators, wet scrubbers, car pooling.

  Ozone layer is the upper layer of atmosphere about 20 km away from the surface of the earth. It protects earth's surface from UV radiations. It is prepared by subjecting pure and dry oxygen to silent electric-discharge in Siemen's ozoniser as

$$SO_2(g) \xrightarrow{hv} 2O_3(g)$$

- Depletion (destruction) of ozone layer is the decrease in quantity of ozone in the stratosphere. This depletion of ozone layer is caused by certain compounds such as chlorofluorocarbon compounds (CFCs), oxides of nitrogen, etc., obtained from various human activities.
- Ozone hole observed due to the depletion of ozone layer in Antarctica over South pole in 1980.
- Effect of depletion of the ozone layer leads to skin cancer, adverse effect on immune system, loss of sight (blindness) etc.

Chapter Practice

Section I

a. Multiple Choice Questions

1. Which of the following is not a green house gas?
   (a) CO
   (b) CO_2
   (c) CH_4
   (d) H_2O/Vapour

Sol. (a)

2. Consider the following measures regarding way to reduce the presence of global warming.
   I. Afforestation
   II. Use of solar energy
   III. Pooling of cars can be practised

   The correct option is
   (a) Only I (b) Only II
   (c) I and III (d) I, II and III

Sol. (d)

3. Which of the following is a green house gas ?
   (a) Methane (b) Oxygen
   (c) Carbon (d) Nitrogen

Sol. (a)

4. Absence of a green house gas will drop the temperature to about
   (a) – 15° C (b) 15°C
   (c) – 18° C (d) 18°C

Sol. (c)

5. The carbon compound, that is responsible for ozone hole in atmosphere.
   (a) Chlorofluorocarbons (CFCs)
   (b) Ethane
   (c) Nitrogen oxide
   (d) Propane

Sol. (a)

6. Chlorofluorocarbons are replaced by
   (a) HCl (b) HCFC
   (c) CClF (d) UV rays

Sol. (b) Hydrochlorofluorocarbons can replace CFC's.

7. A single free radical which can destroy nearly 1 lakh molecules of ozone is produced from
   (a) hydrogen molecule (b) fluorine molecule
   (c) nitrogen molecule (d) chlorine molecule

Sol. (d) chlorine molecule

8. The major sources of water vapours are
   (a) industrial and vehicular exhaust
   (b) burning of fuels
   (c) volcanic eruptions
   (d) All of the above

Sol. (d)

9. For the preparation of ozone, the commonly used ozoniser is/are
   (a) Siemen's ozoniser (b) Brodie's ozoniser
   (c) Both (a) and (b) (d) None of these

Sol. (c)

10. Liquid ozone can be separated by
    (a) fractional distillation
    (b) fractional crystallisation
    (c) liquefaction
    (d) sedimentation

Sol. (a)

10. Bond angle of 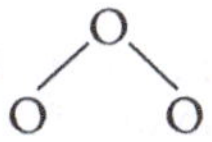 bond is
    (a) 116.8° (b) 114.6°
    (c) 112.8° (d) 116.4°

Sol. (a)

b. Fill in the Blanks

11. Natural pollution is caused by .... (washing clothes, forest fires, smoking)

Sol. forest fires

12. Metals lose .... because of acid present in rain. (lusture, electronegativity, electrons)

Sol. lusture

13. Acid rain is slightly .... due to dissolution of atmospheric gases in water (basic, neutral, acidic).

Sol. acidic

14. The acid present in rain dissolves ...... metals such as Al, Mn, Pb, Zn etc. (light, heavy, noble).

Sol. heavy

15. The acid rain results into the damaging of plants and retard the growth of ....(roots, branches, leaves)

Sol. leaves

16. .... affects yield of crops and cause damage to lungs (Sulphur dioxide, Ozone layer, Nutrient leaching).

Sol. Sulphur dioxide

17. Acid rain is referred to the various ways by which accumulated acid falls from the .... in wet or dry forms (greenhouse, atmosphere, ozone).

Sol. atmosphere

18. .... occurs when acid rain adds hydrogen ions to the soil which interact chemically with existing minerals (Ozonolysis, Greenhouse effect, Nutrient leaching).

Sol. Nutrient leaching

19. Rise in average temperature of the earth's surface is called .... (global warming, ozonolysis, acid rain)

Sol. global warming

20. Carbon dioxide, water vapour, oxides of nitrogen, CH_4, O_3, CFCs, etc., are called .... (noble gases, greenhouse gases, ozones)

Sol. green house gases

21. Absence of green house gases will result in decreasing the surface temperature to about .... (18°C, – 18°C, 15°C)

Sol. – 18°C

22. Supersonic jets release oxides of .... into the atmosphere. (sulphur, carbon, nitrogen).

Sol. nitrogen

23. .... is released from degradable matter. (Methane, Carbon monoxide, Carbon dioxide)

Sol. Methane

24. Bond angle in ozone is .... (110.8°, 116.8°, 122.8°).

Sol. 116.8°

25. Ozone is an .... of oxygen. (isotope, allotrope, isobar).

Sol. allotrope

26. .... are responsible for depletion of ozone layer in upper strata of the atmosphere. (Methane, CO_2, Freons)

Sol. Freons

c. Match the Columns

27. Match the reactions given in Column I with the products given in Column II.

	Column I (Reactions)		Column II (Products)
A.	$4NO_2 + 2H_2O + O_2 \longrightarrow$	1.	$2SO_3$
B.	$2SO_2 + O_2 \xrightarrow{\text{Particulate}}$	2.	H_2SO_4
C.	$SO_2 + H_2O \longrightarrow$	3.	$O_3(g)$
D.	$O(g) + O_2(g) \underset{\text{Light}}{\overset{\text{UV}}{\rightleftharpoons}}$	4.	$4HNO_3$

Sol. A → (4), B → (1), C → (2), D → (3)

d. Give One Word or a Phrase

28. Due to this, Taj Mahal in Agra, is getting discoloured and lustreless.

Sol. Acid rain

29. Acid rain occurs because of the oxides of these two elements mainly.

Sol. Nitrogen and sulphur

30. Effect of ozone hole is maximum in which country?

Sol. Australia

31. Ozone blanket in the upper atmosphere is also called as

Sol. ozone layer

32. This apparatus is used for preparation of ozone.

Sol. Siemen's ozoniser

33. Ozone is separated from oxygen by this process.

Sol. Fractional distillation

Section II

a. 2 Marks Questions

1. Define
(i) Pollution
(ii) Green house effect

Sol. (i) **Pollution** may be defined as contamination of air, water or soil by undesirable amounts of materials or heat and is caused by the concentration of substances that have harmful effects. [1]

(ii) Heating of the earth and its environment due to radiations of the sun trapped by carbon dioxide and water vapour in the atmosphere is called **green house effect**. [1]

2. What is the effect of acid rain on the forest growth?

Sol. The acid rain damages the leaves of plants and retards the growth of forest. The forest deterioration has already taken place in the world because of acid rain. [2]

3. What is the role of CO_2 in the 'greenhouse effect'? Also, write the name of green house gases.

Sol. Heat from the sun after being absorbed by the earth is re-emitted by the earth and absorbed by CO_2 which then radiate it back to the earth, thus, maintaining the constant temperature of the earth.

The greenhouse gases are carbon dioxide, methane, water vapours, nitrous oxide, CFC's and ozone. [2]

4. Why nutrient leaching occurs in heavily polluted areas ?

Sol. Heavily polluted areas contain more amount of acid. When this acid falls on soil it results in nutrient leaching, which is a process that depletes calcium, magnesium and potassium from soil particles and deprives trees of nutrition. [2]

5. What would have happened if the green house gases were totally missing in the earth's atmosphere? Discuss.

Sol. Green house gases are useful in keeping the earth warm, with an average temperature of about 15°C. In their absence, average surface temperature will fall to about – 18°C. This temperature will freeze all water and destroy most of the living beings. [2]

6. Green plants use carbon dioxide for photosynthesis and return oxygen to the atmosphere, even then carbon dioxide is considered to be responsible for green house effect. Explain why?

Sol. The amount of CO_2 produced due to human activity such as burning of fossil fuels like coal, natural gas, petroleum, etc., and production of lime from limestone is much more than that consumed during photosynthesis. The consumption in photosynthesis has further decreased due to deforestation.

Thus, carbon dioxide is considered to be responsible for green house effect. [2]

7. Give reason why chlorofluorocarbons lead to depletion of ozone ?

Sol. Chlorofluorocarbons are very light and reach the second layer of atmosphere. When CFCs reach the ozone layer, the UV rays break apart the CFC's and thus releasing the chlorine atom, which lead to depletion of ozone layer. [2]

8. What are the two forms of oxygen found in the atmosphere?

Sol. The two forms of oxygen found in the atmosphere are

(i) **Elemental oxygen** It is normally found in the form of diatomic molecule (O_2) in the lower part of atmosphere. It constitutes about 20.95% of the atmosphere and is non-poisonous. [1]

(ii) **Ozone** It is found in the stratosphere of atmosphere. It contains three atoms of oxygen (O_3). It is the poisonous form of oxygen. [1]

b. 3 Marks Questions

9. Statues and monuments in India are affected by acid rain. How?

Sol. The air around the statues and monuments in India contains fairly high levels of oxides of sulphur and nitrogen. It is mainly due to a large number of industries and power plants around the areas. Oxides of nitrogen and sulphur are acidic in nature. SO_2 and NO_2 after oxidation and reaction with water are major contributors to acid rain.

$$2\,SO_2(g) + O_2(g) + 2\,H_2O\,(l) \longrightarrow 2\,H_2SO_4(aq)$$
$$4NO_2(g) + O_2(g) + 2\,H_2O\,(l) \longrightarrow 4\,HNO_3(aq)$$

This acid rain reacts with marble of statues and monuments causing damage to these. [2]

$$CaCO_3(s) + H_2SO_4(aq) \longrightarrow CaSO_4(s) + H_2O(l) + CO_2(g)$$ [1]

10. Oxidation of sulphur dioxide into sulphur trioxide in the absence of a catalyst is a slow process but this oxidation occurs easily in the atmosphere. Explain how does this happen? Give chemical reaction for the conversion of SO_2 into SO_3.

Sol. The presence of particulate matter in polluted air catalyses the oxidation of SO_2 to SO_3.

The oxidation of sulphur dioxide into sulphur trioxide can occur both photochemically or non-photochemically. In the near ultraviolet region, the SO_2 molecules react with ozone photochemically.

$$SO_2 + O_3 \xrightarrow{h\nu} SO_3 + O_2$$
$$2SO_2 + O_2 \xrightarrow{h\nu} 2SO_3$$ [2]

Non-photochemically, SO_2 may be oxidised by molecular oxygen in the presence of dust and soot particles.

$$2SO_2 + O_2 \xrightarrow{\text{Particulates}} 2SO_3$$ [1]

11. Give some effects of ozone depletion.

Sol. Following are effects of ozone depletion

(i) **Skin cancer** Depletion of ozone layer will allow ultraviolet rays to enter the earth atmosphere due to which it affects our skin and causes skin cancer. [1]

(ii) **Effect on immune system** Uultraviolet radiations also suppresses immune system. Due to which immunity against certain diseases decreases. [1]

(iii) **Loss of sight** The depletion of ozone layer result in weakening of eye sight and ultimately to blindness. [1]

C. 4 Marks Questions

12. (i) List any four methods used to reduce formation of acid rain?

(ii) List any four methods that can be used to reduce global warming?

Sol. (i) (a) By using less vehicles working on fossil fuels.

(b) By using catalytic converters in cars to reduce the effect of exhaust.

(c) By adding powdered limestone to neutralise the acidic soil.

(d) By spreading information about the harmful effects of oxides of N and S. [2]

(ii) The methods that can be used to reduce the global warming are as follows

(a) Use of solar energy

(b) Afforestation

(c) Use of wet scrubbers

(d) Use of public transport [2]

13. With respect to acid rain, answer the following questions.

(i) What do you mean by acid rain?

(ii) Name the acids formed when acidic oxides dissolves in water.

(iii) Which oxides are released by vehicular exhaust?

(iv) Give chemical equation for the formation of the following acids.

(a) Carbonic acid

(b) Sulphurous acid

(c) Nitric acid

(d) Sulphuric acid

Sol. (i) Acid rain is the rain which carries large amount of acid than normal. pH range is between 5.6 and 3.5. [1]

(ii) Carbonic acid, sulphurous acid, nitric acid etc. [1/2]

(iii) Oxides of nitrogen are released by vehicular exhaust. [1/2]

(iv) (a) $\underset{\text{Carbon dioxide}}{CO_2} + \underset{\text{Water}}{H_2O} \longrightarrow \underset{\text{Carbonic acid}}{H_2CO_3}$

(b) $\underset{\text{Nitrogen dioxide}}{NO_2} + \underset{\text{Oxygen}}{O_2} + \underset{\text{Water}}{2H_2O} \longrightarrow \underset{\text{Nitric acid}}{4HNO_3}$

(c) $\underset{\text{Sulphur dioxide}}{SO_2} + \underset{\text{Water}}{H_2O} \longrightarrow \underset{\text{Sulphurous acid}}{H_2SO_3}$

(d) $\underset{\text{Sulphur trioxide}}{SO_3} + \underset{\text{Water}}{H_2O} \longrightarrow \underset{\text{Sulphuric acid}}{H_2SO_4}$ [2]

14. What is greenhouse effect and what are the sources of green house gases?

Sol. Green house effect is a naturally occurring phenomenon that is responsible for heating of earth's surface and atmosphere due to the presence of certain gases in the atmosphere.

In the absence of green house effect, the average temperature of earth would have been chilly – 18°C rather than the present average temperature of 15°C. [2]

Various sources of green house gases are as follows

(i) **Water vapours** The main sources of water vapour are industrial exhaust, vehicular exhaust, burning of fuels and volcanic eruptions.

(ii) **Carbon dioxide** (CO_2) Photosynthesis, respiration, burning of fossil fuels for energy, decomposition of limestone, volcanic eruptions, etc., all processes proceed with the evolution of carbon dioxide into the atmosphere.

(iii) **Hydrocarbons** (Methane, CH_4) These are obtained by the incomplete combustion of fossil fuels in the automobile engines and by anaerobic decomposition of organic matter or vegetation.

(iv) **Oxides of nitrogen** These are produced by the reaction of dinitrogen and dioxygen at higher altitudes when lightening strikes in atmosphere. Other sources are combustion of fossil fuels, automobile engines, tobacco smoke, denitrifying bacteria and other industrial processes. [2]

15. What do you mean by global warming? State the causes and effects of global warming.

Sol. The gradual and continuous rise in average temperature of the earth's surface is called global warming.

Causes of Global Warming

(i) High levels of gases, such as carbon dioxide (CO_2), methane (CH_4), ozone (O_3), nitrous oxide (N_2O), chlorofluorocarbons (CFCs) are responsible for global warming.

(ii) Burning of fossil fuels in homes and industries, deforestation, etc., increases the level of carbon dioxide and methane in atmosphere. [2]

Effects of Global Warming

(i) An increase in temperature would lead to melting of polar ice caps and consequent rise in sea levels.

(ii) Increase in temperature of earth can cause change in weather and precipitation patterns on the earth. [2]

Chapter Assessment

Section I

a. Multiple Choice Questions

1. The main sources of global warming is/are
   (a) water vapours (b) CO_2
   (c) methane (d) All of these
2. Chlorofluorocarbons (CFCs) are widely used in air conditioners, refrigerators etc. because they are
   (a) highly reactive (b) flammable
   (c) non-reactive (d) All of these
3. Ozone hole refers to
   (a) increase concentration of ozone in the atmosphere
   (b) decrease of thickness of ozone in troposphere
   (c) decrease in thickness of ozone layer in stratosphere
   (d) black hole
4. In which country the effect of ozone hole is maximum?
   (a) Australia (b) Europe
   (c) Germany (d) Norway
5. Which of the following is an Ozone Depleting Substance (ODS)?
   (a) Carbon tetrachloride (b) Methane
   (c) Carbon dioxide (d) Nitrogen

b. Fill in the Blanks

6. The percent proportion of nitrogen in dry air is .... (20.95%, 78.08%, 0.93%)
7. pH of acid rain usually ranges between .... and .... (5.6 and 6; 7 and 7.4; 0.1 and 3.2).
8. .... causes extensive damage to buildings and sculptural materials. (Green house effect, Global warming, Acid rain).
9. Absence of green house gases will result in decreasing the surface temperature to .... (15°C, – 15°C, – 18° C)
10. The percent proportion of oxygen in pure air is .... (20.95%, 80.05%, 72%).

c. Match the Columns

11. Match the phenomenon/pollutants gives in Column I with example/cause given in Column II.

	Column I (Phenomenon)		Column II (Examples/Cause)
A.	Acid rain	1.	Carbon dioxide, methane
B.	Green house gases	2.	Nitric acid and sulphuric acid
C.	Ozone depletion	3.	Solids suspended in smoke, dust and vapour
D.	Suspended particulate nature	4.	Freons

d. Give One Word or a Phrase

12. Oxide cause damage to lungs, headache, vomiting.
13. Elements that impair body's metabolic activities.
14. The substance that can replace CFC's.
15. Any one disease caused due to ozone hole.

Section II

a. 2 Marks Questions

1. The Taj Mahal is turning yellow.
2. Stone cancer is more prominent now-a-days.
3. How environmental pollution is caused?
4. How does acid rain affect aquatic life?

b. 3 Marks Questions

5. Write the ways that can be used to reduce the global warming.
6. What would have happened if the green house gases were totally missing in the earth's atmosphere? Discuss.

c. 4 Marks Questions

7. Define acid rain and what are its causes?
8. What are the pollutants attacking Taj Mahal? How are they being produced in the atmosphere ?

For explanations scan the given QR Code

Olympiad Section*

Brain Teasing Questions asked in Previous Olympiads

1. Which of the following gases does not cause global warming? (NTSE)
(a) CO_2
(b) O_3
(c) CO
(d) Chlorofluorocarbons

2. Which is a natural source of atmospheric pollution? (INJSO)
(a) Disintegration of rocks and soil
(b) Industrial processes
(c) Automobiles
(d) Photosynthesis

3. The main constituent(s) of acid rain is/are (NTSE)
(a) H_2SO_4 (b) HNO_3
(c) HCl (d) Both (a) and (b)

4. Name the gas that caused the Bhopal gas tragedy.(INJSO)
(a) Carbon cioxide (b) Methyl isocyanate
(c) Carbon monoxide (d) Sulphur dioxide

5. Which acid is not present in acid rain? (NTSE)
(a) HNO_3 (b) H_2SO_3
(c) H_2SO_4 (d) CH_3COOH

6. Which of the following green house gas is released in paddy field ? (INJSO)
(a) CFCs (b) CH_4
(c) SO_2 (d) All of these

7. Which of the following is responsible for damaging Taj Mahal and other monuments near Agra? (NTSE)
(a) SO_2
(b) NO_2
(c) Industrial pollutants
(d) All of the above

8. Which of the following statement(s) is/are wrong?(INJSO)
(a) Ozone is not responsible for green house effect
(b) Ozone can oxidise sulphur dioxide present in the atmosphere to sulphur trioxide
(c) Ozone hole is thinning of ozone layer present in stratosphere
(d) Ozone is produced in upper stratosphere by the action of UV rays on oxygen

9. Which of the following reaction(s) is/are carried out during the formation of O_3 layer in stratosphere? (NTSE)
(a) $O_2(g) \xrightarrow{UV} O(g) + O(g)$ (b) $O(g) + O_2 \xrightarrow{UV} O_3(g)$
(c) $O_3(g) \xrightarrow{UV} O_2(g) + O(g)$ (d) All of these

10. Which main compounds are causing damage to ozone layer? (INJSO)
(a) Nitric oxide (b) Freons
(c) Both (a) and (b) (d) Carbon dioxide

11. CFCs deplete the ozone layer because (NTSE)
(a) they release Cl_2 gas
(b) they release chlorine free radical
(c) they release F_2 gas
(d) Both (a) and (b)

12. Name the disease caused due to hole in the ozone layer. (INJSO)
(a) Skin cancer (b) Plague
(c) Huntington's chorea (d) Cholera

13. Excessive release of CO_2 into the atmosphere results in (NTSE)
(a) polar vortex (b) formation of smog
(c) global warming (d) depletion of ozone

Answers

1. (c)	2. (a)	3. (d)	4. (b)	5. (d)	6. (b)	7. (d)	8. (a)	9. (d)	10. (c)
11. (b)	12. (a)	13. (c)							

* *These questions may or may not be asked in the examination, have been given just for additional practice required for olympiads Scholarship Exams etc. For detailed explanations refer Page No. 136.*

Explanations of Olympiad Sections

Chapter 1

1. (*c*) Mass per cent of an element

$$= \frac{\text{Atomic mass of the element present in the compound}}{\text{Molar mass of the compound}} \times 100$$

(i) Relative molecular mass of NH_4NO_3

$= 2 \times \text{Atomic mass of N} + 4 \times \text{Atomic mass of H} + 3 \times \text{Atomic mass of O.}$

$= 2 \times 14 + 4 \times 1 + 3 \times 16$

$= 28 + 4 + 48$

$= 80\ u$

Mass per cent of nitrogen

$$= \frac{2 \times (\text{Atomic mass of nitrogen})}{\text{Molecular mass of } NH_4NO_3} \times 100$$

$$= \frac{2 \times 14}{80} \times 100 = 35\%$$

(ii) Molecular mass of $(NH_4)_2SO_4$

$= 2 \times \text{atomic mass of N} + 8 \times \text{atomic mass of H} + \text{atomic mass of S} + 4 \times \text{atomic mass of O.}$

$= 2 \times 14 + 8 \times 1 + 32 + 4 \times 16$

$= 28 + 8 + 32 + 64 = 132\ u$

Mass per cent of nitrogen

$$= \frac{2 \times (\text{Atomic mass of nitrogen})}{\text{Molecular mass of } (NH_4)_2SO_4} \times 100$$

$$= \frac{2 \times 14}{132} \times 100 = 21.2\ \%$$

2. (*a*) To equalise oxygen atoms, multiply H_2O by 4, i.e.

$$Fe^{2+} + MnO_4^- + H^+ \longrightarrow Mn^{2+} + Fe^{+3} + 4H_2O$$

To equalise hydrogen atoms, multiply H^+ by 8, i.e.

$$Fe^{2+} + MnO_4^- + 8H^+ \longrightarrow Mn^{2+} + Fe^{+3} + 4H_2O$$

Hence, the equation is balanced now.

So, the sum of coefficients in this equation is 16.

3. (*b*) Valence electrons are the electrons present in outermost shell of an atom. Cl^- ion is formed when Cl atom gains an electron. The atomic number of Cl is 17, it has $17e^-$, when it gains one e^-, it becomes Cl^- ion and has $18e^-$.

Thus, electronic configuration of Cl^- atom and Cl^- ion are as follow:

Cl (atom) = 2, 8 7; Valence electrons = 7

Cl^- (ion) = 2, 8, 8 Valence electrons = 8

Hence, Cl^- ion has 8 valence electrons.

4. (*a*) Formula of oxide = *MO*

Valency of *M* will be 2.

So, formula of phosphate

$$M^{2+} \times PO_4^{3-} \longrightarrow M_3(PO_4)_2$$

5. (*a*) Carbon tetrachloride

$$C^{4+} \times Cl^{-1} \longrightarrow CCl_4$$

6. (*a*) Ozone is made up of oxygen atom only.

7. (*b*) $CaCO_3$ is lime stone.

8. (*d*) Statement (d) is not true.

The correct statement is as The molecules and ions aggregate together in large number to form the matter. We cannot see the individual molecules/ions with our eyes, only we can see the various substances which are a big collection of molecules/ions.

Chapter 2

1. (*d*) A decomposition reaction can be characterised as a type of chemical reaction in which one single compound splits into several simpler compounds under suitable conditions.

The reaction stated above is

$$2Pb(NO_3)_2 \longrightarrow 2PbO + 4NO_2 + O_2$$

Here, lead (II) nitrate undergo decomposition reaction to give yellow colour lead (II) oxide, colourless gas of oxygen and brown coloured nitrogen dioxide gas.

In the above-balanced reaction, the coefficient of nitrogen dioxide is 4.

2. (*b*) Endothermic reactions occur by the absorption of heat/energy, so *Y* will be higher in energy than *X*. But exothermic reactions are accompanied by the evolution of heat in which products are lower in energy than the reactants. So, *Z* should be lower in energy than *X* which is option (b).

3. (*c*) A reddish brown compound formed on iron due to its oxidation. On corrosion, ferric hydroxide $[Fe(OH)_3]$ is formed and it forms rust, i.e. $Fe_2O_3 \cdot xH_2O$.

4. (*b*) Decomposition reactions require energy in the form of heat for the decomposition of reactants to form two or more products, so these reactions are endothermic and irreversible. Some of these are exothermic reactions also because they evolve heat after completion of the reaction.

5. (*a*) I. On thermal decomposition, NH_4NO_3 produces N_2, O_2 and H_2O.

$$2NH_4NO_3(s) \xrightarrow{\Delta} 2N_2(g) + O_2(g) + 4H_2O(g)$$

II. Thermal decomposition of ammonium chlorate, i.e. NH_4ClO_3 produces nitrogen gas, chlorine gas, oxygen gas and water.

$$2NH_4ClO_3(s) \longrightarrow N_2(g) + Cl_2(g) + O_2(g) + 4H_2O(l)$$

6. (*b*) $Fe_2O_3 + 2Al \longrightarrow Al_2O_3 + 2Fe$

The above equation is an example of displacement reaction as according to activity series.

Al is more reactive than Fe, so displaces Fe from its compound.

7. (*a*) In test tube I, aluminium being more reactive than zinc, displaces zinc metal from aqueous zinc sulphate solution. So, here chemical reaction takes place.

$$2Al(s) + 3ZnSO_4(aq) \longrightarrow Al_2(SO_4)_3(aq) + 3Zn(s)$$

In test tube II, Lead (Pb) is less reactive than Fe, so it can't displaces iron metal from its sulphate solution.

$$Pb + FeSO_4 \longrightarrow \text{No reaction}$$

In test tube III, reaction occurs because iron is more reactive than lead and displaces it from its nitrate solution.

$$Fe + Pb(NO_3)_2 \longrightarrow Fe(NO_3)_2 + Pb$$

In test tube IV, chemical reaction will not occur because Ag is less reactive than copper (Cu), so, it can't displace copper from its sulphate solution.

$$Ag + CuSO_4 \longrightarrow \text{No reaction.}$$

8. (*b*) In double displacement reaction, two compounds exchange their ions to form two new compounds. Only in reaction (ii), exchange of ions is taking place (cations and anions of both reactants are exchanged).

$$Na_2SO_4 + BaCl_2 \longrightarrow \underset{\text{White ppt.}}{BaSO_4} + 2NaCl$$

9. (*b*) When quicklime reacts with water, a large amount of heat is released along with the formation of calcium hydroxide.

Similarly, the process of dissolving an acid or base in water is a highly exothermic reaction. Evaporation of water and sublimation of camphor are endothermic reaction.

10. (*d*) When copper is heated in presence of air very slowly at high temperature, a layer of brown black copper oxide is formed which protect the copper from extensive corrosion.

Chapter 3

1. (*c*) Maximum amount of a solid that can be dissolved in a specified amount of a given solvent does not depend upon pressure. This is because solid and liquid are highly incompressible and practically remain unaffected by change in pressure.

2. (*c*) Phase transformation takes place at constant temperature. So, temperature remains same.

3. (*d*) At 0°C, water exists as solid, liquid or gas depending upon the conditions.

4. (*b*) Concentration of solution$= \dfrac{\text{Mass of solute}}{\text{Mass of solution}} \times 100$

Mass of common salt (solute) = 50 g

Mass of water = 450 g

Mass of solution = 50 + 450 = 500 g

$$\text{Concentration of solution} = \frac{50}{500} \times 100 = 10\%$$

5. (*b*) The major part of all living organisms is made up of water. Human body has about 65% and some plants have as much as 95% water.

6. (*d*) Temporary hardness of water is due to the presence of calcium and magnesium hydrogen carbonates.

7. (*a*) The substance which can remove chemically combined water molecules from compound is called dehydrating agent. Hot aluminium oxide is an example of dehydrating agent.

8. (*d*) The chemical name of white vitriol is zinc sulphate heptahydrate ($ZnSO_4 \cdot 7H_2O$).

9. (*d*) Glauber's salt is an example of efflouresence because when it is exposed to dry air, it becomes a powdery anhydrous sodium sulphate.

$$\underset{\substack{\text{Hydrated sodium sulphate} \\ \text{(Glauber's salt)}}}{Na_2SO_4 \cdot 10H_2O} \xrightarrow{\text{Dry air}} \underset{\text{Anhydrous}}{Na_2SO_4} + 10H_2O$$

10. (*a*) When more amount of solute can be added to the solution at a particular temperature, then it is called as unsaturated solution.

Chapter 4

1. (*d*) As we move from top to bottom in group, the atomic radius will be increased because the incoming electron enters into a new subshell.

Li, Na, K, Rb, Cs are IA group elements. From Li to Cs, the atomic radius will be increased. So, the correct order of atomic radii is Li < Na < K < Rb < Cs.

Hence, option (d) is correct.

2. (*c*) The oxides of alkali metals are more basic than alkaline earth metals. On moving down the group of alkali metals or alkaline earth metals, the basic character increases.

Hence, the increasing order of basic character is $MgO < SrO < K_2O < Cs_2O$.

3. (*b*) P has 5 valence electrons and instead of losing 5 valence electrons, it will favourably gain 3 electrons to complete its octet and forming P^{3-}.

4. (*d*) An element *X* combines with hydrogen to form a compound XH_3. The element *X* is placed on the right side of the periodic table.

So, the element *X* can be aluminium, i.e. belongs to group III A or 13. As the electronic configuration of Al is 2, 8, 3. So, it has three valence electrons and is a metal and a solid. AlH_3 reacts with water to form a basic compound $Al(OH)_3$.

$$AlH_3 + 3H_2O \longrightarrow Al(OH)_3 + 3H_2$$

5. (*d*) An element *X* belongs to group 2 and period 3 of the periodic table, so it have valency of +2 (due to 2 valence electron) and will form $X(NO_3)_2$, XSO_4, $X_3(PO_4)_2$.

6. (*d*) In the group 17, element in period three has atomic number = 17, i.e. (electronic configuration is 2, 8, 7).

The element in period four will have electronic configuration as 2, 8, 18, 7, i.e. atomic number = 35 and the element in period five will have electronic configuration as 2, 8, 18, 18, 7, i.e. atomic number = 53.

7. (*a*) Beryllium is kinetically inert to oxygen and water as it forms oxide film on the surface. But powdered beryllium burns brightly on ignition in the air to give oxides and nitrides of beryllium.

8. (*b*) Group 17 element (halogens) are highly reactive due to the presence of seven electrons in their valence shell.

9. (c) Noble gas have completely filled valence shell. Due to this reason, they are stable and do not react with other elements.
Hence, noble gases are called inert gases means they do not react with other elements to form chemical compounds.
10. (b) The melting and boiling points of alkali metals are low due to weak metallic bonding and they decrease further down the group due to simultaneous weakening of their metallic bonds.
11. (d) Alkali metals and their salts impart colours to the flame because the outer electrons get excited to higher energy levels. When the electrons return to the original state, it releases visible light of a characteristic wavelength which provides colour to the flame. The colour of the flame of caesium is blue.
12. (b) The normal oxide formed by the element present on the extreme left of periodic table is the most basic, e.g. Na_2O.

Chapter 5

1. (d) Mass of an atom is due to neutrons and protons since mass of electron is almost 1/1833 times of mass of neutron and proton, so we can neglect mass of electron.
In ${}_{18}Ar^{40}$ number of protons = 18
Number of neutrons = 40 – 18 = 22
Let us take mass of proton and mass of neutron as 'm' because both have equal masses.
Atomic mass (M) of Ar = 18 m + 22 m = 40 m
When mass of neutron in argon is made half, i.e. $\left(\frac{m}{2}\right)$, then, change in atomic mass (M) or Ar
$$= 18\,m + 22\left(\frac{m}{2}\right) = 29\,m$$
So, % change $= \left[\frac{(40+29)\,m}{40\,m}\right] \times 100 = 27\%$
Hence, atomic mass of ${}_{18}Ar^{40}$ will be reduced by 27%.
2. (b) Atomic number of Fe = 26
i.e. Number of proton = number of electrons = 26
Mass number of Fe = 56
So, number of neutrons
= mass number – number of protons = 56 – 26 = 30
Fe^{2+} (ferrous ion) is formed when Fe loses it's two electrons, i.e. now, number of electrons becomes 24.
Hence, in haemoglobin there are 26 protons, 24 electrons and 30 neutrons.
3. (a) Atoms having same atomic number but different mass numbers are termed as isotopes.
4. (b) 8
5. (d) Fact (based)
6. (b) Mass number = Number of protons + Number of neutron
$$27 + P + N$$
$$27 - 14 = P \Rightarrow P = 13$$
In an neutral atom, number of proton = number of electrons. The ion of this element has three positive charge. Thus, number of electrons present in ion
$$= 13 - 3 = 10$$
The element is Al and ion is Al^{3+}.
7. (b) Neon is an inert gas and has no isotope.
8. (d) The elements having different atomic number but same mass number are called isobars.
9. (c) Tritium is ${}_1^3H$.
Mass number option : (A)
= Number of neutron + proton = 3
Atomic number option : (Z) = Number of proton = 1
Number of neutron = A – Z = 3 – 1 = 2
10. (c) Isotopes have same number of protons and different number of neutrons or mass number is different.
11. (b) Cl^- ion = $\begin{matrix} K & L & M \\ 2 & 8 & 8 \end{matrix}$ so, valence electrons are 8.
12. (d) $Na \Rightarrow (Z = 11)$; $\begin{matrix} K & L & M \\ 2 & 8 & 1 \end{matrix}$
13. (a) Electron is discovered by J.J. Thomson by plum pudding model.
14. (a) $C(Z = 6)$ has electronic configuration = $\begin{matrix} K & L \\ 2 & 4 \end{matrix}$

Chapter 6

1. (a) Hydrogen has resemblance to the alkali metals, which lose one electron to form unipositive ions, as well as with halogens, which gain one electron to form uninegative ion.
2. (c) In atomic form, hydrogen (${}_1H^1$ or ${}_1H^2$ or ${}_1H^3$) consists of only one proton and one electron.
3. (a) Hydrogen has three isotopes–protium (${}_1^1H$), deuterium (${}_1^2H$) and tritium (${}_1^3H$). These isotopes differ from one another in respect to the presence of neutrons. In protium, deuterium and tritium number of neutrons respectively are 0,1 and 2.
4. (c) Ordinary hydrogen, protium, has no neutrons, deuterium (also known as heavy hydrogen) has one and tritium has two neutrons in the nucleus.
5. (c) Tritium is the radioactive isotope of hydrogen which emits low energy β-particle whose half-life period ($t_{1/2}$) is 12.33 years.
6. (b) Oxides of Zn are amphoteric in nature, i.e. reacts with both acid as well as base. Therefore, they react with both HCl and NaOH.

7. (c) Hydrogen is highly combustible and even the slightest of spark can set it on fire.
Hence, helium is preferred over hydrogen for filling balloons.

8. (c) Active metals like sodium, potassium and calcium are highly reactive, so they react with water producing bases and releasing hydrogen gas.

9. (d) Hydrogen is an inflammable and one of the lightest gas. Cooling gaseous hydrogen below –253°C (–423°F) causes it to liquefy. Hydrogen gas is a reducing agent.
Hence, statement (d) is incorrect.

10. (c) $\overset{+2}{Pb}O + \overset{0}{H_2} \longrightarrow \overset{0}{Pb} + \overset{+2}{H_2}O$
Hence, PbO is oxidising agent and PbO is reduced to Pb. So, statement (c), i.e. PbO is oxidised to Pb is incorrect.

11. (b) Zinc (Zn) is the only metal among these which gives hydrogen on reaction with water, acids and alkalis.

12. (b) Copper (Cu) does not give hydrogen with acids because it comes below hydrogen in the activity series. So, it is least reactive with water.

Chapter 7

1. (d) All gases obey Charles' law at very low pressures and high temperatures.

2. (a) $pV = nRT$ (ideal gas equation)
If n is constant, then $\frac{p_1V_1}{T_1} = \frac{p_2V_2}{T_2} \Rightarrow \frac{p_1V_1}{p_2V_2} = \frac{T_1}{T_2}$

3. (a) When gases expand, they occupy all the available space. So, the volume of gases increases.

4. (c) Pressure is the force exerted by the gas molecules on the wall by virtue of momentum change during their elastic collision with the wall atoms.

5. (c) The average kinetic energy of a gas molecule is directly proportional to the absolute temperature of the gas. An increase in temperature, increases the speed in which the gas molecules move.

6. (c) The conversion of °C in Kelvin takes place by adding 273.
$$58°C = 58 + 273 = 331\,K$$

7. (b) The unit of pressure is atmosphere (atm).

8. (a) Boyle's law tells us the pressure temperature relationship which states that at constant temperatures, the product of pressure and volume of a fixed amount of a gas is constant.

9. (c) The lowest hypothetical or imaginary temperature at which all molecular motion ceases is called absolute zero, i.e. –273.16°C.

10. (b) $\because$ pV = constant, so if p becomes 4 times then V will become 1/4 time.

Chapter 8

1. (c) Heat trapping gases such as CO_2, CH_4, O_3, CFCs and water vapour present in the atmosphere can cause global warming. CO does not cause global warming.

2. (a) The disintegration of rocks and soil by the action of moisture, heat, frost, air, etc., is the natural source of air pollution.

3. (d) SO_2 and NO_2 undergo oxidation followed by reaction with H_2O produces H_2SO_4 and HNO_3 respectively which are major contributors of acid rain, because polluted air usually contains particulate matter that catalyse their oxidation.
$$2SO_2(g) + O_2(g) + 2H_2O(l) \longrightarrow 2H_2SO_4(aq)$$
$$4NO_2(g) + O_2(g) + 2H_2O(l) \longrightarrow 4HNO_3(aq)$$

4. (b) Bhopal gas tragedy caused due to leakage of Methyl Isocyanate (MIC).

5. (d) CH_3COOH (acidic acid) is not present in acid rain.

6. (b) Rice paddy fields are a source of the green house gases such as carbon dioxide (CO_2), methane (CH_4) and nitrous oxide (N_2O).

7. (d) Agra has a number of industries. The pollutants from industries are released in the air which includes oxides of sulphur and nitrogen. This leads to acid rain which is responsible for damaging Taj Mahal and other monuments near Agra.

8. (a) O_3 is responsible for greenhouse effect. Its contribution is about 8%.

9. (d) The UV radiations split O_2 into free O-atoms. These O-atoms combine with the O_2 to form ozone.
$$O_2(g) \xrightarrow{UV} O\,(g) + O\,(g)$$
$$O\,(g) + O_2(g) \xrightleftharpoons{UV} O_3(g)$$

10. (c) Depletion of ozone layer is being caused by certain compounds such as chlorofluorocarbon compounds (CFCs) i.e. freons, oxides of nitrogen etc.obtained from various human activities.

11. (b) CFCs after reaching the stratosphere get broken down by powerful UV radiations and release chlorine free radicals which is responsible for the depletion of ozone layer.

12. (d) Acid rain results from acids such as sulphuric acid and nitric acid present in polluted air. These acids are formed when oxides of sulphur and nitrogen come into contact with rain water.

13. (a) Depletion of ozone layer results in entering of ultraviolet rays into the atmosphere which causes various diseases and skin cancer is one of them.

14. (c) CO_2 has the property of traping heat from the sun. So, higher the level of carbon dioxide, the higher will be the heat trapped. This leads to the rise in the temperature of the earth, resulting in global warming.

Internal Assessment of Practical Work

Experiment 1

Identification of Gases

S. No.	Experiment	Observations	Inferences
1.	**Detection of Hydrogen** (H_2)		
	• Dilute hydrochloric acid (HCl) or dilute sulphuric (H_2SO_4) acid is added to one of the active metals (e.g. Mg). • **Reaction** $Mg + \underset{\text{dil.}}{H_2SO_4} \longrightarrow MgSO_4 + H_2 \uparrow$ • Moist blue litmus and a burning splinter is brought near to the mouth of test tube.	• A colourless, odourless gas is evolved which is neutral towards litmus. • It put off the burning wooden splinter after giving a pale blue flame and producing a pop sound.	Presence of H_2 is confirmed.
2.	**Detection of Oxygen** (O_2)		
	• Lead dioxide is strongly heated in a boiling tube. • **Reaction** $2PbO_2 \xrightarrow{\Delta} 2PbO + O_2 \uparrow$ • Moist blue litmus paper and a burning splinter is brought near to the mouth of test tube.	• A colourless, odourless gas is evolved which is neutral towards litmus.It increased the glow of burning wood splinter.	Presence of O_2 is confirmed.
3.	**Detection of Carbon Dioxide** (CO_2)		
	• Dilute sulphuric acid (H_2SO_4) or dilute hydrochloric acid (HCl) is added to metal carbonate. • **Reaction** $ZnCO_3 + \text{Dil. } 2HCl \longrightarrow ZnCl_2 + CO_2 + H_2O$ • Moist blue litmus paper is brought near to the mouth of the test tube. • Pass the evolved gas through lime water, $Ca(OH)_2$.	• A colourless, odourless gas is evolved which turned moist blue litmus paper red. • It put off the burning wooden splinter and turned lime water milky.	Presence of CO_2 is confirmed.
4.	**Detection of Chlorine** (Cl_2)		
	• Concentrated HCl is added to the lead oxides (Pb_3O_4 or PbO_2) or manganese oxide (MnO_2). • **Reaction** $PbO_2 + 4HCl \longrightarrow PbCl_2 + 2H_2O + Cl_2 \uparrow$ $Pb_3O_4 + 8HCl \longrightarrow 3PbCl_2 + 4H_2O + Cl_2 \uparrow$ $MnO_2 + 4HCl \longrightarrow MnCl_2 + H_2O + Cl_2 \uparrow$ • Moist blue litmus paper and moist a stach iodide paper is brough near to the mouth of test tube.	• A greenish yellow gas with pungent smell is evolved which turned moist blue litmus paper first red and then decolourised it. • It turned moist starch iodide paper blue black.	Presence of Cl_2 is confirmed.

S. No.	Experiment	Observations	Inferences
5.	**Detection of Hydrogen Chloride** (HCl)		
	• Concentrated H_2SO_4 is added to sodium chloride (NaCl) or potassium chloride (KCl). • **Reaction** $NaCl + conc. H_2SO_4 \longrightarrow NaHSO_4 + HCl\uparrow$ $KCl + conc. H_2SO_4 \longrightarrow KHSO_4 + HCl\uparrow$ • Moist litmus paper or rod dipped in ammonium hydroxide is brought near to the mouth of test tube.	• A colourless gas with pungent smell is evolved. It turned moist blue litmus paper red. • It produced dense white fumes when a glass rod dipped in ammonium hydroxide solution is brought near to it.	Presence of HCl is confirmed
6.	**Detection of Sulphur Dioxide** (SO_2)		
	• Dilute HCl or dilute H_2SO_4 is added to the sodium sulphite. • **Reaction** $Na_2SO_3 + dil. 2HCl \longrightarrow 2NaCl + H_2O + SO_2\uparrow$ $Na_2SO_3 + dil. H_2SO_4 \longrightarrow Na_2SO_4 + H_2O + SO_2\uparrow$ $\underset{\text{(Orange)}}{K_2Cr_2O_7} + 3SO_2 + H_2SO_4 \longrightarrow K_2SO_4 + H_2O + \underset{\text{(Green)}}{Cr_2(SO_4)_3}$ $\underset{\text{(Purple)}}{2KMnO_4} + 2H_2O + 5SO_2 \longrightarrow K_2SO_4 + \underset{\text{(Colourless)}}{2MnSO_4} + 2H_2SO_4$ • Blue litmus paper, a paper dipped in acidified $K_2Cr_2O_7$ and in $KMnO_4$ and *a* burning splinter is brought near to the mouth of test tube.	• A colourless gas with pungent suffocating smell, similar to that of burning sulphur is evolved. • This gas turned moist blue litmus paper red. • It put off burning splinter of wood, turned lime water milky, decolourised $KMnO_4$ solution and turned orange solution of acidified $K_2Cr_2O_7$ green.	Presence of SO_2 is confirmed.
7.	**Detection of Hydrogen Sulphide** (H_2S)		
	• Dilute HCl or dilute H_2SO_4 is added to a metal sulphide. • **Reaction** $Na_2S + 2HCl \longrightarrow 2NaCl + H_2S\uparrow$ $ZnS + H_2SO_4 \longrightarrow ZnSO_4 + H_2S\uparrow$ • Blue litmus paper or filter paper dipped in lead acetate is brought near to the mouth of test tube.	• A colourless gas with smell of rotten eggs is evolved. • It turned moist blue litmus paper red. • It also turned lead acetate paper black.	Presence of H_2S is confirmed.
8.	**Detection of Ammonia** (NH_3)		
	• Ammonium salts is heated with alkalies. • **Reaction** $NH_4Cl + NaOH \xrightarrow{\Delta} NaCl + H_2O + NH_3\uparrow$ $(NH_4)_2SO_4 + 2KOH \xrightarrow{\Delta} K_2SO_4 + 2H_2O + 2NH_3\uparrow$ • Red litmus paper and a rod dipped in conc. HCl is brought near to the mouth of test tube.	• A colourless gas with pungent smell is evolved. • It turned moist red litmus paper blue. • It produced dense fume, when brought in contact with a rod dipped in conc. HCl.	Presence of NH_3 is confirmed.
9.	**Detection of Water Vapour** (H_2O)		
	• Heat a salt containing water of crystallisation (like hydrated sodium carbonate or hydrated copper sulphate). • **Reaction** $CuSO_4 \cdot 5H_2O \xrightarrow{\Delta} CuSO_4 + 5H_2O$ • Litmus paper is brought near to the mouth of test tube. The condensed liquid is dropped anhydrous copper sulphate.	• A colourless, odourless gas is evolved which has no effect on litmus. It condensed to liquid state at room temperature. • It turned anhydrous $CuSO_4$ (from white) to blue.	Presence of H_2O is confirmed.

S. No.	Experiment	Observations	Inferences
10.	**Detection of Nitrogen Dioxide** (NO_2)		
	• Concentrated nitric acid is added to copper turnings. The contents of the test tube is heated. • **Reaction** $Cu + Conc.\,4HNO_3 \longrightarrow Cu(NO_3)_2 + 2H_2O + 2NO_2\uparrow$ • Blue litmus paper and iodide paper is brought near to the mouth of test tube. • The evolved gas is passed through acidified ferrous sulphate solution.	• A reddish brown gas with pungent smell is evolved which turned moist blue litmus paper red. • It also turned iodide paper blue and acidified $FeSO_4$ solution brown.	Presence of NO_2 is confirmed.

Experiment 2

Action of Heat on Given (Unknown) Substances

Heating causes both physical and chemical changes. Physical changes usually involve melting and evaporation while chemical changes involve decomposition of a substance, dehydration of hydrated crystals of substance. Observations of change in colour during the heating, gas evolved, etc., helps to identify the heated substance.

S. No.	Observations	Inferences
1.	**Action of Heat on $CuCO_3$ and $ZnCO_3$**	
	(a) Copper Carbonate ($CuCO_3$)	
	(i) The given substance is light green amorphous powder which turns black on heating.	The black residue is CuO.
	(ii) A colourless, odourless gas evolves on heating which turns lime water milky.	The gas evolved is CO_2.
	Chemical reactions $\underset{\text{Light green}}{CuCO_3} \xrightarrow{\Delta} \underset{\text{Black}}{CuO} + CO_2\uparrow$ $\underset{\text{Lime water}}{Ca(OH)_2} + CO_2 \longrightarrow CaCO_3\downarrow + H_2O$	The substance heated is $CuCO_3$.
	(b) Zinc Carbonate ($ZnCO_3$)	
	(i) The given substance is white amorphous solid which turns to pale yellow solid on strong heating.	
	(ii) A colourless, odourless gas evolves which turns lime water milky.	The gas evolved is CO_2.
	(iii) The residue turns white on cooling. **Chemical reaction** $ZnCO_3 \xrightarrow{\Delta} ZnO + CO_2$	The white residue is ZnO. The substance heated is $ZnCO_3$.
2.	**Action of Heat on $Na_2CO_3 \cdot 10\,H_2O$ and $CuSO_4 \cdot 5\,H_2O$**	
	(a) Washing Soda ($Na_2CO_3 \cdot 10\,H_2O$):	
	(i) The given substance is white, crystalline solid which on heating gives steamy vapour and subsequently melts. On cooling, the residue left is white amorphous solid.	The white residue is Na_2CO_3.
	(ii) The vapour that evolves, condenses into liquid upon cooling and turns white anhydrous $CuSO_4$ to blue hydrated $CuSO_4$.	The vapour evolved is H_2O.

S. No.	Observations	Inferences
	Chemical reaction $Na_2CO_3 \cdot 10\,H_2O \xrightarrow{\Delta} Na_2CO_3 + 10\,H_2O \uparrow$	The substance heated is washing soda (hydrated sodium carbonate - $Na_2CO_3 \cdot 10\,H_2O$)
	(b) Copper Sulphate Crystals ($CuSO_4 \cdot 5\,H_2O$)	
	(i) The given substance is blue crystalline solid which produces steamy vapour and white residue on heating.	The white residue is $CuSO_4$.
	(ii) The vapour that evolves, condenses into liquid upon cooling and turns blue cobalt chloride paper pink.	The vapour evolved is H_2O.
	Chemical reaction $CuSO_4 \cdot 5\,H_2O \xrightarrow{\Delta} CuSO_4 + 5\,H_2O \uparrow$	The substance heated to give white residue is copper sulphate crystal.
3.	**Action of Heat on $Zn(NO_3)_2 \cdot 6H_2O$, $Cu(NO_3)_2 \cdot 6H_2O$ and $Pb(NO_3)_2$**	
	(a) Zinc Nitrate Hexahydrate $[Zn(NO_3)_2 \cdot 6H_2O]$	
	(i) The given substance is white, crystalline, deliquescent solid which on heating, produces steamy vapour and melts to form a white viscous liquid.	The initially evolved steamy vapour is H_2O.
	(ii) The vapour that evolves, condenses into liquid and turns white anhydrous $CuSO_4$ to blue hydrated $CuSO_4$.	
	(iii) When the residue is heated more strongly, it produces a new pale yellow residue along with reddish brown fumes which turns moist blue litmus paper red.	The reddish brown fumes are mixture of NO_2 and O_2.
	(iv) On bringing a glowing wood splinter in the fumes, it inflames, which suggest the presence of oxygen in the fumes.	
	(v) The pale yellow residue turns white on cooling.	The final residue is ZnO.
	Chemical reactions $Zn(NO_3)_2 \cdot 6\,H_2O \xrightarrow{\Delta} Zn(NO_3)_2 + 6\,H_2O$ $Zn(NO_3)_2 \xrightarrow{\Delta} 2\,ZnO + 4NO_2 + O_2 \uparrow$	The given substance is $Zn(NO_3)_2 \cdot 6\,H_2O$.
	(b) Copper Nitrate Hexahydrate $[Cu(NO_3)_2 \cdot 6H_2O]$	
	(i) The given substance is bluish green crystalline solid which produces steamy vapour and turns to bluish green amorphous solid on heating.	
	(ii) The vapour that evolves, condenses into liquid and turns white anhydrous $CuSO_4$ to blue hydrated $CuSO_4$.	
	(iii) On heating the residue even more strongly, it produces a new black residue along with reddish brown fumes which turn moist blue litmus paper red.	The initially evolved steamy vapour is H_2O. The reddish brown fumes are mixture of NO_2 and O_2.
	(iv) On bringing a glowing wood splinter in the fumes, it inflames, which suggest the presence of oxygen in the flame.	The final residue is CuO.
	Chemical reactions $Cu(NO_3)_2 \cdot 6\,H_2O \xrightarrow{\Delta} Cu(NO_3)_2 + 6\,H_2O$ $2Cu(NO_3)_2 \xrightarrow{\Delta} 2\,CuO + 4NO_2 \uparrow + O_2 \uparrow$	The given substance is $Cu(NO_3)_2 \cdot 6\,H_2O$.
	(c) Lead Nitrate $[Pb(NO_3)_2]$	
	(i) The given substance is white, crystalline solid which fuses on heating to produce reddish brown residue along with reddish brown fumes which turn moist blue litmus paper red.	The residue formed is PbO.
	(ii) On bringing a glowing wood splinter in the fumes, it inflames, which suggest the presence of oxygen in the fumes.	The reddish brown fumes are mixture of NO_2 and O_2.

S. No.	Observations	Inferences
	(iii) The reddish brown residue changes to light yellow colour on cooling. **Chemical reaction** $2Pb(NO_3)_2 \xrightarrow{\Delta} 2PbO + 4NO_2\uparrow + O_2\uparrow$	The given substance is $Pb(NO_3)_2$.
4.	**Identification of NH_4Cl, I_2 and $(NH_4)_2Cr_2O_7$**	
	(a) Ammonium Chloride (NH_4Cl) (i) The given substance is white crystalline solid which sublimes to produces dense white fumes on heating, leaving no residue behind.	The fumes consist of NH_3 and HCl.
	(ii) The white fumes condenses to form white powdery solid on cooling. **Chemical reaction** $NH_4Cl \underset{\text{Cool}}{\overset{\Delta}{\rightleftharpoons}} NH_3\uparrow + HCl$	The given substance is NH_4Cl.
	(b) Iodine (I_2) (i) The given substance is greyish brown crystalline solid, which sublimes to produce violet vapours on heating, leaving no residue behind. (ii) The violet vapours turn the white filter paper, dipped in starch solution, blue. (iii) The vapours condense to form greyish brown crystalline solid. **Chemical reaction** $I_2 \xrightarrow{\Delta} 2I\uparrow$	The vapours and the given solid substance are I_2.
	(c) Ammonium Dichromate [$(NH_4)_2Cr_2O_7$] (i) The given substance is reddish orange, crystalline solid which give steamy fumes on heating, leaving greenish grey residue.	The residue formed is Cr_2O_3.
	(ii) On cooling, fumes produce a colourless liquid and a colourless gas.	The liquid and the gas are H_2O and N_2, respectively.
	(iii) The colourless liquid turns white anhydrous $CuSO_4$ to blue hydrated $CuSO_4$. (iv) The colourless, odourless gas neither burns nor supports combustion. It also does not have any effect on lime water. **Chemical reaction** $(NH_4)_2Cr_2O_7 \xrightarrow{\Delta} Cr_2O_3 + N_2\uparrow + 4H_2O\uparrow$	The given substance is $(NH_4)_2Cr_2O_7$.

Experiment 3

Action of Dilute Sulphuric Acid on Unknown Substance

S. No.	Experiment	Observations	Inferences
1.	**Action on Metals**		
	$\underset{\text{Magnesium}}{Mg} + \underset{\text{Dil. sulphuric acid}}{H_2SO_4} \rightarrow MgSO_4 + H_2 \uparrow$ $\underset{\text{Zinc}}{Zn} + \underset{\text{Dil. sulphuric acid}}{H_2SO_4} \rightarrow ZnSO_4 + H_2 \uparrow$ The burning splinter is brought near to gas evolved.	A brisk effervescence of colourless, odourless gas is evolved which burns with a sound of pop.	The evolved gas is hydrogen (H_2). The given substance is a metal.
2.	**Action on Carbonate**		
	$\underset{\text{Sodium carbonate}}{Na_2CO_3} + \underset{\text{Dil. sulphuric acid}}{H_2SO_4} \longrightarrow Na_2SO_4 + H_2O + CO_2 \uparrow$ The gas evolved is passed through lime water.	A brisk effervescence of colourless, odourless gas is evolved which turns lime water milky.	The evolved gas is carbon dioxide (CO_2). The given substance is a carbonate salt.
3.	**Action on Sulphide**		
	$\underset{\text{Sodium sulphide}}{Na_2S} + \underset{\text{Dil. sulphuric acid}}{H_2SO_4} \longrightarrow Na_2SO_4 + H_2S \uparrow$ $\underset{\text{Zinc sulphide}}{ZnS} + \underset{\text{Dil. sulphuric acid}}{H_2SO_4} \longrightarrow ZnSO_4 + H_2S \uparrow$ Brought the lead acetate paper and burning wooden splinter one by one near to the gas evolved.	• A colourless gas having odour of rotten eggs is evolved, which turns lead acetate paper black. • It burns with a pop sound.	The evolved gas is hydrogen sulphide (H_2S). The given substance is a sulphide salt.
4.	**Action on Sulphite**		
	$K_2SO_3 + H_2SO_4 \longrightarrow K_2SO_4 + 2H_2O + SO_2$ The gas evolved is passed through lime water and is also brought near to lead acetate paper.	A colourless gas is evolved having suffocating odour of burning sulphur, which turns lime water milky and lead acetate paper black.	The evolved gas is sulphur dioxide (SO_2). The given substance is sulphite salt.

Experiment 4

AIM

To apply the flame test to identify the metal in the unknown substance.

(i) A sodium salt

(ii) A potassium salt

(iii) A calcium compound

Theory

If a given salt consists of metal ion, then it can be detected by the flame test. In this test, certain metals impart characteristic colour to the flame, which becomes basis of their identification.

Procedure

(i) Take a thin platinum wire and make a circular loop at its end.

(ii) Clean it by dipping it in concentrated hydrochloric acid and subsequently heating in the non-luminous flame of the burner.

(iii) This process is repeated until the platinum wire does not impart any colour to the flame.

(iv) Make a thin paste of given salt with concentrated hydrochloric acid.

(v) Apply this paste on the loop of the wire.

(vi) Bring this loop of wire (containing paste) in the flame.

(vii) Observe and note the colour imparted to the flame.

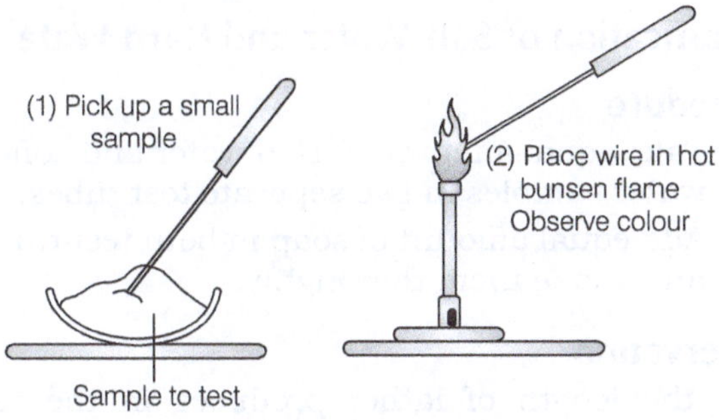

Performing flame test

Observation Table

S. No.	Observation		Inference
	Colour Imparted to the Flame		
	Colour observed with Naked Eyes	Colour seen through a blue Glass	Presence of metal ion
(i)	Golden yellow (Persistent)	Pale yellow (Vanishes)	Sodium ion (Na^+)
(ii)	Lilac (voilet)	Lilac (voilet)	Potassium ion (K^+)
(iii)	Brick red	Pale green	Calcium ion (Ca^{2+})

Experiment 5

AIM

To carry out simple experiments based on hard water and soft water.

Theory

On the basis of action with soaps, there are two types of water

(i) Hard Water

This kind of water does not form lather or foam with soap, easily.

e.g. Ground water, river water, sea water, etc.

(ii) Soft Water

This kind of water readily produces lather with soap. e.g. Rain water and distilled water.

Cause of Hardness of the Water

Hard water consists of dissolved salts, i.e. bicarbonates [$Ca(HCO_3)_2$, $Mg(HCO_3)_2$], chlorides ($CaCl_2$, $MgCl_2$) and sulphates ($CaSO_4$, $MgSO_4$). These salts form complex with soap molecule which prevents soap from dissolving in water and hence reduces its cleansing capacity.

Types of Hardness of Water

There are two types of hardness of water which are as follows

(i) Temporary Hardness

This kind of hardness can be removed easily by boiling the water. It is caused due to presence of Ca and Mg bicarbonates.

(ii) **Permanent Hardness**

This kind of hardness of water cannot be removed by boiling the water. It is caused due to presence of chlorides and sulphates of calcium and magnesium.

Identification of Soft Water and Hard Water

Procedure

(i) Take equal amount of hard water and soft water samples in two separate test tubes.

(ii) Add equal amount of soap in both test tubes and shake them thoroughly.

Observation

Note the length of lather produces in the test tubes.

Inference

The sample of water which produce more lather in the test tube is soft water while the other one is hard water.

Identification of Temporary and Permanent Hard Water

Procedure

(i) Take equal amount of temporary and permanent hard water samples in two separate test tubes.

(ii) Boil both the samples and let them cool down to room temperature.

(iii) Filter both the sample in different separate test tubes and add little but equal amount of soap to each sample.

(iv) Shake both the tubes thoroughly.

Observation

Note down the length of laher formed in each case.

Inference

Heating temporary hard water removes its hardness and makes it soft, as bicarbonates convert into carbonates and settled down.

$$Ca(HCO_3)_2 \xrightarrow{\Delta} CaCO_3 \downarrow + H_2O + CO_2 \uparrow$$

Thus, the sample which formed more lather is temporary hard while the other one is permanent hard water.

Removal of Hardness of Water

Following methods can be implied to soften a hard water

(i) **Boiling the Temporary Hard Water**

As discussed above, boiling a temporary hard water precipitate the bicarbonates in the form of carbonates. By filtering out the insoluble carbonates we get soft water.

(ii) **Removing Temporary as well as Permanent Hardness of Water**

As discussed in the experiment, the hardness of water cannot be removed easily by boiling the water.

Procedure

(i) Take about 100 mL of permanent (or temporary) hard water in a beaker and add about 2 g of washing soda in it.

(ii) Stir the mixture well and filter out the insoluble salt from it.

(iii) Mix this soften water with soap to test whether the lather is formed easily.

Observation

The soften water form lather readily with a soap.

Inference

Washing soda forms percipitate with hardening agents of hard water as follows

(a) **In case of temporary hard water**

$$\underset{\text{Bicarbonate (present in temporary hard water)}}{Ca(HCO_3)_2} + \underset{\text{Washing soda}}{Na_2CO_3} \longrightarrow \underset{\text{Insoluble calcium carbonate (precipitat)}}{CaCO_3} \downarrow + 2\,NaHCO_3$$

(b) **In case of permanent hard water**

$$CaCl_2 + \underset{\text{Washing soda}}{Na_2CO_3} \longrightarrow \underset{\text{Insoluble calcium carbonate (precipitat)}}{CaCO_3} \downarrow + 2\,NaCl$$

Advantage of Using Detergents over Soap in Hard Water

Sodium or potassium salt of higher fatty acids are called **soaps**. e.g. Sodium stearate, potassium palmate etc. where as, sodium salts of alkyl sulphonic acids are called **detergents**. e.g. Sodium dodecyl benzene sulphonate.

The main advantage of using detergents over soap is that detergents form lather even in hard water and hence are more effective cleaning agent.

Comparision of Lather Formation by Soaps and Detergents

Procedure

(i) Take about 20 mL of hard water in each of two test tubes.

(ii) Add about 1 g of soap in one of the test tubes and about 1 g to detergent in the other test tube. Shake both the tubes properly.

(iii) Note the length of lather formed in each test tube.

Observation

The test tube consisting detergent formed lather while soap did not form lather with hard water.

Inference

Detergents form more lather in hard water in comparision to soaps hence can act as better cleansing agent.

Experiment 6

AIM

To find out the sources of pollution of water bodies in the locality. Suggest preventive steps to control it.

Theory

Mixing of undesirable and usually harmful substances in natural source of water is called water pollution. A polluted water can be identified by the presence of unusual colour, smell, taste and visible mixed substances. A polluted water causes serious health hazards to living beings.

Common Sources of Water Pollution

(i) Soaps and detergents used for washing clothes, utencils, etc., causes serious kind of water pollution.

(ii) Sewage and domestic wastes flushed into a river or a pond makes water unfit for creatures dependent on these water bodies.

(iii) Industries releases wastes containing heavy metals, inorganic and organic compounds are so hazardous and persistent that they enter aquatic food chains and get accumulated there.

(iv) Oil spills, usually by oil carrying ships in sea, causes death of living creatures searching for foods in water.

Quality of Water

To assess the quality of water from a water body in your locality, follow the steps written below

Procedure

(i) Take water sample from a water body (like pond, river, well, etc.)

(ii) Filter the sample and fill it in two or three different test tubes.

(iii) Add a small amount of soap in one of the test tube and shake it thoroughly.

Observation

(i) Note the colour of water.

(ii) Notice, if there are any visible suspended particles.

(iii) Note the odour of water, if any.

(iv) Dip an universal pH paper in a test tube (other than the one having dissolved soap) and note the pH of water normal (pH is 7 for pure water.)

(v) Note the length of the foam formed in the test tube having dissolved soap.

(vi) Repeat all the above observation with purified drinking water.

Inference

Any significant or noticeable deviation in observation of water sample from that of drinking water, suggests the quality of water is unfit for drinking, cooking, etc.

Preventive Steps to Control Water Pollution

(i) Proper treatment of sewage should be done, before releasing it into water bodies.

(ii) Ultraviolet radiations can be used to destroy pathogens present in water.

(iii) Methods like oxidation or precipitation can be used to remove organic matter.

(iv) Gravity settlement and screening can be used to remove heavier floating solids.

(v) Toxic substances from factories should be treated so as to reduce their toxicity.

Viva-Voce

Q 1. Name the gas evolved when dilute sulphuric acid is added to magnesium granules.

Ans. Hydrogen (H_2)

Q 2. Name a gas which increase the glowing wood splinter.

Ans. Oxygen (O_2)

Q 3. Name a metal salt which would produce carbon dioxide gas upon heating.

Ans. Zinc carbonate ($ZnCO_3$)

Q 4. Name a gas which turns lime water milky.

Ans. Carbon dioxide (CO_2)

Q 5. What effect does chlorine gas have on moist starch iodide paper?

Ans. It turns the paper blue black.

Q 6. Name the acidic gas formed upon action of common salt on concentrated sulphuric acid.

Ans. Hydrogen chloride (HCl)

Q 7. Name a gas which decolourise $KMnO_4$ solution and tuns acidified solution of $K_2Cr_2O_7$ green.

Ans. Sulphur dioxide (SO_2)

Q 8. What are the products formed upon action of acid on metal sulphides?

Ans. Metal sulphides like Na_2S and ZnS on reacting with dil. HCl gives NaCl and $ZnCl_2$ respectively alongwith H_2S gas.

Q 9. How can the ammonia gas be prepared?

Ans. Heating ammonia salts with alkalies.

Q 10. How can we turn white $CuSO_4$ solid to blue?

Ans. By adding slight amount of water to the $CuSO_4$.

Q 11. What action does a gas, produced by reaction of nitric acid on copper turning, have on iodide paper?

Ans. The gas (NO_2) turns iodide paper blue.

Q 12. What are the products formed on thermal decomposition of copper (II) carbonate?

Ans. CuO and CO_2 ($CuCO_3 \xrightarrow{\Delta} CuO + CO_2$)

Q 13. How the colour changes during decomposition of $CuCO_3$?

Ans. Colour changes form light green ($CuCO_3$) to black (CuO).

Q 14. How can you distinguish between $ZnCO_3$ and $CuCO_3$?

Ans. $ZnCO_3$ is white and turns pale yellow on heating while $CuCO_3$ is light green and turns black on heating.

Q 15. How many water of crystallisation is associated with each molecule of sodium carbonate in washing soda crystal?

Ans. 10 molecules; ($Na_2CO_3 \cdot 10H_2O$)

Q 16. What colour change is observed when copper sulphate crystal is heated?

Ans. Blue molecules; crystals turn to white solid.

Q 17. Strong heating of zinc nitrate results in evolution of brown fumes. What compose(s) the brown furmes?

Ans. The brown fumes are the mixture of nitrogen dioxide (NO_2) and oxygen (O_2).

Q 18. Name a bluish green crystal which produces fumes of NO_2 and O_2.

Ans. Copper nitrate hexahydrate [$Cu(NO_3)_2 \cdot 6H_2O$].

Q 19. Name a metal nitrate crystal which does not have any water of crystallisation.

Ans. Lead nitrate [$Pb(NO_3)_2$]

Q 20. Name the reddish brown oxide formed after thermal decomposition of a white crystalline nitrate.

Ans. Lead oxide (PbO)

Q 21. Name the process by which ammonium chloride forms ammonia and hydrogen chloride.

Ans. Sublimation

Q 22. Name a substance that sublimes into violet vapour.

Ans. Iodine (I_2)

Q 23. Name the products formed after the thermal decomposition of ammonium dichromate.

Ans. Chromium oxide (Cr_2O_3), nitrogen (N_2) and water (H_2O).

$$(NH_4)_2Cr_2O_7 \xrightarrow{\Delta} Cr_2O_3 + N_2 + 4H_2O$$

Q 24. What effect does H_2S have on lead acetate paper?

Ans. It turns lead acetate paper black.

Q 25. What is the cause of brisk effervescence, when dilute sulphuric acid is added to sodium carbonate?

Ans. Evolution of carbon dioxide gas (CO_2).

Q 26. Name the salt formed in a displacement reaction between zinc metal and dilute sulphuric acid.

Ans. Zinc sulphate

Q 27. Name the colours imparted by salts of sodium, potassium and calcium to the flame.

Ans. Salts of sodium, potassium and calcium impart pale yellow, lilac (violet) and pale green colour respectively to the flame.

Q 28. Why platinum wire is used in a flame test?

Ans. Because platinum does not impart any colour to the flame.

Q 29. Name a gas that turns lime water milky and lead acetate paper black.

Ans. Sulphur dioxide (SO_2)

Q 30. Give examples of sources of hard water and soft water.

Ans. Sources of hard : from pond, well, etc.

Sources of soft water : Rain water, distilled water, etc.

Q 31. Give atleast one example each of substances which causes temporary hardness and permanent hardness.

Ans. Temporary hardness is caused by calcium bicarbonate $[Ca(HCO_3)_2]$.

Permanent hardness is caused by calcium sulphate ($CaSO_4$).

Q 32. How can we removed temporary hardness?

Ans. By boiling the water.

Q 33. Name a method to remove temporary as well as permanent hardness of water.

Ans. Adding washing soda $[Na_2CO_3 \cdot 10\ H_2O]$ into the water.

Q 34. Give one examples of both soap and detergents.

Ans. Soap : Sodium stearate

Detergent : Sodium dodecyl benzene sulphonate.

Q 35. Give examples of sources that cause

(a) pollution on water surface.

(b) hazard to food chain.

Ans. (a) Oil spills

(b) Heavy metals, organic compounds, etc., released from industries.

Q 36. What is the percipitate product formed in the process of softening of hard water?

Ans. Calcium carbonate ($CaCO_3$).

Q 37. Name a cleansing agent effective in hard water.

Ans. Detergents

Q 38. Which produces more lather in hard water soaps or detergents?

Ans. Detergent form more lather in hard water than soap, hence acts as better cleansing agent.

Q 39. Give preventive steps to control water pollution.

Ans. (i) Proper treatment of sewage should be done, before releasing it into water bodies.

(ii) Oxidation or percipitation methods can be used to remove organic matter.

Q 40. How will you distinguish hard water from soft water?

Ans. By dissolving soap in water samples. Hard water does not make lather easily while soft water does.

SAMPLE QUESTION PAPER 1

A HIGHLY SIMULATED Sample Question Paper for ICSE Class IX

Chemistry (Fully Solved)

Time : 2 hours | Max. Marks : 80

GENERAL INSTRUCTIONS

- Answer to this Paper must be written on the paper provided separately.
- You will not be allowed to write during first 15 minutes.
- This time is to be spent in reading the question paper.
- The time given at the head of this Paper is the time allowed for writing the answers.
- **Section A** is compulsory. Attempt any **four** questions from **Section B**.
- The intended marks for questions or parts of questions are given in brackets [].

Section-A [40 Marks]

(Attempt **all** questions from this section.)

1. Choose the correct answers to the questions from the given options. [15]

(i) The formula of calcium hydrogen carbonate is • *Recall*

(a) $CaHCO_3$ (b) $Ca(HCO_3)_2$
(c) Ca_2HCO_3 (d) $Ca(HCO_3)_3$

(ii) An alkaline earth metal is • *Recall*

(a) potassium (b) calcium
(c) lead (d) copper

(iii) In the periodic table, alkali metals are placed in the group • *Recall*

(a) 1 (b) 11 (c) 17 (d) 18

(iv) The products of neutralisation reaction are • *Understanding*

(a) salt and oxygen (b) salt and hydrogen
(c) hydrogen and oxygen (d) salt and water

(v) The reaction, $2Cu + O_2 \longrightarrow 2CuO$ is an example of • *Understanding*

(a) oxidation reaction (b) reduction reaction
(c) redox reaction (d) None of these

(vi) **Assertion** (A) Hydrogen gas can be prepared by the reaction of active metals with cold water.

Reason (R) The reaction of active metals like sodium, potassium and calcium with cold water produces bases and releases hydrogen gas. • *Understanding & Application*

(a) Both A and R are true and R is the correct explanation of A.
(b) Both A and R are true, but R is not the correct explanation of A.
(c) A is true, but R is false.
(d) A is false, but R is true.

(vii) Which of the following is not a balanced equation? • *Understanding*

(a) $Ca(OH)_2 + CO_2 \longrightarrow CaCO_3 + H_2O$
(b) $Fe + Cl_2 \longrightarrow FeCl_3$
(c) $Zn + H_2SO_4 \longrightarrow ZnSO_4 + H_2$
(d) $2KBr + Cl_2 \longrightarrow 2KCl + Br_2$

(viii) Which among the following carbonates do not decompose on heating ? • *Understanding*

(a) Magnesium carbonate (b) Zinc carbonate
(c) Calcium carbonate (d) Potassium carbonate

(ix) Sulphur dioxide combines with oxygen and water to form • *Understanding*

(a) H_2SO_4 (b) H_2SO_3
(c) H_2S (d) H_2O

(x) The metal which burns with lilac flame is • *Recall*

(a) sodium
(b) chromium
(c) potassium
(d) sodium and potassium both

(xi) Which of the following isotope is used for determination of age of fossil fuels? • *Application*

(a) ${}^{12}_{6}C$ (b) ${}^{14}_{6}C$ (c) ${}^{14}_{7}N$ (d) ${}^{13}_{6}C$

(xii) Elements which loose electrons are known as
(a) ionic atom • *Understanding*
(b) electropositive elements
(c) electronegative element
(d) covalent

(xiii) **Assertion** (A) The volume of gas decreases when the pressure is decreased.
Reason (R) According to Boyle's law, pressure and volume are inversely proportional. • *Understanding*
(a) Both A and R are true and R is the correct explanation of A.
(b) Both A and R are true, but R is not the correct explanation of A.
(c) A is true, but R is false.
(d) A is false, bu R is true.

(xiv) When a metal '*X*' reacts with water, the reaction is exothermic and violent. Identify *X*. • *Understanding*
(a) Copper (b) Calcium
(c) Potassium (d) Iron

(xv) 78°C is equal to • *Application*
(a) 351 K
(b) 330 K
(c) 376 K
(d) 350 K

2. (i) Match the Column A with Column B. **[5]** • *Recall*

Column A	Column B
A. Reducing agent	1. Addition of oxygen
B. Oxidation	2. Removal of oxygen
C. Reduction	3. Sodium zincate
D. Amphoteric substance	4. Hydrogen sulphide
E. Water gas	5. Reaction of steam with red hot coke

(ii) The following diagram illustrates the process of reduction of copper from its oxide. **[5]**

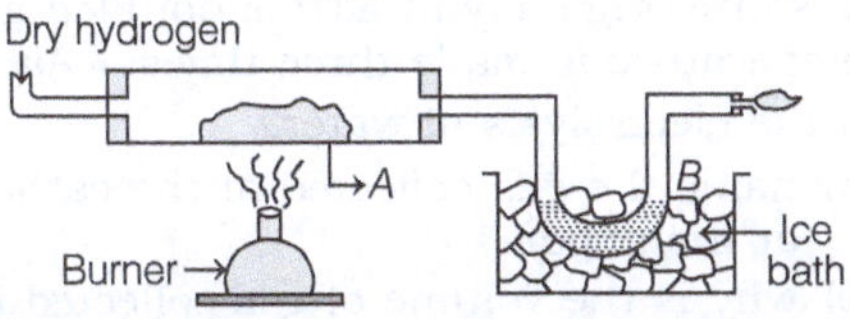

A black coloured substance '*A*' was taken in the combustion tube and heated strongly with H_2 gas, when pinkish red residue was left in the combustion tube and a colourless liquid collected in the *U* tube. Answer the following questions based on the above experiment • *Analysis & Application*
(a) Identify *A* and *B*.
(b) How will you support your answer for *B* ?
(c) What is the nature of hydrogen gas ?
(d) Give the chemical reaction taking place.

(iii) Complete the following by choosing the correct answer from the bracket. **[5]**
(a) All protons are identical and have a charge equal to ………… . (electrons/protons)
(b) ……… is released from degradable matter. (Methane/Carbon dioxide)
(c) Reactive metals like potassium, sodium and calcium react with ……… water forming their corresponding hydroxides and evolving hydrogen. (cold/hot)
(d) The molecular formula of potassium zincate is ……… . [K_2ZnO_2 / $KZnO_2$]
(e) If an element has one electron in its outermost shell, then it is likely to be ……. . [metallic/non-metallic] • *Recall & Understanding*

(iv) Name the gas evolved in each of the following cases. **[5]**
(a) Nitrogen and hydrogen, when subjected to high pressure and iron as catalyst and molybdenum as a promoter.
(b) On passing current through molten sodium chloride.
(c) When zinc reacts with dilute sulphuric acid.
(d) When dilute hydrochloric acid is added to calcium carbonate.
(e) Strong heating of crystals of lead nitrate. • *Recall & Understanding*

(v) (a) Balance each of the chemical equations given below: **[5]** • *Understanding*
1. $Al + KOH + H_2O \longrightarrow KAlO_2 + H_2$
2. $Al + H_2SO_4 \longrightarrow Al_2(SO_4)_3 + 3H_2$

(b) Identify the substance which matches the description given below.
1. A neutral oxide which exists in liquid state at room temperature.
2. The gas used during the process of photosynthesis. It turns lime water milky.
3. The catalyst and promoter used during water gas shift the reaction. • *Recall & Understanding*

Section-B **[40 Marks]**

(Attempt **any four** questions from this section.)

3. (i) Write the formula of the following compounds. **[2]**
(a) Iron (III) sulphide • *Recall*
(b) Calcium hydrogen sulphite

(ii) Fill in the blanks by choosing the correct answer from the brackets : **[2]**
(a) Valency of iron in $FeCl_3$ is ……… [+ 3/ + 2].
(b) Moving from left to right in a period, atomic size ……… [decreases/increases]. • *Understanding*

(iii) Arrange the following as per the instructions given in the brackets: [3]
• *Understanding & Application*
(a) Li, Be, F, N (increasing order of atomic radii)
(b) Cl, At, Br, I, (increasing order of atomic radii)
(c) Be, C, O, N (increasing order of size of atom)

(iv) Write the balanced chemical equations for each of the following: [3]
(a) Dilute hydrochloric acid when added to calcium carbonate salt in a test tube.
(b) Magnesium chloride solution is mixed with sodium carbonate solution.
(c) Addition of dilute nitric acid to magnesium.
• *Recall & Understanding*

4. (i) State a relevant reason for the following. [2]
(a) Mass of an atom is concentrated inside the nucleus of an atom.
(b) Hydrogen obtained by the reaction of zinc and dilute sulphuric acid has a peculiar (fishy) smell. • *Understanding*

(ii) Name the following: [2]
(a) Chemicals responsible for ozone layer depletion.
(b) Green house gases. • *Recall*

(iii) A gas occupies 800 cm^3 under 760 mm of Hg pressure. Calculate the pressure of the gas that will occupy 380 cm^3, the temperature remaining same. • *Application* [3]

(iv) A part of periodic table is shown below with one element missing. [3]

H												He
Li	Be											Ne
Na	Mg											Ar
K	Ca	Sc	Ti	V	Cr	Mn	—	Co	Ni	Cu	Zn	—
Rb	Sr											
Cs	Ba											

Based on the above table, answer the following questions. • *Analysis & Understanding*
(a) Name one element that has, octet structure.
(b) Name the alkali metal present in third period.
(c) Identify the two missing elements.

5. (i) Write one use of the following. [2]
(a) Argon gas (b) Neon gas. • *Application*

(ii) Write the electronic configuration of the following. [2]
(a) $^{27}_{13}X$ (b) $^{35}_{17}Y$ • *Understanding*

(iii) Complete and balance the following equations [3]
(a) $N_2 + O_2 \longrightarrow$ (b) $Ca(NO_3)_2 \xrightarrow{\Delta}$
(c) $PbO_2 \xrightarrow{\Delta}$ • *Recall*

(iv) (a) Explain fractional atomic mass. [3]
(b) Give two uses of isotopes.
(c) Give two examples of radio isotopes.
• *Recall & Understanding*

6. (i) Define/State. [2]
(a) Solute (b) Solvent • *Recall*

(ii) Calculate the percentage of nitrogen in urea $(CO(NH_2)_2$ (Molecular mass of urea = 60). [2]
• *Understanding*

(iii) Choose the substances given in the box below to answer the following questions. [3]

Combination, decomposition, displacement or double displacement.

(a) $NH_3(g) + HCl(g) \longrightarrow NH_4Cl(g)$
(b) $2FeSO_4(s) \xrightarrow{\text{Heat}} Fe_2O_3(s) + SO_2(g) + SO_3(g)$
(c) $Pb + CuCl_2 \longrightarrow PbCl_2 + Cu$
• *Understanding & Application*

(iv) State one relevant observation for each of the following: [3]
(a) Carbon dioxide is passed through lime water first a little, then in excess.
(b) Sulphur dioxide is passed through acidified $K_2Cr_2O_7$ solution.
(c) Hydrochloric acid is added to lead nitrate solution. • *Understanding*

7. (i) Name the following. [2]
(a) An element which does not contain any neutron in its nucleus.
(b) An element having valency 'zero'.
• *Recall & Understanding*

(ii) Give reason for the following. [2]
(a) On mixing and grinding the iron filings with sulphur, a physical change takes place, however if we heat this mixture a chemical change takes place.
(b) Metals act as reducing agents. • *Understanding*

(iii) Find out the final volume of a gas, 'Y', if the pressure originally at STP is doubled and its temperature is made three times. • *Application* [3]

(iv) In the electrolysis of water, [3]
(a) name the gas collected at the cathode and at the anode.
(b) why is the volume of gas collected at one electrode is double of the other?
(c) why are a few drops of dil. H_2SO_4 added to the water? • *Understanding & Application*

8. (i) Arrange the following according to the instructions given in brackets : [2]
(a) Li, Be, C, O (in the increasing order of size of atom)
(b) O, S, Se, Te (in the increasing order of atomic radii) • *Understanding & Application*

(ii) Can the following groups of elements be classified as Dobereiner's triad? **[2]**

(a) Na, Si, Cl (b) Be, Mg, Ca

(Atomic mass of Be 9; Na 23; Mg 24; Si 28; Cl 35; Ca 40)

Explain by giving reason. • *Application*

(iii) Write the balanced chemical equation for the following and identify the type of reaction in each case. • *Understanding* **[3]**

(a) Lead nitrate (aq) + Potassium iodide (aq) ⟶ Lead iodide + Potassium nitrate (aq)

(b) Zinc carbonate (s) $\xrightarrow{\Delta}$ Zinc oxide(s) + Carbon dioxide (g)

(c) Hydrogen (g) + Chlorine (g) ⟶ Hydrogen chloride (g)

(iv) Elements from A to F have the distribution of electrons, protons and neutrons in the following way. **[3]**

Atom/Ion	Number of electrons	Number of protons	Number of neutrons
A	4	3	4
B	10	11	12
C	17	17	18
D	17	17	20
E	18	18	22
F	19	19	21

From the table, find

(a) a pair of ions.

(b) a pair of isobars.

(c) a pair of isotopes. • *Understanding & Analysis*

Solutions

1. (i) (b) $Ca(HCO_3)_2$ (ii) (b) Calcium

(iii) (a) Group 1 (iv) (d) Salt and water

(v) (a) Oxidation reaction

(vi) (a) Active metals like Na, K and Ca are highly reactive and thus they react with cold water to produce bases or hydroxides of metals and releases hydrogen gas. Thus, Both A and R are true and R is the correct explanation of A.

(vii) (b)

(viii) (d) Potassium carbonate

(ix) (a) H_2SO_4 (x) (c) Potassium

(xi) (b) $^{14}_{6}C$

(xii) (c) electropositive element

(xiii) (d) According to Boyle's law pressure and volume are inversely proportional $\left(P \propto \frac{1}{V}\right)$ thus when the volume of gas decreases then the pressure will increase and not decrease. Thus, A is false, but R is true.

(xiv) (c) Potassium

(xv) (a) 351 K

Formula used is 0°C + 273 = 273 K

78°C + 273 = 351 K.

2. (i) A → 4, B → 1, C → 2, D → 3, E → 5.

(ii) (a) A is CuO and B is H_2O.

(b) When a drop of B is added to anhydrous copper sulphate, it turns blue.

$$\underset{\text{Anhydrous copper sulphate (White)}}{CuSO_4} + 5H_2O \longrightarrow \underset{\text{Hydrated copper sulphate (Blue)}}{CuSO_4 \cdot 5H_2O}$$

(c) Hydrogen gas acts as a strong reducing agent as it reduces copper oxide to copper.

Loss of oxygen — Reduction (CuO → Cu)

$$CuO + H_2 \longrightarrow Cu + H_2O$$

Gain of oxygen — Oxidation (H_2 → H_2O); H_2: Reducing agent

Note Reducing agent is a substance which reduces other substances but itself gets oxidised.

(d) $$\underset{\text{(Black)}}{CuO} + H_2 \longrightarrow \underset{\text{(Pinkish red)}}{Cu} + H_2O$$

(iii) (a) electrons (b) Methane (c) cold

(d) K_2ZnO_2 (e) metallic

(iv) (a) NH_3 (ammonia gas)

$$N_2 + 3H_2 \underset{200\text{ atm}}{\overset{\text{Fe-Mo}}{\rightleftharpoons}} 2NH_3$$

(b) Cl_2 (chlorine gas)

$$\underset{\text{Molten sodium chloride}}{2NaCl(l)} \xrightarrow{\text{Electric current}} \underset{\text{Sodium}}{2Na(s)} + \underset{\text{Chlorine}}{Cl_2(g)}$$

(c) H_2 (hydrogen gas)

$$\underset{\text{Zinc}}{Zn} + \underset{\text{Sulphuric acid}}{H_2SO_4} \longrightarrow \underset{\text{Zinc sulphate}}{ZnSO_4} + H_2\uparrow$$

(d) CO_2 (carbon dioxide gas)

$$CaCO_3 + 2HCl \longrightarrow CaCl_2 + H_2O + CO_2\uparrow$$

(e) NO_2 (nitrogen dioxide)

$$\underset{\text{Lead nitrate}}{2Pb(NO_3)_2(s)} \xrightarrow{\Delta} \underset{\text{Lead oxide}}{2PbO} + \underset{\text{Nitrogen dioxde (Brown fumes)}}{4NO_2(g)}$$

(v) (a) 1. $2Al + 2KOH + 2H_2O \longrightarrow 2KAlO_2 + 3H_2$

2. $2Al + 3H_2SO_4 \longrightarrow Al_2(SO_4)_3 + 3H_2$

(b) 1. Water

2. Carbon dioxide gas (CO_2)

3. $\underbrace{CO + H_2 + H_2O}_{\text{Water gas}} \xrightarrow[450°C]{Fe_2O_3/Cr_2O_3} CO_2 + 2H_2$

Catalyst used = Fe_2O_3

Promoter = Chromium oxide

3. (i) (a) Iron sulphide

Fe (+3), S (−2) → Fe_2S_3

(b) Calcium hydrogen sulphite

Ca (+2), HSO_3 (−1) → $Ca(HSO_3)_2$

(ii) (a) +3 (b) decreases

(iii) (a) F < N < Be < Li (b) Cl < Br < I < At

Because atomic radii decreases along a period and increases on moving down a group.

(c) Atomic radii decreases along the period. O < N < C < Be.

(iv) (a) $CaCO_3(s) + 2HCl(aq) \longrightarrow CaCl_2(aq) + H_2O(l) + CO_2(g)$

(b) $MgCl_2(aq) + Na_2CO_3(aq) \longrightarrow MgCO_3(s) + 2NaCl(aq)$

(c) $Mg + \underset{\text{Very dil.}}{2HNO_3} \longrightarrow Mg(NO_3)_2 + H_2(g)$

4. (i) (a) Mass of an atom is contributed by the mass of protons and neutrons present inside the nucleus of an atom and the electrons present outside the nucleus are of negligible mass therefore, mass of an atom is concentrated inside the nucleus of an atom.

(b) Because it contains the impurities of arsine and phosphine.

(ii) (a) Chemicals such as chlorofluorocarbons (CFCs) and nitric oxides.

(b) CO_2, methane, nitric oxide and water vapours.

(iii) $p_1 = 760$ mm Hg, $V_1 = 800\ cm^3$, $p_2 = ?$

$V_2 = 380 cm^3$

From Boyle's law, $p_1V_1 = p_2V_2$

Putting the values, we get

$$760 \times 800 = p_2 \times 380$$

$$p_2 = \frac{760 \times 800}{380} = 1600 \text{ mm Hg} = 160 \text{ cm Hg}$$

Hence, required pressure is 160 cm Hg.

(iv) (a) Ne (Neon) (b) Sodium (Na)

(c) Iron (Fe), Krypton (Kr)

5. (i) (a) Argon gas because of its inert nature is used to provide an inert atmosphere in high temperature metallurgical process.

(b) Neon gas is used in discharge tubes.

(ii) (a) $^{27}_{13}X \longrightarrow 2, 8, 3$ (b) $^{35}_{17}X \longrightarrow 2, 8, 7$

(iii) (a) $N_2 + O_2 \longrightarrow 2NO$

(b) $2Ca(NO_3)_2 \xrightarrow{\Delta} 2CaO + 4NO_2 + O_2$

(c) $2PbO_2 \xrightarrow{\Delta} 2PbO + O_2$

(iv) (a) Fractional atomic mass is the average atomic mass of all the naturally occurring isotopes of an element. e.g. the atomic mass of chlorine of is 35.5 due to the presence of two isotopes with atomic masses of 35 and 37.

(b) **Uses of isotopes**

- Isotopes of cobalt $^{60}_{27}Co$ is used in radiotherapy for treating cancer and other diseases.
- $^{14}_{6}C$ is used for determining the age of historical and geological materials.

(c) C-14 and tritium ($^{3}_{1}H$) are known as radioisotopes.

6. (i) (a) **Solute** The component of the solution that is dissolved in the solvent.

(b) **Solvent** The component of the solution that dissolves the other component in it.

(ii) % of nitrogen

$$= \frac{\text{Mass of nitrogen in the compound}}{\text{Molecular mass}} \times 100$$

$$= \frac{28}{60} \times 100 = 46.67\%$$

(iii) (a) Combination reaction

(b) Decomposition reaction

(c) Displacement reaction

(iv) (a) Milkiness appears, which disappears in excess.

(b) Orange solution of acidified $K_2Cr_2O_7$ turns green.

(c) White ppt. of $PbCl_2$ is formed.

7. (i) (a) Hydrogen

(b) Any noble gas, e.g., He, Ne, Ar, etc.

(ii) (a) On heating powdered iron and sulphur, chemical reaction takes place.

i.e. $Fe + S \xrightarrow{\Delta} FeS$

While on grinding, no chemical reaction takes place.

(b) Metals can easily lose their outermost 1, 2 or 3 electrons to complete their outermost octet and undergoes oxidation hence, they act as reducing agents.

(iii) Suppose that initial volume (V_1) = x

Final volume (V_2) = ?

Initial temperature (T_1) = T_1

Final temperature (T_2) = $3T_1$

Initial pressure (p_1) = 1 atm

Final pressure (p_2) = 2 atm

Applying ideal gas equation, $\frac{p_1V_1}{T_1} = \frac{p_2V_2}{T_2}$

or $\frac{1 \times x}{T_1} = \frac{2 \times V_2}{3T_1}$

$\Rightarrow \quad V_2 = \frac{3T_1 \times x}{T_1 \times 2}$

or $V_2 = \frac{3}{2}$ times of original volume (V_1)

(iv) (a) Gas collected at cathode – Hydrogen
Gas collected at anode – Oxygen

(b) On electrolysis, water decomposes according to the following reaction

$$2H_2O \xrightarrow[\text{Electric current}]{\text{On passing}} 2H_2(g) + O_2(g)$$

This water decomposes to given hydrogen and oxygen in the ratio 2:1 by volume. So, double volume of the gas collected is hydrogen.

(c) A few drops of dil. H_2SO_4 are added to water to make it a better conductor of electricity.

8. (i) (a) Size of atom decreases when moving left to right in a period (increase in the number of protons increases nuclear pull which decreases the size)
Increasing order is

O < C < Be < Li

(b) Atomic radii increases along a group.

O < S < Se < Te

(ii) (a) No, because atomic (Si) has an average atomic mass 28 close to that the average of Na (23) and Cl (35) which is 29.
But they do not resemble in their properties.
Na (23); Si (28); Cl (35).

Atomic mass of Si = $\frac{23 + 35}{2} = \frac{58}{2} = 29$

(b) Yes, Be (9); Mg (24); Ca (40)

Atomic mass of Mg $= \frac{9 + 40}{2} = \frac{49}{2} = 24.5$

It can be classified as Dobereiner's triads because the middle element of the triad had both atomic mass and properties similar to average of the two other elements of the triad.

(iii) (a) $Pb(NO_3)_2 + 2KI \longrightarrow PbI_2 + 2KNO_3$
Type Double displacement reaction.

(b) $ZnCO_3(s) \xrightarrow{\Delta} ZnO\,(s) + CO_2(g)$
Type Thermal decomposition reaction.

(c) $H_2(g) + Cl_2(g) \longrightarrow 2HCl\,(g)$
Type Combination reaction.

(iv) (a) *A* and *B*, because number of electrons and protons are different for these elements.

(b) *E* and *F*, because these have same mass number (number of protons + number of neutrons) but different atomic number.

(c) *C* and *D*, because these have same atomic number (number of protons) but different mass number.

SAMPLE QUESTION PAPER 2

A HIGHLY SIMULATED Sample Question Paper for ICSE Class IX

Chemistry (Unsolved)

General Instructions : See Sample Paper 1

Section-A

[40 Marks]

(Attempt **all** questions from this section.)

1. Choose the correct answer from the options given below. **[15]**

(i) $N_2 + 3H_2 \underset{\substack{450\text{-}500°C \\ 200\text{-}900 \text{ atm}}}{\overset{\text{Catalyst}}{\rightleftharpoons}} 2NH_3$

Identify catalyst in the above reaction. • *Recall*

(a) Platinum with carbon
(b) Palladium with carbon
(c) Iron with molybdenum
(d) Iron

(ii) Which of the following statement is incorrect? • *Recall & Understanding*

(a) Reduction is the process in which an atom gain electrons.
(b) Oxygen is an oxidising agent.
(c) Addition of oxygen is oxidation.
(d) Addition of electropositive atom or iron is oxidation.

(iii) The number of electrons present in *N*-shell of atom is • *Application*

(a) 2 (b) 8 (c) 18 (d) 32

(iv) An element *X* has atomic mass 40, while the element *Y* has atomic mass 137. Then, the atomic mass of the intermediate element *Z* is nearly equal to • *Understanding & Application*

(a) 88 (b) 128
(c) 62 (d) 84

(v) **Assertion** (A) The relative molecular mass of carbon dioxide (CO_2) is 44u.

Reason (R) The relative molecular mass depends only on the number of molecules present in a substance. • *Understanding & Application*

(a) Both A and R are true is the correct explanation of A.
(b) Both A and R are true, but R is not the correct explanation of A.
(c) A is true, but R is false.
(d) A is false, bu R is true.

(vi) Which of the following is an example of Greenhouse gas? • *Recall*

(a) Oxygen (b) Ammonia
(c) Methane (d) Nitrogen

(vii) The chemical reactions in which heat is absorbed are • *Recall*

(a) exothermic (b) oxidation
(c) endothermic (d) thermal

(viii) Which among the following is a monovalent radical? • *Recall & Understanding*

(a) Nitrite (b) Nitride
(c) Sulphate (d) Hydrogen phosphate

(ix) An element that shows variable valency is • *Understanding*

(a) sodium (Na) (b) gold (Au)
(c) potassium (K) (d) magnesium (Mg)

(x) Nucleus consists of • *Recall*

(a) neutrons (b) protons
(c) neutrons and protons (d) electrons

(xi) A compound having 2 double bonds is • *Recall & Understanding*

(a) oxygen
(b) carbon tetrachloride
(c) carbon dioxide
(d) carbon monoxide

(xii) Name the halogen which is liquid at room temperature. • *Recall*

(a) Bromine (b) Chlorine
(c) Iodine (d) Fluorine

(xiii) **Assertion** (A) When zinc reacts with copper sulphate, zinc sulphate and copper metal are obtained. • *Understanding & Application*

Reason (R) This reaction is an example of double displacement reaction.

(a) Both A and R are true and R is the correct explanation of A.
(b) Both A and R are true, but R is not the correct explanation of A.
(c) A is true, but R is false.
(d) A is false, but R is true.

(xiv) The relationship $\frac{p_1V_1}{T_1} = \frac{p_2V_2}{T_2}$ is known as • *Application*

(a) Boyle's law
(b) Charles' law
(c) Ideal gas equation
(d) None of the above

(xv) Ozone layer is found in • *Recall*

(a) troposphere (b) atmosphere
(c) stratosphere (d) ionosphere

2. (i) Match the following columns. • *Recall* **[5]**

	Column I		Column II
A.	Epsom salt	1.	$ZnSO_4 \cdot 7H_2O$
B.	Glauber's salt	2.	$FeSO_4 \cdot 7H_2O$
C.	Blue vitriol	3.	$CuSO_4 \cdot 5H_2O$
D.	Green vitriol	4.	$Na_2SO_4 \cdot 10H_2O$
E.	White vitriol	5.	$MgSO_4 \cdot 7H_2O$

(ii) What do you observe, when **[5]**

(a) solution of hydrogen peroxide are exposed in light?
(b) mercuric chloride and potassium iodide when crushed together in a mortar?
(c) concentrated sulphuric acid is added to a piece of copper?
(d) silver nitrate is added to a solution of sodium chloride?
(e) ferrous sulphate solution is added to sodium hydroxide solution?

• *Recall & Understanding*

(iii) Fill in the blanks. **[5]**

(a) Atoms of same elements may differ from one another in terms of number of neutrons are called .... (isotopes/isotones)
(b) Atoms of different elements may be similar in terms of mass number are called .... (isotopes/isobars)
(c) Atomic number is equal to number of .... (protons/neutrons)
(d) The subscript number shows the .... of an element. (atomic number/mass number)
(e) Proton is discovered by .... (Goldstein, Chadwick) • *Recall*

(iv) Write the name of the following. **[5]**

(a) A metal whose oxide is reduced by electrolysis.
(b) One metal which can be displaced by copper.
(c) One metal which do not rust.
(d) One oxide which can be reduced.
(e) One oxide which can not be reduced by common reducing agent.

• *Recall & Understanding*

(v) (a) Give the formula for the following. **[5]**

1. Water gas 2. Acetylene
3. Calcium chloride • *Recall*

(b) Give the name of the following.

(a) CCl_4 (b) $Na_2SO_4 \cdot 10H_2O$ • *Recall*

Section-B **[40 Marks]**

(Attempt **any four** questions from this section.)

3. (i) Identify the substance which matches the description given below: **[2]**

(a) Gas which is also called inflammable air.
(b) Two metals which react with dilute nitric acid to liberate hydrogen.

• *Understanding & Recall*

(ii) (a) Hydrogen is ...... soluble in water [sparingly, highly] **[2]**

(b) A metal above hydrogen in the activity series gives hydrogen with .... acid. [dil.H_2SO_4/conc.H_2SO_4] • *Understanding*

(iii) Arrange the following as per the instruction given in the brackets. **[3]**

(a) Ca, Ba, Sr, Mg (increasing order of metallic character)
(b) N, Be, O, C (increasing order of non-metallic character)
(c) H, Be, Cl, K (increasing order of period)

• *Understanding & Application*

(iv) Balance each of the chemical equations given below: **[3]**

(a) $KNO_3(s) \xrightarrow{Heat} KNO_2(s) + O_2(g)$
(b) $2FeSO_4 \xrightarrow{Heat} Fe_2O_3(s) + SO_2(g) + SO_3(g)$
(c) $NH_3 + O_2 \longrightarrow NO + H_2O$ • *Understanding*

4. (i) Give a reason for each of the following: **[2]**

(a) Though lead is placed above hydrogen in the activity series, it is not used to prepare hydrogen.
(b) Table salt becomes sticky on exposure to humid air during the rainy season.

• *Understanding & Application*

(ii) The formula of the aluminate of metal '*M*' is $MAlO_3^{3-}$, state the formula of its **[2]**

(a) hydrogen sulphite.
(b) hydrogen sulphate.

• *Analysis & Understanding*

(iii) Write the relative molecular mass of each of the following. **[3]**

(a) Magnesium nitrate $Mg(NO_3)_2$
(b) Zinc sulphate $ZnSO_4$

[S = 32, O = 16, Mg = 24, N = 14, Zn = 65]

• *Application*

(iv) Write balanced equations for each of the following: **[3]**

(a) Reaction of potassium with cold water.
(b) Reaction of magnesium sulphate with sodium hydroxide.
(c) Heating of iron with sulphur. • *Understanding*

5. (i) Calculate the mass number of neon and argon from the data given below. • *Analysis* [2]

Element	Number of protons	Number of neutrons
Neon	10	10
Argon	18	22

(ii) Write the electronic configuration of the following. • *Understanding* [2]

(a) $^{14}_{7}N$ (b) $^{31}_{15}P$

(iii) Write the complete balanced equation of the following. [3]

(a) $Pb(NO_3)_2 \xrightarrow{\Delta}$ (b) $MgO \xrightarrow{\text{Combustion}}$

(c) $NaCl + AgNO_3$ • *Recall & Understanding*

(iv) The electronic configuration of an element *X* is 2, 8, 7.

Answer the following questions.

(a) What is the group of *X*?

(b) What is the period of *X*?

(c) Whether '*X*' is a metal or a non-metal?

• *Analysis & Understanding* [3]

6. (i) Define/State. • *Recall* [2]

(a) Isotopes (b) Isobars

(ii) An atom *X* has electronic configuration 2, 8, 7. It combines with *Y* having 1 electron in its outermost shell. • *Understanding & Application* [2]

(a) What type of bond will be formed between *X* and *Y*?

(b) Write the formula of the compound formed.

(iii) Classify the following reaction by choosing the reactions given in the box below. [3]

(combination, decomposition, displacement or double displacement)

• *Understanding & Application*

(a) $2AgCl(s) \xrightarrow{\text{Sunlight}} 2Ag(s) + Cl_2(l)$

(b) $2Fe(s) + 3Cl_2(g) \longrightarrow 2FeCl_3(s)$

(c) $AgNO_3 + NaCl \longrightarrow AgCl\downarrow + NaNO_3$

(iv) State one relevant observation for each of the following. [3]

(a) When lead nitrate crystals are heated strongly.

(b) When washing soda is heated.

(c) When HCl is added to lead nitrate solution.

• *Understanding*

7. (i) Name the following. [2]

(a) Metalloid in period 3.

(b) Noble gas with configuration: 2, 8, 8. • *Recall*

(ii) Give reason for the following. [2]

(a) Generally most of the alkali metals are kept in inert solvent.

(b) Rain water does not leave behind concentric rings when boiled. • *Understanding*

(iii) Calculate the minimum pressure required to compress 500 dm^3 of air pressure at 1 bar and to 200 dm^3 at 30°C. • *Application* [3]

(iv) Answer the following questions. [3]

(a) Why hydrogen is used as fuel?

(b) Explain the role of hydrogen in producing artificial petrol from coal.

(c) Hydrogen is no longer used in meteorological balloons.

• *Understanding & Application*

8. (i) When sodium hydroxide solution is added to an aqueous solution of copper sulphate, a bluish-white precipitate is obtained. [2]

(a) How is this precipitate get separated?

(b) Write the name and formula of the precipitate. • *Understanding*

(ii) Differentiate between the following. [2]

(a) Hard and soft water.

(b) Efflorescence and deliquescence. • *Recall*

(iii) The schematic atomic structure of element '*X*' and '*Y*' are given, based on these structures answer the following questions. [3]

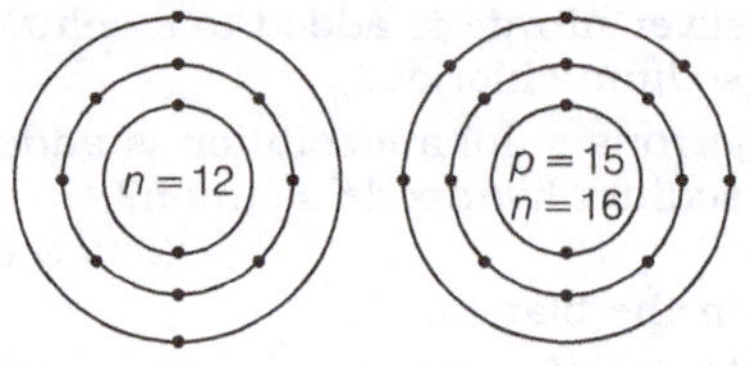

(X) (Y)

(a) Identify the element '*X*' and '*Y*'.

(b) The electronic configuration of *X*.

(c) The electronic configuration of *Y*.

• *Analysis & Understanding*

(iv) Choose the answer from the list which fits in the description. [3]

[H_2SO_3, H_2SO_4, H_3PO_4, HCl] • *Understanding*

(a) When SO_2 is dissolved in water form.

(b) When SO_3 is dissolved in water form.

(c) When P_2O_5 is dissolved in water form.

Answers

1. (i) (c) (ii) (d) (iii) (d) (iv) (a)
(v) (c) (vi) (c) (vii) (c) (viii) (a)
(ix) (b) (x) (c) (xi) (c) (xii) (a)
(xiii) (c) (xiv) (d) (xv) (c)

SAMPLE QUESTION PAPER 3

A HIGHLY SIMULATED Sample Question Paper for ICSE Class IX

Chemistry (Unsolved)

General Instructions : See Sample Paper 1

Section-A **[40 Marks]**

(Attempt **all** questions from this section.)

1. Choose the correct answer from the options given below. **[15]**

(i) What is the percentage composition of hydrogen in water? • *Application*

(Relative atomic mass of H = 1, O = 16)

(a) 22.7 % (b) 18.4 %

(c) 11.1 % (d) 16.2 %

(ii) What is the chemical formula of soap? • *Recall*

(a) $C_{16}H_{33}COONa$ (b) $C_{17}H_{35}COONa$

(c) $C_{15}H_{31}COONa$ (d) $C_{14}H_{29}COONa$

(iii) Which of the following is an ionic compound? • *Understanding*

(a) C_2H_4 (b) $MgCl_2$

(c) NH_3 (d) CCl_4

(iv) The correct order regarding size of atom is • *Application & Understanding*

(a) Li ≈ Be > C ≈ O

(b) Li > Be > C ≈ O

(c) Li > Be > C > O

(d) Be > Li > C > O

(v) **Assertion** (A) When silver chloride (AgCl) is exposed to sunlight, it turns grey.

Reason (R) This happens because silver chloride decomposes into silver and chlorine gas in the presence of sunlight. • *Understanding & Application*

(a) Both A and R are true and R is the correct explanation of A.

(b) Both A and R are true, but R is not the correct explanation of A.

(c) A is true, but R is false.

(d) A is false, but R is true.

(vi) $$H_2S + Cl_2 \longrightarrow 2HCl + S$$

In the above reaction, the substance shows reduction is • *Understanding & Application*

(a) H_2S (b) S (c) HCl (d) Cl_2

(vii) Modern atomic symbols are based on the method proposed by • *Recall*

(a) Bohr (b) Dalton

(c) Berzelius (d) Alchemist

(viii) Thermal decomposition of sodium carbonate will produce • *Understanding*

(a) carbon dioxide (b) oxygen

(c) sodium hydroxide (d) no other product

(ix) **Assertion** (A) Helium is used in filling balloons for meteorological observations.

Reason (R) Helium is not flammable and lighter than air. • *Application*

(a) Both A and R are true and R is the correct explanation of A.

(b) Both A and R are true, but R is not the correct explanation of A.

(c) A is true, but R is false.

(d) A is false, but R is true.

(x) Which of the following metals does not give hydrogen with acids? • *Application*

(a) Iron (b) Copper

(c) Magnesium (d) Zinc

(xi) Volume-temperature relationship is given by • *Recall*

(a) Boyle (b) Gay Lussac

(c) Dalton (d) Charles

(xii) Decrease in amount of ozone in stratosphere is called depletion in ozone and it is caused by • *Understanding*

(a) UV radiations of sun.

(b) excessive use of detergents.

(c) burning coal and wood.

(d) use of CFC compounds.

(xiii) Which alkali metal is stored in kerosene? • *Understanding*

(a) Sodium (b) Magnesium

(c) Boron (d) Beryllium

(xiv) The symbol for carbonate ion is • *Recall*

(a) CO_3^- (b) CO_3^{2-}

(c) CO_2^- (d) CO^-

(xv) Hardness of water is due to • *Recall*

(a) chlorides of sodium

(b) chlorides of calcium

(c) sulphates of aluminium

(d) calcium oxide

2. (i) Match the following columns. • *Recall* [5]

Column I	Column II
A. Carbon monoxide	1. Small particles get logged in the lungs and gradually damage the functioning of lungs.
B. Chlorofluorocarbons	2. Burning, itching, watery eyes and lowered resistance to respiratory diseases.
C. Lead	3. Depletion of ozone layer.
D. Ozone in the troposphere	4. Damages the nervous and digestive systems and can causes cancer
E. Suspended particle matter	5. Reduces oxygen in blood causing retardation and dizziness.

(ii) What do you observe when • *Understanding* [5]

(a) lead sulphide is heated in a test tube.

(b) magnesium ribbon is burnt on a flame.

(c) electric current is passed through acidulated water.

(d) carbon compound when heated in presence of air.

(e) ammonium chloride solution is heated.

(iii) Fill in the blanks with the correct choice given in the brackets. [5]

(a) Neutrons and protons are found in .... of the atom. (orbit, nucleus)

(b) The reaction of lead sulphide with oxygen to form lead sulphate shows .... (combination/decomposition) reaction.

(c) The number of protons present in an atom is called .... number of an atom. (atomic, mass)

(d) The molecular formula of the compound lead nitrate is .... [$Pb(NO_3)_2$/$PbNO_3$].

(e) An atom having eight electrons and eight protons can be represented by the symbol as .... ($^{16}_{8}O$, $^{8}_{16}O$). • *Recall &Understanding*

(iv) Name the gas evolved in each of the following cases. • *Recall & Understanding* [5]

(a) Lead nitrate is heated strongly.

(b) On combustion of magnesium oxide.

(c) Action of sulphuric acid on copper granules.

(d) Zinc metal when reacted with dil. H_2SO_4.

(e) A gas evolved which contribute towards green house effect.

(v) (a) Explain the following. • *Understanding* [5]

(a) Mass of an atom is concentrated inside the nucleus of the atom.

(b) Atoms combine by transfer and sharing of electron(s).

(c) An element has atoms with different mass number.

(b) Answer the following question based on the given diagram.

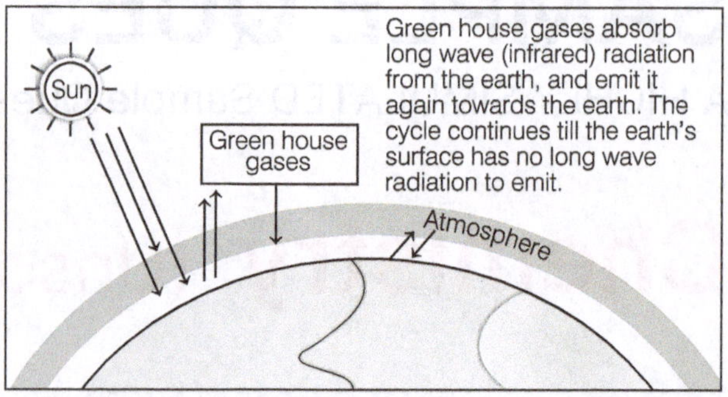

Green house effect

(i) Name the effect described in the diagram.

(ii) Name a green house gas that is released by excessive burning of fossil fuels.

• *Recall & Understanding*

Section-B [40 Marks]

(Attempt **any four** questions from this section.)

3. (i) Identify the following reactions as either oxidation or reduction: • *Understanding* [2]

(a) $O + 2e^- \longrightarrow O^{2-}$

(b) $K - e^- \longrightarrow K^+$

(ii) (a) Hydrogen is .... soluble in H_2O. [2] (sparingly, highly)

(b) Sodium .... reacts smoothly with cold water. (metal, amalgam)

• *Recall & Understanding*

(iii) Arrange the following. • *Understanding & Application* [3]

(a) Elements of group 1, in increasing order of reactivity.

(b) Elements of group 17, in decreasing order of reactivity.

(c) He, Na, Mg (increasing order of melting point).

(iv) Write balanced chemical equations for each of the following • *Understanding* [3]

(i) Decomposition of calcium bicarbonate.

(ii) Reaction of potassium iodide with hydrogen peroxide.

(iii) Reaction of quicklime with carbon dioxide.

4. (i) Give a reason for each of the following. • *Understanding* [2]

(a) Ozone gas is heavier than air. Why does ozone not settle down near the earth?

(b) Why should an equation be balanced?

(ii) (a) Identify odd one out from the following [2]

I. Zn, Fe, Mg and Na

II. SO_2, H_2S, NH_3 and CO_2

• *Analysis & Understanding*

(iii) Calculate the temperature at which 500 cm^3 of a gas measured at 20°C occupy half its volume. • *Application* [**Ans.** *–126.5°C]*
Assume pressure is remain constant. **[3]**

(iv) The formula of the chloride of a metal '*M*' is *M*Cl. State the formula of its **[3]**
(a) carbonate (b) nitrate
(c) hydroxide • *Understanding*

5. (i) Write one use of the following. **[2]**
(a) Soft water (b) Hydrogen gas • *Application*

(ii) Write the electronic configuration of the following : **[2]**
(a) $^{31}_{15}P$ (b) $^{39}_{19}K$ • *Understanding*

(iii) Complete and balance the following equations.
(a) $KCl \xrightarrow{\text{Electricity}}$ • *Recall & Understanding* **[3]**
(b) $Zn + H_2SO_4 \longrightarrow$
(c) $BaCl_2 + H_2SO_4 \longrightarrow$

(iv) Atomic number of the elements of III period of modern periodic table are listed below. Study the data carefully and answer the questions that follows **[3]**

Period 3 elements	Na	Mg	Al	Si	P	S	Cl	Ar
Atomic number	11	12	13	14	15	16	17	18

(i) What are the atomic number of sodium and phosphorus respectively? Write their respective electronic configurations.
(ii) Write down the number of valence electrons in an atom of sodium and phosphorus respectively.
(iii) What are the valencies of sodium and phosphorus? • *Analysis & Understanding*

6. (i) State/define. **[2]**
(a) Diffusion
(b) Standard temperature and pressure • *Recall*

(ii) Calculate the relative molecular mass of each of the following. **[2]**
(a) Calcium chloride hexahydrate : $CaCl_2 \cdot 6H_2O$
(b) Glauber's salt : $Na_2SO_4 \cdot 10H_2O$
[Ca = 40, Cl = 35, H = 1, O = 16, Na = 23, S = 32]
• *Understanding & Application*

(iii) Classify each of the following reactions as (combination, decomposition, displacement or double displacement). **[3]**
• *Understanding & Application*
(a) $2Fe + 3Cl_2 \longrightarrow 2FeCl_3$
(b) $2HgO \xrightarrow{\Delta} 2Hg + O_2$
(c) $BaCl_2 + Na_2SO_4 \longrightarrow BaSO_4 + 2NaCl$

(iv) State one relevant observation for each of the following • *Understanding* **[3]**
(a) When hydrogen is passed over litharge.
(b) When water is added to calcium hydride.
(c) HCl passed through silver nitrate solution.

7. (i) State the type of covalent bonding in the following molecules. • *Understanding* **[2]**
(a) Nitrogen
(b) Ammonia

(ii) Give reason for the following. • *Understanding* **[2]**
(a) Silver nitrate solution is kept in coloured bottles.
(b) Isotopes occupy the same position in the periodic table.

(iii) The capacity of one cylinder is 4 dm^3 and that of the other is 1 dm^3; their are pressure 560 mm Hg and 1000 mg Hg respectively. Both of these cylinders, containing carbon dioxide, are connected together by a tube fitted with a tap. What will be the final pressure in either cylinder on opening the tap if the temperature remains constant? • *Application*
[**Ans.** 648 mm Hg] **[3]**

(iv) State, if the solubility increases, decreases or remains the same with rise in temperature for each of the following compounds : **[3]**
(a) Sodium nitrate
(b) Slaked lime
(c) Ceric sulphate • *Analysis & Understanding*

8. (i) Arrange the following. • *Understanding* **[2]**
(a) $^{13}_{6}C, ^{12}_{6}C, ^{14}_{6}C$ (increasing order of neutrons)
(b) $^{14}_{7}N, ^{18}_{8}O, ^{16}_{7}N$ (increasing order of neutrons)

(ii) Differentiate between the following. • *Recall* **[2]**
(a) Distilled and potable water.
(b) Permanent and temporary harness.

(iii) Write the balanced chemical equations of the following word equations. **[3]**
(a) Sodium hydroxide + Sulphuric acid ⟶ Sodium sulphate + Water
(b) Silver nitrate ⟶ Silver + Nitrogen dioxide + Oxygen
(c) Iron + sulphuric acid ⟶ Ferrous sulphate + Hydrogen • *Understanding*

(iv) Choose the answer from the list which fits in the description. **[3]**
[HCFC's, harmful, fractional distillation, column chromatography, chlorine, methane].
(a) Substance which are replacing CFCs.
(b) How can ozone be separated from the oxygen?
(c) When *X* reacts with ozone it converts into simple oxygen? • *Understanding & Application*

Answers

1. (i) (c) (ii) (b) (iii) (b) (iv) (c)
(v) (a) (vi) (d) (vii) (c) (viii) (a)
(ix) (a) (x) (b) (xi) (d) (xii) (d)
(xiii) (a) (xiv) (b) (xv) (b)

SAMPLE QUESTION PAPER 4

A HIGHLY SIMULATED Sample Question Paper for ICSE Class IX

Chemistry (Unsolved)

General Instructions : See Sample Paper 1

Time : 2 Hrs **Max. Marks : 80**

Section-A

[40 Marks]

(Attempt **all** questions from this section.)

1. Choose the correct answer from the options given below. **[15]**

(i) In Mendeleev's periodic table, gap was not left for one of the following elements. This element is • *Recall*

(a) gallium (b) beryllium
(c) germanium (d) scandium

(ii) Which of the following is a deliquescence substance? • *Recall*

I. NaOH II. KOH
III. $MgCl_2$ IV. $ZnCl_2$

(a) I and II only (b) III and IV only
(c) II and IV (d) All of these

(iii) Which of the following statements is incorrect about hydrogen? • *Recall & Understanding*

(a) It is combustible but it does not support combustion.
(b) It burns silently in air with a pale blue flame.
(c) Its density is 0.0899 g/mL.
(d) It is yellow in colour.

(iv) 120 cm^3 of a gas is taken at 27.3 K. The temperature is then raised to 0°C. What is the new volume of the gas? The pressure is kept constant. • *Application*

(a) 1200 cm^3 (b) 1400 cm^3
(c) 1100 cm^3 (d) 1000 cm^3

(v) **Assertion (A)** Acid rain is harmful to plants, aquatic life and infrastructure.

Reason (R) Acid rain contains sulphuric acid and nitric acid, formed when sulphur dioxide and nitrogen oxides react with water present in the atmosphere. • *Understanding*

(a) Both A and R are true and R is the correct explanation of A.
(b) Both A and R are true, but R is not the correct explanation of A.
(c) A is true, but R is false.
(d) A is false, but R is true.

(vi) Which of the following is not indicating an isotopes of hydrogen? • *Recall*

(a) ^1_1H (b) ^2_1H
(c) ^3_1H (d) ^4_1H

(vii) Reacting with water, an active metal produces • *Understanding*

(a) oxygen
(b) nitric acid
(c) a base
(d) None of the above

(viii) If the volume of gas at 27°C is doubled at constant pressure. What is the new temperature? • *Application*

(a) 327°C (b) 255°C
(c) 300°C (d) 450°C

(ix) In which layer of atmosphere, ozone is present? • *Recall*

(a) Troposphere (b) Stratosphere
(c) Mesosphere (d) Ionosphere

(x) Name the gas used for filling balloons. • *Application*

(a) Helium
(b) Hydrogen
(c) Argon
(d) Hydrogen sulphide

(xi) The temperature of 273 K on the Celcius scale is equal to: • *Application*

(a) −273°C (b) −100°C
(c) 0°C (d) +298°C

(xii) **Assertion (A)** $^{40}_{18}Ar$ and $^{40}_{20}Ca$ are isobars.

Reason (R) Isobars are the atoms of different elements with the same atomic number but different mass numbers. • *Understanding*

(a) Both A and R are true and R is the correct explanation of A.
(b) Both A and R are true, but R is not the correct explanation of A.
(c) A is true, but R is false.
(d) A is false, but R is true.

(xiii) The valency of N in NO_3 is • *Understanding*
(a) four (b) three
(c) five (d) two

(xiv) The chemical formula of lead nitrate is • *Recall & Understanding*
(a) $Pb(NO_3)_2$ (b) $PbNO_3$
(c) Pb_2NO_3 (d) $Pb_3(NO_3)_2$

(xv) The metal which forms a protective layer of oxide. • *Recall*
(a) Al (b) Zn
(c) Mg (d) Fe

2. (i) Match the following columns. • *Recall* **[5]**

Column I (Element)	Column II (Symbol)
A. Titanium	1. K
B. Scandium	2. Sc
C. Argon	3. Ar
D. Potassium	4. Si
E. Silicon	5. Ti

(ii) What do you observe, when **[5]**
(a) crystals of copper (II) sulphate are heated in a test tube strongly?
(b) sodium is added to cold water ?
(c) sodium hydrogen carbonate is heated strongly?
(d) washing soda is exposed to atmosphere for sometime?
(e) ammonia gas when passed to container containing quicklime? • *Recall & Understanding*

(iii) Fill in the blanks with the correct choice given in brackets. **[5]**
(a) All protons are identical and have a charge equal to ……… . (electrons/neutrons)
(b) Hydrogen gas is a strong ……… . (reducing agent/oxidising agent)
(c) ……… is the strong reducing agent present in activity series. (Potassium/Copper).
(d) The molecular formula of potassium metaaluminate is ……… . ($KAlO_2$ / $KMnO_4$)
(e) The chemical reaction in which a compound splits into two or more simpler substances is called ……….. reaction. (decomposition/ displacement)
• *Recall & Understanding*

(iv) Name the following: **[5]**
(a) Two metals which do not displace hydrogen from dilute acids.
(b) A gas which forms explosive mixture with air.
(c) A gas having rotten egg smell.
(d) A gas evolved when mercuric oxide is heated.
(e) A metal that does not react with water under any condition. • *Recall & Understanding*

(v) (a) Write the chemical formula for the following compounds. **[5]**
1. Aluminium phosphate
2. Potassium nitrate
3. Sodium phosphate • *Understanding*
(b) Give the names of the following compounds.
1. $HClO_3$ 2. $HClO_2$ • *Recall*

Section-B **[40 Marks]**

(Attempt **any four** questions from this section.)

3. (i) Identify the charge in each of the following cases: **[2]**
(a) When the number of electrons is less than the number of protons, the atom carries *X* charge.
(b) When the number of electrons is greater than the number of protons, the atom carries *Y* charge. • *Understanding*

(ii) Observe the two test tubes *A* and *B* in the diagram given below and answer the following questions. **[2]**
(a) In which test tube, reaction will take place?
(b) Name the type of reaction.

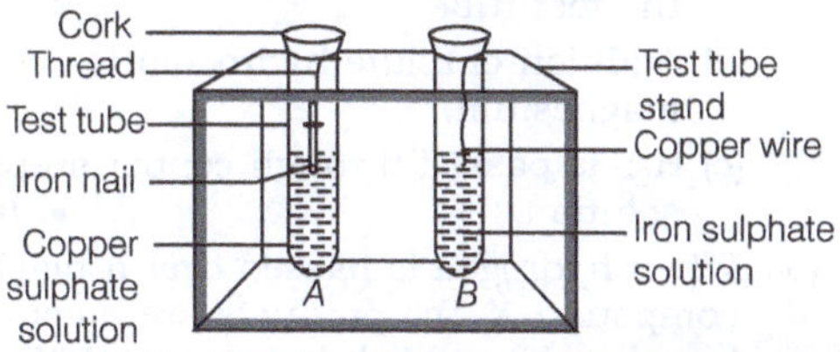

• *Understanding & Application*

(iii) Arrange the following. **[3]**
(a) Thallium, Indium, Gallium, Boron (decreasing order of metallic character).
(b) F, Cl, Br, I (decreasing order of electronegativity)
(c) Li, Rb, Cs, Fr (increasing order of non- metallic character).
• *Understanding & Application*

(iv) Complete and balance the following equations. **[3]**
(a) $PbO_2 + SO_2 \longrightarrow PbSO_4$
(b) $2KClO_3 \longrightarrow 2KCl + 3O_2$
(c) $2H_2O_2 \longrightarrow 2H_2O + O_2$ • *Understanding*

4. (i) Give a reason for each of the following. **[2]**

(a) Washing soda loses its weight when exposed to atmosphere.

(b) Anode rays also called as 'canal rays'.

• *Understanding*

(ii) Write the chemical formula of the following salts. • *Recall*

(a) Glauber's salt (b) Epsom salt **[2]**

(iii) At a constant temperature, the volume of a gas was found to be 800 cm^3 at a pressure of 76 cm of Hg. If the pressure of the gas is increased by 25%, calculate the new volume. • *Application*

[**Ans.** 640 cm^3] **[3]**

(iv) An atom of an element is represented as $^{23}_{11}Y$. Answer the following questions.

(a) What does the subscript 11 indicate?

(b) What does the superscript 23 indicate?

(c) What is the number of electrons present in *Y*? • *Analysis & Understanding*

[3]

5. (i) Write one use of the following gases. **[2]**

(a) Carbon dioxide (b) Methane • *Application*

(ii) The elements *X* and *Y* have electronic configuration (2, 8, 18, 2) and (2, 6) respectively, then • *Analysis & Understanding*

[2]

(a) in which period *X* and *Y* belong?

(b) in which group *X* and *Y* belong?

(iii) Write the balanced chemical equations for each of the following. **[3]**

(a) A burning magnesium wire is introduced in the test tube evolving steam and then a burning candle is brought near the mouth of the test tube'.

(b) Addition of dilute hydrochloric acid in magnesium.

(c) H_2S is passed through copper sulphate solution. • *Understanding*

(iv) When hydrogen is passed over a black solid compound *X*, the products are a colourless liquid and a reddish brown metal '*Y*'. Metal '*Y*' is divided into two parts and each placed in separate test tubes. Dilute HCl is added to one part of substance and dilute HNO_3 to the other.

(a) Write the name of substances *X* and *Y*. **[3]**

(b) Write two tests for the colourless liquid formed in the experiment.

(c) What happen to substances *X* when it reacts with hydrogen? • *Analysis & understanding*

6. (i) Define/State. **[2]**

(a) Electronegativity (b) Absolute zero • *Recall*

(ii) Calculate the percentage composition of each element in potassium chlorate, $KClO_3$. • *Application*

(K = 31.83%, Cl = 28.97%, O = 39.18%) **[2]**

(iii) Complete, balance and classify each of the following chemical reaction as **[3]**

Combination, decomposition, displacement and double displacement.

(a) $Pb_3O_4 \xrightarrow{\Delta}$ .... + ...

(b) $PCl_5 \underset{\text{Cool}}{\overset{\Delta}{\rightleftharpoons}}$ .... + ...

(c) $2H_2O \xrightarrow[\text{Current}]{\text{Electric}}$ .... • *Recall & Understanding*

(iv) State one relevant observation for each of the following. **[3]**

(a) When sodium is added to cold water.

(b) When calcium is added to cold water.

(c) When metal reacts with dil. HNO_3.

• *Understanding*

7. (i) Give one word for the following.

• *Recall & Understanding*

[2]

(a) An element whose isotope has mass number 14 and 8 neutrons.

(b) Species having same number of neutrons.

(ii) Give reason for the following. • *Understanding*

[2]

(a) Hydrogen is not collected in air.

(b) Boiled or distilled water tastes flat.

(iii) Calculate the relative molecular mass of each of the following. • *Understanding*

(a) Ammonium sulphate. [**Ans.** 132]

(b) Sodium carbonate decahydrate [**Ans.** 286] ($Na_2CO_3 \cdot 10H_2O$).

[N = 14, H = 1, S = 32, O = 16, Na = 23, C= 12]

[3]

(iv) Answer the following question with reference to table. • *Analysis & Understanding*

[3]

Group 1	Group 2	Group 16	Group 17
—	—	—	*D*
—	*B*	*C*	—
A	—	—	*E*

(a) State which are metals, non-metals and noble gas in the above table.

(b) Which type of ion will be formed by element *A*, *B* and *C*?

(c) Which is larger in size (I) *D* or *E* (II) *B* or *C*?

8. (i) Arrange the following according to the instructions given • *Understanding & Application*

[2]

(a) Na, Al, Mg, Si (decreasing order of valency)

(b) MgO, CaO, BaO, SrO (increasing order of basic oxide)

(ii) Differentiate between the following pairs. [2]
(a) Sodium and potassium (inflammable nature).
(b) Acid radical and basic radical. • *Recall*

(iii) Convert the following reactions into a balanced chemical equation. • *Understanding* [3]
(a) Water gas to methanol using zinc oxide.
(b) Head oxide to lead.
(c) Iron to iron oxide using steam and heat.

(iv) Choose the answer from the list which fits in the description. [3]
[I, Kr, Ar, Be, Si]
(a) Rare gas other than neon, krypton and xenon.
(b) A non-metal having properties similar to carbon.
(c) One halogen other than fluorine and chlorine. • *Understanding & Recall*

Answers

1. (i) (b)	(ii) (d)	(iii) (d)	(iv) (a)
(v) (a)	(vi) (d)	(vii) (c)	(viii) (a)
(ix) (b)	(x) (a)	(xi) (c)	(xii) (c)
(xiii) (c)	(xiv) (a)	(xv) (a)	

SAMPLE QUESTION PAPER 5

A HIGHLY SIMULATED Sample Question Paper for ICSE Class IX

Chemistry (Unsolved)

General Instructions : See Sample Paper 1

Section-A

[40 Marks]

(Attempt **all** questions from this section.)

1. Choose the correct answer from the options given below. **[15]**

(i) The property which characteristic of an electrovalent compound is that • *Understanding*

(a) it is easily vapourised
(b) it has a high melting point
(c) it is a weak electrolyte
(d) it often exists as a liquid

(ii) The inert gas with a complete duplet only is • *Recall*

(a) helium (b) argon
(c) krypton (d) neon

(iii) The percentage mass of water in washing soda crystals, $Na_2CO_3 \cdot 10H_2O$ is • *Application*

(a) 52.8 (b) 62.9 (c) 72.3 (d) 79.6

(iv) **Assertion (A)** The relative atomic mass of oxygen 16u.

Reason (R) Relative atomic mass is the average mass of an atom compared to $\frac{1}{12}$th the mass of a carbon-12 atom. • *Recall*

(a) Both A and R are true and R is the correct explanation of A.
(b) Both A and R are true, but R is not the correct explanation of A.
(c) A is true, but R is false.
(d) A is false, but R is true.

(v) The anhydrous salt which is used to test water (as it changes colour when water is added to it is) • *Application & Understanding*

(a) sodium chloride
(b) magnesium sulphate
(c) zinc chloride
(d) copper sulphate

(vi) Which of the following represents the symbol of an element, used in making thermometers ? • *Application*

(a) Ag (b) Au
(c) Hg (d) Mg

(vii) Which is used as a drying agent? • *Recall*

(a) CaO (b) Conc. H_2SO_4
(c) $MgHCO_3$ (d) NO_2

(viii) What is the cause of hardness in water? • *Recall*

(a) Magnesium carbonate
(b) Magnesium bicarbonate
(c) Calcium oxide
(d) Both (a) and (b)

(ix) The lightest alkali metal is • *Recall*

(a) potassium (b) sodium
(c) lithium (d) rubidium

(x) Which of the following represents the formula of sodium hypochlorite? • *Recall*

(a) NaClO (b) $NaClO_2$
(c) $NaClO_3$ (d) $NaClO_4$

(xi) The substance which increases the efficiency of a reaction is • *Understanding*

(a) catalyst (b) receptor
(c) promoter (d) effector

(xii) Which formula represents the water gas? • *Recall*

(a) $CO_2 + H_2$ (b) $CO + H_2O$
(c) $CO + H_2$ (d) $CO + O_2$

(xiii) The element which contains two neutrons and 2 electrons in its nucleus is • *Understanding*

(a) hydrogen (b) helium
(c) deuterium (d) boron

(xiv) **Assertion (A)** Magnesium chloride ($MgCl_2$) is held together by strong electrostatic forces of attraction.

Reason (R) In ionic bond formation, the positively and negatively charged ions attracts each other to form a stable compound.

• *Understanding & Application*

(a) Both A and R are true and R is the correct explanation of A.
(b) Both A and R are true, but R is not the correct explanation of A.
(c) A is true, but R is false.
(d) A is false, but R is true.

(xv) Which symbol represents the nitride ion? • *Recall*
(a) N^{3-} (b) NO^{2-} (c) N^{2-} (d) N^{-}

2. (i) Match the following columns. • *Recall* [5]

Column I	Column II
A. Boyle's law	1. 373 K
B. Charles' law	2. $V \propto T$
C. Boiling point of water	3. $pV = K$
D. Freezing point of water	4. $-273°C$
E. Absolute zero	5. 273 K

(ii) What do you observe, when • *Recall & Understanding* [5]
(a) barium chloride is added to sodium sulphate solution?
(b) hydrogen peroxide is exposed to sunlight.
(c) chlorine water is exposed to sunlight.
(d) crystals of copper (II) sulphate and iron (II) sulphate are separately heated in two test tubes.
(e) iron sulphide is added to nitric acid.

(iii) Fill in the blanks with the correct choice given in brackets. • *Recall & Understanding* [5]
(a) The atomic number of atom of an element has three electrons in the *M*-shell is .... (13, 14)
(b) Tendency of metal to lose electron is called .... (oxidation/reduction)
(c) The negatively charged particle of atom has ...... charge. (-1.602×10^{-19}C/$+1.9 \times 10^{-19}$C).
(d) .... will not show deflection from the path on passing through an electric field. (neutrons/protons)
(e) Atomic size .... on moving across a period from left to right. (increases/decreases)

(iv) State the name of the following cases. [5]
(a) An alkaline earth metal except calcium, strontium and barium.
(b) An alkali metal except lithium, sodium and potassium.
(c) The group number of periodic table in which alkali metals are placed.
(d) The phenomenon in which a compound loses its water of crystallisation on exposure to dry air.
(e) The water free from soluble salts of calcium and magnesium. • *Recall & Understanding*

(v) (a) Give the formula of the following compounds. [5]
1. Sodium chlorate
2. Sodium perchlorate
3. Calcium phosphate • *Recall*

(b) Give the names of the following compounds.
1. $NaClO_3$ 2. $NaClO_2$ • *Recall*

Section-B [40 Marks]

(Attempt **any four** questions from this section.)

3. (i) Identify the element in each of the following cases. [2]
(a) An element *A* has 2 electrons in its fourth shell.
(b) Element *B* of having zero valency.
• *Analysis & Understanding*

(ii) Answer the following questions based on the figure given below. • *Analysis & Understanding* [2]

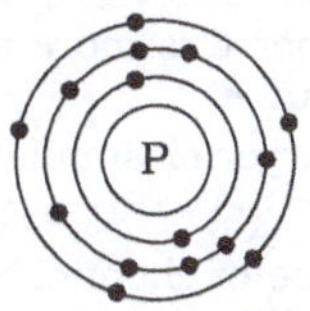

(a) What charge would be attained by the ion of the element P during a reaction?
(b) Write the number of electrons present in the element P.

(iii) Arrange the following as per the instructions gives in the brackets. • *Understanding & Application* [3]
(a) Cl, Na, Mg (decreasing order of reducing character)
(b) Li, Be, F, N (decreasing order of atomic radii)
(c) Na, P, S, Cl (increasing metallic character)

(iv) Complete and balance the equation. [3]
(a) $AgNO_3(aq) + NaCl(aq) \longrightarrow$
(b) $CaO(s) + H_2O \longrightarrow$
(c) $KClO_3(s) \xrightarrow{\Delta}$ • *Recall & Understanding*

4. (i) Give a reason for each of the following. [2]
(a) Chalk deposits slowly and dissolves in rain water.
(b) Though aluminium is above zinc in the activity series, it requires higher temperature to react with water. • *Understanding & Application*

(ii) Write the formulae of each of the following. [2]
(a) Magnesium hydroxide
(b) Chromium oxide • *Understanding*

(iii) A gas occupies 400 cm^3 under 760 mm Hg pressure. Find under what pressure the gas will occupy 380 cm^3, the temperature remains constant. [**Ans.** 800 mm Hg] • *Application* [3]

(iv) Sodium chloride reacts with silver nitrate to produce silver chloride and sodium nitrate [3]
(a) Write the equation.
(b) Check whether it is balanced, if not, balance it.
(c) State the law that this equation satisfies.
• *Understanding & Application*

5. (i) Write one use of the following. [2]
(a) Co-60 (b) U-235 • *Application*

(ii) Write the electronic configuration, electron, proton and neutron of the following **[2]**

(a) $^{48}_{22}T$ (b) $^{40}_{18}Ar$ • *Understanding*

(iii) The position of three elements *A*, *B* and *C* in the periodic table are shown below. **[3]**

Group 16	Group 17
—	—
—	*A*
—	—
B	*C*

(a) State whether *A* is a metal or non-metal.

(b) State whether *C* is more reactive or less reactive than *A*.

(c) Will *C* be larger or smaller in size than *B* ?

• *Analysis & Understanding*

(iv) Identify the type of chemical reaction taking place in each of the following. **[3]**

(a) Barium chloride solution is mixed with copper sulphate solution and a white precipitate is observed.

(b) On heating copper powder in air in a china dish, the surface of copper powder turns black.

(c) On heating green coloured ferrous sulphate crystals, reddish brown solid is left and smell of a gas having odour of burning sulphur is experienced.

• *Understanding & Application*

6. (i) Define/State. **[2]**

(a) Hydrated substance

(b) Anhydrous substance • *Recall*

(ii) Calculate the percentage of iron in iron (III) oxide (Fe_2O_3) [O = 16, Fe = 56]. [**Ans.** 70%]

• *Application*

[2]

(iii) Choose the atomic number given in the box below to answer the questions. **[3]**

13, 8, 15, 4, 12

(a) A solid non-metal of valency 3.

(b) A gas of valency 2.

(c) A metal that belongs to group 2 and 2nd period.

• *Understanding & Recall*

(iv) State one relevant observation for each of the following. **[3]**

(a) HCl is passed through silver nitrate solution?

(b) Cl_2 is passed through potassium iodide (KI) solution?

(c) Nitric acid, even in its dilute form, is not used in the preparation of hydrogen from metals.

• *Understanding*

7. (i) Name an example **[2]**

(a) A photochemical reaction involving a salt of silver.

(b) A catalytic reaction involving two gaseous reactants. • *Recall & Understanding*

(ii) Give reason for the following. **[2]**

(a) Hydrogen is kept in the metal activity series of metals.

(b) Equilibrium is reached when red hot iron reacts with steam. • *Understanding*

(iii) Calculate the relative molecular mass of each of the following. **[3]**

(a) $C_{12}H_{22}O_{11}$ (b) Lead nitrate • *Understanding*

[C = 12, H = 1, O = 16, Pb = 207, N = 14]

(iv) State the following with reference to the elements of first and three periods of the periodic table **[3]**

(a) A metalloid in period 3

(b) The valency of elements in group 14.

(c) Noble gas having electronic configuration 2,8,8.

• *Understanding & Recall*

8. (i) Arrange the following according to the instructions given in brackets. • *Understanding & Applicaiton* **[2]**

(a) Cu, Ge, Mn, Sc, (decreasing order of atomic size)

(b) Hf, Cs, Ba, Tl (increasing order of valency)

(ii) Differentiate between the following pairs. • *Recall* **[2]**

(a) Ammonium chloride and iodide (heating dry test tube test)

(b) Copper and magnesium [using dil. H_2SO_4]

(iii) Convert the following reactions into a balanced chemical equations. • *Understanding* **[3]**

(a) Magnesium + Silver nitrate $\longrightarrow$ Magnesium nitrate + Silver

(b) Chlorine + Sodium hydroxide $\longrightarrow$ Sodium chloride + Sodium chlorate + H_2O

(c) Red lead oxide $\longrightarrow$ lead monoxide + oxygen.

(iv) [K, Na, Ca, Mg, Al, Zn, Fe, Sn, Pb, H, Cu, Hg, Ag and Au].

Choose the answers from list which fits in the description. **[3]**

(a) The metal which does not react with cold water, but reacts with boiling hot water slowly.

(b) A metal which displaces hydrogen very slowly from dilute HCl.

(c) The metal which on heating reacts with steam, but reaction is reversible.

• *Understanding*

Answers

1. (i) (b) (ii) (a) (iii) (b) (iv) (a)
(v) (d) (vi) (c) (vii) (a) (viii) (d)
(ix) (c) (x) (a) (xi) (a) (xii) (c)
(xiii) (b) (xiv) (a) (xv) (a)